Schriften zum Migrationsrecht

edited by

Prof. Dr. Jürgen Bast, Universität Gießen
Prof. Dr. Ulrike Davy, Universität Bielefeld
Prof. Dr. Anuscheh Farahat, Universität Erlangen-Nürnberg
Prof. Dr. Andreas Fischer-Lescano, Universität Bremen
Prof. Dr. Marie-Claire Foblets,
MPI für ethnologische Forschung, Halle
Prof. Dr. Thomas Groß, Universität Osnabrück
Dr. Konstanze Jüngling,
Akademie der Diözese Rottenburg-Stuttgart
Prof. Dr. Winfried Kluth, Universität Halle-Wittenberg
Prof. Dr. Nora Markard, Universität Münster
Prof. Dr. Daniel Thym, Universität Konstanz
Prof. Dr. Mattias Wendel, Universität Leipzig

Volume 36

Jürgen Bast | Frederik von Harbou | Janna Wessels

Human Rights Challenges to European Migration Policy

The REMAP Study

HART

Nomos

The Deutsche Nationalbibliothek lists this publication in the Deutsche Nationalbibliografie; detailed bibliographic data are available on the Internet at http://dnb.d-nb.de

ISBN:	HB (Nomos)	978-3-8487-8244-4
	ePDF (Nomos)	978-3-7489-2674-0

British Library Cataloguing-in-Publication Data
A catalogue record for this book is available from the British Library.

ISBN:	HB (Hart)	978-1-5099-6486-4

Library of Congress Cataloging-in-Publication Data
Bast, Jürgen / Harbou, Frederik von / Wessels, Janna
Human Rights Challenges to European Migration Policy
The REMAP Study
Jürgen Bast / Frederik von Harbou / Janna Wessels
292 pp.
Includes bibliographic references.

ISBN 978-1-5099-6486-4 (hardcover Hart)

Second revised edition 2022

Published by
Nomos Verlagsgesellschaft mbH & Co. KG
Waldseestraße 3–5 | 76530 Baden-Baden
www.nomos.de

Production of the printed version:
Nomos Verlagsgesellschaft mbH & Co. KG
Waldseestraße 3–5 | 76530 Baden-Baden

ISBN 978-3-8487-8244-4 (Print)
ISBN 978-3-7489-2674-0 (ePDF)

ISBN 978-1-5099-6486-4 (hardcover Hart)

DOI https://doi.org/10.5771/9783748926740

Onlineversion
Nomos eLibrary

Preface

This study is co-authored by three researchers originally based at Justus Liebig University Gießen (JLU), Germany. Jürgen Bast is Professor of Public Law and European Law at this university. Frederik von Harbou and Janna Wessels were Postdoctoral Researchers when the project started in 2018; by now, they have become Professor of Law at the University of Applied Sciences Jena (EAH) and Assistant Professor of Migration Law at Vrije Universiteit Amsterdam (VU) respectively. From the beginning we have been supported by Saskia Ebert, who started as an undergraduate student assistant. After having received her law degree, she left the REMAP team in January 2021 to work for the Refugee Law Clinic at the JLU.

The REMAP study was generously funded by Stiftung Mercator. We are grateful for the professional support, the Foundation's appreciation of independent research, and its flexibility when the pandemic affected the original timetable of the project. Stiftung Mercator's continuous support has made it possible for us to publish this volume under a Creative Commons license with Nomos and Bloomsbury, which kindly accepted and skillfully processed the manuscript.

We also gratefully acknowledge the support from a panel of experts composed of academics and practitioners, who shared their experience in a series of workshops and gave most valuable comments on earlier versions of the study (for a full list of experts, see the Annex). The input from our friends and colleagues was so profound that we are somewhat reluctant to assume exclusive responsibility for the content. Of course, all remaining errors are ours.

The first edition of the study was presented to the public in October 2020, in cooperation with the German Institute for Human Rights (DIMR). The earlier version focused on access to asylum, deprivation of liberty, procedural rights, non-discrimination, and the infrastructure necessary to render the Human Rights of migrants effective. These chapters have been updated and partly revised for the present second edition. Our findings on the protection of social and family ties of migrants and of their economic and social rights – with particular attention to the situation of irregular migrants – are presented for the first time in the context of this edition. It represents the state of our legal knowledge by the end of 2021.

The authors, April 2022

Table of Contents

Introduction: Nature and Purpose of this Study

The REMAP study is placed at the crossroad of academic and political discourse. The project aims at re-mapping the legal framework of Human Rights law applicable to European migration policy and examines the implications of this framework in practice. In this introduction, we shall reflect on the context of the study, define core concepts and doctrinal premises, and explain its methods and structure.

0.1 Why re-mapping the role of Human Rights in European migration policy?

When discussing the aim of this project within our academic communities, virtually nobody doubted that such a study is a timely endeavor that could deliver meaningful outcomes, although many found it overly ambitious given the wealth of material. Twenty-five years ago, the reaction probably would have been different. A European migration policy was practically non-existent at the time, and it was far from obvious that Human Rights law had much to say about the governance of migration. This indicates that fundamental changes in the basic legal structures of an entire policy field, and the related legal discourse, have occurred within a fairly short period of time.

Today, the European Union (EU) has established itself as a powerful actor in migration policy, although it still struggles to meet public expectations of delivering 'solutions'. In any case, the EU's role in migration policy has vastly expanded in terms of its substantive and territorial scope, including extraterritorially. Both forms of expansion have intensified the reach of the EU's regulatory power over, and the impact on, migrants' individual rights. Looking at EU policy in this field, hardly anyone today would contemplate the EU's role in migration governance as a sort of regional Human Rights organization, as Alston and Weiler did back in 1999.[1] Rather, much of the policy is guided by concerns that potentially conflict with individual rights of migrants. The EU has yet to adjust to its new role as a potential threat to the Human Rights of migrants.

---

1 Ph. Alston and J.H.H. Weiler, *An 'Ever Closer Union' in Need of a Human Rights Policy: The European Union and Human Rights* (1999).

An equally important shift has taken place in Human Rights discourse. The rights and interests of migrants are not a 'classic' topic of Human Rights. For a long time the discourse was implicitly based on the fictitious model of an immobile society with borders controlled by sovereign states, regardless of the fact that Human Rights have always been meant to apply to non-nationals residing within their territories as well. Only with the onset of globalization in the 1980s, as the static attribution of territory, public authority and rights started to loosen,[2] space was created for a Human Rights framing of migration processes.[3] Today, Human Rights guarantees are frequently invoked in migration-related issues. Such claims are also increasingly being recognized by courts as forming a part of the applicable law.[4] The case-law of the European Court of Human Rights (ECtHR) has been critical to this development, although the future direction of its jurisprudence is subject to debate.[5] Individual and collective actors of civil society also play an important role in 'universalizing Human Rights through processes driven by non-State actors'.[6] This new paradigm is reflected in the wealth of legal scholarship dedicated to the Human Rights of migrants.[7] In particular the ECtHR's case-law has received widespread at-

2 S. Sassen, *Territory, Authority, Rights: From Medieval to Global Assemblages* (2008), at 143 et seq.

3 A. Farahat, *Progressive Inklusion: Zugehörigkeit und Teilhabe im Migrationsrecht* (2014), at 104 et seq.

4 See, e.g., R. Rubio-Marín (ed.), *Human Rights and Immigration* (2014).

5 See, e.g., B. Çali, L. Bianku and I. Motoc (eds), *Migration and the European Convention on Human Rights* (2021).

6 B. Leisering, *Menschenrechte an den europäischen Außengrenzen: Das Ringen um Schutzstandards für Flüchtlinge* (2016), at 195; trans. by the authors; on strategic litigation, see, e.g., Schüller, 'Strategien und Risiken zur Durchsetzung migrationsrelevanter Menschenrechte vor dem EGMR', *Zeitschrift für Ausländerrecht (ZAR)* (2015) 64.

7 For example, Cholewinski, 'Human Rights of Migrants: The Dawn of a New Era?', 24 *Georgetown Immigration Law Journal* (2010) 585; M.-B. Dembour and T. Kelly (eds), *Are Human Rights for Migrants?* (2011); A.R. Gil, *Imigração e Direitos Humanos* (2017); E. Guild, S. Grant and K. Groenendijk (eds), *Human Rights of Migrants in the 21st Century* (2017).

tention,[8] with an outstanding study by Dembour.[9] In international refugee law, a Human Rights-based approach has largely replaced an older, intergovernmental paradigm.[10] The shift to a Human Rights paradigm is also reflected in research on the prohibition of refoulement.[11]

These two complementary processes sit at the heart of this study: the increasing density of obligations under Human Rights law that are recognized as relevant to migration, and the new role of the EU as a powerful player in migration policy. This has resulted in a growing number of instances in which EU migration policies potentially conflict with Human Rights. The purpose of the present study is to identify these instances, outline the applicable legal standards, and provide recommendations to ease the tension.

0.2 What is our understanding of 'Human Rights'?

In the context of this study, we consistently distinguish between Human Rights and fundamental rights (i.e., legal norms of EU law or national constitutional law), irrespective of the closely interwoven nature of these legal layers. According to our understanding, Human Rights are legal norms that have their basis in public international law. The EU and its Member States are legally bound by these norms: As a subject of international law, the EU is obliged to respect, protect, and promote Human Rights to the

8 See, e.g., C. Costello, *The Human Rights of Migrants and Refugees in European Law* (2016); Spijkerboer, 'Analysing European Case-Law on Migration', in L. Azoulai and K. de Vries (eds), *EU Migration Law: Legal Complexities and Political Rationales* (2014) 188; Viljanen and Heiskanen, 'The European Court of Human Rights: A Guardian of Minimum Standards in the Context of Immigration', 34 *Netherlands Quarterly of Human Rights* (2016) 174.

9 M.-B. Dembour, *When Humans Become Migrants: Study of the European Court of Human Rights with an Inter-American Counterpoint* (2015).

10 See, seminally, J. Hathaway, *The Law of Refugee Status* (1st ed. 1991); *The Rights of Refugees under International Law* (2nd ed. 2021); as to the pitfalls, see J. Wessels, *The Concealment Controversy: Sexual Orientation, Discretion Reasoning and the Scope of Refugee Protection* (2021).

11 J. McAdam, *Complementary Protection in Refugee Law* (2007); K. Wouters, *International Legal Standards for the Protection from Refoulement* (2009); E. Hamdan, *The Principle of Non-Refoulement under the ECHR and the UN Convention against Torture and Other Cruel, Inhuman or Degrading Treatment or Punishment* (2016); F. de Weck, *Non-Refoulement under the European Convention on Human Rights and the UN Convention against Torture* (2017).

extent that they are part of the unwritten body of customary international law.[12] For the EU Member States, these and other obligations primarily follow from the Human Rights treaties to which they are a party. In addition, both for the EU and for its Member States, the commitment to Human Rights is constitutionally entrenched as a foundational value (cf. Art. 2 TEU).

The study makes a contribution to the *legal* discourse: it identifies legal imperatives on the basis of the law as it stands, and against this yardstick it judges laws and practices adopted by public authorities as lawful or unlawful. At the same time, we are aware that any appeal to Human Rights always simultaneously invokes the special moral persuasiveness inherent in Human Rights as the 'universal language of justice'.[13] Indeed, for the authors – this must be openly stated at this point – endorsing a Human Rights-based migration policy is both a moral imperative and a guideline for political action. However, we claim to move within the rules of legal discourse with this study. Our statements claim to be professionally objective, in that they are based on recognized methods of interpretation of positive law. We acknowledge the relative indeterminacy of the law, which is particularly pronounced for Human Rights norms given the open formulation of many of its provisions. The inherent logic of the law includes the contestability of legal claims. However, it provides all participants in the discourse with the kind of arguments on the basis of which contestation can occur, if they do not want to leave the frame of reference of the legal discourse. In this sense, we look forward to an open discussion with all critics of the study.

However, we emphasize that the study does not pursue a 'maximalist' agenda in the sense of transcending the limits of what can be argued legally.[14] Nor do we want to declare the optimal realization of Human Rights to be the only legitimate orientation for politics. There are two reasons for this. First, we were surprised to see to what extent even a 'conservative' interpretation of the applicable law has already revealed considerable po-

---

12 Uerpmann-Wittzack, 'The Constitutional Role of International Law', in A. von Bogdandy and J. Bast (eds), *Principles of European Constitutional Law* (2009) 131, at 135 et seq.

13 M. Ignatieff, *Human Rights as Politics and Idolatry* (2001); Cassel, 'The Globalization of Human Rights: Consciousness, Law and Reality', 2(1) *Northwestern Journal of International Human Rights* (2004), article 6.

14 For a nuanced defense of Human Rights maximalism, see Brems, 'Human Rights: Minimum and Maximum Perspectives', 9 *Human Rights Law Review* (2009) 349.

tential for conflict with current practices. There is no reason to weaken the persuasive force of these findings by offering excessively 'progressive' proposals for interpretation. Second, we recognize that migration policy has the legitimate task of reconciling public interests in shaping migration processes with the interests of migrants protected by Human Rights. We therefore in no way negate political discretion in making European migration policy, which must be exercised in democratically legitimized processes by politically responsible decision-makers.

At the same time, however, we reject a 'minimalist' understanding of Human Rights according to which Human Rights merely provide a justiciable external framework for policy, and otherwise contain no – or only a few – substantially relevant statements regarding the contents of migration policy.[15] This view is based on an overly strict separation of law and politics and, as a consequence, the tasks of (constitutional) courts and politically responsible bodies. Such a minimalist understanding of Human Rights underestimates the extent to which they depend on legislative concretization. The *legal* significance of Human Rights is not limited to serving as a yardstick for a court judgment. The program of duties derived from Human Rights goes far beyond the simple omission of infringing acts; rather, they are dependent on the active exercise of legislative powers and, thus, open up spaces for Human-Rights-led policy-making, for which we make proposals in this study (on this 'objective dimension' of Human Rights, see again below).

In sum, our study is based on an understanding of Human Rights as legal norms of international law that are rich in content but that must be construed by means of interpretation that are methodologically sound – a 'positivist Human Rights maximalism', as it were.

0.3 *What do we mean by 'European Migration Policy'?*

In this study we use the term 'migration policy' in its broadest sense. We consider various forms of migration and categories of migrants, including

15 See, e.g., Thym, 'EU Migration Policy and its Constitutional Rationale: A Cosmopolitan Outlook', 50 *Common Market Law Review (CMLRev.)* (2013) 709; Thym, 'Migrationssteuerung im Einklang mit den Menschenrechten', *Zeitschrift für Ausländerrecht (ZAR)* (2018) 193; for an approach located halfway between maximalism and minimalism, see Groß, 'Menschenrechtliche Grenzen der Migrationssteuerung', in J. Markow and F. von Harbou (eds), *Philosophie des Migrationsrechts* (2020) 133.

but not limited to asylum seekers and refugees. The latter concept includes all forms of international protection – that is, it covers refugees in a wider sense, including persons relying on 'subsidiary' protection grounds. Throughout the study we give considerable attention to migrants who find themselves in circumstances that render them particularly vulnerable, although we use the concept of 'vulnerability' with due caution as it tends to establish arbitrary distinctions that may even lead to false assumptions of non-vulnerability of 'ordinary' migrants (or humans at large). We specifically focus on classes of migrants with a precarious legal status, such as irregular migrants and asylum seekers, and to a certain extent also on persons facing intersectional disadvantages, such as migrant women, children and people of color, although we do not systematically deal with issues of intersectionality.

A more detailed explanation is required regarding the notion of 'European' in the title of the study. Ever since the EU legislature started to use its new competences, conferred on it by the Treaty of Amsterdam and subsequently expanded by the Treaties of Nice and Lisbon, a highly complex and constantly changing system of multi-level governance has emerged in the field of migration. The relevant powers of legislation, rule-making and enforcement are shared between the EU and its Member States, to a degree that varies over time and according to the respective subfields. This study mainly focuses on the responsibility of the EU for the conduct of Human Rights-based policies in this increasingly Europeanized field.

Accordingly, we look into acts or omissions that, according to our legal evaluation, actually violate Human Rights obligations, or instances in which current policies and practices run the risk of doing so. We do not only focus on acts or omissions attributable to the EU but also on the EU Member States acting 'within the scope of EU law' – that is, in situations covered by existing EU legislation – and partly also beyond, as we shall explain in the following discussion. Our core assumption is that the EU is primarily accountable for European migration policy being in conformity with Human Rights. This assumption builds on a somewhat complex legal argument of EU constitutional law. Specific variations of the argument will be provided in the various chapters, but the general argument runs as follows.

Obviously, the EU is legally responsible for its own action – that is, any measures taken by, or otherwise attributable to, any of its own institutions, bodies, offices, and agencies (cf. Art. 51(1) EU-CFR). Moreover, it is beyond dispute that the EU is responsible where EU law requires the Member States to take certain action and where that law determines the contents of those actions – that is, where state authorities act as mere 'agents' of the EU. However, we argue that the EU is also accountable where the existing legislative framework, as laid down in EU acts, does not prevent the Member States from taking decisions that violate Human Rights, or seemingly even invites them to do so. We call such situations 'underinclusive legislation' since the EU has failed to enact a comprehensive legal framework that is sufficiently specific (first instance) or sufficiently broad (second instance) to address cases in which Human Rights violations by States frequently occur in a field principally covered by EU law.

In the first instance, the matter is covered by EU legislation and Member State action therefore constitutes 'implementation' for the purposes of Art. 51(1) EU-CFR. Still, the relevant pieces of legislation often include discretionary or optional clauses, or simply lack sufficient detail, which may in effect lead to Human Rights violations on the part of the implementing Member States that are seemingly in accordance with the letter of the law. However, such practices simultaneously violate EU law given that, according to the EU Court of Justice (CJEU), EU legislation must always be construed in conformity with EU fundamental rights, which in substance mirror Human Rights (on the relevant sources and their interplay, see below).[16] This rule of interpretation established by the CJEU effectively shields underinclusive EU legislation from being regarded as unlawful per se, provided that it is sufficiently undetermined to enable a lawful interpretation by incorporating EU fundamental rights. Still, this study argues that the EU is accountable for addressing situations where, on a regular basis, the silence of the EU legislature coincides with results that are actually inconsistent with EU fundamental rights and Human Rights. In cases of systematic violations, this amounts to a legal obligation to amend the existing legislative framework.

In the second instance, Member State action in the field of migration policy does not (yet) fall within the scope of EU law although the EU is vested with the necessary legislative powers to regulate the issue. Accordingly, EU fundamental rights are not applicable, and the EU is not empowered to take supervisory measures to ensure compliance with EU law. One may argue that this is the normal state of affairs in a federal polity in which migration is a matter of shared competence governed by

16 See, e.g., CJEU, Case C-540/03, *Parliament v. Council* (EU:C:2006:429), at para. 61 et seq. and 104–105 (re family reunification); Case C-305/05, *Ordre des barreaux francophones et germanophones* (EU:C:2007:383), at para. 28.

the principle of subsidiarity (cf. Art. 5(3) TEU, Art. 2(2) and 4(2)(j) TFEU). However, the EU's incremental or fragmentary exercise of its legislative powers may lead to an incoherent situation in terms of Human Rights, leaving 'gaps' that are filled by Member States with problematic practices. We have identified such tensions in cases where the EU has regulated certain aspects of migration policy in quite some detail, while other, closely related aspects are not covered. This not only constitutes a strong case in favor of EU action in terms of the principle of subsidiarity, but arguably also suggests a duty to take action in accordance with the values of Art. 2 TEU and the related objectives of Art. 3(1) and (2) TEU and Art. 67(1), 78(1) and/or 79(1) TFEU.

In sum, we hold that the EU is under a legal obligation, derived from EU constitutional law, to use its legislative powers in the field of migration to prevent systematic Human Rights violations on the part of the Member States wherever the EU has (fully or partly) occupied the field by its previous legislative action. In these situations, underinclusive legislation must be specified or broadened, as the case may be.

0.4 What do we mean by the 'challenges' identified in each chapter?

This study is organized according to the interests of migrants protected by Human Rights guarantees (the relevant *Schutzgut*, in German). Having established the extent to which the EU is accountable for ensuring this protection, each chapter starts with our conclusions on what the main 'challenges' to these protected interests are. In these sections, we identify the relevant policy trends as they emerged from our analysis of the respective fields of migration governance.

The temporal scope of the 'trends' varies. Some of them crystalized only in recent years, sometimes involving a dramatic escalation. Others reflect unresolved issues of a more structural nature. We therefore title these sections 'Structural challenges and current trends', to cover both types of challenges. We aim at identifying major trends in European migration policy that may pose – increasing and/or structural – conflicts with Human Rights.

For this purpose we have consulted various empirical and comparative studies, along with legal scholarship reporting on cases and legislative developments. In addition, we relied heavily on the experience assembled in the panel of experts who supported the authors. In our presentation we provide evidence and examples where appropriate for illustrative purposes, but with no intention of singling out individual Member States.

Selecting certain topics as a subject of further investigation while leaving others aside necessarily involves a subjective element of choice. Our selection represents what we consider the most pressing issues in terms of the Human Rights of migrants, with the aim of directing public and scholarly attention toward them. Some of them are highly topical (such as access to asylum), while other issues are less visible and have yet to be discussed extensively (such as non-discrimination among migrants). In any event, a worrying picture emerges in which Human Rights challenges are not limited to singular events or States but, rather, concern European migration policy as a whole.

0.5 What are the sources of the 'legal evaluation' provided in each chapter?

In the second section of each chapter, we outline the relevant sources of Human Rights based in Public International Law and identify the provisions of EU constitutional law, in particular the EU Charter of Fundamental Rights (EU-CFR). The latter mirror the former in the EU legal order. These Human Rights provide the basis of a more detailed legal analysis of the specific issues raised by the trends and patterns identified in the first section.

The outline of sources lists the relevant guarantees of universal international law that Chetail calls the 'fundamental principles of International Migration Law'[17] derived from customary international law and reflected in the trinity of documents that constitute the 'International Bill of Rights' – the Universal Declaration of Human Rights (UDHR), the International Covenant on Civil and Political Rights (ICCPR), and the International Covenant on Economic, Social and Cultural Rights (ICESCR). Reference is also made to other universal Human Rights treaties to which all EU Member States are a party, such as the Convention against Torture (CAT) and the Convention on the Elimination of All Forms of Racial Discrimination (ICERD). According to our understanding, the Geneva Refugee Convention (GRC) of 1951/1967 also constitutes such a Human Rights treaty. Next to these sources of universal international law we identify the relevant guarantees of regional Human Rights law, with special regard to the European Convention of Human Rights (ECHR). Other international

17 V. Chetail, *International Migration Law* (2019), at 76 et seq.

treaties are referred to with somewhat more caution due to the more limited number of ratifications – these include relevant ILO conventions, the UN Migrant Workers Convention, and the revised European Social Charter.

The ECHR has by far the strongest legal force within the EU legal order, since all relevant rights laid down in the ECHR are expressly mirrored in the EU Charter. According to Art. 52(3) EU-CFR, the meaning and scope of those rights shall be the same as those laid down by the said Convention. The same holds true for the unwritten general principles of Union law, which provide an additional source of fundamental rights. According to Art. 6(3) TEU, and in line with the settled case-law of the CJEU, the provisions of the ECHR are the most important source of inspiration in clarifying the meaning and scope of EU fundamental rights. Consequently, the EU is legally obliged to fully observe the Human Rights guaranteed in the ECHR, although the EU has so far failed to become a party to this Convention. Similar arguments can be made in respect of Human Rights guarantees derived from other treaties to which all, or almost all, Member States are parties. They are relevant sources of inspiration in construing the meaning of the 'mirror provisions' in the EU Charter, particularly where they provide a broader scope of protection than the ECHR (in particular in respect of social and economic rights) or where they provide a higher level of protection (in particular derived from the ICCPR). The same assumption of substantive homogeneity of Human Rights and EU fundamental fights applies, unless it is rebutted by a detailed analysis of the relevant provisions.[18]

In discussing the meaning of the provisions of the ECHR, the case-law of the European Court of Human Rights in Strasbourg plays a paramount role that is also recognized by the EU Court of Justice in Luxembourg. Technically, the judgments of the ECtHR are only binding upon the parties of the respective dispute (Art. 46(1) ECHR). However, the case-law developed by the ECtHR is generally accepted as precedent with *erga omnes* effect for all Convention States, thus providing mandatory guidance on the interpretation of the ECHR. It is, therefore, appropriate to consider the ECtHR as a constitutional court in the legal architecture of Europe whose leading role in matters of Human Rights is accepted both by the

18 For a different approach, highlighting the functional differences between the levels of migration governance, see Nettesheim, 'Migration im Spannungsfeld von Freizügigkeit und Demokratie', 144 *Archiv des öffentlichen Rechts (AöR)* (2019) 358.

CJEU and most constitutional or supreme courts in Europe when dealing with the provisions of their domestic bill of rights.

Accepting this leading role also for the purposes of this study, we heavily rely on case-law of the ECtHR in our own legal evaluation. In the rare instances in which we take the scholarly liberty to deviate from the established jurisprudence of the Strasbourg Court and side with minority voices within the Court, we will mark this expressly. Apart from that, the crucial importance of the ECHR does not rule out that other sources of international law and/or EU law provide higher levels of protection that must be met by EU policy.

Another source of interpretation that we consult to give meaning to a relevant provision of Human Rights is the interpretative practice of treaty bodies established to monitor compliance with a particular Human Rights treaty, most prominently the Human Rights Committee (HR Committee) serving the ICCPR. Such interpretative practice can be derived from their findings in quasi-judicial complaint procedures and from so-called General Comments, despite the fact that they are non-binding under international law.[19] Moreover, we refer to other documents of 'soft law' when they express an existing or emerging consensus of the international community of States. One important example is the Global Compact for Migration (GCM) adopted by a large majority of members in the UN General Assembly. While a legal obligation cannot be derived from this type of act in its own right, it does constitute a legitimate argument when discussing the provisions of binding international law, in line with the rules of interpretation laid down in the Vienna Convention on the Law of Treaties.[20]

0.6 What is the nature of the 'recommendations' provided in each chapter?

Based on the findings of what we consider the law in view of the trends and patterns challenging the Human Rights of migrants, we offer specific recommendations at the end of each chapter.

---

19 Çalı, Costello and Cunningham, 'Hard Protection through Soft Courts? Non-Refoulement before the United Nations Treaty Bodies', 21 *German Law Journal (GLJ)* (2020), Special Issue: Border Justice: Migration and Accountability for Human Rights Violations, 355.

20 Goldmann, 'We Need to Cut Off the Head of the King: Past, Present, and Future Approaches to International Soft Law', 25 *Leiden Journal of International Law* (2012) 335.

The content of these recommendations automatically follows from those findings where the EU, either in its laws or through action taken by its executive bodies, violates Human Rights. Given the fact that EU fundamental rights mirror Human Rights as a minimum standard owed to citizens and non-citizens alike, such action is almost automatically unlawful under EU law. Hence, for this type of findings the recommendation is straightforward: the EU must stop violating Human Rights immediately and ensure restitution and/or compensation to those whose rights have been infringed.

A more complex situation arises where our findings indicate that positive action on the part of the EU is required. The situation of underinclusive legislation discussed above is a prime example. Other examples include the failure of the EU to adequately address structural challenges that create a risk of repeating Human Rights violations that occurred in the past.

The doctrine of Human Rights is well equipped to deal with situations that require action of the obliged legal person (States or other subjects of international law). In the context of the ECHR, the ECtHR has consistently recognized that Convention rights entail so-called positive obligations – the duty of parties to take the measures within their power in order to ensure respect for the rights guaranteed by the Convention. In universal Human Rights law, legal scholarship and UN treaty bodies have developed the notion that Human Rights are characterized by the threefold duty to 'respect, protect and fulfill', of which the latter two require taking action. In German constitutional jurisprudence this is called the 'objective dimension' of rights, according to which a constitutionally protected right entails 'duties to protect' (*Schutzpflichten*) and may require 'statutory fleshing-out' (*gesetzliche Ausgestaltung*), i.e. implementing legislation to give effect to a particular right.

However, meeting a positive obligation usually involves a higher degree of discretion on the part of the competent authority, and this authority is often a legislative body rather than part of the executive or judicial branches of government. Accordingly, courts that have the power to adjudicate on matters of Human Rights are more reluctant to determine a failure to act, or to issue a specific order to take action, because such determinations and orders may tilt the constitutional balance between the branches of government. Arguably, such deference is even more justified in the European multi-level system of government, in which legislative powers are shared between the Member States' and the EU's legislatures.

In our study we point to such positive obligations nevertheless, even when they are not justiciable due to the degree of discretion involved. According to our understanding, Human Rights are not only 'guardrails' that set strict outer limits to policy choices, but are also 'directive principles' that legally guide policy-making.[21] Metaphorically, one may distinguish between a justiciable 'core' of Human Rights and a non-justiciable 'corona' of principles. Accordingly, we include in our study a set of recommendations that are based upon, and derived from, our legal findings but that involve policy choices on the part of the addressee. We acknowledge that the objective dimension of Human Rights constitutes a space in which policy and law overlap, in particular when it comes to recommendations on the legislative action the EU should take. We do not hold that our recommendations are the *only* lawful response to remedy a legally problematic situation, but we argue that it is not merely a matter of politics but also a matter of law – that is, that there is a legal obligation to take remedial action.

Some of our recommendations may sound politically naïve, given that the current political climate tends to lower Human Rights standards for migrants rather than raising them. One may even argue, as some members of our panel of experts did, that certain recommendations are dangerous, as they may trigger a political dynamic in which the legislative framework becomes more restrictive than before. Still, at a time when Human Rights of migrants are increasingly in peril, we find it even more important to contribute to a discourse on a European migration policy faithfully implementing the EU's foundational commitment to Human Rights. We are imagining ourselves being the trusted legal advisors of a 'bona fide' policy-maker who would like to know what a European migration policy based on Human Rights must and should entail.

21 See Kälin, 'Menschenrechtsverträge als Gewährleistungen einer objektiven Ordnung', 33 *Berichte der Deutschen Gesellschaft für Völkerrecht: Aktuelle Probleme des Menschenrechtsschutzes* (1994) 9, at 38.

Chapter 1 – Ensuring Access to Asylum

Asylum policy is the subfield of European migration policy that most strongly demands that Human Rights serve as guardrails and guiding principles.[22] Refugee law and Human Rights law are intrinsically linked: Refugees are persons who ask for international protection against the threat of serious Human Rights violations in their home country, and due to the forced nature of their mobility they are typically a particularly vulnerable class of migrants.[23]

There are three fundamental questions any asylum system must answer regarding the protection of refugees: who deserves protection (Who is a 'refugee' in the eyes of that system?), the required content of the protection (What is the 'asylum status' offered to refugees?), and the issue of entering the protection system and having an asylum claim processed (How do refugees gain 'access to asylum'?).

In the European context, the EU has taken the primary political responsibility for answering all three questions. The EU Treaties have assigned the EU the task of establishing a Common European Asylum System (CEAS) in order to implement the fundamental right to asylum in accordance with Human Rights law, in particular the Geneva Convention of 1951/1967 (Art. 18 EU-CFR). According to this constitutional commitment, the Union shall develop a common policy with a view to offering appropriate status to any third-country national requiring international protection and ensuring compliance with the principle of non-refoulement (Art. 78(1) TFEU). The EU has all legislative powers necessary to formulate a comprehensive asylum policy (Art. 78(2) TFEU).

---

22 For an overview, see C. Costello, *The Human Rights of Migrants and Refugees in European Law* (2016), at 171–277; V. Moreno-Lax, *Accessing Asylum in Europe: Extraterritorial Border Controls and Refugee Rights under EU Law* (2017).

23 See ECtHR, *M.S.S. v. Belgium and Greece*, Appl. no. 30696/09, Grand Chamber Judgment of 21 January 2011, at para. 233 and 251, on the *inherent* vulnerability of asylum-seekers. The narrower understanding of vulnerability in Art. 21 Reception Conditions Directive 2013/33/EU (mentioning as examples sub-classes of asylum seekers such as minors, disabled and elderly people, and pregnant women) may obscure the fact that asylum seekers are per se structurally susceptible to rights violations.

In the two decades since the entry into force of the Amsterdam Treaty, the EU legislature has consistently addressed the aforementioned first and second questions. Broadly speaking, the EU has adopted a Human-Rights-based approach to defining the European concept of refugee, and it has set a fairly high minimum standard for the asylum status of those eligible for international protection in the EU.[24] However, the EU struggles in tackling the third question. In this chapter, we therefore focus on the issue of gaining access to asylum – notwithstanding the fact that other aspects would also deserve critical evaluation from a Human Rights perspective.[25]

1.1 Structural challenges and current trends

The EU's approach to granting asylum on EU territory seems to contradict its liberal approach to eligibility and status, to the extent that it almost appears paradoxical. The EU not only fails to effectively offer legal and safe passages to asylum but has actively implemented policies that aim at preventing access to asylum. The CEAS defines the EU as a single jurisdictional space in order to collectively fulfill the international obligations of its Members, yet the EU adopts policies that aim at circumventing these obligations by way of non-exercise of asylum jurisdiction.

We observe a consistent pattern of policies, both at the level of the EU and among its Member States, that prevent potential asylum seekers from gaining access to refugee status determination procedures in EU Member States and, hence, from seeking and enjoying asylum in the EU as promised in Art. 18 EU-CFR. While visa requirements coupled with carrier sanctions have served for decades to exclude most would-be asylum seekers from legally traveling to European States in the first place,[26] new

24 However, severe deficits in the implementation of these standards persist in individual Member States, leading to disparities between EU Member States as to the application of the refugee definition, sometimes described as 'asylum lottery'; see European Council on Refugees and Exiles, Asylum Statistics in Europe: Factsheet, June 2020, available at https://bit.ly/30zw2IH.

25 Some of the latter will be addressed in subsequent chapters, such as the issues of detention (Chapter 2), inadequate procedural safeguards (Chapter 3), inequalities regarding the right to family reunification (Chapter 4), and the undermining of institutionalized support for refugees (Chapter 7).

26 See, e.g., Neumayer, 'Unequal Access to Foreign Spaces: How States Use Visa Restrictions to Regulate Mobility in a Globalized World', 31 *Transactions of the Institute of British Geographers* (2006) 72.

forms of containment of migrants have emerged in recent years. According to our analysis, these policies take three forms: avoiding, contesting and transferring jurisdiction.

Trend 1: Avoiding jurisdiction through cooperative externalization of mobility control

We observe increased efforts among the EU and its Member States to avoid international jurisdiction to assess an asylum claim through the externalization of mobility control via cooperation with third countries.

Such policies of cooperative externalization may aim either at preventing migrants from leaving the country of origin or a transit country in the first place ('non-departure policies') or at 'pulling back' migrants before arrival on EU territory ('non-arrival-policies'). The common rationale of these policies is that jurisdiction in the meaning of international law is not triggered. Jurisdiction usually requires the physical presence of a person on State territory or, in certain instances, the extraterritorial exercise of public authority of the State concerned. Both triggers are apparently avoided when the authority is exercised by other States (for details, see section 1.2.2).

The most prominent example of non-departure policy is the cooperation with Turkey, as laid down in the EU–Turkey 'statement' in March 2016,[27] although it also contains elements of the 'protection elsewhere' approach. The aim of non-departure is expressly declared in the commitment of the Turkish government to prevent new routes for 'irregular migration' being opened.[28] The general subtext of the statement is directed at deterring attempts by migrants to depart from Turkey to access EU territory (for a more extensive discussion of the EU–Turkey 'statement', see below in this section as well as the section on trend 3).

While the cooperation with Turkey is meant to limit the access of irregular migrants to Greece, European cooperation with Libyan authorities is supposed to do the same with regard to Italy and Malta – that is, to

27 European Council, 'EU-Turkey Statement', Press release, 18 March 2016, available at https://www.consilium.europa.eu/en/press/press-releases/2016/03/18/eu-turkey-statement/.

28 Ibid., at para. 3.

achieve the closure of the 'central Mediterranean route'.[29] Bilateral cooperation between Italy and Libyan authorities on questions of border control started as early as in 2012.[30] A Memorandum of Understanding between Libya and Italy of 2017[31] refers to and reactivates a number of formal and informal agreements on mobility control, inter alia the 2008 Treaty of Friendship, Partnership and Cooperation[32] concluded with Libya before the civil war, during the reign of Gaddafi. The Treaty of Friendship, a formal international agreement, contains provisions on the cooperation regarding both the enhanced control of Libyan maritime and land borders.[33]

---

29 Cf. the extensive report by Forensic Oceanography (C. Heller and L. Pezzani), *Mare Clausum: Italy and the EU's undeclared operation to stem migration across the Mediterranean* (2018), available at https://content.forensic-architecture.org/wp-content/uploads/2019/05/2018-05-07-FO-Mare-Clausum-full-EN.pdf; Moreno-Lax, Ghezelbash and Klein, 'Between Life, Security and Rights: Framing the Interdiction of "Boat Migrants" in the Central Mediterranean and Australia', 32 *Leiden Journal of International Law* (2019) 715.

30 For a reference to the 'Tripoli Declaration of 21 January 2012' see E. Paoletti, *Migration Agreements between Italy and North Africa: Domestic Imperatives versus International Norms*, 20 December 2012, available at https://www.mei.edu/publications/migration-agreements-between-italy-and-north-africa-domestic-imperatives-versus. For another early example, see Italian Ministry of Defence, 'Italy – Libya: cooperation agreements', Press statement, 29 November 2013, available at https://www.difesa.it/EN/Primo_Piano/Pagine/20131129_Italy%E2%80%93Libyacooperationagreements.aspx.

31 Memorandum d'intesa, 2 February 2017, available at http://itra.esteri.it/vwPdf/wfrmRenderPdf.aspx?ID=50975; for an English translation, see 'Memorandum of understanding on cooperation in the fields of development, the fight against illegal immigration, human trafficking and fuel smuggling and on reinforcing the security of borders between the State of Libya and the Italian Republic', available at http://eumigrationlawblog.eu/wp-content/uploads/2017/10/MEMORANDUM_translation_finalversion.doc.pdf.

32 Cf. the unofficial translation of the 'Treaty of Friendship, Partnership, and Cooperation between the Great Socialist People's Libyan Arab Jamahiriya and the Republic of Italy', 30 August 2008, available at https://security-legislation.ly/sites/default/files/lois/7-Law%20No.%20%282%29%20of%202009_EN.pdf.

33 According to Art. 19(2) of the Treaty, establishing the control of the Libyan land borders is supposed to be 'entrusted to Italian companies' while 'the Italian government shall assume fifty percent of the costs thereof, and the Parties shall ask the European Union to bear the remaining fifty percent'. Art. 19(1) of the Treaty refers inter alia to 'protocols of cooperation signed in Tripoli on 29/12/2007'. This agreement on bilateral maritime cooperation allowed Italian boats to patrol in Libyan territorial waters and provided for the creation of joint maritime patrols by the Italian police and Libyan coast guard in order to apprehend and push back migrants leaving the Libyan shores, see S. Klepp, *Italy and its Libyan Cooperation Program: Pioneer of the European Union's Refugee Policy?*, 1 August

The 2017 memorandum, which was tacitly renewed in February 2020, forms the basis of the since-intensified cooperation between Italy and Libya on maritime and land border controls as well as for the financing of such measures.[34]

Meanwhile, not only Member States but also the EU itself had become engaged in various forms of cooperations with Libya in the field of migration control. In 2017, the European Council, in its Malta Declaration, promised EU support for the 'training, equipment and support' of the Libyan coastguard.[35] Through the EU Emergency Trust Fund for Africa,[36] the European Commission adopted the program 'Support to Integrated border and migration management in Libya' in order to 'strengthen the capacity of relevant Libyan authorities in the areas of border and migration management'.[37] Both Italy and the EU are engaged in the funding, deliv-

2010, available at https://www.mei.edu/publications/italy-and-its-libyan-cooperation-program-pioneer-european-unions-refugee-policy.

34 Art. 1(c) and Art. 2(1), Art. 4 of the Memorandum.

35 European Council, 'Malta Declaration', Press release, 3 February 2017, available at https://www.consilium.europa.eu/en/press/press-releases/2017/02/03/malta-declaration/, at para. 6.

36 For a broader assessment of the EU Trust Fund, see Oxfam International, *The EU Trust Fund for Africa. Trapped between aid policy and migration politics*, Briefing Paper (2020), available at https://reliefweb.int/sites/reliefweb.int/files/resources/bp-eu-trust-fund-africa-migration-politics-300120-en.pdf. The possible violation of EU financial regulations by the use of the Trust Fund was subject to a complaint filed with the European Court of Auditors (ECA) in April 2020, see GLAN/ASCI/ARGI, 'Legal Complaint against EU Financial Complicity in Illegal Push-Backs to Libya', Press statement, 27 April 2020, available at https://www.glanlaw.org/eu-complicity-in-libyan-abuses. The ECA however, refused to initiate a special review of the program, referring to limited resources, prompting the NGOs involved in the case to file a petition to the European Parliament, see GLAN, 'Petition to European Parliament Challenging EU's Material Support to Libyan Abuses Against Migrants', Press statement, 11 June 2020, available at https://www.glanlaw.org/single-post/2020/06/11/petition-to-european-parliament-challenges-eu-s-material-support-to-libyan-abuses-against.

37 Since 2015 until early 2021, the total sum allocated by the EU to Libya for migration control under the EU Emergency Trust Fund for Africa amounted to around EUR 455 million of which around EUR 57 million were invested in the Libyan border management system, cf. EEAS, Factsheet EU–Libya Relations, 2 March 2021, available at https://eeas.europa.eu/headquarters/headquarters-homepage_en/19163/EU-Libya%20relations.

ery, and maintenance of coast guard equipment – such as vessels – and the training of Libyan coast guard personnel.[38]

Following these developments, the Libyan government declared a Search and Rescue (SAR) zone to the International Maritime Organization in 2017,[39] but it has yet to establish adequate rescue coordination facilities as required by international maritime law.[40] The Italian Maritime Rescue Coordination Center (MRCC) in Rome cooperates with the Libyan coast guard in asking them to pick up rescues.[41] Cases of coordination and cooperation have been well documented, such as the sharing of information about the position of migrant vessels detected by EU aerial surveillance under the Frontex Multipurpose Aerial Surveillance (MAS) framework.[42]

The logistical support and operational cooperation with the Libyan coast guard by EU Member States and the EU itself in order to have 'pull-back' operations conducted raises serious questions regarding their international responsibility for ensuing Human Rights violations in Libya. Numerous reports bear testimony to the devastating Human Rights situa-

38 More than 238 Libyan coast guards were trained by the end of 2018, with training conducted by European Union Naval Force Mediterranean Operation Sophia; see European Commission, Action Document for EU Trust Fund to be used for the decisions of the Operational Committee (2018), available at https://ec.europa.eu/trustfundforafrica/sites/euetfa/files/t05-eutf-noa-ly-07.pdf.

39 European Parliament, Parliamentary questions, available at http://www.europarl.europa.eu/doceo/document/E-8-2018-000547_EN.html, answer given by Mr. Avramopoulos on behalf of the Commission, 26 April 2018, available at http://www.europarl.europa.eu/doceo/document/E-8-2018-000547-ASW_EN.pdf.

40 In March 2021, the European Commission described the Libyan Maritime Rescue Coordination Centre (MRCC) as 'very basic', cf. European Parliament, Parliamentary questions, available at https://www.europarl.europa.eu/doceo/document/E-9-2021-000027_EN.html, answer given by Mr Várhelyi on behalf of the European Commission, 30 March 2021, available at https://www.europarl.europa.eu/doceo/document/E-9-2021-000027-ASW_EN.html.

41 Pijnenburg, 'From Italian Pushbacks to Libyan Pullbacks: Is Hirsi 2.0 in the Making in Strasbourg?', 20 *European Journal of Migration and Law (EJML)* (2018) 396, at 405.

42 See e.g. Alarm Phone et al., *Remote Control: the EU-Libya Collaboration in Mass Interceptions of Migrants in the Central Mediterranean* (2020), available at https://eu-libya.info/img/RemoteControl_Report_0620.pdf; United Nations High Commissioner for Human Rights, *'Lethal Disregard': Search and Rescue and the Protection of Migrants in the Central Mediterranean Sea* (2021), at 20, available at https://www.ohchr.org/Documents/Issues/Migration/OHCHR-thematic-report-SAR-protection-at-sea.pdf.

tion of (retained or returned) migrants in Libya, including their systematic subjection to arbitrary detention and torture.[43]

Both types of cooperation – with Turkey on the one hand, with Libya on the other – are regarded as models for future relations with other third countries bordering the Mediterranean Sea in order to further implement non-departure and non-arrival policies. In June 2016, the Commission referred to the EU–Turkey statement when presenting ideas for a new 'partnership framework' for the cooperation with third countries on mobility control.[44] The Commission's plans to conclude 'regional disembarkation arrangements' with all North African Mediterranean countries, and to refer asylum seekers to procedures on the African continent, are also based on this.[45] However, the plans on the part of the EU are opposed by many African countries of origin and transit, so that the swift implementation of further 'disembarkation arrangements' – or even the establishment of the 'regional disembarkation platforms' in North Africa originally called for by the European Council[46] – appears uncertain. At a summit in November 2015, representatives of European and African States agreed on an action plan (the 'Valletta Principles') based on the previous cooperation formats on migration issues (the so-called Rabat and Khartoum Processes and the Joint EU–Africa Strategy) and providing for, among other things, a more intensive fight against irregular migration, and greater cooperation in the readmission of irregular migrants and in border protection (including the training of border guards).[47] As an example, in May 2021, Home Affairs

43 See, e.g., Human Rights Watch, *No Escape from Hell: EU Policies Contribute to Abuse of Migrants in Libya* (2019), available at https://www.hrw.org/sites/default/files/report_pdf/eu0119_web2.pdf; United Nations Security Council, United Nations Support Mission in Libya, Report of the Secretary-General, UN Doc. S/2020/41, 15 January 2020.

44 European Commission, 'Towards a new Partnership Framework with third countries under the European Agenda on Migration', Press release, 7 June 2016, available at http://europa.eu/rapid/press-release_MEMO-16-2118_en.htm; European Council, Conclusions, 28 June 2016, at para. 2, available at https://www.consilium.europa.eu/media/21645/28-euco-conclusions.pdf.

45 European Commission, 'Managing migration: Commission expands on disembarkation and controlled centre concepts', Press release, 24 July 2018, available at http://europa.eu/rapid/press-release_IP-18-4629_en.htm.

46 European Council, 'Conclusions on: migration, security and defence, jobs, growth and competitiveness, innovation and digital, and on other issues', Press release, 28 June 2018, at para. 5, available at https://www.consilium.europa.eu/en/press/press-releases/2018/06/29/20180628-euco-conclusions-final/.

47 Valletta Summit on Migration, Action Plan, 11–12 November 2015, available at https://www.consilium.europa.eu/media/21839/action_plan_en.pdf.

Commissioner Ylva Johansson declared that she was seeking a deal with Tunisia allowing for EU economic support in exchange for a commitment from the Tunisian government to 'engage in managing the borders'. The EU's push to conclude further 'arrangements' with North African countries is an example of the wider trend toward an informalization of the EU's external migration policy and the proliferation of soft-law cooperation on migration issues, apparently intended by the EU.[48]

These developments were supplemented by Frontex's considerable increase in power over the recent years. The successive extension of the European Border and Coast Guard Agency's mandate and equipment is also reflected in its power to conclude working arrangements with authorities from third countries. The 2019 Frontex Regulation (Regulation 1869/2019) permits cooperation with third countries that are not directly neighboring EU Member States. Among other things, the new regulation explicitly authorizes the Union to conclude status agreements with these third countries for Frontex operations on their territories and the deployment of border management and repatriation teams there.[49] Since 2019, a considerable number of new (or renewed) status agreements and working arrangements have been concluded with third countries by the Union and Frontex respectively.[50] On the basis of such agreements, Frontex launched its first three official operations on the territory of third countries, in

48 Such cooperation arrangements have been concluded with, for example, Afghanistan, Niger, and Sudan; for an overview, see Molinari, 'The EU and its Perilous Journey through the Migration Crisis: Informalisation of the EU Return Policy and Rule of Law Concerns', 44 *European Law Review (E.L.Rev.)* (2019) 824. On a recent push of the Commission toward concluding an agreement with Tunisia, see Deutsche Welle, 'EU Seeks Migration Deals with Libya and Tunisia', 20 May 2021, available at https://www.dw.com/en/eu-seeks-migration-deals-with-libya-and-tunisia/a-57592161.

49 See Art. 73(3) Frontex Regulation, in comparison to Art. 54(4) interpreted in light of Art. 54(3) of the repealed Regulation 1624/2016. The latter provision referred to 'neighbouring' third countries.

50 Since 2019, the EU has negotiated five agreements with the Western Balkan states Albania, Montenegro, Serbia, Bosnia and Herzegovina, and North Macedonia (the latter two not yet entered into force), cf. Statewatch, *Blackmail in the Balkans: How the EU is Externalising its Asylum Policies* (2021), available at https://www.statewatch.org/analyses/2021/blackmail-in-the-balkans-how-the-eu-is-externalising-its-asylum-policies/#_ftnref41. A list of working arrangement, such as the 2020 arrangement with Georgia, is available at https://frontex.europa.eu/about-frontex/key-documents/?category=working-arrangements-with-non-eu-countries.

Albania (2019), Montenegro (2020) and Serbia (2021).[51] Further, the European Border Surveillance System (Eurosur) was integrated into the Frontex framework in 2019.[52] Eurosur is a mechanism for information exchange and cooperation between different Member State authorities involved in border surveillance as well as with Frontex. Its purpose is notably to detect and prevent irregular immigration, a term that is applied also to forced migration of individuals entitled to international protection. Both developments should be regarded as aspects of non-departure as well as non-arrival policies. Increased operational and informational cooperation with countries of origin and transit aims either at finding and stopping migrant boats before entering European territorial waters, or at discouraging migrants from leaving in the first place by establishing comprehensive border regimes, including in countries remote from Europe.

Trend 2: Contesting jurisdiction by failing to comply with Human Rights obligations

We observe that actors of European migration policy actually contest the applicability of Human Rights norms, in particular the principle of non-refoulement, when confronted with claims to refuge on their territory or at their part of the EU's external border. This reflects a growing trend among EU Member States of disregarding their Human Rights obligations (and corresponding obligations under EU law) toward migrants who demand access to asylum. We read this as political attempts at challenging, and possibly reversing, Human Rights jurisprudence on asylum jurisdiction.

Such practices of resistance include push-back measures toward migrants at or near the border ('hot returns') and the closure of ports to the disembarkation of migrants saved at sea ('non-disembarkation policy'). Those are carried out despite the settled case-law of the ECtHR post-*Hirsi* and provisions of the CEAS requiring Member States to ensure the

51 Frontex, Press statements of 21.05.2019, 14.10.2020, and 16.06.2021, available at https://frontex.europa.eu/media-centre/news/news-release/frontex-launches-first-operation-in-western-balkans-znTNWM; https://frontex.europa.eu/media-centre/news/news-release/frontex-launches-second-operation-in-montenegro-C0Pc3E; https://frontex.europa.eu/media-centre/news/news-release/frontex-expands-presence-in-western-balkans-with-operation-in-serbia-9WRMiW.

52 Art. 18–23 Frontex Regulation.

possibility of applying for asylum at the border (Art. 3(1) and 43 Asylum Procedures Directive).[53]

As regards push-back measures, an increasing number of incidents have been reported since 2015 at land borders in Central and South-Eastern Europe. Numerous accounts of migrants trying to enter Hungarian territory being pushed back to Serbia have been reported.[54] Such push-backs have continued even after the CJEU ruled, in December 2020, that the underlying Hungarian legislation breached EU law.[55] As the practice is still prescribed by national law, the Hungarian Police continues to publish daily statistics, and reported more than 10.000 push-backs in the first three months of 2021 alone.[56] The ECtHR also found the practices of 'hot returns' conducted by the Hungarian authorities to be in violation of the ECHR – in particular, the prohibition of collective expulsions (see Chapter 3).[57] The Court determined that Hungary had failed to secure effective means of legal entry to lodge an application for international protection.[58] Beyond Hungary, many other instances in EU Member States have been reported, such as thousands of push-back operations at the Croatian border with Bosnia-Herzegovina, often involving violence against migrants.[59]

As regards non-disembarkation policies, Italy and Malta, among other European countries bordering the Mediterranean, have also resorted to policies such as the closure of their ports to the entry of migrants saved at sea, mainly by NGO-chartered rescue ships. While already threatening to do so in 2017[60], Italy in 2018 and 2019 repeatedly closed its ports to NGOs and other vessels conducting SAR operations, such as the *Aquarius*,

---

53 Directive 2013/32/EU on common procedures for granting and withdrawing international protection (Asylum Procedures Directive).

54 Hungarian Helsinki Committee, *Pushed Back at the Door: Denial of Access to Asylum in Eastern EU Member States* (2017), available at https://www.refworld.org/docid/5888b5234.html.

55 CJEU, Case C-808/18, *Commission v. Hungary* (EU:C:2020:1029).

56 ASGI et al., *Pushing Back Responsibility*, April 2021, 10, available at https://helsinki.hu/en/pushing-back-responsibility/.

57 ECtHR, *Shahzad v. Hungary*, Appl. no. 12625/17, Judgment of 8 July 2021.

58 Ibid., at para. 62–66.

59 European Center for Constitutional and Human Rights, *Push-Backs in Croatia: Complaint before the UN Human Rights Committee*, 11 December 2020, available at https://www.ecchr.eu/en/case/push-backs-croatia-complaint-un-human-rights-council/; Human Rights Watch, *Violent Pushbacks on Croatia Border Require EU Action*, 22 October 2020, available at https://www.hrw.org/news/2020/10/29/violent-pushbacks-croatia-border-require-eu-action.

60 European Parliament: Parliamentary questions, Immigration emergency in Italy: closure of Italian ports to prevent clandestine migrants from disembarking, 28

the *Lifeline*, the *Sea-Watch*, the *Sea Eye*, and the *Diciotti*. This policy led to a 'disembarkation crisis',[61] leaving rescued migrants on those ships 'stranded at sea for weeks'[62] and in limbo regarding their access to asylum in the EU. EU Member States reacted with a 'ship by ship' approach to their disembarkation and relocation.[63] This ad hoc approach – a de facto exception of the 'first country of entry' principle of the Dublin system – points to a structural lack of a safe, fair, and predictable allocation and relocation mechanism for such cases.[64] A Joint Declaration of Intent by Italy, Malta, France, and Germany signed at an informal summit in September 2019 in Malta was intended to alleviate the situation by promising a limited solidarity mechanism for persons disembarked following SAR operations conducted in the high seas, and falling under the responsibility of the Italian and Maltese governments, but lacks a firm legal basis and sufficient consent across EU Member States necessary to provide for a stable mechanism.[65] In March and April 2020, Italy and Malta temporarily closed their ports to SAR vessels, arguing that they had stopped being a 'place of safety' due to the COVID-19 pandemic.[66]

July 2017, available at https://www.europarl.europa.eu/doceo/document/E-8-2017-005108_EN.pdf.

61 European Council on Refugees and Exiles (ECRE), *'Relying on Relocation': ECRE's Proposal for a predictable and fair relocation arrangement following disembarkation* (2019), at 3, available at https://www.ecre.org/wp-content/uploads/2019/01/Policy-Papers-06.pdf.

62 UNHCR, Italy Fact Sheet (2019), at 2, available at https://data2.unhcr.org/en/documents/download/68161.

63 ECRE, *'Relying on Relocation': Proposal for a predictable and fair relocation arrangement following disembarkation* (2019), at 3 et seq., available at https://www.ecre.org/wp-content/uploads/2019/01/Policy-Papers-06.pdf.

64 Ibid., at 4 et seq.; UNHCR, Italy Fact Sheet (2019), at 2.

65 Joint declaration of intent on a controlled emergency procedure – voluntary commitments by member states for a predictable temporary solidarity mechanism, 23 September 2019, available at http://www.statewatch.org/news/2019/sep/eu-temporary-voluntary-relocation-mechanism-declaration.pdf; see S. Carrera and R. Cortinovis, *The Malta declaration on SAR and relocation: A predictable EU solidarity mechanism? CEPS Policy Insights* No. 14 (2019), available at https://www.ceps.eu/wp-content/uploads/2019/10/PI2019_14_SCRC_Malta-Declaration-1.pdf.

66 On the development and possible further conflicts with international law, see A. Farahat and N. Markard, *Closed Ports, Dubious Partners: The European Policy of Outsourcing Responsibility: Study Update* (2020), available at https://eu.boell.org/sites/default/files/2020-05/HBS-POS%20study-A4_25-05-20-2.pdf.

Trend 3: Transferring jurisdiction by referring migrants to other States

We observe increased efforts to implement schemes that refer migrants to (presumed) protection in countries other than their place of actual residence. This leads to situations in which access to adequate asylum procedures and/or effective protection is not ensured. Measures shifting jurisdiction (re-)delegate responsibilities within Europe, or even beyond to non-European countries.

While in these cases jurisdiction is neither silently avoided nor normatively contested in principle, such arrangements provide either the EU as a whole or particular EU Member States with an exemption from being in charge of processing the asylum applications of certain migrants. Thus, EU Member States try to deny jurisdiction by referring migrants either to third countries ('protection elsewhere' in a supposedly safe third country) or to other European States within the Dublin system (that is, within the ambit of Regulation 604/2013, the so-called Dublin III Regulation).[67]

As mentioned above, referring migrants who try to reach EU territory to 'protection elsewhere', in this case Turkey, is a key element of the EU–Turkey statement, concluded in March 2016.[68] It raises the question of whether the required level of protection for refugees is met by Turkey.[69] This concern is linked to the fact that Turkey maintains a geographical limitation to the 1951 Refugee Convention, such that it only applies to events in Europe. Furthermore, there are reports that Turkish authorities forcibly returned Syrian refugees after coercing them to sign 'voluntary return' forms.[70] Nonetheless, the EU–Turkey statement seems to be regarded as a model for EU migration policy during the process of reforming the CEAS. For instance, in the revision process of the Asylum Procedures Directive, it was proposed to lower the standards for a 'safe third country',

---

67 Regulation 604/2013 establishing the criteria and mechanisms for determining the Member State responsible for examining an application for international protection lodged in one of the Member States by a third-country national or a stateless person (Dublin III Regulation).

68 European Council, 'EU–Turkey Statement', Press release, 18 March 2016, available at https://www.consilium.europa.eu/en/press/press-releases/2016/03/18/eu-turkey-statement/.

69 For a detailed socio-legal analysis, see H. Kaya, *The EU-Turkey Statement on Refugees: Assessing Its Impact on Fundamental Rights* (2020).

70 Human Rights Watch, *Turkey Forcibly Returning Syrians to Danger*, 26 July 2019, available at https://www.hrw.org/news/2019/07/26/turkey-forcibly-returning-syrians-danger.

by requiring only that parts of that country meet the requirements for protection.[71]

But even for those who have reached European soil, access to an adequate asylum procedure may be thwarted by the Dublin system determining the Member State responsible for examining an application for asylum. While the asylum procedure and reception of refugees in a given Member State in charge according to the Dublin system may be malfunctioning and unacceptable,[72] an asylum application in another Member State would be inadmissible in most cases, preventing de facto effective access to asylum. At the same time relocation is also malfunctioning, as demonstrated by the failure of the 2015 refugee relocation scheme,[73] which was meant to remedy some of the deficiencies of the Dublin system.[74]

Furthermore, as the Dublin system is being amended it becomes clear that the Commission holds on to what has been described as the 'no choice, first entry' logic of the existing system, rather than envisaging a distribution mechanism that actually guarantees the rights of migrants to

71 Council of the EU, Proposal for a Regulation of the European Parliament and of the Council establishing a common procedure for international protection in the Union and repealing Directive 2013/32/EU (First reading), 6238/18, 19 February 2018, Art. 45(1a), available at http://www.statewatch.org/news/2018/mar/eu-council-asylum-procedures-asylum-6238-18.pdf.

72 Examples of severe and systemic deficiencies in the asylum systems of different EU Member States are manifold and a long-standing issue; see ECtHR, *M.S.S. v. Belgium and Greece*, Appl. no. 30696/09, Grand Chamber Judgment of 21 January 2011; on the more recent situation in Greece, see Commissioner for Human Rights of the Council of Europe, Report following her visit to Greece from 25 to 29 June 2018, 6 November 2018, available at https://rm.coe.int/report-on-the-visit-to-greece-from-25-to-29-june-2018-by-dunja-mijatov/16808ea5bd; UNHCR, 'Act now to alleviate suffering at reception centres on Greek islands – UNHCR's Grandi', Press Statement, 21 February 2020, available at https://www.unhcr.org/news/press/2020/2/5e4fe4074/act-alleviate-suffering-reception-centres-greek-islands-unhcrs-grandi.html; on Hungary, see UN Special Rapporteur on the human rights of migrants, End of visit statement, 17 July 2019, available at https://www.ohchr.org/EN/NewsEvents/Pages/DisplayNews.aspx?NewsID=24830&LangID=E.

73 Council Decision 2015/1601 establishing provisional measures in the area of international protection for the benefit of Italy and Greece.

74 E. Guild, C. Costello and V. Moreno-Lax, *Implementation of the 2015 Council Decisions establishing provisional measures in the area of international protection for the benefit of Italy and of Greece* (2017), available at https://www.europarl.europa.eu/RegData/etudes/STUD/2017/583132/IPOL_STU(2017)583132_EN.pdf.

access a functioning asylum system.[75] Some highly problematic provisions have so far been proposed in the CEAS reform process, aimed at a new Regulation replacing the current Dublin III Regulation: For example, in its 2016 draft the European Commission proposed to restrict the scope of the discretionary clause for the assumptions of responsibility by Member States,[76] thus possibly reducing Member State flexibility to comply with Human Rights norms, particularly in cases of emergency. At the same time, the draft aimed at imposing extended duties on the Member State where an asylum application is first lodged to mandatorily apply the 'safe third country' rule when examining admissibility prior to the actual Dublin procedure.[77] In a similar vein, it was proposed to shorten or eliminate time limits for transfers from one Member State to another,[78] which would lead to longer periods 'in limbo' for individual migrants. Although the Commission withdrew many of these suggestions in its 2020 proposal for a Regulation on Asylum and Migration Management,[79] these ideas may re-emerge at any time during the legislative process and, if realized, create serious problems in terms of access to protection.

1.2 Legal evaluation

1.2.1 General legal framework regarding access to asylum

Ensuring access to asylum should be the core content of the Human Right to asylum, next to guaranteeing a particular status after having completed a procedure determining the need for international protection. However, such a Human Right has yet to emerge as an undisputed part of international law.[80] The Universal Declaration of Human Rights, in Art. 14, postulates only the right 'to seek' asylum, a carefully drafted compromise

---

75 See F. Maiani, *A 'Fresh Start' or One More Clunker? Dublin and Solidarity in the New Pact* (2020), available at https://eumigrationlawblog.eu/a-fresh-start-or-one-more-clunker-dublin-and-solidarity-in-the-new-pact/.

76 European Commission, Proposal for a recast Dublin Regulation, COM(2016) 270, 4 May 2016, Art. 19.

77 Ibid., Art. 3(3).

78 Ibid., Art. 30.

79 European Commission, Proposal for a Regulation on Asylum and Migration Management, COM(2020) 610, 23 September 2020, Art. 25, Art. 8(5), Art. 35.

80 On the relations between asylum and non-refoulement, see V. Chetail, *International Migration Law* (2019), at 190–194.

that leaves in abeyance the corresponding duty of the requested State to actually provide protection. Ensuing attempts in the 1970s at drafting a binding convention on territorial asylum have failed, both in the UN and the Council of Europe.[81]

The most important rule of international law that, to some extent, ensures access to asylum is the principle of non-refoulement – that is, the prohibition on expelling or returning a person to a State in which his or her fundamental Human Rights are threatened. The principle of non-refoulement has developed into an independent Human Right. It includes an unconditional right to be admitted and protected, including of persons arriving at the borders of a State, whenever the possible alternatives to provisionally granting access to the territory would entail the risk of Human Rights violations.[82] This principle not only protects persons from being transferred to a State that itself threatens the individual, but also to a State that would not protect the person against onward transfer in violation of the principle of non-refoulement (so-called chain refoulement). The prohibition of refoulement is explicitly provided for in Art. 33(1) of the 1951 Refugee Convention and Art. 3 CAT. The principle of non-refoulement can also be inferred from the right to life and the prohibition of torture, cruel, inhuman, or degrading treatment, as guaranteed in Art. 6 and 7 ICCPR as well as – very relevantly – Art. 3 ECHR.

Procedural safeguards, such as the prohibition of collective expulsion (Art. 4 Protocol No. 4 ECHR), also play an important role in ensuring effective access to asylum; they are discussed in detail in Chapter 3 of this volume. Standing out among the various other Human Rights affected by policies preventing access to asylum is the right to leave any country, including one's own, as protected by Art. 13(2) UDHR, Art. 12(2) ICCPR, and Art. 2(2) of Protocol No. 4 ECHR.

The Global Compact on Refugees (GCR) recognizes the principle of non-refoulement as the 'cardinal principle' of the international refugee protection regime (GCR, para. 5). The Global Compact for Migration (GCM) contains commitments to the protection of migrants' right to life (GCM, para. 24, point a) as well as upholding the 'prohibition of collective

---

81 A. Hurwitz, *The Collective Responsibility of States to Protect Refugees* (2009), chapter 1.

82 J. Hathaway, *The Rights of Refugees under International Law* (2nd ed. 2021), at 313–464; Lauterpacht and Bethlehem, 'The Scope and Content of the Principle of Non-Refoulement: Opinion', in E. Feller, V. Türk and F. Nicholson (eds), *Refugee Protection in International Law: UNHCR's Global Consultations on International Protection* (2003) 87.

expulsion and of returning migrants when there is a real and foreseeable risk of death, torture and other cruel, inhuman and degrading treatment or punishment, or other irreparable harm' (GCM, para. 37) – that is, a commitment, among other things, to the principle of non-refoulement.

The EU Charter of Fundamental Rights does, in Art. 18 EU-CFR, guarantee the right to asylum. In the case-law of the CJEU thus far, this has not been used as an independent source of a fundamental right ensuring access to asylum.[83] However, as a constitutional guarantee having the same legal value as the EU Treaties (Art. 6(1) TEU), it at any rate informs the construction of the relevant legislation of the Common European Asylum System. The principle of non-refoulement is firmly established as a fundamental right of EU law: While Art. 4 EU-CFR mirrors (with the very same wording) Art. 3 ECHR,[84] Art. 19(2) EU-CFR mirrors the case-law of the ECtHR on Art. 3 ECHR[85] as well as the non-refoulement principle from international Human Rights law by explicitly prohibiting any removal, expulsion, or extradition if there is a serious risk of inhuman or degrading treatment or punishment of the person concerned.

In light of the legal constraints imposed by international and EU law, the cooperation between the EU or its Member States on the one side and third countries on the other directed at non-departure or non-arrival of migrants thus raises numerous concerns. Apart from possible violations of the principle of non-refoulement, especially through the risk of chain refoulement, such practices may also affect the Human Right to leave any country including one's own, especially where effective protection is not available in the country concerned.[86] Furthermore, the treatment of migrants pulled back or hindered from departure in the third county (the country of transit, e.g., Libya) may itself amount to Human Rights violations, including by subjecting migrants to torture or inhuman or degrading treatment.

83 Cf. CJEU, Case C-528/11, *Zuheyr Frayeh Halaf* (EU:C:2013:342).

84 See Explanations relating to the Charter of Fundamental Rights, 2007/C 303/02, on Art. 4 EU-CFR.

85 See ibid., on Art. 19(1) EU-CFR.

86 For details, see Markard, 'The Right to Leave by Sea: Legal Limits on EU Migration Control by Third Countries', 27 *European Journal of International Law (EJIL)* (2016) 591; V. Moreno-Lax, *Accessing Asylum in Europe* (2017), chapter 9.

1.2.2 Specific issue: Attributing responsibility for acts of third countries

The cooperation of the EU or its Member States with third countries raises difficult questions of attribution of responsibility.[87] Such attribution also depends on the kind and degree of support from European actors for the country concerned (e.g., deployment of vessels, training of coast guards, sharing of information regarding the location of migrant boats etc.). This is because ultimate and effective operational control in such cases usually rests with the third country engaged in pull-back measures (e.g., the control of Libya over the boats of its coast guard). Establishing 'jurisdiction' of the European country as required for the applicability of the ECHR according to Art. 1 ECHR will often be difficult.[88] In addition, the multiplicity of actors in this area may lead to a diffusion of responsibilities – and it is exactly for this reason that the EU Member States employ these strategies.[89]

The accountability of States and International Organizations in cooperative scenarios is governed by the principles of responsibility in international law. These principles are restated in the 2001 Articles on State Responsibility (ASR) and the 2011 Articles on the Responsibility of International Organizations (ARIO). Both were drafted by the International Law Commission (ILC) and for the most part reflect customary international law.[90] According to these principles, direct responsibility for the acts of another State is only incurred in very limited circumstances. Pursuant to Art. 6 ASR, 'the conduct of an organ placed at the disposal of a State by another State shall be considered an act of the former State under international law if the organ is acting in the exercise of elements of the government authority of the State at whose disposal it is placed'. It is hard to imagine

87 On the following considerations, see M. Fink, *Frontex and Human Rights: Responsibility in 'Multi-Actor Situations' under the ECHR and EU Public Liability Law* (2018); R. Mungianu, *Frontex and Non-Refoulement: The International Responsibility of the EU* (2016).

88 However, under specific circumstances 'contactless control' may also amount to 'effective control' in the sense of Art. 1 ECHR; see Moreno-Lax and Giuffré, 'The Rise of Consensual Containment: From "Contactless Control" to "Contactless Responsibility" for Migratory Flows', in S. Juss (ed.), *Research Handbook on International Refugee Law* (2019) 81.

89 Moreno-Lax and Lemberg-Pedersen, 'Border-induced Displacement: The Ethical and Legal Implications of Distance Creation through Externalization', 56 *Questions of International Law* (2019) 5, at 19 et seq.

90 M. Fink, *Frontex and Human Rights: Responsibility in 'Multi-Actor Situations' under the ECHR and EU Public Liability Law* (2018), at 84.

situations of migration control measures in which third countries fully place their agents at the disposal of an EU Member State. However, the concept of joint responsibility (Art. 47(1) ASR),[91] which allows attributing a single internationally wrongful act to a plurality of States, confirms that responsibility is not diminished or reduced by the fact that one or more other States are responsible for the same act. According to the principle of independent responsibility, each State continues to be separately responsible for conduct attributable to it.[92]

This still leaves the possibility of indirect (derivative) responsibility of the EU or its Member States for Human Rights violations committed by third countries. Notably, liability could be established by the facilitation of the commission of Human Rights violations (e.g., by supplying equipment to the Libyan coast guards, enabling them to pull back migrants to Libya). While this type of support will not constitute direction or control (Art. 17 ASR), it may constitute an act of 'aid or assistance' according to Art. 16 ASR, which reads:

> *A State which aids or assists another State in the commission of an internationally wrongful act by the latter is internationally responsible for doing so if: (a) that State does so with knowledge of the circumstances of the internationally wrongful act; and (b) the act would be internationally wrongful if committed by that State.*

There is a controversy regarding the criterion of 'knowledge' in Art. 16 ASR, with some scholars requiring actual intent to facilitate the commission of a Human Rights violation.[93] However, as with other violations of international law, motivation – notoriously hard to prove, especially where State actions are concerned – is not necessary; what matters is the

---

91 Or Art. 48(1) ARIO, respectively.

92 International Law Commission, *Yearbook of the International Law Commission* (2001), vol. II, Part Two, commentary on Art. 47 ASR, at para. 1 and 3.

93 The argument is based on the wording of the ILC's Commentary on Art. 16(5) ASR, which states that a 'State is not responsible for aid or assistance under article 16 unless the relevant State organ intended, by the aid or assistance given, to facilitate the occurrence of the wrongful conduct'. However, even scholars who require 'intent' argue that, under certain conditions, the criterion should be interpreted broadly, so that one may infer the intention from objective criteria, particularly when internationally wrongful acts are committed 'manifestly' or 'systematically'; see H.P. Aust, *Complicity and the Law of State Responsibility* (2011), at 230 et seq. and 245; Nolte and Aust, 'Equivocal Helpers: Complicit States, Mixed Messages and International Law', 58 *International & Comparative Law Quarterly (ICLQ)* (2009) 1, at 15.

effect of the action, the knowledge of its causation, and the possibility of acting differently.[94] Therefore, a due diligence standard must be applied. This is also in line with a more recent General Comment of the Human Rights Committee on the right to life (Art. 6 ICCPR), according to which the obligation of States Parties to respect and ensure the Human Right to life extends to 'reasonably foreseeable threats'.[95] Applying this standard, it would be hard to deny the fulfillment of the knowledge criterion in respect of lasting cooperation regarding migration control with third countries, such as Libya, that have a well-documented record of Human Rights violations in the treatment of migrants pulled back when trying to reach Europe (see above, section 1.1, on trend 1).[96]

However, it is not yet fully established how the general principles on State responsibility and responsibility of International Organizations – as laid down in ASR and ARIO – relate to the special regime of the ECHR. Does the jurisdiction clause in Art. 1 ECHR create a *lex specialis* that limits state responsibility to cases where jurisdiction exists, or is it not meant to limit other responsibility rules? The ECtHR has explicitly invoked the ASR in the past[97] when discussing the establishment of jurisdiction under Art. 1 ECHR. The question of attribution was discussed as a preliminary question for establishing jurisdiction when multiple actors are involved in a possible Human Rights violation. In line with this case-law, one may also

94 See, for a similar standard, M. Fink, *Frontex and Human Rights. Responsibility in 'Multi-Actor Situations' under the ECHR and EU Public Liability Law* (2018); R. Mungianu, *Frontex and Non-Refoulement. The International Responsibility of the EU* (2016), at 80 et seq.

95 HR Committee, General Comment No. 36 on Article 6 ICCPR on the Right to Life, CCPR/C/GC/36, at para. 7; see also Moreno-Lax and Lemberg-Pedersen, 'Border-induced Displacement: The Ethical and Legal Implications of Distance creation through Externalization', 56 *Questions of International Law* (2019) 5, at 19.

96 In the case of Libya, this result may follow even if one interprets Art. 16 ASR as requiring intent, see H.P. Aust, *Complicity and the Law of State Responsibility* (2011), at 245.

97 Namely Art. 6 ASR, see ECtHR, *Jaloud v. the Netherlands*, Appl. no. 47708/08, Grand Chamber Judgment of 20 November 2014, at para. 151; on the implications of this decision, see Rooney, 'The Relationship between Jurisdiction and Attribution after Jaloud v. Netherlands', 62 *Netherlands International Law Review (NILR)* (2015) 407.

invoke Art. 16 ASR for the interpretation of Art. 1 ECHR and thus extend the notion of jurisdiction as 'effective control' to cases of complicity.[98]

Following another line of argument, it is also possible to refer directly to Art. 16 ASR as applicable independently of Art. 1 ECHR. In a more recent decision, the ECtHR again situated the ECHR within the general framework of international law:

> *Despite its specific character as a human rights instrument, the Convention is an international treaty to be interpreted in accordance with the relevant norms and principles of public international law.*[99]

Hence, we hold that Art. 1 ECHR should not be interpreted so as to limit international responsibility for Human Rights violations. Such an interpretation would open up a pathway for the extensive circumvention of Convention rights by the employment of third countries. Consequently, the ECHR is also applicable when a State Party to the Convention is responsible for complicity to Human Rights violations under Art. 16 ASR.

1.2.3 Specific issue: 'Push-backs' on the High Seas and at land borders

Push-back practices indisputably constitute violations of the principle of non-refoulement. They have already been outlawed by the ECtHR in its *Hirsi* decision in 2012 for cases on the high seas.[100] In that decision, the Court also declared push-backs at sea a violation of the prohibition of collective expulsions as laid down in Art. 4 Protocol No. 4 ECHR (for details, see Chapter 3).

The same rationale applies to cases concerning measures at land borders. This was confirmed by the ECtHR's Grand Chamber decision in the case of *N.D. and N.T.*[101] In this decision, however, the Court established a new criterion for the assessment of violations of the prohibition of collective expulsions: States may refuse entry to aliens and may even push back

---

98 M. den Heijer, *Europe and Extraterritorial Asylum* (2012); Markard, 'The Right to Leave by Sea: Legal Limits on EU Migration Control by Third Countries', 27 *European Journal of International Law (EJIL)* (2016) 615.

99 ECtHR, *N.D. and N.T. v. Spain*, Appl. no. 8675/15 and 8697/15, Grand Chamber Judgment of 13 February 2020, at para. 172.

100 ECtHR, *Hirsi Jamaa and others v. Italy*, Appl. no. 27765/09, Judgment of 23 February 2012.

101 ECtHR, *N.D. and N.T. v. Spain*, Appl. no. 8675/15 and 8697/15, Grand Chamber Judgment of 13 February 2020.

persons who have already entered the State's territory without individual removal decisions if the State provides 'genuine and effective access to means of legal entry'. In its assessment, the Court considers whether there were 'cogent reasons' for the person concerned not to make use of these means of legal entry.[102] The limits of this newly established exception are far from clear, given that the Court highlighted several aspects of the particular case.[103] In any case, the Court established this criterion for the interpretation of Art. 4 Protocol No. 4 ECHR 'without prejudice to the application of Articles 2 and 3' of the Convention.[104] Given the absolute nature of these rights and the resulting prohibitions on refoulement, the standards established by the ECtHR in *N.D. and N.T* do not apply to persons in need of protection.[105]

Thus, as far as access to asylum is concerned, the standard set out in the *Hirsi* decision remains unchanged both at sea and on land. This means that push-backs violate Art. 3 ECHR insofar as they expose persons to risks of inhuman or degrading treatment.

EU legislation mirrors this finding, as Art. 4 of the Schengen Borders Code[106] commits EU Member States, when conducting any measure to control the external borders of the Union, to fully comply with the EU-CFR, relevant international law (including the 1951 Refugee Convention), and 'obligations related to access to international protection, in particular the principle of non-refoulement'. Art. 3 point (b) of the Schengen Borders Code further confirms that the Regulation applies 'without prejudice to the rights of refugees and persons requesting international protection, in particular as regards non-refoulement'. As Art. 4 of the Schengen Borders Code also affirms that 'decisions under this Regulation shall be taken on

---

102 Ibid., at para. 201.

103 Thym, 'Menschenrechtliche Trendwende? Zu den EGMR-Entscheidungen über "heiße Zurückweisungen" an den EU-Außengrenzen und humanitäre Visa für Flüchtlinge', 80 *Zeitschrift für ausländisches öffentliches Recht und Völkerrecht (ZaöRV)* (2020) 989, at 996 et seq.; cf. ECtHR, *Shahzad v. Hungary*, Appl. no. 12625/17, Judgment of 8 July 2021, at para. 60 et seq.

104 ECtHR, *N.D. and N.T. v. Spain*, Appl. no. 8675/15 and 8697/15, Grand Chamber Judgment of 13 February 2020, at para. 201.

105 This is the general view of the legal commentators, see, e.g., ECRE, *Across Borders: The Impact of N.D. and N.T. v. Spain in Europe*, Legal Note 10 (2021), at para. 7–9; Thym, 'Menschenrechtliche Trendwende?', 80 *ZaöRV* (2020) 989, at 999; Lübbe, 'Unklares zu den Pushbacks an den Außengrenzen', *Europarecht* (2020) 450, at 456 et seq.

106 Regulation 2016/399 on a Union Code on the rules governing the movement of persons across borders (Schengen Borders Code).

an individual basis', it leaves no doubts about the illegality of push-backs without any individual assessment of possible grounds for international protection.

1.2.4 Specific issue: Entry of vessels into the territorial waters and disembarkation at EU ports

Disembarkation in the EU is another highly controversial issue, particularly given the fact that the international law of the sea – most importantly, the 1982 United Nations Convention on the Law of the Sea (UNCLOS) – does not explicitly oblige any specific State to permit disembarkation. While UNCLOS obliges States to cooperate in order to promote a swift disembarkation, this obligation toward other States Parties is impossible to address by an individual claimant. However, even UNCLOS (in Art. 2(3)) affirms that the Convention must not be interpreted in isolation but in line with other rules of international law. The application of the law of the sea thus does not preclude the application of international refugee and Human Rights law. The law of the sea, therefore, must be interpreted in conjunction with the principle of non-refoulement (Art. 3 ECHR)[107] as well as positive duties attached to the right to life (Art. 2 ECHR).[108] These may well leave a coastal state with no other option but to allow for disembarkation on its own soil.

The same may follow from the duty to render assistance to persons in distress at sea,[109] an obligation both under customary international law and under a number of provisions in international treaties, such as Art. 98(1) UNCLOS, Annex 2.1.10 of the 1979 International Search and

---

107 See Moreno-Lax, 'Seeking Asylum in the Mediterranean: Against a Fragmentary Reading of EU Member States' Obligations Accruing at Sea', 23 *International Journal of Refugee Law* (2011) 174.

108 Komp, 'The Duty to Assist Persons in Distress: An Alternative Source of Protection against the Return of Migrants and Asylum Seekers to the High Seas?', in V. Moreno-Lax and E. Papastavridis (eds), *'Boat Refugees' and Migrants at Sea: A Comprehensive Approach: Integrating Maritime Security with Human Rights* (2016) 222.

109 For the following, see also A. Farahat and N. Markard, *Places of Safety in the Mediterranean: The EU's Policy of Outsourcing Responsibility* (2020), at 14–18, available at https://eu.boell.org/en/2020/02/18/places-safety-mediterranean-eus-policy-outsourcing-responsibility; see also the Study Update (2020), available at https://eu.boell.org/sites/default/files/2020-05/HBS-POS%20study-A4_25-05-20-2.pdf?dimension1=anna2020.

Rescue Convention (SAR Convention),[110] and Regulation V/33 of the 1974 International Convention for the Safety of Life at Sea (SOLAS).[111] Rescues must be delivered to a 'place of safety'.[112] This has been characterized by the Maritime Safety Committee (MSC) of the International Maritime Organization (IMO) as a 'place where the survivors' safety of life is no longer threatened and where their basic human needs (such as food, shelter and medical needs) can be met'. Governments have the duty to 'co-operate with each other with regard to providing suitable places of safety for survivors after considering relevant factors and risks'. Where asylum seekers and refugees recovered at sea are affected, the governments must consider the 'need to avoid disembarkation in territories where the lives and freedoms of those alleging a well-founded fear of persecution would be threatened'.[113] More specifically, the Rescue Co-ordination Centre (RCC) of the State responsible for a particular SAR zone in which an incident takes place (and possibly also other RCCs confronted with a distress situation) is obliged to initiate not only the rescue operation but also the process of identifying a place of safety and delivering the person to that place.[114]

A recent study, taking into account numerous reports on the current Human Rights situation in Northern African Mediterranean countries, concluded that none of these countries generally qualify as 'places of safety' in the sense of the aforementioned provisions.[115] While this result seems obvious for Libya, given its record of Human Rights violations,

---

110 International Convention on Maritime Search and Rescue (SAR), 1979, 1405 UNTS 97, modified by Res. MSC Res. 155(78), 20 May 2004 (SAR Convention 2004). The Convention was ratified by all Mediterranean States except for Egypt and Israel. The 2004 amendments were not ratified by Malta.

111 International Convention for the Safety of Life at Sea (SOLAS), 1974, 1184 UNTS 278. The 1974 Convention was ratified by all Mediterranean States except for Bosnia and Herzegovina; the 2004 amendments (hereafter referred to as SOLAS (2004)) were not ratified by Malta.

112 SOLAS (2004) regulation V/33, para. 1.1; SAR Convention (2004), Annex 3.1.9.

113 MSC.Res. 167(78), 20 May 2004, (MSC 78/26/Add.2, Annex 34, para. 6.12., 6.16 and 6.17). These Guidelines were passed by the IMO Member States with the exception of Malta and were later affirmed by the UN General Assembly, GA Res. 16/222, 16 March 2007, UN doc. A/RES/61/222, para. 70.

114 SAR Convention (2004), Annex 3.1.9 and 4.8.5.

115 A. Farahat and N. Markard, *Places of Safety in the Mediterranean: The EU's Policy of Outsourcing Responsibility* (2020), available at https://eu.boell.org/en/2020/02/18/places-safety-mediterranean-eus-policy-outsourcing-responsibility; see also the Study Update (2020) available at https://eu.boell.org/sites/default/files/2020-05/HBS-POS%20study-A4_25-05-20-2.pdf?dimension1=anna2020.

an analysis of the situation in Algeria, Egypt, Morocco and Tunisia – albeit less devastating – likewise showed an overall lack of functioning asylum systems as well as numerous severe Human Rights violations, such as incidences of chain refoulement, detention of migrants in inhuman and degrading conditions, and the use of torture. This was especially the case for LGBTIQ migrants, who face persecution in all Northern African countries. At the same time, it seems impossible to provide a reliable screening procedure onboard rescuing ships to determine refugee status and comprehensively assess the risk of torture or a particular vulnerability.[116] This is why EU Member States, in order to comply with their duty to render assistance to persons in distress at sea, would have to allow for disembarkation on the soil of an EU Member State.

Based on the EU's general commitment to the protection and promotion of Human Rights (Art. 2 TEU), to the right of life (Art. 2 EU-CFR), the right to asylum (Art. 18 EU-CFR) and the principle of non-refoulement (Art. 19(2) EU-CFR), the EU is accountable for possible violations of these rights in the context of (non-)disembarkation policies. It should, therefore, enact a set of rules according to which Member States must allow migrants to disembark, combined with a mechanism of transfer (for example, by quota) based on the principle of solidarity among Member States.[117] In this respect, the 2019 Malta Declaration on SAR and relocation (see above 1.1, Trend 2) is not an adequate substitution for a stable mechanism with a firm legal basis and general applicability in all (coastal) EU Member States.

Clear-cut and legally binding rules on disembarkation already exist for a limited number of situations, namely, where Frontex-coordinated missions are concerned. Here, the 2014 Maritime Surveillance or External Sea Borders Regulation (Regulation 656/2014) provides for two options: disembarkation may take place in the country from whence the migrants came and, that failing (e.g., if this would violate the principle of non-refoulement or other Human Rights), disembarkation shall take place in the Member State hosting the Frontex operation.[118] This provision could serve

116 Ibid., at 18–31.

117 Cf. European Commission, COM(2020) 610, 23 September 2020. The Commission proposes a solidarity mechanism for cases of disembarkation but builds largely on the goodwill of Member States once the particular situation arises instead of sufficiently anticipating conflict between Member States by providing for clear-cut rules for actual burden sharing; see Art. 45–49.

118 Art. 4 and 10 Regulation 656/2014 establishing rules for the surveillance of the external sea borders.

as a model for a codification that allows disembarkation in costal Member States in general.

1.2.5 Specific issue: Limits to 'protection elsewhere'

Based on the concept of 'protection elsewhere', refugees are referred or transferred to third countries that are said to provide sufficient protection. The idea of excluding persons from refugee status by referring him or her to 'protection elsewhere' – mostly applied as a rule of (in)admissibility of protection claims[119] – has no firm and explicit basis in international law. It is built on the silence on this matter of the 1951 Refugee Convention, which neither expressly permits nor prohibits such policies. The concept remains contested to this day.[120] Among other things, it may be fundamentally at odds with the principles of international solidarity, burden- and responsibility-sharing among UN Member States, and some of the 'guiding principle' of the 2018 Global Compact on Refugees (GCR, para. 5). However, based on the argument that the 1951 Refugee Convention does not grant a right to asylum and that asylum seekers must not be entitled to 'choose' their specific country of refuge, the concept of 'protection elsewhere' is mostly accepted – for example, by the United Nations High Commissioner for Refugees (UNHCR)[121] and by the authors of the 2007 Michigan Guidelines, a highly relevant scholarly opinion.[122] However, constraints are imposed on its application – that is, there are criteria for the permissibility of a referral or transfer of asylum seekers to a particular third country.[123]

In the context of the EU, the concept of 'protection elsewhere' is applied by referring or transferring refugees to third countries that are identified

---

119 See, e.g., Art. 33(2) Asylum Procedures Directive.

120 Moreno-Lax, 'The Legality of the "Safe Third Country" Notion Contested: Insights from the Law of Treaties', in G.S. Goodwin-Gill and P. Weckel (eds), *Migration & Refugee Protection in the 21st Century: Legal Aspects* (2015) 663.

121 UNHCR, Position on Readmission Agreements, 'Protection Elsewhere' and Asylum Policy (1994), at 465, available at https://www.refworld.org/docid/3ae6b31cb8.html.

122 University of Michigan Law School, *The Michigan Guidelines on Protection Elsewhere* (2007), at 211, available at https://www.refworld.org/docid/4ae9acd0d.html.

123 On the general legitimacy of the concept, see also Foster, 'Protection Elsewhere: The Legal Implications of Requiring Refugees to Seek Protection in Another State', 28 *Michigan Journal of International Law* (2007) 223, at 230.

either as the 'country of first asylum' (Art. 35 Asylum Procedures Directive 2013/32/EU), implying that the person concerned has already found protection in that country, or as a 'safe third country' (Art. 38 and 39 Asylum Procedures Directive), where it is presumed that the person concerned *could have* found protection. A number of normative problems arise regarding both the interpretation of the current versions and the possible reform of these provisions, particularly the 'safe third country' rule.

While Art. 38(1)(c) Asylum Procedures Directive requires that a Member State may only apply the 'safe third country' rule if the third country respects the principle of non-refoulement 'in accordance with the Geneva Convention', it is unclear whether this requires actual ratification of the Geneva Convention by the receiving state or only an equivalent protection standard. This question is relevant for the case of Turkey, whose geographical limitation of the Geneva Convention to refugees from Europe excludes those from Syria, for example. An expansion of the safe third country concepts seems also to be intended by the Commission's proposal of 2016 and 2020 to replace the wording in Art. 38(1)(c) Asylum Procedures Directive by a provision that only refers to the 'substantive standards of the Geneva Convention' or 'sufficient protection' provided that further criteria are met.[124] Such a widening of the concept would be at odds with Art. 78(1) TFEU, which continues to require the EU's asylum policy to be 'in accordance' with the Geneva Convention. Furthermore, the EU's commitments to the protection and promotion of Human Rights in general (Art. 2 TEU), as well as to the right to asylum (Art. 18 EU-CFR) and the principle of non-refoulement (Art. 19(2) EU-CFR) in particular, require a narrow interpretation of the current provision of Art. 38(1)(c) Asylum Procedures Directive and set limits for legislative amendments.

In the ongoing process of reforming the CEAS, it was additionally proposed to make the application of the (nowadays optional) 'safe third country' rule mandatory for all EU Member States as well as to lower the standard for referrals to 'safe third countries' by assuming a necessary 'connection'[125] between any asylum seeker and a third country solely on the basis that the country was transited by, and is geographically close

124 European Commission, Proposal for an Asylum Procedures Regulation, COM(2016) 467, 13 July 2016, Art. 45(1)(e). The Commission's amended proposal of 23 September 2020, COM(2020) 611, leaves the relevant parts unchanged.

125 On the concept, see Lübbe, 'Das Verbindungsprinzip im fragmentierten europäischen Asylraum', 50 *Europarecht (EuR)* (2015) 329.

to the country of origin of, the asylum seeker.[126] Again, these proposals seem to contradict the EU's endorsement of a positive contribution to the protection of Human Rights and are at odds with the principle of burden- and responsibility-sharing as expressions of international solidarity (GCR, para. 5).

Another important issue regarding the application of the 'safe third country' rule concerns the actual empirical determination of the Human Rights situation (or 'safety') in a given third country and the burden of proof in this regard. The 2007 Michigan Guidelines require, for permitting the referral of an asylum seeker to 'protection elsewhere', a 'good faith empirical assessment' by the sending state that refugees will enjoy Refugee Convention rights in the receiving state.[127] Similarly, UNHCR maintains that

> *the country to which an asylum application has been submitted is primarily responsible for considering it. Accordingly, if that country wants to transfer that responsibility to a third country, in addition to securing the agreement of that country to receive and consider the asylum application, it must establish that such third country is "safe" with respect to that particular asylum-seeker. The burden of proof does not lie with the asylum-seeker (to establish that the third country is unsafe), but rather with the country which wishes to remove the asylum-seeker from its territory (to establish that the third country is safe).*[128]

The burden of proof in this respect lies with the country where the asylum application was filed, as it retains the responsibility for any action in violation of its obligation from international law, most notably the principle of non-refoulement. This may also follow from the practical consideration

126 European Commission, Proposal for an Asylum Procedures Regulation, COM(2016) 467, 13 July 2016, Art. 45(3)(a). The amended proposal of 23 September 2020, COM(2020) 611, leaves the relevant parts unchanged.

127 University of Michigan Law School, *The Michigan Guidelines on Protection Elsewhere* (2007), at 211, available at https://www.refworld.org/docid/4ae9acd0d.html.

128 UNHCR, Observations on the European Commission's Proposal for a Council Directive on Minimum Standards on Procedures for Granting and Withdrawing Refugee Status (2001), at para. 36, available at https://www.refworld.org/docid/3c0e3f374.html; for a similar standard, see Foster, 'Protection Elsewhere: The Legal Implications of Requiring Refugees to Seek Protection in Another State', 28 *Michigan Journal of International Law* (2007) 223, at 281.

that the refugee affected cannot be required to provide comprehensive information about the Human Rights situation in the third country.[129]

In the context of the EU, Art. 38 Asylum Procedures Directive states that Member States may only apply the third country rule where the competent authorities are 'satisfied' that a person seeking protection will be treated in accordance with the principles named in Art. 38 in the third country concerned. According to EASO (the European Asylum Support Office), Member States therefore must 'substantiate any finding that the country concerned is sufficiently safe to remove the applicant' if they wish to apply the safe country concept.[130] This requires the 'determination of more than the mere absence of persecution or serious harm'[131] and obliges Member States to show that the safeguards provided for in Art. 38 would be met in the third country concerned – a requirement practically impossible to accomplish aboard a ship on a SAR mission, for instance. This sets a high standard that must be observed both in future EU legislation and in any conclusion or application, by the EU or its Member States, of cooperation arrangements with third countries on matters of migration control.

1.2.6 Specific issue: Allocating asylum jurisdiction within the EU (Dublin system)

Other legal problems arise as to the internal European dimension of referring asylum seekers to other countries in the framework of the Dublin system. Depending on the circumstances of the applicant concerned, as well as of the conditions of the asylum system in the specific EU Member State to which a person is supposed to be referred, the ECtHR has in the past found that Dublin referrals may violate Art. 3 ECHR, both on its own and in conjunction with Art. 13 ECHR (right to an effective remedy) as well as Art. 4 of Protocol No. 4 ECHR (prohibition of collective expulsion).[132]

The rights from the ECHR are mirrored and partly expanded by the safeguards enshrined in the EU-CFR. The current Dublin III Regulation

---

129 Foster, ibid.

130 EASO, *Evidence and Credibility Assessment in the Context of the Common European Asylum System* (2018), at 164.

131 Ibid., at 167.

132 ECtHR, *M.S.S. v. Belgium and Greece*, Appl. no., 30696/09, Judgment of 21 January 2011; *Sharifi and others v. Italy and Greece*, Appl. no. 16643/09, Judgment of 21 October 2014; *Tarakhel v. Switzerland*, Appl. no. 29217/12, Grand Chamber Judgment of 4 November 2014.

(Regulation 604/2013) explicitly refers to the EU-CFR when it states that the Regulation 'seeks to ensure full observance of the right to asylum guaranteed by Art. 18 of the Charter as well as the rights recognized under Articles 1 [dignity], 4 [prohibition of torture, inhuman or degrading treatment or punishment], 7 [respect for private and family life], 24 [rights of the child] and 47 thereof [right to an effective remedy and to a fair trial]'.[133] While the CJEU has hitherto left open the question of whether Art. 18 EU-CFR amounts to a free-standing right to asylum,[134] it is clear that the Dublin Regulation has to be construed in light of this constitutional guarantee. Moreover, the Court confirmed that in order to ensure compliance with the fundamental rights of asylum seekers, EU Member States, when applying the Dublin Regulation, may not transfer asylum seekers to other Member States 'where they cannot be unaware that systemic deficiencies in the asylum procedure and in the reception conditions of asylum seekers in that Member State amount to substantial grounds for believing that the asylum seeker would face a real risk of being subjected to inhuman or degrading treatment within the meaning of Art. 4 of the Charter'.[135]

The Dublin system must fully respect the aforementioned Human Rights and fundamental rights. A revised Dublin Regulation, or its successor, must be particularly sensitive to the protection of family union as part of the respect for private and family life enshrined in Art. 8 ECHR and Art. 7 EU-CFR, and to the rights of – particularly unaccompanied – minors, in order to fully take into account the rights of the child as provided for in the Convention on the Rights of the Child (CRC) and Art. 24 EU-CFR. Proposals such as the 2016 Commission proposal to shorten or eliminate time limits for transfers from one Member State to another[136] may not only lead to violations of procedural rights such as the right to an effective remedy (Art. 13 ECHR, Art. 47 EU-CFR) but also to the guarantee of access to a fair asylum procedure that is implied in Art. 18 EU-CFR. Accordingly, access to a functioning asylum procedure must be provided by a new Dublin system.[137]

133 Dublin III Regulation, recital 39.

134 CJEU, Case C-528/11, *Zuheyr Frayeh Halaf* (EU:C:2013:342).

135 CJEU, Cases C-411/10 and C-493/10, *N.S. and M.E.* (EU:C:2011:865), at para. 94.

136 European Commission, Proposal for a recast Dublin Regulation, COM(2016) 270, 4 May 2016, at 16.

137 Cf. E. Guild, C. Costello and V. Moreno-Lax, *Implementation of the 2015 Council Decisions establishing provisional measures in the area of international protection for the benefit of Italy and of Greece* (2017), available at https://www.europarl.europa.

In order to guarantee these rights, including under exceptional circumstances, and to avoid leaving persons in limbo as 'refugees in orbit', the Dublin Regulation must also provide for sufficiently flexible rules for one Member State to be able to step in for another if needed by applying escape clauses such as, for example, the discretionary or 'humanitarian' clauses in the current Dublin system (Art. 17 Dublin III Regulation). Depriving the future Dublin system of such flexibility would inevitably lead to situations where EU Member States would have to choose between compliance with EU law and their obligations under the ECHR. A new Dublin Regulation that does not systematically avoid such conflict would be unlawful.[138]

1.2.7 Specific issue: International obligations to provide for safe and legal access to asylum?

Due to the lack of safe and regular options for access to protection in Europe, the vast majority of asylum seekers nowadays reach Europe as irregular migrants.[139] This has provoked calls for opening or extending safe and regular pathways such as quota-based governmental admission, resettlement programs, ad hoc humanitarian admission programs, or admission on the basis of private or community sponsorship.[140] At the same time the ECtHR, in the 2020 decision in *N.D. and N.T. v. Spain*, held that certain coercive measures of migration control (in that case, actual push-backs without individual assessment; see above, section 1.2.3, and Chapter 3) may only be employed by States that at the same time provide

---

eu/RegData/etudes/STUD/2017/583132/IPOL_STU(2017)583132_EN.pdf, 43, at 51.

138 M. Pelzer, *Die Rechtsstellung von Asylbewerbern im Asylzuständigkeitssystem der EU* (2020), at 148 et seq. and 243 et seq.; L.-M. Lührs, *Überstellungsschutz und gegenseitiges Vertrauen* (2021), at 52 and 244 et seq.

139 V. Moreno-Lax, *The Added Value of EU Legislation on Humanitarian Visas: Legal Aspects* (2018), at 34 et seq., available at https://www.europarl.europa.eu/RegData/etudes/STUD/2018/621823/EPRS_STU%282018%29621823_EN.pdf.

140 For an overview, see M.-C. Foblets and L. Leboeuf (eds), *Humanitarian Admission to Europe: The Law between Promises and Constraints* (2020), and L. Ansems de Vries, J.P. Gauci and H. Redwood, *Legal Pathways to Protection* (2018), available at https://www.biicl.org/documents/24_2042_legal_pathways_policy_brief_final_complete_27feb2018.pdf.

'genuine and effective access to means of legal entry'.[141] Arguably, this line of reasoning implies a broadly framed positive obligation of States, derived from Human Rights, to facilitate legal pathways of accessing the asylum system.[142] This calls for legislation in the EU to provide for such forms of regular access to protection, which notably must also be 'effective'.[143]

One of the safe and regular pathways to protection frequently discussed is humanitarian visas – that is, permits to enter the territory of a state in order to ask for asylum. Humanitarian visas stand out among other pathways in that they are based on a well-established legal instrument (visas) and existing governmental institutions (embassies and consulates). Moreover, this instrument allows for the external pre-assessment of individual protection claims, taking into account both urgent need and existing (e.g., family or economic) ties. If founded on a legal basis applicable in all EU Member States, rather than on unilateral ad hoc measures, this pathway could also provide for an accessible, fair, and reliable mechanism for the individual and contribute to burden sharing among the EU Member States. The question of humanitarian visas also specifically calls for the EU legislature because – unlike in resettlement programs – UNHCR is typically not involved here. Such legislation could build upon rich experiences from Member States, given that 16 of them have, or have had, schemes for issuing humanitarian visas.[144]

In fact, in 2018 the European Parliament issued an initiative report calling on the Commission to table a legislative proposal establishing a

141 ECtHR, *N.D. and N.T. v. Spain*, Appl. no. 8675/15 and 8697/15, Grand Chamber Judgment of 13 February 2020, at para. 201; confirmed in *Shahzad v. Hungary*, Appl. no. 12625/17, Judgment of 8 July 2021, at para. 62.

142 Daniel Thym has called it a doctrinal 'seed' (*Samen*) planted by the Court which may sprout in its later case-law, although he doubts that this will actually happen; see Thym, 'Menschenrechtliche Trendwende?', 80 *Zeitschrift für ausländisches öffentliches Recht und Völkerrecht (ZaöRV)* (2020) 989, at 1007 and 1010.

143 However, the reluctance of EU Member States in this respect is considerable. For example, in a 2019 hearing before the ECtHR, representatives of Belgium and France, among other Member States, reaffirmed their rejection of any interpretation of the ECHR that would require Member States to issue humanitarian visa; see the public hearing in the case *M.N. and others v. Belgium*, Appl. no. 3599/18, webcast available at https://www.echr.coe.int/Pages/home.aspx?p=hearings&w=359918_24042019&language=en. See below, section 3.2.2 on the ECtHR decision which, in 2020, declared the complaints by M.N. and others to be inadmissible.

144 U. Iben Jensen, *Humanitarian Visas: Option or Obligation?* (2014), at 48 et seq., available at https://www.europarl.europa.eu/RegData/etudes/STUD/2014/509986/IPOL_STU(2014)509986_EN.pdf.

'European Humanitarian Visa' that gives access to the territory of the Member State issuing the visa for the purpose of submitting an application for international protection.[145] This call to provide a regular pathway to access international protection in the EU is based on the duty of the EU to take positive action to guarantee the principle of non-refoulement,[146] but other human and fundamental rights may also require the EU to become active as a legislator in the field.

It has been argued, for example, that in light of the EU-CFR a duty to issue visas to ensure safe access to the European asylum already follows from the interpretation of EU law as it stands, in particular the EU Visa Code (Regulation 810/2009). In the case of a Syrian family who had applied for visas at the Belgian embassy in Lebanon in order to seek asylum in Belgium, Paolo Mengozzi, Advocate General at the CJEU, argued that in cases where its rejection would expose a person to a serious risk of inhuman or degrading treatment, a legal right to a visa flows from the EU-CFR, which applies in the ambit of the EU Visa Code.[147] The Advocate General held that the denial of visas may violate the applicants' rights as protected by Art. 1 (right to dignity), Art. 2 (right to life), Art. 3 (right to the integrity of the person), Art. 4 (prohibition of torture and inhuman and degrading treatment) and Art. 24(2) EU-CFR (the child's best interest). The CJEU, in its 2017 decision, did not follow the Advocate General's Opinion. However, it did not rule on the substance of the case but rather rejected the view that the Visa Code, and hence the EU-CFR, applied to the particular case.[148] Given the ongoing structural risk of human and fun-

---

145 European Parliament, Resolution 2018/2271(INL) of 11 December 2018 with recommendations to the Commission on Humanitarian Visas, available at https://www.europarl.europa.eu/doceo/document/TA-8-2018-0494_EN.pdf; European Parliament, 'Humanitarian visas', European Added Value Assessment accompanying the European Parliament's legislative own-initiative report (Rapporteur: Juan Fernando López Aguilar), Study, October 2018, available at https://publications.europa.eu/en/publication-detail/-/publication/a3b57ef6-d66d-11e8-9424-01aa75ed71a1/language-en/format-PDF.

146 V. Moreno-Lax, *The Added Value of EU Legislation on Humanitarian Visas: Legal Aspects* (2018), at 69 et seq., available at https://www.europarl.europa.eu/RegData/etudes/STUD/2018/621823/EPRS_STU%282018%29621823_EN.pdf.

147 Opinion of Advocate General Mengozzi in Case C-638/16 PPU, *X & X v. Belgium* (EU:C:2017:93).

148 The Court held that the Visa Code was not applicable to such visa applications as in the case decide upon filed with the purpose to seek international protection after arrival in the EU: CJEU, Case C-638/16-PPU, *X & X v. Belgium* (EU:C:2017:173). In a similar vein, the ECtHR in 2020 decided that due to the lack of 'jurisdiction' in such cases, the ECHR does not apply to State Parties'

damental rights violations referred to by AG Mengozzi, in cases of denial of visa applications the EU remains accountable for not having provided a firm legal basis for humanitarian visas across EU Member States.

1.3 Recommendations

Recommendation 1: Strictly condition cooperation with third countries on Human Rights compliance

The EU and its Member States must immediately cease to support, directly or indirectly, any measures of migration control by third countries that constitute breaches of international law. Accordingly, cooperation in this regard with States known for their systematic violations of Human Rights must be suspended.

In deciding on the establishment of any other 'migration partnerships' with third countries, Human Rights provisions should always be strictly observed as legal guardrails and should also be carefully considered as policy guidelines. Following such assessments, cooperation with third countries may appear to be inappropriate in the first place. Any form of cooperation by the EU or its Member States with third countries in the field of migration control should only be considered when the third country is able and willing to effectively protect Human Rights and is politically sufficiently stable at the time of concluding the agreement.

Furthermore, to guarantee a certain level of protection over time, an effective mechanism to monitor respect for Human Rights in such third countries would need to be established. Such a mechanism should provide for an objective and independent evaluation. It would have to consist of a politically responsible management body (under the direction of the Commission or Frontex) as well as an independent body of experts for risk assessment of Human Rights violations (e.g., delegated by the EU Fundamental Rights Agency (FRA) in cooperation with UNHCR as well as experts from NGOs). The body of experts would need to have full access to empirical data in the third country (e.g., prison conditions) allowing for a continuous and precise evaluation of conformity with Human Rights standards in that country.

---

diplomatic and consular missions, ECtHR, *M.N. and others v. Belgium*, Appl. no. 3599/18, Grand Chamber Decision of 5 May 2020, at para. 112 et seq.

Any future arrangements on migration cooperation between the EU or its Member States and third countries should, therefore, contain provisions on the establishment of such a mechanism and should be conditional upon the continuous respect for Human Rights in that country. The cooperation should automatically end if the management body, following the risk assessment of the independent expert body, comes to the conclusion that the third country does not sufficiently observe Human Rights provisions, namely, in cases of severe or systematic violations of Human Rights.

Recommendation 2: End push-backs and closure of ports

Member States must refrain from any push-back measures as such practices violate the ECHR and the EU-CFR. This should be fostered by new EU legislation specifying the conditions for the respect of Human Rights, such as the principle of non-refoulement, during border control measures conducted by Member States. While such conditions are enumerated in detail for measures involving the coordination of Frontex, the same is not true for measures conducted by Member States independently – the vast majority of all (sea) border control measures.[149] While these must also respect the principle of non-refoulement and other human and fundamental rights when undertaking controls of the EU external borders (with or without Frontex involvement), the respective provisions in the Schengen Borders Code are rather general and make no provision for search and rescue incidents in the course of border control operations. Such legislation should also specify the Human Rights obligations that apply when EU agencies or Member States call on third country authorities for pull-back measures.

In a similar vein, while Member States should refrain from the closure of their ports to the disembarkation of migrants rescued at sea by NGO vessels conducting SAR operations, such non-disembarkation policies also point to the structural lack of a safe, fair, and predictable allocation and relocation mechanism following disembarkation.[150] Establishing such an

149 Den Heijer, 'Frontex and the Shifting Approaches to Boat Migration in the European Union', in R. Zaiotti (ed.), *Externalizing Migration Management* (2016) 53, at 67.

150 ECRE, *'Relying on Relocation': ECRE's Proposal for a predictable and fair relocation arrangement following disembarkation* (2019), at 4 et seq., available at https://www.ecre.org/wp-content/uploads/2019/01/Policy-Papers-06.pdf; UNHCR, Italy Fact

allocation mechanism should be an integral part of any reform of the Dublin System.

Recommendation 3: Establish a high standard for the assumption of safe third countries

Any attempt at lowering standards with regard to the concept of a 'safe third country', such as the current proposal for a Regulation replacing the Asylum Procedures Directive, should be thoroughly reconsidered. In particular, the new concept of partial territorial protection must be formulated in such a way as to exclude the dangers of referring migrants to overall unstable third countries and of their confinement in parts of that third country. Furthermore, any proposals for revising the connection clause in Art. 38 of the Asylum Procedure Directive must take into account the right to respect for the applicant's family and social ties.

Recommendation 4: Keep the Dublin system flexible to effectively ensure access to asylum

Any reform of the Dublin system must duly take into account the Human Rights of asylum seekers, including the right to access a functioning asylum procedure and reception system, while strengthening the respect for family and social ties.

A new Dublin Regulation must not reverse the achievements in terms of Human Rights and EU fundamental rights brought about through case-law – most notably, the protection against transfers to Member States where there is a threat of Human Rights violations and the guarantee of effective legal remedies, including with suspensive effect. A new Regulation must also strictly guarantee that the responsibility to process an asylum application falls back upon a Member State in the case of deficits of the asylum system in the responsible Member State. In a similar vein, in order to guarantee sufficient flexibility of Member States to comply with Human Rights obligations, particularly under exceptional circumstances, a new Dublin Regulation must continue to provide for an open-ended discretionary clause for the assumption of responsibility by Member States.

Sheet (2019), at 2, available at https://data2.unhcr.org/en/documents/download/68161.

Overall, a new Regulation should reduce rather than expand coercive elements and provide for ways to take due account of the individual interests and agency of asylum seekers.

Recommendation 5: Establish safe and legal pathways to asylum in the EU

In order to comply with its claim to protect and promote Human Rights, the EU must not only refrain from certain measures but also become proactive in providing safe and legal pathways to refuge in the EU.

There are a number of avenues to reach this goal. For example, quota-based governmental admission may guarantee such pathways for those in urgent need of protection. Massively expanding resettlement programs or ad hoc humanitarian admission programs – for example, in cooperation with UNHCR – could be one solution. This could also be combined with facilitating individual admission based on personal links to the receiving state by family reunification and private sponsorship.

However, external assessment of individual protection claims with a realistic chance of obtaining a humanitarian visa is, in our view, the preferable option for providing an accessible, fair, and reliable mechanism of access based on considerations of both urgent need and existing ties. Conditions for issuing such visas should be laid down in a Regulation, following the initiative report by the European Parliament for a legislative proposal for a European Humanitarian Visa.

Chapter 2 – Ensuring Liberty and Freedom of Movement

The authority to admit and expel non-nationals is generally regarded as a key element of state sovereignty. To enforce such decisions, States often resort to administrative detention. EU Member States were initially reluctant to lose control over the legal exercise of physical force toward migrants. However, immigration detention is not only instrumental in enforcing a given policy aim but also a tool of migration policy in its own right, used for a variety of purposes.[151] Accordingly, regulating immigration detention is a necessary corollary of the EU's task of developing a common immigration policy according to Art. 79 TFEU.

Since the second phase of legislation in the field of migration policy, the EU has exercised its respective powers and developed a broad – albeit fragmented – regulatory framework in relation to administrative detention of migrants. Immigration detention is treated as an adjunct to the reception of asylum seekers (Reception Conditions Directive),[152] including the EU-wide mechanism for allocating asylum jurisdiction (Dublin Regulation),[153] and to the legislative act regulating the procedure on terminating illegal residence, including deportations (Return Directive).[154] Other related instruments touch on the issue of detention indirectly, such as the Schengen Borders Code[155] or, briefly, the Asylum Procedures Directive.[156] As a result, EU law has established a regulatory framework on detention that covers all relevant situations and, hence, has assumed for itself primary responsibility for Human Rights compliance in this field of European migration policy.

---

151 Leerken and Broeders, 'A Case of Mixed Motives? Formal and Informal Functions of Administrative Immigration Detention', 50 *British Journal of Criminology* (2010) 830.

152 Directive 2013/33/EU, recitals 15–20 and Art. 8–11.

153 Regulation 604/2013, recital 20 and Art. 28.

154 Directive 2008/115/EC, recitals 16–17 and Art. 15–17.

155 Regulation 2016/399, Art. 14, Annex V and VI: Border guards must prevent the entry of persons without a right to enter 'in accordance with national, Union and international law'.

156 Directive 2013/32/EU, Art. 26: a person shall not be detained for the sole reason that he or she is an applicant; speedy judicial review must be ensured; cross-reference to Reception Conditions Directive for grounds, conditions and guarantees.

2.1 Structural challenges and current trends

In public discourse, migration has increasingly been assimilated to security. Migrants, especially those who are undocumented or otherwise irregular, are presented as a danger to society. Detention policies have become emblematic in an attempt to show control and respond to the threat of terrorism as well as to mounting political pressures regarding border security.[157] There is also an increasing trend of EU Member States using detention as a deterrence policy with a view to managing the numbers of 'undesirable' migrants, by seeking to push those present in their territory to leave, and to deter future arrivals.[158] Thus, detention is portrayed as a legitimate response to protecting national interests and serves to further a variety of broader strategies of migration management. It is implemented toward migrants, including refugees and asylum seekers, at all stages of their migration process: upon seeking entry to a territory or pending deportation, removal or return from a territory,[159] but also during asylum procedures (e.g., the special form of detention pending transfer to another Dublin State).[160]

Detention, defined here as 'deprivation of liberty or confinement to a particular place'[161], can take place in a variety of locations – from specialized administrative facilities to prisons, airport transit zones, or remand

157 Sampson and Mitchell, 'Global Trends in Immigration Detention and Alternatives to Detention: Practical, Political and Symbolic Rationales', 1 *Journal on Migration and Human Security* (2013) 97; see also Leerken and Broeders, 'A Case of Mixed Motives? Formal and Informal Functions of Administrative Immigration Detention', 50 *British Journal of Criminology* (2010) 830, at 842–844; Ph. de Bruycker et al., *Alternatives to Immigration and Asylum Detention in the EU: Time for Implementation* (2015), at 19.

158 See, e.g. for Denmark, J. Suarez-Krabbe, J. Arce and A. Lindberg, *Stop Killing Us Slowly: A Research Report on the Motivation Enhancement Measures and Criminalization of Rejected Asylum Seekers in Denmark* (2018), available at http://refugees.dk/media/1757/stop-killing-us_uk.pdf.

159 A. Edwards, *Back to Basics: The Right to Liberty and Security of Person and 'Alternatives to Detention of Refugees, Asylum-Seekers, Stateless Persons and Other Migrants'* (2011), available at https://www.unhcr.org/4dc949c49.pdf.

160 Dublin detention is a special form of detention that should only serve the purpose of facilitating a transfer to the responsible Dublin State and falls within neither the categories of restrictions of liberty for asylum seekers nor detention in the context of return; see Art. 28(2) Dublin III Regulation.

161 UNHCR, Guidelines on the Applicable Criteria and Standards relating to the Detention of Asylum-Seekers and Alternatives to Detention (2012), at 9, available at https://www.refworld.org/docid/503489533b8.html.

facilities.[162] States justify detention measures with practical considerations – such as having the migrant at the disposal of the authorities for identity checks or public health screenings at arrival – as well as enforcement-related motivations such as securing public order, or political objectives such as protecting host societies.[163]

The three key pieces of legislation at EU level that pertain to detention are subject to ongoing reform efforts,[164] which tend toward a tightening of the regime. Whereas in the context of the second phase of CEAS, the European Commission still displayed a fundamental rights approach to migration detention (albeit one met with skepticism by some Member States),[165] more recently the Commission has adopted a more restrictive and repressive approach that moves further away from an administrative law rationale and integrates the punitive logic of criminal law, captured by the term 'crimmigration'.[166]

We observe three key trends in which this plays out: (1) an increased use of immigration detention for a wider range of reasons, (2) a proliferation of area-based restrictions and other measures limiting migrants' freedom of movement short of detention, and (3) problematic conditions in immigration detention facilities. These trends naturally increase the tension between the expanding scope of EU migration policy and its commitment to Human Rights.

---

162 Ph. de Bruycker et al., *Alternatives to Immigration and Asylum Detention in the EU: Time for Implementation* (2015), at 15.

163 G. Cornelisse, *Immigration Detention and Human Rights: Rethinking Territorial Sovereignty* (2010), at 247; Vohra, 'Detention of Irregular Migrants and Asylum Seekers', in R. Cholewinski, R. Perruchoud and E. McDonald (eds), *International Migration Law: Developing Paradigms and Key Challenges* (2007) 49.

164 European Commission, Proposal for a recast Reception Conditions Directive, COM(2016) 465, 13 July 2016; European Commission, Proposal for a recast Return Directive, COM(2018) 634, 12 September 2018; European Commission, Proposal for a recast Dublin Regulation, COM(2016) 270, 4 May 2016.

165 See Tsourdi, 'Asylum Detention in EU Law: Falling between Two Stools?' 35 *Refugee Survey Quarterly* (2016) 7, at 11.

166 Costello, 'Immigration Detention: The Grounds Beneath Our Feet', 68 *Current Legal Problems* (2015) 143; citing Legomsky, 'The New Path of Immigration Law: Asymmetric Incorporation of Criminal Justice Norms', 64 *Washington & Lee Law Review* (2007) 469.

Trend 1: More frequent and systematic use of detention for a wider range of reasons

We observe that Member States are more frequently and systematically resorting to immigration detention based on a wider range of grounds. This trend is buttressed by EU legislation and policy.

First, we observe an expansion of the reasons for detention. Although the relevant Directives establish lists of permissible detention grounds,[167] and recourse to detention is to some extent subject to political economies,[168] there is ample evidence indicating that the use of immigration detention is on the rise quantitatively, both for those seeking asylum and in the context of returns. For example, in Greece, immigration detention remains systematic and arbitrary, and some forms of detention lack a legal basis altogether.[169] Germany has expanded its use of detention with a view to deportation with the introduction of a new 'Orderly Return Act' adopted in 2019.[170] Denmark explicitly used detention as a deterrence measure when reopening old military camps and prisons to house rejected asylum seekers with a view to making life so 'intolerable' for them that they would leave Denmark 'voluntarily'.[171] Immigration detention affects not only asylum seekers or rejected asylum seekers but also migrants of any kind of status. A particularly egregious example is the Windrush scandal in the United Kingdom, then still an EU Member State. In the course of the so-called 'hostile environment policy', which involved administrative

---

167 Art. 8(3) Reception Conditions Directive; Art. 15(1) Return Directive.

168 Prior to 2015, in some Member States the number of migrants in detention went down sharply after the high costs and low effectiveness became clear (NL) or the judicial control became stricter (Germany). See I. Majcher M. Flynn and M. Grange, *Immigration Detention in the European Union: In the Shadow of the Crisis* (2020), at 1–4.

169 See Greek Refugee Council, *Administrative Detention in Greece: Field Observations (2018)* (2019), available at https://www.gcr.gr/media/k2/attachments/GCR_Ekthesi_Dioikitik_Kratisi_2019.pdf.

170 *Zweites Gesetz zur besseren Durchsetzung der Ausreisepflicht* (*Geordnete-Rückkehr-Gesetz*), 15 August 2019; for critique, see Pro Asyl, *Stellungnahme zur Sachverständigenanhörung des Ausschusses für Inneres und Heimat des Deutschen Bundestages am 03.06.2019*, 29 May 2019, available at https://www.proasyl.de/wp-content/uploads/PRO-ASYL_Stellungnahme-zum-Geordnete-R%C3%BCckkehr-Gesetz_Sachverst%C3%A4ndigenanh%C3%B6rung.pdf.

171 J. Suarez-Krabbe, J. Arce and A. Lindberg, *Stop Killing Us Slowly: A Research Report on the Motivation Enhancement Measures and Criminalization of Rejected Asylum Seekers in Denmark* (2018), available at http://refugees.dk/media/1757/stop-killing-us_uk.pdf.

and legislative measures to make staying in the UK as difficult as possible for people so as to induce them to 'voluntarily leave', dozens of people, many of whom had been born British subjects, were wrongly detained and deported.[172]

At EU level, reform efforts reinforce restrictive State practice, in particular with a view to a more expansive use of detention. Specifically, regarding pre-deportation detention, the Commission's 2018 proposal for a recast Return Directive would make the list of grounds for detention explicitly non-exhaustive. In addition, it would add a new, broadly framed ground for detaining irregular migrants, namely, the option to detain individuals posing a threat to public order or national security. It also proposes a non-exhaustive list of 'objective' criteria for determining the risk of absconding, which is one of the existing grounds for detention, as well as a new requirement of setting a maximum detention period of at least three months, with a view to giving States sufficient time to organize deportations.[173]

Second, we observe a wider and more arbitrary use of detention for asylum seekers upon entry specifically. This trend is reflected in EU as well as Member State policy. Examples of this development are national legislative reforms in countries such as Hungary and Poland to the effect that asylum procedures are conducted almost exclusively at the border, involving detention on a regular basis. The EU's policies echo the restrictive turn, as both the 'hotspot' approach[174] and the follow-up proposal

---

172 W. Williams, *Windrush Lessons Learned Review, Independent Review, Ordered by the House of Commons*, 19 March 2020, available at https://assets.publishing.service.gov.uk/government/uploads/system/uploads/attachment_data/file/876336/6.5577_HO_Windrush_Lessons_Learned_Review_LoResFinal.pdf.

173 European Commission, 'Fact Sheet: State of the Union 2018: Stronger EU rules on return: Questions and Answers', 12 September 2018, available at https://ec.europa.eu/commission/presscorner/detail/en/MEMO_18_5713.

174 European Commission, A European Agenda On Migration, COM(2015) 240, 13 May 2015; European Commission, Explanatory note on the 'hotspot' approach, 15 July 2015, available at https://www.statewatch.org/media/documents/news/2015/jul/eu-com-hotsposts.pdf; S. Silverman, *The EU's Hotspot Approach: Questionable Motivations and Unreachable Goals* (2018), available at https://www.e-ir.info/2018/04/17/the-eus-hotspot-approach-questionable-motivations-and-unreachable-goals/; Markard and Heuser, '"Hotspots" an den EU-Außengrenzen: Menschen- und europarechtswidrige Internierungslager', *Zeitschrift für Ausländerrecht (ZAR)* 165.

of 'controlled centres'[175] build on the detention of asylum seekers.[176] The increased use of so-called border procedures, which almost automatically entail liberty-restricting measures, is one of the major trends in European asylum policy (we shall return to this issue in sections 2.2.3 and 2.2.4, below).[177]

EU legislation paves the way for expanded use of detention for asylum seekers. For example, in the Reception Conditions Directive the permitted derogations from the required level of reception conditions seem to open up to the option that housing is provided in detention.[178] These provisions create a legal ambiguity that appears to allow Member States to lawfully

175 European Council, European Council meeting (28 June 2018): Conclusions, EUCO 9/18, at 6; European Commission, Migration: 'Controlled Centres' in EU Member States: Follow-up to the European Council Conclusions of 28 June 2018, available at https://ec.europa.eu/info/sites/default/files/controlled_centres_en.pdf; European Commission, Non-paper on 'controlled centres' in the EU: interim framework, 24 July 2018, available at https://ec.europa.eu/home-affairs/system/files/2020-09/20180724_non-paper-controlled-centres-eu-member-states_en.pdf; see F. Maiani, *'Regional Disembarkation Platforms' and 'Controlled Centres': Lifting The Drawbridge, Reaching out Across The Mediterranean, or Going Nowhere?* (2018), available at https://eumigrationlawblog.eu/regional-disembarkation-platforms-and-controlled-centres-lifting-the-drawbridge-reaching-out-across-the-mediterranean-or-going-nowhere/.

176 Campesi, 'Normalising The Hotspot Approach? An Analysis of the Commission's Most Recent Proposals', in S. Carrera, D. Curtin and A. Geddes (eds), *20 Year Anniversary of the Tampere Programme: Europeanisation Dynamics of the EU Area of Freedom, Security and Justice* (2020) 93; Ziebritzki, 'The Integrated EU Hotspot Administration and the Question of the EU's Liability', in M. Kotzur et al. (eds) *The External Dimension of EU Migration and Asylum Policies* (2020) 253.

177 See European Parliament Research Service, *Asylum Procedures at the Border: European Implementation Assessment* (2020), at 74–95, available at https://www.europarl.europa.eu/RegData/etudes/STUD/2020/654201/EPRS_STU(2020)654201_EN.pdf.; European Commission, Proposal for a Regulation introducing a screening of third country nationals at the external borders, COM(2020) 612, 23 September 2020; Amended proposal for an Asylum Procedures Regulation, COM(2020) 611, 23 September 2020.

178 Art. 18(1)(a) of the Directive allows housing in kind to be provided, among others, in 'premises used for the purpose of housing applicants during the examination of an application made at the border or in transit zones' or 'other premises adapted for housing applicants'; other provisions of the Directive refer to derogations from certain conditions in cases where 'the applicant is detained at a border post or in a transit zone' (see, e.g., Art. 10(5) and 11(6) Reception Conditions Directive).

detain asylum seekers at the external borders.[179] The proposal for a new Reception Conditions Directive does not address the expanding use of detention.[180] Instead, the proposal emphasizes the risk of absconding as a ground for detention. Under the current legislation, an asylum seeker not respecting a reporting obligation can already be considered as absconding.[181] 'Absconding' remains a fuzzy ground for detention. It could be interpreted sufficiently broadly to render the vast majority of irregular migrants and asylum seekers susceptible to detention.[182] For example, if payment of a smuggler is seen as an objective indicator of a risk of absconding, this would in principle allow for the detention of almost all asylum seekers. However, due to a lack of capacity in detention facilities not all individuals meeting such broad criteria could actually be put in detention. Therefore, there is a risk of arbitrariness, as it cannot be predicted whether a person will be detained or not. Such a wide degree of discretion in the context of the deprivation of liberty is highly problematic.

Trend 2: Increasing use of area-based restrictions not amounting to detention

In addition to the wider use of detention, the second trend we observe relates to the fact that States increasingly make use of area-based restrictions – that is, liberty-restricting measures that fall short of detention narrowly defined.

These measures involve a range of policies and practices reflecting different degrees of coerciveness.[183] They include designated residence (often coupled with conditionality for the provision of material reception conditions), as well as registration requirements, deposit of documents, bond/

---

179 M. Mouzourakis and K. Pollet, *Boundaries of Liberty: Asylum and* de facto *Detention in Europe (2018)*, at 15, available at https://www.asylumineurope.org/sites/default/files/shadow-reports/boundariesliberty.pdf.

180 European Commission, Proposal for a recast Reception Conditions Directive, COM(2016) 465, 13 July 2016.

181 The CJEU established this in the *Jawo* case in the context of the Dublin procedure: CJEU, Case C-163/17, *Jawo* (EU:C:2019:218).

182 See on asylum seekers: Costello and Mouzourakis, 'EU Law and the Detainability of Asylum-Seekers', 35 *Refugee Survey Quarterly* (2016) 47, at 65–70.

183 C. Costello and E. Kaytaz, *Building Empirical Research into Alternatives to Detention: Perception of Asylum Seekers and Refugees in Toronto and Geneva* (2013), at 10–11, available at https://www.refworld.org/docid/51a6fec84.html.

bail or surety/guarantor, reporting requirements, case management/supervised release, electronic monitoring, and home curfew/house arrest.[184] We observe that Member States have increasingly put in place such liberty-restricting measures, either as alternative pathways to detention or in addition to detention.[185] This is warranted by the Reception Conditions Directive as it generally allows Member States to subject asylum seekers to geographical and residence restrictions, even without there being a ground for detention.[186] Such practices expand the scope and intensity of coercive measures vis-à-vis migrants.

The failure to respect such restrictive measures may lead to detention. In this case, they function as a pathway to detention. In this way, recourse to liberty restrictions as a general means of migration control actually facilitates detention (this aspect thus relates back to the developments described above). As a consequence, the legal constraints applicable to immigration detention are turned on their head – rather than being a measure of last resort, permissible on strictly circumscribed grounds, detention seems increasingly legitimized as a punitive measure per se, justified by the individual's failure to comply with an alternative.[187] Austria, for example, has introduced legislative reforms to codify systematic residence restrictions and a corollary power to detain those who fail to observe them.[188] In France, the '*assignations a residence*' (house arrest with reporting obligations) easily lead to findings of absconding, which in turn warrants detention.[189]

---

184 UNCHR, Detention Guidelines: Guidelines on the Applicable Criteria and Standards relating to the Detention of Asylum-Seekers and Alternatives to Detention (2012), at 40, available at https://www.unhcr.org/publications/legal/505b10ee9/unhcr-detention-guidelines.html; C. Costello and E. Kaytaz, *Building Empirical Research into Alternatives to Detention: Perception of Asylum Seekers and Refugees in Toronto and Geneva* (2013), at 6, available at https://www.refworld.org/docid/51a6fec84.html.

185 Asylum Information Database, *The Detention of Asylum Seekers in Europe: Constructed on Shaky Ground?* (2017), available at http://www.refworld.org/docid/595a23ef4.html.

186 Art. 7 Reception Condition Directive.

187 Asylum Information Database, *The Detention of Asylum Seekers in Europe: Constructed on Shaky Ground?* (2017), at 11.

188 Asylum Information Database, *Country Report: Austria* (2017), available at https://asylumineurope.org/wp-content/uploads/2018/03/report-download_aida_at_2017update.pdf.

189 La Cimade, *La Machine Infernale de l'Asile Européen: Dissuader et exclure: analyse des impacts d'une procédure sur les droits des personnes exilées en France* (2019),

This trend is also reflected at EU level. In its 2016 proposal for a recast Reception Conditions Directive, the Commission broadens the scope for Member States to impose residence restrictions on asylum seekers and even proposes *requiring* them to do so.[190] The rationale is explicitly stated in the accompanying Commission document:

> *[I]n order to tackle secondary movements and absconding of applicants, an additional detention ground has been added. In case an applicant has been assigned a specific place of residence but has not complied with this obligation, and where there is a continued risk that the applicant may abscond, the applicant may be detained in order to ensure the fulfilment of the obligation to reside in a specific place.*[191]

The new ground for detention foreseen in Art. 8(3)(c) of the proposal constructs a legal obligation to comply with residence restrictions.[192] This would enable Member States to bypass the requirement of satisfying the existing grounds for detention under the Reception Conditions Directive and the obligation to consider an alternative beforehand.[193]

Moreover, area-based restrictions are used to manage the migration process more broadly – for example, to prevent 'ghettoization' or to avoid overburdening individual municipalities. Such policies and practices involve measures aimed at restricting migrants' freedom of movement, but do not necessarily amount to detention. Rather, they are widening the network of available restrictions of migrants' liberty of movement, in addition to detention.

---

available at https://www.lacimade.org/wp-content/uploads/2019/04/La_Cimade_Rapport_Dublin_2019.pdf.

190 Proposal for a recast Reception Conditions Directive, COM(2016) 465, 13 July 2016, Art. 7: The Commission proposes to include that Member States 'shall' decide on the residence of asylum seekers, instead of the current language on the basis of which Member States 'may' decide on that. The objective is to reduce reception-related incentives for secondary movements within the EU (on this subject, see Chapter 6).

191 Ibid., at 14.

192 Ibid., Art. 8(3)(c) reads: 'in order to ensure compliance with legal obligations imposed on the applicant through an individual decision in accordance with Art. 7(2) in cases where the applicant has not complied with such obligations and there is a risk of absconding of the applicant.'

193 European Council on Refugees and Exiles (ECRE), *Comments on the Commission proposal to recast the Reception Conditions Directive* (2016), at 12, available at https://www.ecre.org/wp-content/uploads/2016/10/ECRE-Comments-RCD.pdf.

Various EU Member States[194] have such policies in place or are planning to implement them, both upon arrival (detention in camps on islands, on ships, in camps with restricted opening hours, in airports) and in the context of enforcing returns (camps in remote areas, on islands, in police stations and airports, etc.). Sometimes migrants are legally free to leave the assigned places but will lose essential benefits – such as access to status determination procedures or social assistance – if they actually do so. Examples of 'soft' restrictions of liberty include the 'AnkER Centres' in place in some German regional states,[195] which de facto require asylum seekers to stay in a reception facility. Such 'semi-carceral spaces'[196] provide limited space to move but are different from the clearly delineated practice of detention. Accordingly, these measures are not subject to the same legal requirements; often, there is not even a clear legal basis for imposing them.[197] The proposal from the Commission for an Asylum Procedures Regulation, as amended in September 2020, follows the same line. The Commission now proposes a more extensive use of integrated (asylum and return) procedures at the external borders, during which certain categories of asylum seekers shall be 'kept' at the borders or in transit zones in order to make return policies more effective.[198] For the first time, Member States would be obliged, according to an EU Regulation, to impose restrictions on movement of asylum seekers.

194 For example, Greece, Italy, Denmark as well as at the border between Hungary and Serbia.

195 ECRE, *The AnkER centres: Implications for asylum procedures, reception and return* (2019), available at https://www.asylumineurope.org/sites/default/files/anker_centres_report.pdf.

196 Term borrowed from E. Guild, C. Costello, M. Garlick and V. Moreno-Lax, *Enhancing the Common European Asylum System and Alternatives to Dublin* (2015), at 34–35.

197 L. Slingenberg, 'Evaluating "Life Steeped in Power": Non-Domination, the Rule of Law and Spatial Restrictions for Irregular Migrants', 12 *Hague Journal on the Rule of Law* (2020), https://doi.org/10.1007/s40803-020-00147-x.

198 European Commission, Amended proposal for a Regulation establishing a common procedure for international protection in the Union, COM/2020/611, 23 September 2020, Art. 41(13): 'During the examination of applications subject to a border procedure, the applicants shall be kept at or in proximity to the external border or transit zones.'

Trend 3: Persistent pattern of problematic conditions of detention

Whereas the first two trends related to the question of whether to detain, the third challenge relates to the question of *how* migrants are detained. We observe a persistent pattern of problematic conditions of detention in many Member States, both for migrants generally and for vulnerable groups specifically. It is important to recall in this context that immigration detention is a form of administrative detention – that is, migrants are detained for administrative purposes rather than because they committed a crime. Detention conditions should reflect this fact.

First, State practice displays a pattern of detention conditions that are often extremely poor. Particularly egregious examples are the failure to provide food for detained asylum seekers in Hungary[199] or appalling conditions in Spanish immigration detention facilities.[200] Health risks associated with living in overcrowded camps in Greece were highlighted by the COVID-19 pandemic.[201] Further problematic aspects are the absence of contact with the outside world, the impossibility of continuing to manage one's own affairs, loss of any employment, separation from family, and loss of power to decide one's diet, among others.[202] Many EU countries blurred the separation of administrative and criminal detention, such as Germany in 2019 with its 'Orderly Return Act'.[203]

Second, we observe that detention conditions are often particularly critical for migrants in situations of vulnerability, including children. Some

---

199 Hungarian Helsinki Committee, *Hungary Continues to Starve Detainees in the Transit Zones Information update by the Hungarian Helsinki Committee (HHC)*, 23 April 2019, available at https://www.helsinki.hu/wp-content/uploads/Starvation-2019.pdf?utm_source=ECRE+Newsletters&utm_campaign=ad4260b76c-EMAIL_CAMPAIGN_2019_04_26_08_50&utm_medium=email&utm_term=0_3ec9497afd-ad4260b76c-420543949.

200 La Vanguardia, *101 internos del CIE de Aluche denuncian la vulneración de sus derechos*, 2 May 2019, available at https://www.lavanguardia.com/vida/20190502/461997644926/101-internos-del-cie-de-aluche-denuncian-la-vulneracion-de-sus-derechos.html?utm_source=ECRE+Newsletters&utm_campaign=ff2f249c45-EMAIL_CAMPAIGN_2019_05_10_12_46&utm_medium=email&utm_term=0_3ec9497afd-ff2f249c45-420543949.

201 See Tsourdi, 'COVID-19, Asylum in the EU, and the Great Expectations of Solidarity', 32 *International Journal of Refugee Law* (2020) 374.

202 M.-B. Dembour, *When Humans Become Migrants* (2015), at 395–396.

203 *Zweites Gesetz zur besseren Durchsetzung der Ausreisepflicht* (*Geordnete-Rückkehr-Gesetz*), 15 August 2019.

Member States (e.g., Portugal[204] and Poland[205]) continue to detain children without the necessary protections in place. This, too, is apparently permitted by the relevant EU legislation. While the Reception Conditions Directive includes a special provision on the detention of vulnerable persons, it does not prescribe a screening procedure in order to identify them, and it permits the detention of children, albeit 'as a measure of last resort' and 'in exceptional circumstances' only (the latter in the case of unaccompanied minors).[206] In contrast, the provisions in the Return Directive relating to the special needs of vulnerable migrants in detention are minimal, being limited to requiring that 'particular attention shall be paid to the situation of vulnerable persons', and that 'emergency health care and essential treatment of illness shall be provided'.[207]

2.2 Legal evaluation

2.2.1 General framework: The rights to liberty, to freedom of movement, and to adequate treatment

The aim of this section is to develop the standards relevant to determine under which circumstances restrictions on the spatial movement of migrants constitute a Human Rights violation.

We have identified four interrelated layers of Human Rights standards as being particularly relevant in this regard. Human Rights law protects not only against detention unless duly justified (first layer) but also against other forms of arbitrary limitation of movement (second layer). In all situations in which migrants' liberty and freedom of movement is restricted, Human Rights law prohibits inhuman or degrading treatment (third layer), and it precludes other, less severe interferences with private life if they do not meet the requirements of the principle of proportionality (fourth layer). In other words, Human Rights law determines both the question of *whether* a person's spatial movement may be restricted (first

---

204 See, e.g., Asylum Information Database, *Country Report: Portugal* (2017), at 17, available at https://asylumineurope.org/wp-content/uploads/2017/12/report-download_aida_pt.pdf.

205 Cf. ECtHR, *Bilalova and others v. Poland*, Appl. no. 23685/14, Judgment of 26 March 2020.

206 Art. 11(2) and (3) Reception Conditions Directive, respectively.

207 Art. 16 Return Directive.

and second layer) and of *how* such restrictions may be carried out (third and fourth layer).

(1) The right to liberty and security is one of the oldest and most fundamental Human Rights. The guarantee of *habeas corpus* applies to all human beings, regardless of immigration or other status.[208] The right is expressed in two provisions of the Universal Declaration of Human Rights of 1948: 'Everyone has the right to life, liberty and security of person' (Art. 3 UDHR) and 'No one shall be subjected to arbitrary arrest, detention or exile' (Art. 9 UDHR). The prohibition of arbitrary detention is a well-established rule of customary international law and is codified in a broad range of treaties.[209]

At the universal level, it has been included in Art. 9 of the ICCPR.[210] The jurisprudence of the Human Rights Committee (HR Committee, the treaty body entrusted with the supervision of ICCPR) has clarified that in order to comply with the requirements of lawfulness and non-arbitrariness, the principles of reasonableness, necessity, and proportionality apply.[211] While the detention of migrants is not prohibited per se, it must pursue a narrow and specific aim and be necessary and proportionate to reach this aim, taking into account the individual circumstances of the case at hand.[212] Illegal entry by migrants does not in itself justify their detention; additional factors particular to the individual are required, such as the likelihood of absconding or a risk of acts against national security.[213] Following the same line of reasoning, the UN Working Group on Arbitrary Detention, a subsidiary body of the UN, reiterates the principles of reasonableness, necessity, and proportionality in the light of the

---

208 As reaffirmed, for example, in HR Committee, General Comment No. 15: The Position of Aliens under the Covenant, HRI/GEN/1/Rev.1, at para. 1 and 7.

209 V. Chetail, *International Migration Law* (2019), at 133.

210 Art. 9(1) ICCPR: 'Everyone has the right to liberty and security of the person. No one shall be subjected to arbitrary arrest or detention. No one shall be deprived of his liberty except on such grounds and in accordance with such procedures as are established in law.'

211 HR Committee, *Van Alphen v. the Netherlands*, Communication No. 305/1988, CCPR/C/39/D/305/1988, at para. 5.8; *A v. Australia*, Communication No. 560/1993, CCPR/C/59/D/560/1993, at para. 9.2.

212 For a concise overview, see Allinson, Stefanelli and Weatherhead, 'Immigration Detention', in E. Guild, S. Grant and C. A. Groenendijk, *Human Rights of Migrants in the 21st Century* (2017) 27.

213 See. e.g., HR Committee, *A v. Australia*, Communication No. 560/1993, CCPR/C/59/D/560/1993, at para. 9.4; *A.G.F.K. et al. v. Australia*, Communication No. 2094/2011, CCPR/C/108/D/2094/2011, at para. 9.3–9.4.

circumstances specific to the individual case.[214] The UN Working Group recalls that the 'standards restated in the present deliberation apply to all States in all situations, and factors such as the influx of large numbers of immigrants regardless of their status … cannot be used to justify departure from these standards'.[215]

Provisions similar to Art. 9 ICCPR can be found in other universal Human Rights treaties, such as Art. 16 of the Migrant Workers Convention (ICRMW) and Art. 37 of the Convention on the Rights of the Child (CRC).[216] The 'presumption of liberty' for migrants is also reflected in regional Human Rights law, including in Art. 6 of the African Charter on Human and People's Rights (ACHPR, 'Banjul Charter') and in Art. 7 of the American Convention on Human Rights (ACHR). The Inter-American Commission on Human Rights explicitly rejects a 'presumption of detention' for migrants[217] and acknowledges that the constraints on immigration detention must be even stricter than those governing pre-trial or other forms of preventive criminal detention.[218] This international consensus is confirmed in Objective 13 of the Global Compact for Migration: 'Use immigration detention only as a measure of last resort and work towards alternatives' (GCM, para. 29).[219]

To complete the picture of relevant guarantees in universal Human Rights law, reference is made to the 1951 Convention Relating to the Status of Refugees (Geneva Refugee Convention, GRC). Art. 31 GRC exempts refugees from penalties for illegal entry. This provides an additional source

214 Human Rights Council. Working Group on Arbitrary Detention, Revised deliberation No. 5 on deprivation of liberty of migrants, A/HRC/39/45, at para. 14, 19–20 and 22–24.

215 Ibid., at para. 48.

216 E.g., Art. 16 ICRMW; Art. 37 CRC.

217 In the *Mariel Cubans* case, the Inter-American Commission on Human Rights criticized US practice leading to 'a presumption of detention rather than a presumption of liberty', which the Court regarded as 'fundamentally antithetical' to Art. I (liberty), XXV (protection against arbitrary arrest and detention) ADHR. See Gomez, 'The Inter-American System: Report No. 51/01, Case 9903 Rafael Ferrer-Mazorra et al. (United States), Report No. 51/01, 4 April 2001 Inter-American Commission on Human Rights', 2 *Human Rights Law Review* (2002) 117; for an elaborate examination of the presumption of liberty in the Inter-American system, see M.-B. Dembour, *When Humans Become Migrants* (2015), at 369–401.

218 Costello, 'Immigration Detention: The Grounds Beneath Our Feet', 68 *Current Legal Problems* (2015) 143, at 171.

219 See also GCM, Objective 21, para. 37 ('Cooperate in facilitating safe and dignified return and readmission, as well as sustainable reintegration').

of protection against detention of asylum seekers upon entry. According to legal scholarship, depriving asylum seekers or refugees of their liberty for the mere reason of having entered or stayed illegally would amount to a penalty under Art. 31(1) GRC.[220] In addition, Art. 31(2) GRC entails a necessity requirement regarding refugees unlawfully in the country, but only if they come directly from a territory where their life was in danger. In its 2012 Revised Guidelines on Detention of Asylum Seekers, UNHCR confirmed the principle that asylum seekers should not be detained for the sole reason of seeking asylum and that detention is only permissible in exceptional circumstances, when it is reasonable, necessary, and proportionate in order to attain a limited range of objectives.[221]

In the European legal space, Art. 5 ECHR incorporates the right to liberty and security of the person. Rather than a generic prohibition of arbitrariness, however, it provides an exhaustive list of six situations of when detention may lawfully occur. In the context of immigration detention, the relevant provision is point (f) of Art. 5(1) ECHR, which reads: 'the lawful arrest or detention of a person to prevent his effecting an unauthorised entry into the country or of a person against whom action is being taken with a view to deportation or extradition'.

The original intent, in 1950, to draft an exhaustive list of detention grounds was to provide for more specific regulation than the generic clauses of the UDHR, but the ensuing case-law on Art. 5(1)(f) has some difficulties in keeping track with developments in universal Human Rights law. The ECtHR only reluctantly applies the principles of necessity and proportionality to cases of immigration detention. While the ECtHR has recognized in non-migration contexts that 'it does not suffice that the deprivation of liberty is executed in conformity with national law but it

220 Noll, 'Article 31 (Refugees unlawfully in the country of refuge/Réfugiés en situation irrégulière dans le pays d'accueil)', in A. Zimmermann (ed.), *Commentary on the 1951 Convention relating to the Status of Refugees* (2011) 1243, at para. 96; see also Goodwin-Gil, 'Article 31 of the 1951 Convention Relating to the Status of Refugees: Non-penalisation, Detention and Protection', in E. Feller, V. Türk and F. Nicholson, *Refugee Protection in International Law: UNHCR's Global Consultations on International Protection* (2003) 185, at 195–196; A. Grahl-Madsen, *The Status of Refugees in International Law* (1972), at 209; A. Edwards, *Back to Basics: The Right to Liberty and Security of Person and 'Alternatives to Detention of Refugees, Asylum-Seekers, Stateless Persons and Other Migrants'* (2011), at 11, available at https://www.unhcr.org/4dc949c49.pdf.

221 UNHCR, Guidelines on the Applicable Criteria and Standards relating to the Detention of Asylum-Seekers and Alternatives to Detention (2012), available at https://www.refworld.org/docid/503489533b8.html.

must also be necessary in the circumstances',[222] the Court has accepted the practice of detention for bureaucratic convenience in the migration context.[223] In its *Saadi* judgment, the Grand Chamber explicitly held that necessity is not a requirement under Art. 5(1)(f) ECHR for the lawfulness of immigration detention upon entry.[224]

This line of reasoning was widely challenged in legal scholarship.[225] It also has outspoken critics within the Court[226] and the Council of Europe more widely. The Parliamentary Assembly of the Council of Europe has expressly criticized the *Saadi* judgment,[227] and the European Commissioner for Human Rights and the European Committee for the Prevention of Torture have expressed their opposition to the use of immigration detention as a first response and deterrent to migrants reaching Europe irregularly.[228] In its more recent case-law, albeit not decisively, the Strasbourg Court has been cautiously resiling from its previous position and

222 ECtHR, *Witold Litwa v. Poland*, Appl. no. 26629/95, Judgment of 4 April 2000, at para. 78.

223 ECtHR, *Chahal v. UK*, Appl. no. 22414/93, Judgment of 15 November 1996 (regarding pre-removal detention), and *Saadi v. Italy*, Appl. no. 37201/06, Judgment of 28 February 2008 (regarding detention upon entry).

224 ECtHR, *Saadi v. Italy*, Appl. no. 37201/06, Judgment of 28 February 2008, at para. 72–74.

225 G. Cornelisse, *Immigration Detention and Human Rights: Rethinking Territorial Sovereignty* (2010); Moreno-Lax, 'Beyond Saadi v UK: Why the "Unnecessary" Detention of Asylum Seekers is Inadmissible under EU Law', 5 *Human Rights and International Legal Discourse* (2011) 166; Costello, 'Human Rights & the Elusive Universal Subject: Immigration Detention under International Human Rights and EU Law', 19 *Indiana Journal of Global Legal Studies* (2012) 257; see also D. Wilsher, *Immigration Detention: Law, History, Politics* (2014).

226 In the *Saadi* case, by reference to international law documents, judges Rozakis, Tulkens, Kovler, Hajiyev, Spielman and Hiverlä formulated a joint partly dissenting opinion that ended on the oft-cited words 'Is it a crime to be foreigner? We do not think so', ECtHR, *Saadi v. Italy*, Appl. no. 37201/06, Judgment of 28 February 2008, dissent.

227 A. C. Mendonça, *The Detention of Asylum Seekers and Irregular Migrants in Europe*, 11 January 2010, available at https://assembly.coe.int/nw/xml/XRef/Xref-XML2HTML-en.asp?fileid=12435&lang=en, at 14 and 20.

228 Memorandum by Thomas Hammarberg, Commissioner for Human Rights of the Council of Europe, following his visits to the United Kingdom on 5–8 February and 31 March–2 April 2008, as cited in London Detainee Support Group, *Detained Lives: The Real Cost of Indefinite Immigration Detention* (2009), at 11, available at https://detentionaction.org.uk/wp-content/uploads/2018/12/Detained-Lives-report1.pdf.

increasingly incorporates elements of a full proportionality test (including the element of necessity).[229]

To sum up the Human Rights standard regarding immigration detention, the prohibition of arbitrary detention is an absolute norm of customary international law. In the language of the UN Working Group on Arbitrary Detention, '[a]rbitrary detention can never be justified, including for any reason related to national emergency, maintaining public security or the large movements of immigrants or asylum seekers'.[230] In order not to be considered arbitrary, detention measures must adhere to the principles of reasonableness, necessity, and proportionality (i.e., in the doctrinal language of EU law, all elements of the principle of proportionality must be tested). Accordingly, the lower standard provided in the ECHR is superseded by the higher level of protection in universal Human Rights law.

In EU law, the latter standard is mirrored in Art. 6 EU-CFR, which replicates the plain wording of Art. 3 UDHR and Art. 9(1) ICCPR, without further qualifications or special provisions on immigration detention. Regardless of the general rule of interpretation established in the first sentence of Art. 52(3) EU-CFR, according to which the provisions of the EU Charter are presumed to have the same meaning as the corresponding provisions of the ECHR, we hold that the second sentence of Art. 52(3) EU-CFR applies. According to this clause, the above-mentioned rule of interpretation shall not prevent Union law providing more extensive protection. We argue that in respect of the prohibition of arbitrary detention, the relevant EU fundamental right in substance is consistent with the UN standard rather than with the *Saadi* case-law of the ECtHR. In any case, the EU is legally bound to follow the rules of customary international law that are an integral part of the EU legal order and are binding upon the institutions of the Union, including its legislative bodies.

---

229 ECtHR, *Suso Musa v. Malta*, Appl. no. 42337/12, Judgment of 23 July 2013; *Yoh-Ekale Mwanje v. Belgium*, Appl. no. 10486/10, Judgment of 20 December 2011, at 124.

230 Human Rights Council: Working Group on Arbitrary Detention, Revised deliberation No. 5 on deprivation of liberty of migrants, A/HRC/39/45, at para. 8; and see HR Committee, General Comment No. 35: Article 9 Liberty and Security of Person, CCPR/C/GC/35, at para. 66: 'The fundamental guarantee against arbitrary detention is non-derogable, insofar as even situations covered by Art. 4 cannot justify a deprivation of liberty that is unreasonable or unnecessary under the circumstances.'

(2) Human Rights law also prohibits arbitrary limitations on the freedom of movement in the form of 'area-based restrictions'[231] even if they do not constitute detention. In its initial form, the relevant right can be found in Art. 13 UDHR, which provides that '[e]veryone has the right to freedom of movement and residence within the borders of each state'. The main difference in relation to the concept of detention is the wider geographical scope of the bordered space ('territory') to which the guarantee of mobility relates.

However, subsequent instruments incorporating this right have conditioned it on lawful stay of the protected person. Art. 12(1) ICCPR limits freedom of movement and choice of residence to those 'lawfully within the territory of a State'. A similar qualification is laid down in Art. 26 GRC, which requires a State to 'accord to refugees lawfully in its territory the right to choose their place of residence to move freely within its territory, subject to any regulations applicable to aliens generally in the same circumstances'. At the level of the Council of Europe, freedom of movement was added to the ECHR only in 1963 through Protocol No. 4, which entered in force in 1968. Likewise, Art. 2 of that Protocol grants freedom of movement to 'everyone lawfully within the territory of a State'.

In contrast to the prohibition of arbitrary detention, the right to intra-territorial mobility is not an absolute right. Once a person is lawfully within a State, restrictions on his or her right guaranteed by Art. 12(1) ICCPR, as well as any treatment different from that accorded to nationals, must be justified under the rules provided for by Art. 12(3) ICCPR. This provision restricts permissible limitations to those 'provided by law' and necessary to protect national security, public order, health or morals, or the rights and freedoms of others; such limitations must also be consistent with the other rights recognized in the ICCPR.[232] Thus, restrictions applied in the individual case must have a clear legal basis, serve one of the listed grounds, meet the test of necessity and the requirements of proportionality, and be governed by the need for consistency with the other rights recognized in the Covenant.[233] The ECHR has a comparable limitation clause in Art. 2(3) of Protocol No. 4 ECHR. In addition, Art. 2(4) Protocol No. 4

231 Todt, 'Area-based Restrictions to Maintain Public Order: The Distinction Between Freedom-restricting and Liberty-depriving Public Order Powers in the European Legal Sphere', 4 *European Human Rights Law Review* (2017) 376.

232 HR Committee, CCPR General Comment No. 27: Article 12 (Freedom of Movement), CPR/C/21/Rev.1/Add.9, at para. 4.

233 Ibid., at para. 2 and 16.

ECHR permits restrictions in certain areas as justified by 'the public interest in a democratic society'. This wider scope of permissible restrictions is not warranted by the ICCPR.

In EU law, the right to intra-territorial mobility tends to be overlooked, as it is not explicitly mirrored in one of the provisions of the EU-CFR. Applying the presumption of substantive homogeneity between EU fundamental rights and Human Rights, its sources nonetheless are incorporated into EU law as general principles in the sense of Art. 6(3) TEU. A distinction must be drawn here between the territory of each Member State, on the one hand, and Union territory as a whole (as defined in Art. 52(2) TEU and Art. 355 TFEU), on the other hand.[234] Given that all EU Member States are party to the ICCPR, the GRC and to Protocol No. 4 ECHR (except for Greece, which did not sign Protocol No. 4) we assume that the right to freedom of movement within the territory of each Member State is a general principle of EU law, subject to the qualifications and permissible restrictions laid down in these instruments. In respect of the freedom of movement within the territory of the EU as a whole, Art. 45(1) EU-CFR grants this right to all EU citizens. For third-country nationals, Art. 45(2) EU-CFR incorporates the proviso of legal residence, stating that '[f]reedom of movement may be granted … to nationals of third countries legally resident in the territory of a Member State'. This provision refers to the competence conferred on the Union by Art. 77, 78 and 79 TFEU. Consequently, the granting of this right depends on the EU institutions exercising those powers.[235] A discussion of the extent to which a positive obligation exists to exercise these powers is beyond the scope of this chapter (it may follow from the principle of non-discrimination; see Chapter 4).

Two main issues of construction arise from this overview. The first question is who is to be considered lawfully present on state territory. In principle, this matter is governed by national law, provided it complies with international obligations.[236] On the other hand, this cannot imply unlimited discretion on the part of the States. Since 'lawful stay' is a concept laid down in an instrument of international law, it can have an

---

234 On the legal concept of Union territory, see Bast, 'Völker- und unionsrechtliche Anstöße zur Entterritorialisierung des Rechts', 76 *Veröffentlichungen der Vereinigung Deutscher Staatsrechtslehrer (VVDStRL)* (2017) 277.

235 See Explanations relating to the Charter of Fundamental Rights, 2007/C 303/02, on Art. 45 EU-CRC.

236 HR Committee, General Comment No. 27: Article 12 (Freedom of Movement), CPR/C/21/Rev.1/Add.9, at para. 4.

autonomous meaning and is ultimately a matter for international interpretation.[237] According to legal scholarship, migrants whose right to stay is subject to determination or adjudication should be considered as lawfully on territory.[238] The same rationale applies to those migrants who are qualified as non-deportable, such as people with toleration status (*Duldung*) in Germany or Austria.[239] However, the right to freedom of movement does not apply to those who have entered or are present irregularly and do not have a pending request for regularization of their stay, or to those whose request has been rejected and who are not considered unreturnable.

The second issue relates to the delimitation of restrictions of movement – which are justifiable for a larger range of reasons – from deprivations of liberty that constitute detention. In that regard, the Strasbourg Court has stated that the difference is one of degree rather than substance.[240] The label of the measure is irrelevant; determination requires a factual assessment of the concrete situation (type, duration, effects, and manner of implementation).[241] This line of reasoning is significant in the context of this study in two respects. First, it implies that a measure that is not explicitly labeled as detention may nonetheless be subject to the stricter test provided by Art. 9 ICCPR and Art. 5 ECHR. Second, the so-called alternatives to detention are not exempted from observing Human Rights standards. Arguably, the closer a liberty-restricting measure comes to being a detention measure, the stricter these standards must be. We return to this issue in more detail below when discussing border procedures in European asylum law.

---

237 L. Slingenberg, *The Reception of Asylum Seekers under International Law* (2014), at 110–111.

238 Costello, 'Immigration Detention: The Grounds Beneath Our Feet', 68 *Current Legal Problems* (2015), at 147 and 174.

239 See Report of the Special Rapporteur for the Human Rights of Migrants, Francois Crépeau, A/HRC/20/24, at para. 54; HR Committee, *Celepli v. Sweden*, CCPR/C/51/D/456/1991, at para. 9.2; for an extensive consideration on the meaning of lawful stay in the context of the Refugee Convention, see J. Hathaway, *The Rights of Refugees under International Law* (2nd ed. 2021), at 176–219.

240 See ECtHR, *Khlaifia and others v. Italy*, Appl. no. 16483/12, Judgment of 15 December 2016, at para. 64.

241 ECtHR, *Z.A. and others v. Russia*, Appl. no. 61411/15, 61420/15, 61427/15 and 3028/16, Judgment of 21 November 2019, at para. 138; *Ilias and Ahmed v. Hungary*, Appl. no. 47287/15, Judgment of 21 November 2019, at para. 217–218; see Tsourdi, 'Asylum Detention in EU Law: Falling between Two Stools?' 35 *Refugee Survey Quarterly* (2016) 7, at 11.

(3) As to the conditions of detention or other forms of mobility restrictions, any deprivation of liberty must respect the detainee's dignity and cannot be in conflict with the prohibition of torture or inhuman or degrading treatment. That prohibition is laid down in numerous universal instruments, such as Art. 5 UDHR, Art. 7 ICCPR and Art. 1 and 16 CAT, as well as regional instruments such as Art. 3 ECHR, Art. 5 ACHR and Art. 5 ACHPR. The prohibition of torture and inhuman or degrading treatment or punishment is mirrored in Art. 4 EU-CFR. It is considered to be an absolute guarantee. If detention conditions are found to amount to such treatment, detention will automatically be unlawful.

In its case-law regarding Art. 3 ECHR in the context of detention,[242] the ECtHR has developed a number of important and detailed positive obligations of States. In order to establish whether the required level of severity has been reached, the Court considers the cumulative effect of detention conditions, ranging from sufficient and adequate living space, including sanitary products and meals, to medical care and assistance.[243] However, even though the Court has found violations in numerous cases, it has so far failed to derive general principles regarding the required standards. This has enabled some more controversial judgments in which the Court has found that the situation fell short of a violation of Art. 3 ECHR.[244]

(4) While Art. 3 ECHR (and its counterparts in universal Human Rights law) constitutes an absolute standard for detention conditions, other provisions of Human Rights law provide further limitations on such measures. They serve to fill a gap in protection where the threshold of severity that constitutes inhuman treatment is not exceeded.

Art. 10(1) ICCPR enshrines a right to humane treatment in detention. It states in positive terms: 'All persons deprived of their liberty shall be

---

242 See, e.g., ECtHR, *M.S.S. v. Belgium and Greece*, Appl. no. 30696/06, Grand Chamber Judgment of 21 January 2011, at para. 205–234; *S.Z. v. Greece*, Appl. no. 66702/13, Judgment of 21 June 2019, and *HA.A. v. Greece*, Appl. no. 58387/11, Judgment of 21 April 2016.

243 L. Slingenberg, *The Reception of Asylum Seekers under International Law* (2014), at 300–304 and 310.

244 Such as ECtHR, *J.R. and others v. Greece*, Appl. no. 22696/16, Judgment of 25 January 2018. For discussion concerning in particular Greece, see Vedsted-Hansen, 'Reception Conditions as Human Rights: Pan-European Standard or Systemic Deficiencies?', in V. Chetail, Ph. de Bruycker, F. Maiani (eds), *Reforming the Common European Asylum System: The New European Refugee Law* (2016) 317.

treated with humanity and with respect for the inherent dignity of the human person.' Case-law of the HR Committee demonstrates that breaches of this Article need not reach the threshold of inhuman treatment.[245] Art. 10(1) ICCPR does not have an explicit equivalent in other Human Rights instruments.

At the European regional level, the ECtHR combines the assessment of the lawfulness of detention with the adequacy of detention conditions, to a similar effect. The safeguard provided by Art. 5(1) ECHR is that the detention must be 'in accordance with law'. As the Strasbourg Court has established, lawfulness involves a requirement of non-arbitrariness, which amounts to a compendium of factors, including those relating to the place and duration of detention: 'the place and conditions of detention should be appropriate', bearing in mind that asylum seekers are not convicted of a criminal offense; and 'the length of the detention should not exceed that reasonably required for the purpose pursued'.[246] In other words, the Court clarified that there must be a link between the ground of permitted deprivation of liberty, on the one hand, and the place and conditions of detention, on the other hand.[247] It has repeatedly held that detaining children in closed centers designed for adults does not take account of their extreme vulnerability and that their detention is therefore disproportionate and unlawful under Art. 5(1)(f) ECHR.[248] Although the Court does not label it that way, this essentially constitutes a proportionality assessment, allowing the ECtHR to measure detention conditions not only in terms of Art. 3 ECHR (which precludes any balancing with the public interest pursued) but also in terms of a more flexible standard derived

245 HR Committee, *Penarrieta, Pura de Toro et al. v. Bolivia*, Communication No. 176/1984, CCPOR/C/31/D/176/1984; *Francesco Madafferi et al. v. Australia*, Communication No. 1011/2001, CCPR/C/81/D/1011/2001: the HR Committee found that the separation of a family pending removal causing financial and psychological difficulties would violate Art. 10(1) ICCPR.

246 ECtHR, *Saadi v. Italy*, Appl. no. 37201/06, at para. 74. In addition, detention must be carried out in good faith and be closely connected to the purpose of preventing entry (or facilitating return).

247 ECtHR, *Popov v. France*, Appl. no. 39472/07, Judgment of 19 January 2012, at para. 118; *Mubilanzila Mayeka and Kaniki Mitunga v. Belgium*, Appl. no. 13178/03, Judgment of 12 October 2006, at para. 102; *Muskhadzhiyeva and others v. Belgium*, Appl. no. 41442/07, Judgment of 19 January 2010, at para. 73.

248 ECtHR, *Popov v. France*, Appl. no. 39472/07, Judgment of 19 January 2012, *Muskhadzhiyeva and others v. Belgium*, Appl. no. 41442/07, Judgment of 19 January 2010, *Mubilanzila Mayeka and Kaniki Mitunga v. Belgium*, Appl. no. 13178/03, Judgment of 12 October 2006.

from Art. 5(1)(f) ECHR. If detention conditions were adequate, the detention measure would not be disproportionate and thence would be lawful.

Restrictions on movement may also interfere with other Human Rights, in particular the right to private and family life. The most developed jurisprudence in this regard stems from the ECtHR case-law on Art. 8 ECHR (mirrored in Art. 7 EU-CFR; for details, see Chapter 5). According to the settled case-law, private life includes a person's physical and mental integrity and encompasses the development, without outside interference, of the personality of each individual in their relations with other human beings.[249] Liberty of movement is an indispensable condition for the free development of a person.[250] In several cases the ECtHR has held that detention constituted a disproportionate interference with Art. 8 ECHR if no particular flight risk has been established.[251] Even where there was an indication that a family might abscond, authorities were found to have violated Art. 8 ECHR due to a failure to provide sufficient reasons to justify detention for a lengthy period.[252]

Likewise, Art. 8 ECHR comes into play in the context of area-based restrictions. The Strasbourg Court considers Art. 2 of Protocol No. 4 ECHR and Art. 8 ECHR to be closely linked and regularly considers them together.[253] This is of particular relevance for irregular migrants: although they are excluded from the scope of Art. 2 Protocol No. 4 ECHR due to their unlawful presence, the protection granted under Art. 8 ECHR also extends to them. In a case involving the freedom to leave any country, laid down in Art. 2(2) Protocol No. 4 ECHR, the Court clarified: 'The fact that 'free-

249 ECtHR, *Mubilanzila Mayeka and Kaniki Mitunga v. Belgium*, Appl. no. 13178/03, Judgment of 12 October 2006, at para. 83, citing *Niemietz v. Germany*, Appl. no. 13710/88, Judgment of 16 December 1992, at para. 29; *Botta v. Italy*, Appl. no. 21439/93, Judgment of 24 February 1998, at para. 32; *Von Hannover v. Germany*, Appl. no. 59320/00, 24 June 2004, at para. 50.

250 HR Committee, General Comment No. 27: Article 12 (Freedom of Movement), CCPR/C/21/Rev.1/Add.9, at para. 1.

251 ECtHR, *Popov v. France*, Appl. no. 39472/07, Judgment of 19 January 2012, at para. 147–148, *A.B. and others v. France*, Appl. no. 11593/12, Judgment of 12 July 2016, at para. 155–156; *R.K. and others v. France*, Appl. no. 68264/14, Judgment of 12 July 2016, at para. 114 and 117.

252 ECtHR, *Bistieva and others v. Poland*, Appl. no. 75157/14, Judgment of 10 April 2018, at para. 88.

253 See, e.g., ECtHR, *Olivieira v. the Netherlands*, Appl. no. 33129/96, Judgment of 4 June 2002, at para. 67–69; *Garib v. the Netherlands*, Appl. no. 43494/09, Grand Chamber Judgment of 6 November 2017, at para. 140–141; see also, more extensively, in the preceding Chamber judgment of 23 February 2016: ECtHR, *Garib v. the Netherlands*, Appl. no. 43494/09, at para. 114–117.

dom of movement' is guaranteed as such under Article 2 of Protocol no. 4, which Turkey has signed but not ratified, is irrelevant given that one and the same fact may fall foul of more than one provision of the Convention and its Protocols' and found a violation of Art. 8 ECHR.[254] This reasoning can be extended to area-based restrictions not amounting to detention. In situations where Art. 2(1) of Protocol No. 4 does not apply, restrictions of movement may nonetheless violate other Convention rights, most notably the right to family and private life.[255] Accordingly, any type of area-based restriction for irregular migrants must be in accordance with Art. 8 ECHR.

The above standards to measure the conditions of detention or other forms of liberty-restricting measures imposed on migrants are mainly developed by judicial and quasi-judicial bodies based on broadly framed provisions in international treaties. They are necessarily of a casuistic nature, which makes it difficult for States (or the EU) to implement them in practice. In such situations, international soft law is of key importance to specifying the contents of Human Rights, without imposing obligations in its own right.

The first document to mention in this context is the developed set of standards contained in the Nelson Mandela Rules of 2016 adopted by the UN General Assembly in 2016, which concretizes the right to humane treatment in detention enshrined in Art. 10 ICCPR for the criminal law context.[256] The standards are a revised version of the Standard Minimum Rules for the Treatment of Prisoners, originally adopted by the First UN Congress on the Prevention of Crime and the Treatment of Offenders in 1955. The Nelson Mandela Rules constitute the universally acknowledged minimum standard for the management of prison facilities and the treat-

---

254 The case involved restrictions of movement regarding a Turkish citizen by Turkey, preventing him from leaving Turkey to be with his family in Germany. Turkey had signed but not ratified Protocol No. 4; ECtHR, *Iletmis v. Turkey*, Appl. no. 29871/96, Judgment of 6 December 2005, at para. 50.

255 In this regard, see ECtHR, *Battista v. Italy*, Appl. no. 43978/09, Judgment of 2 December 2014, at para. 51–52, where the applicant complained against compulsory residence order under both Art. 2(1) Protocol No. 4 ECHR and Art. 8 ECHR. The Court held that the claim raised under Art. 8 ECHR was 'closely linked to the complaint under Article 2 of Protocol No. 4' and therefore needed not be assessed separately.

256 UN General Assembly, United Nations Standard Minimum Rules for the Treatment of Prisoners (the Nelson Mandela Rules), 8 January 2016, A/RES/70/175, available at https://www.refworld.org/docid/5698a3a44.html. For the original version, see https://www.unodc.org/pdf/criminal_justice/UN_Standard_Minimum_Rules_for_the_Treatment_of_Prisoners.pdf.

ment of prisoners. The equivalent standards in the Council of Europe are the European Prison Rules.[257] While it is clear that the quality of immigration detention cannot be lower than that of criminal detention, the established criminal detention standards are neither directly applicable to nor adequate for immigration detainees. Therefore, at the level of the Council of Europe an attempt at codifying specific European Rules on Administrative Detention is currently in progress.[258] A first draft establishes rules of international law pertaining to administrative detention, including immigration detention, though its future normative status is unclear.[259]

2.2.2 Specific issue: Detention grounds

In view of the increasing use of immigration detention in Europe, a more detailed analysis of the permissible grounds for detention seems appropriate to evaluate whether the EU meets the minimum standards established by Human Rights law. Particular attention will be given to the jurisprudence developed by the HR Committee in respect of Art. 9 ICCPR, since this Covenant represents the level of protection incorporated in Art. 6 EU-CFR (see above, 2.2.1, subsection 1).

Current EU law regulates pre-removal detention and detention of asylum seekers in separate legal instruments. However, the CJEU has clarified that the notion of detention is the same across the Asylum Procedures Di-

257 Council of Europe: Committee of Ministers, Recommendation Rec(2006)2 on the European Prison Rules, 11 January 2006, available at https://www.refworld.org/docid/43f3134810.html.

258 Council of Europe, Website 'Administrative Detention of Migrants', available at https://www.coe.int/en/web/cdcj/activities/administrative-detention-migrants.

259 Council of Europe: European Committee on Legal Co-Operation (CDCJ), Codifying instrument of European rules on the administrative detention of migrants, 18 May 2017, available at https://rm.coe.int/european-rules-on-the-administrative-detention-of-migrants-draft-codif/1680714cc1. See also the European Committee for the Prevention of Torture 'Fact Sheet' detailing standards for immigration detention: Council of Europe Committee for the Prevention of Torture, Immigration detention: Factsheet (2017), available at https://www.refworld.org/docid/58ca84894.html. For an assessment and critique of the draft, see International Detention Coalition and ICJ, *European rules for the administrative detention of migrants Written submission to the European Committee on Legal Co-Operation of the Council of Europe* (2017), available at https://idcoalition.org/wp-content/uploads/2017/07/CouncilofEurope-ImmigrationDetentionRules-JointSubmission-ICJIDC-ENG-2017.pdf.

rective, the Reception Conditions Directive, and the Return Directive.[260] This is in line with international law, as the HR Committee does not distinguish either explicitly or in substance between pre-removal detention and detention upon entry. According to the HR Committee, detention of migrants is only permissible if there are circumstances specific to the individual that make it necessary and proportionate to resort to this ultimate measure. While the HR Committee does not develop a closed list of accepted detention grounds, it emerges from its case-law that an individualized risk of absconding[261] or a risk of acts against national security[262] can justify detention measures, provided that less coercive means of achieving the same ends are not available.[263] Although the language of the HR Committee ('reasons such as') concedes that, in principle, other detention grounds are not excluded, the HR Committee has consistently held that detention cannot be 'based on a mandatory rule for a broad category' of situations, but would have to be 'specific to the individual' and meet the strict necessity test.[264] Mere administrative convenience, sanctioning unlawful behavior on the part of the migrant concerned, or general aims of migration policy, such as deterring or educating other migrants, would not meet these standards. Accordingly, other grounds justifying detention have thus far not been accepted by the HR Committee.[265]

Applying these standards to EU legislation on immigration detention, the first thing to note is that any detention governed by EU law can only be imposed by Member State authorities when the decision meets the principle of proportionality, which is a constitutional requirement even in

260 In the *Röszke* case, the CJEU clarified that the notion of detention is the same, CJEU, Cases C-924/19 PPU and C-925/19 PPU, *FMS* (EU:C:2020:367), at para. 224.

261 HR Committee, *Jalloh v. the Netherlands*, Communication No. 794/1998, CCPR/C/74/D/794/1998, at para. 8.2.

262 HR Committee, *A.G.F.K. et al. v. Australia*, Communication No. 2094/2011, CCPR/C/108/D/2094/2011, at para. 9.3–9.4.

263 HR Committee, *C. v. Australia*, Communication No. 900/1999, CCPR/C/74/D/900/1999, at para. 8.2.

264 HR Committee, *A.G.F.K. et al. v. Australia*, Communication No. 2094/2011, CCPR/C/108/D/2094/2011, at para. 9.3.

265 See the HR Committee's own summary of its jurisprudence in General Comment No. 35: Liberty and Security of Person, CCPR/C/107/R.3, at para. 18. Note that in the early case of *A. v. Australia*, CCPR/C/59/D/560/1993, the HR Committee also accepted non-cooperation as a legitimate ground, but has never done so since and does not list non-cooperation as an example for accepted grounds in its General Comment No. 35.

the absence of a statutory provision to this effect. This doctrine is in line with the UN standard and partly compensates for the insufficient protection under Art. 5(1)(f) ECHR. However, the grounds justifying detention appear overly broad, so that they have the potential to undermine the strict standards required by Human Rights law. In the following discussion, we shall consider in detail the relevant legislation and the suggested proposal for its reform.

Detention with a view to deportation is specifically regulated in the Return Directive. The relevant provision in Art. 15(1) states:

> *Unless other sufficient but less coercive measures can be applied effectively in a specific case, Member States may only keep in detention a third-country national who is the subject of return procedures in order to prepare the return and/or carry out the removal process,* in particular when: *(a) there is a risk of absconding or (b) the third-country national concerned avoids or hampers the preparation of return or the removal process.*[266]

The wording of this provision allows for differing views as to whether the listed grounds for detention are exhaustive. A literal reading would suggest that the Directive allows for the detention of third-country nationals 'only' when they are subject to return procedures for the two reasons listed in points (a) and (b). However, prefaced by the non-exhaustive 'in particular when' the reference to these grounds seems to imply that they serve as mere illustrations.[267] In line with the latter reading, some EU Member States have laid down further grounds for detention in their domestic legislation.[268] Hence, the wording is sufficiently vague to allow for alternative readings.[269] The CJEU has indicated in a series of judgments that the

266 Art. 15(1) Return Directive, emphasis added.

267 For an example of this reading, see FRA, Detention of third-country nationals in return procedures (2011), at 15 and 27.

268 Such as investigation of the person's identity (Belgium, Italy), acquisition of travel documents (Italy), unlawful entry (Denmark), or public health considerations (Spain), thus providing a significantly broader basis for detention; see European Parliament, The Return Directive 2008/115/EC: European Implementation Assessment (2020), at 90, available at https://www.europarl.europa.eu/RegData/etudes/STUD/2020/642840/EPRS_STU(2020)642840_EN.pdf.

269 The European Parliament in its Implementation Study is careful not to preclude that reading and somewhat reluctantly notes that '[b]y using the terms "in particular", Article 15(1) of the Directive *appears to* enumerate the two grounds in a non-exhaustive manner'; see ibid., at 90 (emphasis added).

list of grounds is limited to the two laid down in the provision.[270] In its 2020 judgment on the Hungarian transit zone Röszke (the '*Röszke* case'), the CJEU reiterated this reading and stated that Member States may only deprive an individual of their liberty on the basis of Art. 15(1) Return Directive if the deportation may be jeopardized by the behavior of the person concerned.[271]

In response to this ambiguity, the 2018 Commission proposal for a recast Return Directive aims to resolve the issue in favor of a non-exhaustive reading. The Commission not only proposes to strike out the word 'only' but also to expand the illustrative list of possible grounds, which would henceforth include 'the third-country national poses a risk to public policy, public security or national security'.[272] While detention on the basis of risks of 'acts against national security' is warranted by HR Committee jurisprudence, it is highly doubtful that this also extends to any risk to public policy. Public policy is a broadly framed concept covering a wide range of public interests, whereas the HR Committee explicitly requires that the factors justifying detention must be specific to the individual.[273] Even more importantly, the removal of the limiting 'only' while maintaining the illustrative 'in particular when' would emphasize a reading of the provision that detention for the purpose of removal is permitted to pursue policy aims of any kind. Such a reading would certainly not be in line with HR Committee jurisprudence.[274]

As regards asylum seekers, the permissible grounds for detention are unequivocally laid down exhaustively in Art. 8(3) Reception Conditions Directive:

---

270 CJEU, Case C-146/14 PPU, *Bashir Mohamed Ali Mahdi* (EU:C:2014:1320), at para. 61; Case C-61/11 PPU, *Hassen El Dridi, alias Soufi Karim* (EU:C:2011:268), at para. 39; Case C-357/09 PPU, *Saïd Shamilovich Kadzoev (Huchbarov)* (EU:C:2009:741), at para. 70.

271 CJEU, Cases C-924/19 PPU and C-925/19 PPU, *FMS* (EU:C:2020:367), at para. 268–269.

272 European Commission, Proposal for a recast Return Directive, COM(2018) 634, 12 September 2018, at 34 (new Art. 18).

273 HR Committee, *A.G.F.K. et al. v. Australia*, Communication No. 2094/2011, CCPR/C/108/D/2094/2011, at para. 9.3; HR Committee, General Comment No. 35: Liberty and Security of Person, CCPR/C/107/R.3, at para. 18.

274 See HR Committee, *A. v. Australia*, CCPR/C/59/D/560/1993, at para. 9.4; this extends to illegal stay, see subsequent jurisprudence on deportation detention, for example: *Jalloh v. the Netherlands*, Communication No. 794/1998, CCPR/C/74/D/794/1998, at para. 8.2.; *Madafferi v. Australia*, Communication No. 1011/2001, CCPR/C/81/1011/2001, at para. 9.2.

> *An applicant may be detained only:*
> *(a) in order to determine or verify his or her identity or nationality;*
> *(b) in order to determine those elements on which the application for international protection is based which could not be obtained in the absence of detention, in particular when there is a risk of absconding of the applicant;*
> *(c) in order to decide, in the context of a procedure, on the applicant's right to enter the territory;*
> *(d) when he or she is detained subject to a return procedure under Directive 2008/115/EC of the European Parliament and of the Council of 16 December 2008 on common standards and procedures in Member States for returning illegally staying third-country nationals, in order to prepare the return and/or carry out the removal process, and the Member State concerned can substantiate on the basis of objective criteria, including that he or she already had the opportunity to access the asylum procedure, that there are reasonable grounds to believe that he or she is making the application for international protection merely in order to delay or frustrate the enforcement of the return decision;*
> *(e) when protection of national security or public order so requires;*
> *(f) in accordance with Article 28 of Regulation (EU) No 604/2013 of the European Parliament and of the Council of 26 June 2013 establishing the criteria and mechanisms for determining the Member State responsible for examining an application for international protection lodged in one of the Member States by a third-country national or a stateless person.*[275]

Although formulated in an exhaustive manner, this list of grounds covers a wide range of situations that are subject to interpretation and raises a series of issues.

First, the two grounds that are generally accepted by the HR Committee – risk of absconding and acts against national security – are laid down in a convoluted manner. Rather than specifying the risk of absconding as a self-standing ground, as in the Return Directive, the provision in point (b) presents absconding merely as an example of situations in which determination of the actual need of protection supposedly requires detention. It is unclear which 'elements' that would be, especially in light of the fact that detention can in turn impede access to information that is required to evaluate an asylum claim. This appears to be contrary to the principle established by the HR Committee that determination of the

275 Art. 8(3) Reception Conditions Directive.

asylum claim should not take place in detention.[276] Similarly, the wording of the provision in point (e) appears broader than is warranted by the HR Committee. Not only has public order been added to national security, but the provision also does not specify that those considerations must relate to risks posed by acts of the individual concerned. It thus gives way to the interpretation that broader public order considerations could warrant detention of asylum seekers, a reading that would not be in line with international law to the extent that it requires individualized reasons specific to the person concerned.[277]

Second, while detention to determine or verify identity or nationality (see point (a)) may be in line with Human Rights law, it is only acceptable for a brief initial stage.[278] It must, therefore, be interpreted in that light. In contrast, detention to determine the right to enter (see point (c)) is contrary to Human Rights law. This issue will be discussed in more detail in the following section on border procedures (2.2.3).

Third, the remaining two grounds listed in the Reception Conditions Directive give rise to other concerns. Point (d) regulates a situation that could be subsumed under non-cooperation. While Human Rights law does not in principle preclude non-cooperation as a ground for detention, it appears disproportionate in this context absent a risk of absconding. Point (f) makes cross-reference to Dublin procedures. Art. 28(2) Dublin Regulation establishes that the ground for detention under the Regulation is a risk of absconding. It is not clear why a separate ground is necessary for Dublin cases, as the same safeguards should apply, and the risk of absconding laid down in the Reception Conditions Directive should also cover Dublin cases. Thus, neither of these grounds should be interpreted so as to expand the possible grounds for detention but should, rather, be read in the light of the notion of absconding.

Since detention based on a broader notion of non-cooperation – extending beyond a risk of absconding – would often be considered disproportionate, the two most pertinent grounds are the risk of acts against nation-

276 HR Committee, *A.G.F.K. et al. v. Australia*, Communication No. 2094/2011, CCPR/C/108/D/2094/2011, at para. 9.3.

277 Moreover, acts against national security can be prosecuted under criminal law; their inclusion here reflects the 'crimmigration' trend that is so far not excluded by the HR Committee.

278 See the HR Committee jurisprudence, reported above, and also, e.g., UNHCR, Guidelines on the Applicable Criteria and Standards relating to the Detention of Asylum-Seekers and Alternatives to Detention (2012), at 17, para. 24, available at https://www.refworld.org/docid/503489533b8.html.

al security and absconding. As regards the former, such risks would rarely be found. In contrast, a risk of absconding could potentially be found for a large range and number of migrants. A careful definition as well as a thorough proportionality analysis are therefore required in order not to undermine the requirement of an individual assessment.

The Reception Conditions Directive and the Asylum Procedures Directive do not define the notion of 'absconding' at all, whereas the Return Directive and the Dublin Regulation currently merely state that risk of absconding means 'the existence of reasons in an individual case which are based on objective criteria defined by law to believe that a third-country national who is the subject of return procedures and may abscond'.[279] The 'objective criteria' are not defined in the Return Directive or the Dublin Regulation.[280] Hence, the understanding of the concept and the criteria laid down in domestic laws vary between Member States.[281] In its non-binding 2008 Recommendation on Returns, the European Commission calls upon Member States to provide for eight criteria for establishing a risk of absconding in their legislation.[282] The 2018 proposal for a recast Return Directive projects a new article with an even more expansive notion, proposing a non-exhaustive list of sixteen criteria to establish a risk of absconding, four of which lead to a presumption of a risk of absconding.[283] Such broad and non-exhaustive lists – especially if they are only loosely connected with a person's propensity to flee – are contrary to Human Rights law, because they undermine the individual assessment required by the proportionality principle.[284] The risk of absconding as a ground for

279 Art. 3(7) Return Directive; see also Art. 2(n) Dublin Regulation: 'risk of absconding' means the existence of reasons in an individual case, which are based on objective criteria defined by law, to believe that an applicant or a third-country national or a stateless person who is subject to a transfer procedure may abscond.

280 In the *Jawo* case, in the context of the Dublin Regulation, the CJEU clarified that 'absconding' can be assumed when the individual does not remain at the accommodation allocated to them without informing the competent authorities of their absence, CJEU, Case C-163/17, *Jawo* (EU:C:2019:218), at para. 70.

281 European Parliament, The Return Directive 2008/115/EC: European Implementation Assessment (2020), at 86–88.

282 European Commission, Recommendation 2017/432 on making returns more effective when implementing the Directive 2008/115/EC, at para. 15–16.

283 European Commission, Proposal for a recast Return Directive, COM(2018) 634 final, 12 September 2018, Art. 6.

284 European Parliament, The Return Directive 2008/115/EC: European Implementation Assessment (2020), at 89.

detention must be interpreted narrowly and is not amenable to legislative presumptions.[285] In the words of the HR Committee, a determination must carefully 'consider relevant factors case-by-case, and not be based on a mandatory rule for a broad category'.[286] The legislative approach taken by the European Commission is therefore not consonant with Human Rights law.

The reform proposal for a recast Reception Conditions Directive also proposes to expand the grounds of detention. The Commission projects a new ground for detention under Art. 8(3) of this Directive, which explicitly lays down non-compliance with area-based restrictions as a pathway to detention. According to the proposed new Art. 8(3)(c), detention would be permissible 'in order to ensure compliance with legal obligations imposed on the applicant through an individual decision in accordance with Article 7(2) in cases where the applicant has not complied with such obligations and there is a risk of absconding of the applicant'.[287]

2.2.3 Specific issue: Border Procedures

The rise of so-called 'border procedures' to determine an asylum claim is a major trend in European migration policy. Next to concerns related to the principle of solidarity among the Member States, such procedures raise issues of Human Rights in view of the prohibition of arbitrary detention and other non-justified measures restricting liberty.[288]

The EU border procedures regime is scattered across various legal instruments, which must be read together. Art. 8(3)(c) of the Reception Conditions Directive provides that detention is permissible 'in order to *decide*, in the context of a procedure, on the *right to enter* the territory'.[289] A

285 Majcher and Strik, 'Legislating without Evidence: The Recast of the EU Return Directive', 23 *European Journal of Migration and Law (EJML)* (2021) 103, at 115–116.

286 HR Committee, *A.G.F.K. et al. v. Australia*, Communication No. 2094/2011, CCPR/C/108/D/2094/2011, at para. 9.3.

287 European Commission, Proposal for a recast Reception Conditions Directive, COM(2016) 465, 13 July 2016.

288 For a detailed legal assessment, see European Parliament Research Service, Asylum Procedures at the Border: European Implementation Assessment (2020), at 74–95, available at https://www.europarl.europa.eu/RegData/etudes/STUD/2020/654201/EPRS_STU(2020)654201_EN.pdf.

289 Art. 8(3)(c) Reception Conditions Directive (emphasis added).

systematic reading of this somewhat opaque provision reveals that 'procedure' refers to 'border procedures' as defined in the Art. 43 of the Asylum Procedures Directive.[290] According to this provision, Member States may establish border procedures in order to determine the admissibility, and in some cases the substance, of an asylum claim.[291] Although Art. 43 of the Asylum Procedures Directive itself makes no mention of detention, various other provisions of this Directive, read in conjunction with the Reception Conditions Directive, indicate that the EU legislature acknowledged that these procedures entail deprivation of liberty in most cases.[292] For example, some provisions of the Reception Conditions Directive refer to derogations in cases where 'the applicant is detained at a border post or in a transit zone'.[293] In the *Röszke* case, the CJEU explicitly endorsed this interpretation and stated that in light of Art. 8(3)(c) Reception Conditions Directive, Art. 43 Asylum Procedures Directive permits the detention of asylum seekers at the border for the purposes specified in that provision.[294]

The question arises as to whether detention of asylum seekers in the context of a border procedure is in line with Human Rights law. As outlined above (see section 2.2.1), Human Rights law does not preclude the detention of asylum seekers entering a State's territory unlawfully, but does narrowly circumscribe such detention. Such detention is permissible only for a brief initial period in order to *document* their entry, *record* their claims, and determine their identity if it is in doubt.[295] However, to detain

290 See also European Commission, Proposal for a recast Reception Conditions Directive, COM(2016) 465, 13 July 2016, Art. 8(3)(d).

291 Art. 43(1) Asylum Procedures Directive.

292 G. Cornelisse, *The Constitutionalisation of Immigration Detention: Between EU Law and the European Convention on Human Rights* (2016), available at https://research.vu.nl/ws/portalfiles/portal/1522197/Cornelisse-GDP-paper.pdf.

293 E.g., Art. 10(5) and Art. 11(6) Reception Conditions Directive.

294 CJEU, Cases C-924/19 PPU and C-925/19 PPU, *FMS* (EU:C:2020:367), at para. 237–239. This followed the finding that conditions at the transit zone did amount to detention, at para. 226–231; in contrast to the Grand Chamber of the ECtHR in *Ilias and Ahmed*, which controversially overruled a Chamber judgment to hold that asylum seekers were not detained in the Röszke transit zone: ECtHR, *Ilias and Ahmed v. Hungary*, Appl. no. 47287/15, Grand Chamber Judgment of 21 November 2019. However, in *R.R. and others v. Hungary*, Appl. no. 36037/17, Judgment of 2 March 2021, the ECtHR distinguished the case from *Ilias and Ahmed* and held that the situation of the applicants amounted to a de facto deprivation of liberty.

295 HR Committee, *Bakhtiyari v. Australia*, Communication No. 1069/2002, CCPR/C/79/D/1069/2002, at para. 9.2–9.3. In line with HR Committee jurisprudence, the 2017 Michigan Guidelines also accept detention 'during the very

asylum seekers further while their claims are being processed would be arbitrary in the absence of particular reasons specific to the individual.[296] As established above (see section 2.2.2), only individualized reasons specific to the individual can justify detention, such as a risk of absconding or acts against national security. A pending determination on the right to enter is not a sufficient reason to justify detention beyond initial documentation and recording.

Due to the scattered nature of the regulation of border procedures, it is not entirely clear what constitutes the legal basis for the detention in this context. In the *Röszke* case, the CJEU referred to the 'purposes' laid down in Art. 43 Asylum Procedures Directive. These purposes are decisions on the admissibility of claims pursuant to Art. 33 Asylum Procedures Directive[297] or on the substance of an application for the situations listed in Art. 31(8) Asylum Procedures Directive.[298] Both the determination of admissibility pursuant to Art. 33(2) and the accelerated procedure foreseen by Art. 31(8) of the Asylum Procedures Directive require the assessment of core elements of the asylum claim. As established above, determination of the substance of claims is not a valid ground for detention of asylum seekers. Thus, detention in the context of border procedures cannot be based on the mere purposes stated in this Directive.

Alternatively, it may be argued that the basis for the detention of asylum seekers in the context of border procedures is not Art. 43 Asylum Procedures Directive, since that provision merely outlines the procedure. Rather, the relevant ground for detention of asylum seekers would be

---

earliest moments after arrival' but only 'so long as such detention is prescribed by law and is shown to be the least intrusive means available to achieve a specific and important lawful purpose, such as documenting the refugee's arrival, recording the fact of a claim, or determining the refugee's identity if it is in doubt'; see University of Michigan Law School, *The Michigan Guidelines on Refugee Freedom of Movement* (2017), at 15, available at https://www.refworld.org/docid/592ee6614.html; similarly: UNHCR, Guidelines on the Applicable Criteria and Standards relating to the Detention of Asylum-Seekers and Alternatives to Detention (2012), at para. 24, available at https://www.refworld.org/docid/503489533b8.html.

296 HR Committee, *Tarlue v. Canada*, Communication No. 1551/2007, CCPR/C/95/D/1551/2007, at para. 3.3 and 7.6; *Mansour Ahani v. Canada*, Communication No. 1051/2002, CCPR/C/80/D/1051/2002, at para. 10.2; and see UNHCR, Guidelines on the Applicable Criteria and Standards relating to the Detention of Asylum-Seekers and Alternatives to Detention (2012), at 18, para. 28, available at https://www.refworld.org/docid/503489533b8.html.

297 Art. 33(2) Asylum Procedures Directive.

298 Art. 31(8) Asylum Procedures Directive.

found in Art. 8(3)(c) Reception Conditions Directive. Art. 8(3)(c) states: 'An applicant may be detained ... in order to decide, in the context of a [border] procedure, on the applicant's right to enter the territory'.[299] However, this reading also conflicts with Human Rights law. The determination of an applicant's claim is not a sufficient ground to justify detention absent specific and individual reasons. Art. 8 Reception Conditions Directive accounts for this to the extent that it subjects any decision to detain to necessity and proportionality in the individual case, as the CJEU acknowledged in the *Röszke* judgment.[300] Yet such individual assessment could only ever be the result of a proper procedure, which may or may not produce a lawful detention order, rather than the other way around. It follows that in the light of Human Rights law, point (c) of Art. 8(3) Reception Conditions Directive is devoid of meaning.

The question remains whether other grounds laid down in Art. 8 Reception Conditions might serve as a legal basis for detention in the context of border procedures. The most pertinent candidate is Art. 8(3)(a) Reception Conditions Directive, which establishes verification of identity as a detention ground. As long as detention based on this ground remains 'brief' and 'initial', this is warranted under Human Rights law. However, any detention that serves to assess the substance of the asylum claim is unlawful.

In sum, immigration detention can only legally take place if there are individual reasons specific to the person concerned, such as a risk of absconding (which corresponds with Art. 8(3) points (b) and (f) of the Reception Conditions Directive) or of acts against national security (corresponding with Art. 8(3) point (e) Reception Conditions Directive). This must be established in the individual case, including in the context of border procedures. Hence, in order for border procedures to be in line with international law, they cannot summarily resort to detention. In other words, border procedures may be an expedient element of the Common European Asylum System, but this policy choice does not justify quasi-automatic detention of entire classes of asylum seekers.

The remaining scope of application for border procedures is limited to area-based restrictions not amounting to detention.[301] Art. 43(3) Asylum

299 Art. 8(3)(c) Reception Conditions Directive.

300 CJEU, Cases C-924/19 PPU and C-925/19 PPU, *FMS* (EU:C:2020:367), at para. 259 and 266.

301 The CJEU made suggestions to that end in the *Röszke* case, see ibid., at para. 222 and 247.

Procedures Directive allows for 'normal' accommodation near the border or within a transit zone.[302] In parallel, Art. 18(1)(a) of the Reception Conditions Directive allows housing to be provided in kind, among others, in 'premises used for the purpose of housing applicants during the examination of an application made at the border or in transit zones'. In the *Röszke* case, the CJEU clarified that these are different from detention centres as referred to in Art. 10 Reception Conditions Directive and must not lead to deprivations of liberty in the meaning of Art. 5 ECHR.[303] To the extent that such housing is connected with limitations on freedom of movement, they must be duly justified (see next section).

The amended proposal for an Asylum Procedures Regulation of September 2020 appears to acknowledge that in order to be lawful, border procedures must not be accompanied by quasi-automatic detention. Art. 41 of the proposed Asylum Procedures Regulation would make the use of border procedures mandatory for certain types of those claims that are subject to the accelerated procedure, but does not prescribe detention. As per Art. 41(9)(d) of the proposed Regulation, Member States can make use of detention in line with the requirements set out in the Reception Conditions Directive or the Return Directive, as applicable. However, under the Reception Conditions Directive, the ground for detention would still be the self-referential Art. 8(3)(c)[304] – which is unlawful, as we have outlined above (in section 2.2.2).

Moreover, for the mandatory border procedures, Art. 41(13) of the proposed Asylum Procedures Regulation, as amended in 2020, states that: 'During the examination of applications subject to a border procedure, the applicants *shall be kept* at or in proximity to the external border or transit zones.'[305] The proposal uses the somewhat fuzzy wording that the applicant 'shall be kept' at the border. While this is not an established legal term, it is clear that the proposal avoids the term 'detention' – and therefore does not directly require detention either. Nevertheless, it is possible that those measures that Member States must impose on asylum seekers in order achieve the task of 'keeping them at the border' would *in fact* amount to detention nonetheless. As we developed in section 2.2.1,

302 Ibid., at para. 247.

303 Ibid., at para. 254.

304 Renumbered as Art. 8(3)(d) according to the proposal from the European Commission, Proposal for a recast Reception Conditions Directive, COM(2016) 465, 13 July 2016.

305 European Commission, Amended proposal for an Asylum Procedures Regulation, COM(2020) 611, 23 September 2020 (emphasis added).

the distinction between detention in the strict sense (deprivation of liberty) and other restrictions on movement is gradual, not categorical; the classification by the legislator or the ordering authority is irrelevant. The distinction depends on the actual circumstances, including the duration, the threatened sanctions in the event of a violation, and the manner of implementation. Situations of *de facto* detention would regularly be unlawful for failing to be in line with material and procedural standards. However, the question of *de facto* detention would have to be determined in lengthy proceedings for each specific place and person. Suffice it to recall the Hungarian transit zone with conflicting and partly controversial outcomes from the two supranational European Courts. Therefore, it is to be expected that Member States would regularly claim that the measures they impose do not amount to detention. The provision allows the EU to rely on counterfactual expectations of an implementation by EU Member States in accordance with fundamental and Human Rights, specifically the prohibition of arbitrary detention. Furthermore, the Commission's Pontius Pilate approach clouds the fact that the restriction imposed by the new Art. 41(13) of the proposed Asylum Procedures Regulation would violate the EU's own obligation to respect fundamental and Human Rights, as we shall demonstrate in the following section.

2.2.4 Specific issue: Area-based restrictions

EU law permits restrictions on intra-territorial movement of migrants in various instances. Art. 7 of the Reception Conditions Directive lays down the conditions under which Member States may limit the freedom of movement of asylum seekers. Other provisions, such as Art. 18(1)(a) Reception Conditions Directive[306] and Art. 43(3) Asylum Procedures Directive[307] also rely on the assumption that asylum seekers' movement is restricted to a certain area, in that case near the border or transit zone. Such area-based restrictions must be distinguished from so-called alternatives to detention (ATDs). While the principle of proportionality requires the prior consideration of alternatives to detention before a decision to detain a migrant is taken (as discussed above, section 2.2.2), area-based restrictions are not meant to serve as a less onerous measure in response to a situation that, as a rule, would justify issuing a detention order. Rather,

306 Art. 18(1)(a) Reception Conditions Directive.
307 Art. 43(3) Asylum Procedures Directive.

they serve independent aims that, according to a specific legal basis, justify temporarily restricting the spatial movement of individuals to a certain area.

The central provision for this type of measure as regards asylum seekers is Art. 7 Reception Conditions Directive on 'Residence and Freedom of Movement'.[308] It reads, in the relevant parts:

> *1. Applicants may move freely within the territory of the host Member State or within an area assigned to them by that Member State. The assigned area shall not affect the unalienable sphere of private life and shall allow sufficient scope for guaranteeing access to all benefits under this Directive.*
> *2. Member States may decide on the residence of the applicant for reasons of public interest, public order or, when necessary, for the swift processing and effective monitoring of his or her application for international protection.*
> *3. Member States may make provision of the material reception conditions subject to actual residence by the applicants in a specific place, to be determined by the Member States. Such a decision, which may be of a general nature, shall be taken individually and established by national law.*

A series of issues arise when analyzing these provisions in light of Human Rights. The measures foreseen in Art. 7 of the Reception Conditions Directive must pass the test of conformity with Art. 12 ICCPR and Art. 2 of Protocol No. 4 ECHR (and the corresponding fundamental right). Note that, according to Art. 9(1) of the Asylum Procedures Directive, asylum seekers are allowed to remain in the Member State pending a decision on their asylum claim, irrespective of a potentially illegal entry. They are, therefore, 'lawfully within the territory' for the purposes of Art. 12 ICCPR and Art. 2 of Protocol No. 4 ECHR.[309] Were asylum seekers conceived as not being covered by the scope of these guarantees, area-based restrictions on their mobility would have to be tested against Art. 8 ECHR (see above, section 2.2.1).

First, we recall that restrictive measures taken on the basis of Art. 7 of the Reception Conditions Directive – or rather, of national legislation transposing its provisions – may, depending on their degree, intensity, and cumulative impact, nonetheless amount to a deprivation of liberty within the meaning of Art. 9 ICCPR and Art. 5 ECHR. The question of whether

308 Art. 7 Reception Conditions Directive.

309 Art. 9(1) Asylum Procedures Directive; on this point, see Costello, 'Immigration Detention: The Grounds Beneath Our Feet', 68 *Current Legal Problems* (2015) 143, at 147 and 174.

restrictions actually amount to detention irrespective of their designation depends on the specific circumstances in each particular case[310] – for example, whether the building is physically locked is not decisive if the places and time spent away are subject to permissions, controls, and restrictions.[311] Likewise, being held on a small island under strict supervision and curfew, including the requirement to report to the police twice a day, and only being permitted to contact the outside world under supervision, would also amount to deprivation of liberty for the purposes of Art. 5 ECHR.[312] In contrast, night curfew coupled with reporting obligations on certain days and the requirement to inform the police when leaving the house was found to be a mere restriction of movement rather than deprivation of liberty.[313] In light of these criteria, it depends on the specific circumstances whether measures that Member States put in place to restrict the movement of asylum seekers based on Art. 7 Reception Conditions Directive – such as house arrest in France with reporting obligations, restriction of movement to an island in Greece, or accommodation in a remote village in Austria – amount to unlawful deprivation of liberty.

Second, Art. 12 ICCPR and Art. 2 of Protocol No. 4 ECHR require area-based restrictions to be 'provided by law' and 'in accordance with law', respectively. Art. 7(1) and (2) Reception Conditions Directive does not explicitly mention this requirement. Only the decision to make provision of material reception conditions subject to actual residence is constrained by a procedure 'established by national law' (Art. 7(3) of the Directive). However, the requirement of a legal basis in an act of general application can be deduced from general principles of EU law and, more specifically, from the legal regime developed by the CJEU for a proper transposition of directives in accordance with Art. 288(3) TFEU.[314] Notably, this legal regime does not provide for so-called reversed direct effect of directives: absent a sufficient legal basis in national law, the provisions of the Reception Conditions Directive cannot be held against an asylum seeker, that is, it cannot serve as an independent legal basis for a restrictive measure.

310 ECtHR, *Amuur v. France*, Appl. no. 19776/92, Judgment of 25 June 1996; the Court qualified holding persons in the transit zone of an international airport as detention, even though they were 'legally free to leave' toward third countries.

311 ECtHR, *Stanev v. Bulgaria*, Appl. no. 36760/06, Judgment of 17 January 2012, at para. 124.

312 ECtHR, *Guzzardi v. Italy*, Appl. no. 7367/76, Judgment of 6 November 1980.

313 ECtHR, *Raimondo v. Italy*, Appl. no. 12954/87, Judgment of 22 February 1994.

314 See Bast, 'Legal Instruments and Judicial Protection', in A. von Bogdandy and J. Bast (eds), *Principles of European Constitutional Law* (2009) 345, at 355 et seq.

Third, Art. 7(2) Reception Conditions Directive provides that 'Member States may decide on the residence of the applicant for reasons of public interest, public order or, when necessary, for the swift processing and effective monitoring of his or her application for international protection'. This wide scope for the grounds that may justify area-based restrictions raises questions in light of Art. 12(3) ICCPR and Art. 2(3) and (4) of Protocol No. 4 ECHR. According to Art. 12(3) ICCPR, restrictions on the right to freedom of movement must be necessary for the protection of national security, public order, public health or morals, or the rights and freedoms of others. Art. 2(3) Protocol No. 4 ECHR is drafted in a similar way. However, the additional limitation foreseen in Art. 2(4) Protocol No. 4 ECHR, permitting area-based restrictions justified by 'the public interest', is not included in Art. 12(3) ICCPR.

This difference is particularly significant in the context of Art. 7(2) of the Reception Condition Directive. The broad notion of 'public interest' might well cover measures taken for mere bureaucratic convenience that would not qualify for the maintenance of *ordre public*. Arguably, the 'swift processing and effective monitoring' of asylum claims that is explicitly mentioned in Art. 7(2) is but one example, although a swift and fair asylum procedure is also in the interest of bona fide asylum seekers. However, measures that are only supported by public interests, and not by the grounds mentioned in Art. 12(3) ICCPR and Art. 2(3) Protocol No. 4 ECHR, would violate Human Rights law in two respects. First, the Member States are bound to respect their international obligations under the ICCPR in addition to their obligations under the ECHR. Second, the Strasbourg Court has established a narrow reading of the scope of Art. 2(4) Protocol No. 4 ECHR. According to its case-law, the fourth paragraph does not apply to measures directed at particular individuals or groups of individuals – which must be considered in light of the third paragraph, with its narrower scope – but only to measures of general applicability that are limited to discrete areas of a country.[315] Hence, Member States cannot refer to Art. 2(4) Protocol No. 4 ECHR when implementing Art. 7(2) of the Directive. In light of the above jurisprudence, freedom of movement of legally present migrants may only be limited by national security or public order considerations in a stricter sense, as laid down in Art. 12(3) ICCPR and Art. 2(3) Protocol No. 4 ECHR.

---

315 On this distinction in a non-migration case, see ECtHR, Appl. no. 43494/09, *Garib v. the Netherlands*, Judgment of 6 November 2017, at para. 110.

Accordingly, Art. 7(2) of the Reception Condition Directive seemingly permits Member State certain action that is actually unlawful under Human Rights law and EU fundamental rights. This is not merely another example of 'underinclusive legislation', which would be technically lawful according to the jurisprudence of the CJEU when its provisions are sufficiently flexible to incorporate EU fundamental rights (see above, introductory chapter). Rather, in cases such as Art. 7(2) of the Reception Condition Directive, in which the literal transposition of the provision of a Directive would constitute a violation of fundamental rights, this provision must itself be regarded as unlawful.

The reform proposals tabled in 2020 by the European Commission would even expand the use of area-based restrictions. In the specific context of border procedures, the amended proposal for an Asylum Procedures Regulation[316] would make the use of border procedures mandatory for certain types of claims,[317] while Art. 41(13) requires Member States to 'keep' these claimants near the border or transit zones, that is, to implement area-based restrictions. According to Art. 41(2) and (3) of the amended proposal, the use of border procedures would be mandatory for three grounds: Where the applicant is assumed to have misled the authorities by withholding or presenting false evidence, where the applicant is considered a danger to national security and, importantly, according to a new ground added in the 2020 proposal, where the applicant comes from a country with a Union-wide recognition rate of 20 % or lower.[318] Once the determination is made, during a screening procedure or otherwise, that one of these grounds is present, the imposition of an area-based restriction is the immediate and automatic effect according to the Regulation. On the basis of our legal evaluation conducted above, such a provision of EU law would be unlawful for two reasons. First, the grounds laid down in Art. 41(2) and (3) of the amended proposal clearly exceed what is accepted under Art. 12(3) ICCPR and Art. 2(3) Protocol No. 4 ECHR (and the corresponding EU fundamental right). In particular the statistical chances of an asylum claim to be successful does not relate to any of the public

316 Amended proposal for an Asylum Procedures Regulation, COM(2020) 611, 23 September 2020.

317 According to Art 40(1) of the proposal, as amended in 2020, Member States are obliged to apply the accelerated procedure on nine specified grounds that are related to what are considered prima facie manifestly unfounded claims. The accelerated procedure may, but does not have to be, carried out in the form of a border procedure in all cases.

318 Art. 40(1)(c), (f) and (i) of the amended proposal.

order considerations mentioned in these clauses. Second, even if the more lenient test under Art. 8(2) ECHR were applicable due to a presumed 'unlawful' presence of the asylum seekers concerned, the automatic imposition of restriction on the freedom of movement would fail to be 'necessary in a democratic society' (and comply with the corresponding principle of proportionality in EU law). Restrictions on movement that are based on abstractly formulated criteria, that establish irrebuttable presumptions to the detriment of migrants, are inadmissible. In line with Human Rights law, regardless of whether such measures would in fact amount to detention, their blanket imposition without a proportionality assessment on a case-by-case basis is manifestly unlawful.

2.2.5 Specific issue: Detention conditions

(1) The outline of the legal framework has revealed a lack of normative standards on adequate conditions for administrative immigration detention (see above, section 2.2.1). This also holds true in EU legislation. The regulation of detention conditions for asylum seekers (Art. 10 Reception Conditions Directive) and for persons who are subject to return procedures (Art. 16 Return Directive) is rather sparse. Although the requirements laid down in the Reception Conditions Directive are somewhat more detailed than those in the Return Directive, neither provides detailed guidance on how a detention centre is to be designed and what facilities it should provide.[319] Both instruments limit the standards for conditions essentially to one article, and under both instruments many exceptions and derogations are possible.[320]

This is a clear case of underinclusive legislation at the EU level with regard to those standards that do exist in Human Rights law to prevent inhuman or degrading treatment in detention. The European Commission has noted this gap and reminded Member States in its 2017 Recommendation regarding a 'Return Handbook' that Member States must respect the absolute minimum that is required by Art. 4 EU-CFR, even when

319 A. Achermann, J. Künzli and B. von Rütte, *European Immigration Detention Rules: Feasibility Study* (2013), at 20, available at https://www.unine.ch/files/live/sites/ius-migration/files/Publikationslisten/EIDR%20Feasibility%20Study%20MC.pdf.

320 For example, Art. 16(1)(1) Return Directive, and Art. 10(1)(3) Reception Conditions Directive.

the Return Directive does not regulate certain material detention conditions.[321] The Commission makes reference to a series of relevant guidelines and standards. This illustrates that not even the absolute minimum is sufficiently regulated in EU legislation regarding immigration detention.

As outlined above, inadequate conditions in immigration detention can also lead to a breach of Art. 5(1)(f) ECHR or other provisions of Human Rights law, in particular Art. 8 ECHR. In this regard, detention conditions must reflect the administrative character of the measure. Detention is imposed in order to achieve the specific aim of a person not leaving, but otherwise detention conditions should not be of punitive character and be as close as possible to living normally such that other harms are curbed as much as possible. To reflect this, and while other specific legislation is lacking, the provisions on reception conditions of asylum seekers could provisionally serve as a general standard. To this end, the Reception Conditions Directive could be made applicable to all migrants in detention. This would at least ensure compliance with the basic principle of proportionality in most cases, regardless of the requirement also to assess this principle in the individual case.

In addition, there is a need for further concretization. The codification process of the European Rules for Administrative Detention is potentially promising in this regard. However, reports indicate that the process is stagnating just as, somewhat ironically, the EU is blocking the adoption of a Council of Europe resolution on the standards.[322] Moreover, the draft contains little detail on the design and operation of an immigration detention center and on how migrants are to be treated.[323] Rather, the parts of the Rules on the conditions and treatment in detention largely

---

321 European Commission, Recommendation 2017/2338 establishing a common 'Return Handbook' to be used by Member States' competent authorities when carrying out return-related tasks, at para. 149.

322 See Deutscher Bundestag, Bericht der Bundesregierung über die Tätigkeit des Europarats im Zeitraum vom 1. Januar bis 31. Dezember 2018, BT Drucksache 19/9444, 5. April 2019, at 16: '[CDCJ] has continued its work on a codification of existing legal standards in centers for the administrative detention of migrants. The work has been halted shortly before the finalization by interventions lodged by the EU Commission at a late stage. The Committee of Ministers of the Council of Europe is currently examining in what form the work can be taken up again in 2019 and finalized' (trans. by the authors).

323 Council of Europe: European Committee on Legal Co-Operation (CDCJ), Codifying instrument of European rules on the administrative detention of migrants, 18 May 2017, available at https://rm.coe.int/european-rules-on-the-administrative-detention-of-migrants-draft-codif/1680714cc1.

replicate the text of the European Prison Rules, without contextualization or adaptation.[324] Here, a more proactive role of the EU and its Member States would be required from the viewpoint of Human Rights.

(2) Detention of any kind represents a context of particular vulnerability to maltreatment that requires an effective monitoring mechanism. Art. 16(4) Return Directive provides for monitoring but allows for the visits in detention facilities to be conditioned on prior authorization. The Reception Conditions Directive does not specifically foresee a monitoring mechanism. According to Art. 10(3) and (4) Reception Conditions Directive, only UNHCR and NGOs have (in principle) unlimited access to detained asylum seekers. In order to ensure Human Rights compliance, a monitoring mechanism is needed not only for detention centers but also for reception centers and other places of area-based restriction, such as confinement on islands.[325] Such monitoring should be carried out by bodies that also inspect prisons – for example, by national prison monitoring bodies such as the national preventive mechanisms established under the Optional Protocol to CAT.[326]

(3) The Return Directive allows for the detention of children 'as a measure of last resort and for the shortest appropriate period of time' (Art. 17) as well as of persons in situations of vulnerability and with special needs (Art. 16(3) Return Directive). Similarly, the Reception Conditions Directive allows for the detention of both children and persons in situations of vulnerability. The 2017 Commission Recommendation on making returns

---

324 L. McGregor, *An Appraisal of the Council of Europe's Draft European Rules on the Conditions of Administrative Detention of Migrants*, 19 July 2017, available at https://www.ejiltalk.org/an-appraisal-of-the-council-of-europes-draft-european-rules-on-the-conditions-of-administrative-detention-of-migrants/.

325 E. Guild, M. Garlick and V. Moreno-Lax, *Study on Enhancing the Common European Asylum System and Alternatives to Dublin* (2015), available at http://www.europarl.europa.eu/RegData/etudes/STUD/2015/519234/IPOL_STU%282015%29519234_EN.pdf, at para. 30–38. See also the guide for monitoring immigration detention prepared by the Association for the Prevention of Torture (ATP), the International Detention Coalition (IDC) and UNHCR, Monitoring Immigration Detention: Practical Manual (2014), available at https://idcoalition.org/wp-content/uploads/2015/06/Monitoring-Immigration-Detention-Practical-Manual.pdf.

326 Ph. de Bruycker et al., *Alternatives to Immigration and Asylum Detention: Time for Implementation* (2015), at 21.

more effective even states that Member States should not preclude the detention of minors in their legislation.[327]

This raises the issue as to what extent, and under what conditions, the placement in detention of particularly vulnerable migrants can be justified in international law. In Human Rights law as it stands, we were not able to identify a general prohibition of detaining certain classes of persons entirely. The UN Convention on the Rights of the Child establishes that detention of a minor should be a measure of last resort, but it does not explicitly prohibit the practice.[328] The same holds true under the UN Convention on the Rights of Persons with Disabilities; while this document has been specifically designed to address the protection of disabled persons, it does not prohibit resorting to detention.[329] Consequently, establishing a general prohibition to detain certain classes of particularly vulnerable migrants would be the task of domestic legislatures, including the EU.

However, as repeatedly stated, detention must be necessary and proportionate in each case. The individual's specific vulnerability is an important element that needs to be duly considered. Taking into account the administrative purpose of a measure, through a correct reading of the principles of necessity and proportionality, a vulnerable person should be placed under a non-custodial measure from the outset of the procedure.[330] In this light, the Working Group on Arbitrary Detention argues that immigration detention of migrants in situations of vulnerability or at risk, such as unaccompanied children, families with minor children, pregnant women, breastfeeding mothers, elderly persons, persons with disabilities, lesbian, gay, bisexual, transgender and intersex persons, or survivors of trafficking, torture, and/or other serious violent crimes, 'must not take place'.[331] Similarly, for children specifically, the UN Special Rapporteur on the Human Rights of Migrants has argued that children should never be detained for

327 European Commission, Recommendation 2017/432 on making returns more effective when implementing the Directive 2008/115/EC, at para. 14.

328 See Art. 37(c) CRC.

329 See Art. 14 of the Convention on the Rights of Persons with Disabilities (relating to liberty and security).

330 Pétin, 'Exploring the Role of Vulnerability in Immigration Detention', 35 *Refugee Survey Quarterly* (2016) 91, at 98.

331 Human Rights Council: Working Group on Arbitrary Detention, Revised deliberation No. 5 on deprivation of liberty of migrants, A/HRC/39/45, at para. 41; see also Report of the Working Group on Arbitrary Detention, Mission to Malta 2009, A/HRC/13/30/Add.2, at para. 79(f), and Report of the Working Group on Arbitrary Detention, Mission to Malaysia 2011, A/HRC/16/47/Add.2, at para. 119.

immigration purposes, nor can detention ever be justified as being in a child's best interests,[332] a view that is shared by the Committee on the Protection of the Rights of All Migrant Workers and Members of Their Families and the Committee on the Rights of the Child.[333] The ECtHR has also regularly found detention of children to be disproportionate in relevant cases that came before it.[334] In sum, although detention is not categorically prohibited, the requirements of necessity and proportionality renders immigration detention of people in situations of vulnerability, in particular children, almost always unlawful.

Finally, in order to identify migrants in situations of vulnerability, and to prevent their potentially unlawful detention, a screening procedure is required. Some situations of particular vulnerability are more or less obvious, such as old age or physical disability, but others are not, such as mental disorders, or trauma resulting from torture or rape. Identification is a core element without which the provisions aimed at special treatment of persons in situations of vulnerability would lose any meaning.[335]

While Art. 11 of the Reception Conditions Directive includes a special provision on the detention of vulnerable persons, it does not specifically prescribe a screening procedure in order to identify them.[336] Art. 21 and 22 of this Directive require an assessment of special reception needs, and Art. 24(1) of the Asylum Procedures Directive requires an assessment of a need for special procedural guarantees. But the details and design of such mechanisms are not specified in either instrument. The sole prerequisite is the need for a vulnerability assessment.[337] It is unclear whether

332 Report of the Special Rapporteur on the human rights of migrants: Focus Return (2018), at 10.

333 See joint General Comment No. 3 (2017) of the CMW and No. 22 (2017) of the CRC on the general principles regarding the human rights of children in the context of international migration, CMW/C/GC/3-CRC/C/GC/22; joint General Comment No. 4 (2017) of the CMW and No. 23 (2017) of the CRC on State obligations regarding the human rights of children in the context of international migration in countries of origin, transit, destination and return, CMW/C/GC/4-CRC/C/GC/23.

334 For an analysis, see Smyth, 'Towards a Complete Prohibition on the Immigration Detention of Children', 19 *Human Rights Law Review* (2019) 1, at 16–19.

335 Jakuleviciene, 'Vulnerable Persons as a New Sub-Group of Asylum Seekers?', in V. Chetail, Ph. de Bruycker and F. Maiani (eds), *Reforming the Common European Asylum System: The New European Refugee Law* (2016) 353, at 353–373.

336 Art. 11 Reception Conditions Directive.

337 Art. 22 and recital 29 of Reception Conditions Directive, in conjunction with Art. 24 Asylum Procedures Directive.

identification should be a separate step in the asylum procedure and what minimal requirements would suffice to fulfill this obligation. In contrast, the Return Directive makes no mention of any vulnerability assessment procedure at all. Art. 16 of the Return Directive is limited to requiring that 'particular attention shall be paid to the situation of vulnerable persons', and that 'emergency health care and essential treatment of illness shall be provided'. There is thus no explicit legal requirement for a screening procedure in order to identify persons in situations of vulnerability among those who are subject to pre-removal detention based on the Return Directive.

2.3 Recommendations

Recommendation 1: Enact horizontal provisions on detention grounds

We recommend that in order to prevent the disproportionate and expansive use of detention, the EU should regulate the grounds for detention of migrants in a horizontal provision that applies across all instruments. Taking the cue from the exhaustive list in the Reception Conditions Directive and the CJEU's rulings regarding the Return Directive, the provision should exhaustively list the possible grounds for detention. Considering the relevant jurisprudence of the HR Committee, the permissible grounds for detention should be limited to a risk of absconding and a risk of acts against national security. We suggest the following wording:

> *Unless other sufficient but less coercive measures can be applied effectively in a specific case, Member States may keep in detention, for the shortest time possible, a third-country national who is the subject of migration procedures only when strictly necessary in order to prevent (a) absconding or (b) acts against national security. In each individual case, Member States must demonstrate that the detention is necessary in order to meet this aim.*

These two grounds should each be carefully circumscribed and exhaustively defined in EU law in order to ensure that expanding interpretation does not undermine the requirement of an individual assessment. This provision should apply to instances of the detention in the EU related to asylum and immigration matters, including but not limited to the Return Directive, the Reception Conditions Directive, and the Dublin Regulation. The necessary powers of the EU legislature follow from a combined use of the legal bases provided in Art. 78(2) and Art. 79(2) TFEU.

Recommendation 2: Prohibit 'border procedures' based on detention

The EU should abstain from enabling the use of detention as part of border procedures to assess asylum claims. Upholding the current policy that relies on detention for border procedures would violate Human Rights law and, hence, Art. 6 EU-CFR. Accordingly, we recommend deleting Art. 8(3)(c) Asylum Procedures Directive. Accelerated asylum procedures at the external borders of the EU are not per se unlawful, but they must not be accompanied by quasi-automatic detention absent a specific reason to detain a particular individual.

Pending such amendment, EU Member States are obliged, by virtue of Art. 9 ICCPR and their corresponding obligations under EU law, to refrain from detaining asylum seekers upon entry beyond a brief initial stage to register and record their claim. In order to achieve the purposes laid down in Art. 43(1) Asylum Procedures Directive, Member States may only resort to well-justified area-based restrictions, as referred to in Art. 43(3) Asylum Procedures Directive.

Accordingly, the Commission should withdraw its proposal for an Asylum Procedures Regulation, as amended in 2020, since it proposes to expand the use of border procedures and maintains ambiguous wording as regards the question of whether this involves detention.[338] We rather recommend that in its reform efforts regarding border procedures, the EU should explicitly prohibit the use of detention specifically related to asylum claims.

Recommendation 3: Specify legal safeguards for area-based restrictions

We recommend that Art. 7(2) Reception Conditions Directive be revised. First, it should explicitly require a legal basis in national law for any type of area-based restriction imposed on asylum seekers. Second, the permissible grounds for area-based restriction laid down in Art. 7(2) Reception Conditions Directive must be amended, as 'public interest' and 'swift processing and effective monitoring' of asylum applications are not sufficient to justify area-based restrictions. In order to align with EU fundamental rights, read in the light of Art. 12(3) ICCPR and Art. 2(3) Protocol No. 4 ECHR, the revised Reception Conditions Directive should provide for

338 See Art. 41 and 41a of the Amended proposal for an Asylum Procedures Regulation, COM(2020) 611, 23 September 2019.

area-based restrictions only on grounds of national security or for the maintenance of public order.

The same limitations and safeguards should apply to all types of area-based restrictions, including in the context of border procedures, as referred to in Art. 18(1)(a) Reception Conditions Directive and Art. 43(3) Asylum Procedures Directive. The Commission must withdraw its proposal for a mandatory use of area-based restrictions (Art. 41(13) amended proposal for an Asylum Procedures Regulation) since it violates Human Rights and fundamental rights.

Recommendation 4: Ensure adequate conditions in immigration detention and reception centers

We recommend that the EU proactively advance the process of further developing soft law on the conditions of immigration detention. To this end, it should constructively contribute to the process at the Council of Europe with the aim of implementing a Human Rights-based approach to defining the adequate conditions for administrative detention. The EU should define its own position on the draft European Immigration Detention Rules in the form of a decision, which would also be binding upon the negotiating stance of the Member States in all fields governed by EU law, including immigration detention.

In the meantime, we recommend that the general provisions on reception conditions laid down in the Reception Conditions Directive be made applicable to all migrants in detention.

In order to ensure compliance with these standards, we further recommend that the EU require Member States to implement a monitoring mechanism for places of administrative detention and reception centers, including the possibility of inspections without notice.

Recommendation 5: Prohibit detention of persons in situations of particular vulnerability

We recommend that the EU legislature explicitly prohibit the administrative detention of migrants in situations of particular vulnerability, including but not limited to children, in order to comply with the principle of proportionality by way of legislative balancing.

In order to be able to effectively implement this prohibition, this should be coupled with the requirement for Member States to implement an identification mechanism for situations of vulnerability prior to any order to detain, and at regular intervals during detention.

Chapter 3 – Guaranteeing Procedural Standards

Substantive rights need procedural safeguards in order to be effective. Such procedural standards encompass provisions ensuring that individuals are heard before decisions are taken that may adversely affect their legal position, that reasons are given for such decisions, and that the latter are subject to appeal through effective legal remedies. These safeguards recognize the affected person's agency as a legal subject and, thus, his or her human dignity.

In an objective dimension, procedural rights are inherently related to the rule of law, guaranteeing the supremacy of law as well as the equal and predictable application of legal norms to individual cases. The EU has committed itself to respect the rule of law as one of its core values, on equal level with human dignity, freedom, democracy, equality, and respect for human rights (Art. 2 TEU). This foundational value is also reflected in the Union's objectives guiding the creation of an Area of Freedom, Security and Justice, of which the EU's migration policy is a part: respect for fundamental rights, fairness toward migrants from third countries, and the facilitation of access to justice are supposed to be its cornerstones (Art. 3(2) and 67 TFEU).

Ensuring due process of law is one of the most important expressions of any public authority's respect for the rule of law. In the EU legal order, these standards are recognized as fundamental rights. The EU Charter provides for a right to good administration, including certain procedural rights (Art. 41 EU-CFR) as well as a right to an effective remedy and to a fair trial (Art. 47 EU-CFR). According to the EU Court of Justice, these provisions express general principles of EU law.[339]

Accordingly, EU institutions and bodies as well as Members States' authorities must meet the procedural guarantees stipulated in the Charter in all situations governed by EU law. The EU has, therefore, assumed full legal responsibility, and is politically accountable, for ensuring that these standards are observed in all administrative and judicial proceedings that fall within the substantive scope of EU migration law, irrespective of the

339 On the right to good administration, see CJEU, Case C-604/12, *H. N. v. Ireland* (EU:C:2014:302), at para. 49; C-230/18, *PI* (EU:C:2019:383), at para. 57; on the right to an effective remedy: C-556/17, *Torubarov* (EU:C:2019:626), at para. 55.

fact that such processes are mostly conducted by Member States' bodies. As a consequence, all substantive Human Rights of migrants discussed in this study are accompanied by procedural guarantees derived from EU constitutional law. As we shall explain in more detail below, some of these constitutional guarantees mirror Human Rights that are specific to migrants and are recognized as procedural Human Rights per se.

Does the Union live up to these ambitious commitments toward migrants and, if not, how can it make sure it does?

3.1 Structural challenges and current trends

In the context of migration governance, the recognition of a comprehensive set of procedural rights and a strict respect for the rule of law have long been alien to most legal systems, including those of EU Member States. These systems have traditionally been marked by a notorious exceptionalism regarding immigration proceedings. Full protection by procedural guarantees (as well as by substantive rights) were reserved to citizens, allowing for largely unbound discretionary powers of state authorities vis-à-vis foreigners. This exceptionalism was even more marked toward non-residents, that is, when dealing with applications from persons staying abroad.

The belated and still partial assertion of procedural safeguards in immigration proceedings only started after the Second World War, spurred by three, largely simultaneous developments: the constitutionalization of domestic legal systems, with an increasing importance of the rule of law (or *Rechtsstaat* or *État de droit*) in general; the rise of international Human Rights law and its transformative effect on domestic legal systems; and – arguably the most important driver in this respect – the Europeanization of migration law.[340] Today, as a consequence of this Europeanization, numerous EU legal acts provide for specific procedural safeguards and legal remedies in the context of migration law. They concern, inter alia, applica-

340 Bast, 'Of General Principles and Trojan Horses: Procedural Due Process in Immigration Proceedings Under EU Law', 11 *German Law Journal (GLJ)* (2010) 1006; Rochel, 'Working in Tandem: Proportionality and Procedural Guarantees in EU Immigration Law', 20 *GLJ* (2019) 89.

tions for Schengen visas,[341] the refusal of entries at border crossings,[342] the rejection of applications for residence permits for family reunification[343] as well as for long-term residence,[344] and of a number of residence permits related to labor migration (among others, applications to issue, amend or renew a single permit to reside and work in a Member State,[345] applications for EU Blue Cards,[346] and for residence permits for the purposes of research, studies, training, voluntary service, pupil exchange schemes, or educational projects and au pairing[347]). A specific set of procedural provisions apply once an asylum claim is presented – for example, the right to a personal interview.[348] Furthermore, pursuant to the Return Directive Member States must provide for effective remedies to challenge decisions related to return.[349]

The EU has thus already assumed responsibility to safeguard procedural rights regarding a large spectrum of migration statuses and situations, even if some of the explicit regulations in the respective acts may fall short of the level of protection required by EU fundamental rights and/or Human Rights. This raises the question of where the Union must close remaining gaps of protection by comprehensively providing for procedural rights of

341 Art. 32(3) Regulation 810/2009 establishing a Community Code on Visas (Visa Code).

342 Art. 14(3) Regulation 2016/399 on a Union Code on the rules governing the movement of persons across borders (Schengen Borders Code).

343 Art. 5(4), Art. 18 Directive 2003/86/EC on the right to family reunification (Family Reunification Directive).

344 Art. 7(2), Art. 10, Art. 20 Directive 2003/109/EC concerning the status of third-country nationals who are long-term residents (Long-Term Residents Directive).

345 Art. 8 Directive 2011/98/EU on a single application procedure for a single permit for third-country nationals to reside and work in the territory of a Member State and on a common set of rights for third-country workers legally residing in a Member State (Single Permit Directive).

346 Art. 11(3) Directive 2009/50/EC on the conditions of entry and residence of third-country nationals for the purposes of highly qualified employment (Blue Card Directive), replaced by Directive 2021/1883 as of 19 November 2023.

347 Art. 34 Directive 2016/801/EU on the conditions of entry and residence of third-country nationals for the purposes of research, studies, training, voluntary service, pupil exchange schemes or educational projects and au pairing (recast) (REST Directive).

348 Art. 14, 46 Directive 2013/32/EU on common procedures for granting and withdrawing international protection (Qualification Directive).

349 Art. 13 Directive 2008/115/EC on common standards and procedures in Member States for returning illegally staying third-country nationals (Return Directive). For a recent application, see CJEU, Cases C-924/19 PPU and C-925/19 PPU, *FMS* (EU:C:2020:367), at para. 127 et seq.

migrants. This question is all the more pressing as procedural rights have a particularly widespread impact, as they can come into play at all possible stages of immigration proceedings. Most notably, the following types of decisions may lead to the denial or loss of a particular immigration status:

- decisions on visa applications and on admission at the border (decisions on admission)
- decisions on the renewal or extension of residence permits
- decisions on the termination of residence, particularly expulsion and deportation.

Note that we are applying a wide notion of 'decision' for the purposes of this chapter. The failure of an authority to give a person access to a proper procedure amounts to a decision as well.

Today, procedural guarantees seem to be largely respected by Member States in respect of decisions on renewing or extending an existing residence permit. Similar standards are often violated or even negated, however, when it comes to decisions on the admission of migrants (visa applications or territorial admission at the borders) or on the termination of residence. Here, 'immigration exceptionalism' seems to persist as a historically shaped and bequeathed mindset. This chapter therefore focuses on the latter two issues.

While this chapter is mainly concerned with decisions taken by Member States' authorities, an area of growing tension concerns situations where the EU administration is directly involved as an actor. The last two decades have not only produced a general 'agencification' of EU governance but also a particular rise of EU agencies as key actors involved in 'hybrid' (or 'mixed') administrative decision-making in the field of migration.

Trend 1: Denial of procedural standards for decisions on admission

We observe a persistent pattern of denying procedural guarantees in proceedings that may lead to refusing the admission of migrants. This pattern is particularly marked when the place of decision-making is located outside the territory of the Member State, or in close proximity to the external border.

First, in what amounts to a long-term structural deficit, notoriously little attention is given to procedural standards in visa application procedures conducted at Member States' consular or diplomatic missions. The Visa Code (Regulation 810/2009) contains some procedural guarantees, but it only applies to short-stay visas (so-called Schengen visas).[350] There are no equivalent horizontal provisions for long-stay visas (so-called national visas, although the ground of admission may be governed by EU law). Procedural guarantees for applications for residence permits defined in EU legislation (such as Art. 5(4) of the Family Reunification Directive[351] and Art. 11(3) of the Blue Card Directive[352]) are potentially thwarted by Member State laws and practices excluding or limiting procedural rights. For example, a provision in the German Residence Act (*Aufenthaltsgesetz*) waives the requirement to specify the reasons for the decision and to inform applicants about available redress procedures and the time limit for bringing an action, when rejecting applications for national visas (Sec. 77(2) German Residence Act).[353]

---

350 Even regarding the application procedures for Schengen visas, Member States have in some instances tried to limit these guarantees by narrow interpretations of EU law – for example, by excluding access to court procedures in the case of the refusal of a visa application: Art. 5(4) of the Polish *Prawo o postępowaniu przed sądami administracyjnymi* (Law on proceedings before the administrative courts) of 30 August 2002.

351 Cf. Art. 5(4) of the Family Reunification Directive: 'The competent authorities of the Member State shall give the person, who has submitted the application, written notification of the decision as soon as possible and in any event no later than nine months from the date on which the application was lodged. In exceptional circumstances linked to the complexity of the examination of the application, the time limit referred to in the first subparagraph may be extended. Reasons shall be given for the decision rejecting the application. Any consequences of no decision being taken by the end of the period provided for in the first subparagraph shall be determined by the national legislation of the relevant Member State.'

352 Art. 11(3) of the Blue Card Directive: 'Any decision rejecting an application for an EU Blue Card, a decision not to renew or to withdraw an EU Blue Card, shall be notified in writing to the third-country national concerned and, where relevant, to his employer in accordance with the notification procedures under the relevant national law and shall be open to legal challenge in the Member State concerned, in accordance with national law. The notification shall specify the reasons for the decision, the possible redress procedures available and the time limit for taking action.' The new Blue Card Directive 2021/1883, in effect as of 19 November 2023, redrafts this provision, slightly reinforcing the procedural safeguards in requiring Member States to 'provide an effective judicial remedy, in accordance with national law'.

353 Sec. 77(2) of the Act on the Residence, Economic Activity and Integration of Foreigners in the Federal Territory: 'Denial and restriction of a visa and passport substitute before the foreigner enters the federal territory shall not require any statement of grounds or information on available legal remedies; refusal at the

Second, the trend of avoiding asylum jurisdiction (described in Chapter 1) usually encompasses the denial of any individual procedure – that is, such denials amount to decisions of collective non-admission to the territory at the land or sea border. The fact that such decisions do not necessarily qualify as 'decisions' according to the terms of procedural codes is precisely the point of concern. Several manifestations have already been mentioned above, such as the support for pull-back measures conducted by third countries or non-disembarkation-policies toward refugees saved at sea by the closure of ports to SAR vessels (see Chapter 1). In the same vein, individual procedural guarantees are violated by Member State practices of forcible – 'hot' – returns of migrants in immediate proximity to borders, such as the long-running Spanish practice of controlling the border of the Spanish exclaves of Ceuta and Melilla,[354] or the more recent practice of push-backs from Croatia to Serbia or Bosnia and Herzegovina.[355] Similarly, accelerated asylum procedures in transit zones (see Chapter 2) may also lead to an infringement of procedural rights.[356]

Yet even when border guards actually apply EU law to entry decisions at external border crossing, the applicable procedural guarantees often remain rather general and vague. While Art. 14(2) of the Schengen Borders Code (Regulation 2016/399) requires a 'substantiated decision stating the precise reasons for the refusal' for adverse entry decisions, ticking boxes in a standard form is generally supposed to fulfill the requirement. Moreover, the refusal is supposed to take immediate effect. In this regard, Art. 14(3) of the Schengen Borders Code does not set precise conditions for satisfying the guarantee of an effective remedy.

---

border shall not require written form. Formal requirements for the denial of Schengen visas shall be determined by Regulation (EC) No 810/2009.'

354 See, e.g., López-Sala, 'Keeping up Appearances: Dubious Legality and Migration Control at the Peripheral Borders of Europe: The Cases of Ceuta and Melilla', in S. Carrera and M. Stefan (eds), *Fundamental Rights Challenges in Border Controls and Expulsion of Irregular Immigrants in the European Union* (2020) 25.

355 European Council on Refugees and Exiles (ECRE), 'Widespread Pushbacks and Violence Along Borders in the Balkans Continues', Press release, 20 December 2019, available at https://www.ecre.org/widespread-pushback-and-violence-along-borders-in-the-balkans-continues/; ECRE, 'Croatia: Further Evidence of Systemic Push-Backs at the Border with Bosnia', Press release, 5 June 2020, available at https://www.ecre.org/croatia-further-evidence-of-systemic-push-backs-at-the-border-with-bosnia/.

356 See, e.g., CJEU, Cases C-924/19 PPU and C-925/19 PPU, *FMS* (EU:C:2020:367).

Trend 2: Deportation procedures without adequate procedural guarantees

We also observe a persistent pattern of insufficient procedural guarantees in proceedings that may lead to the termination of residence.

The most critical issue in this regard is the procedures of forced returns. Such deportations or 'removals' (the term employed by EU legislation)[357] regularly involve coercive measures, including the use of physical force, by Member State officials. They may lead to irreversible harm on the side of the deported person when she or he fears individual persecution or general insecurity in the destination country. Deportations carry an inherent risk of leading to violations of substantive Human Rights. It is, therefore, essential to provide for comprehensive procedural safeguards in EU law as well as their strict implementation by Member States. Neither requirement, however, is currently fully satisfied.

First, the lack of sufficiently clear procedural guarantees concerns EU legislation on return decisions. According to the Return Directive, such return decisions must precede the actual deportation and should also usually provide for a certain period for voluntary departure.[358] The right to be heard before taking a return decision is not explicitly provided in the Return Directive; it was inferred by the CJEU from general principles of EU law.[359] The Commission's proposal of 2018 for a recast Return Directive still does not contain any such clause.[360] Moreover, the Return Directive currently fails to provide for suspensive effect of appeals against return decisions concerning applicants for international protection.[361]

An even more pressing issue, however, is the actual execution of deportations. Despite being regulated in some detail by the Return Directive, Member States' actual enforcement of returns frequently leads to violations of procedural standards such as safeguards for sufficient access to legal assistance, or even respect for the suspensive effects of appeals against deportation decisions. For example, the European Committee for the Pre-

357 See, e.g., Art. 8 Return Directive.

358 Art. 6–7 Return Directive.

359 CJEU, Case C-249/13, *Boudjlida* (EU:C:2014:2431), at para. 28 et seq.

360 Proposal for a recast Return Directive, COM(2018) 634, 12 September 2018, at 79; European Parliament Research Service, The proposed Return Directive (recast): Substitute Impact Assessment (2019), at 79, available at https://www.europarl.europa.eu/RegData/etudes/STUD/2019/631727/EPRS_STU(2019)631727_EN.pdf.

361 Leading to possible violations of Art. 18, 19, 47 EU-CFR, see CJEU, Case C-181/16, *Gnandi* (EU:C:2018:465), at para. 54.

vention of Torture and Inhuman or Degrading Treatment or Punishment (CPT) mentions in a 2019 report that in 2017 and 2018 seven persons were unlawfully deported from Germany while legal proceedings that had suspensive effect were still pending before a court.[362]

Such cases are often not recognized by the public because of a lack of independent observation. Despite the fact that Art. 8(6) of the Return Directive requires Member States to install an 'effective forced-return monitoring system', an FRA report revealed that in 2018 four Member States did not sufficiently do so, providing either no monitoring at all (Cyprus), a monitoring system belonging to the branch of government responsible for return (Slovakia and Sweden), or a system that only covers parts of the country (Germany).[363]

Trend 3: Blurring accountability by agencification of EU migration policy

An increasing cause of concern is the lack of accountability of EU agencies involved in mixed proceedings implementing EU migration law.

With more than 40 agencies at present, the increasing involvement of EU agencies in European executive governance – its 'agencification' – has become a general trend of EU policy since the 1990s. The term describes a structural process of functional decentralization within the EU executive, shifting executive powers away from the EU Commission and usually implying a higher degree of Member States' control via the agency's governing bodies. This goes hand-in-hand with a process of federal centralization – increasing involvement of EU bodies in composite administrative procedures involving both Member State and EU authorities. EU agencies have their own legal personality and enjoy a certain degree of administrative and financial autonomy. Agencies assist in the implementation of EU law and policy, collect information, provide scientific advice, and help with the coordination of Member State authorities. In some instances, agencies can adopt legally binding acts if the founding legislative act so provides.

362 See for example: European Committee for the Prevention of Torture and Inhuman or Degrading Treatment or Punishment (CPT), Report to the German Government on the visit to Germany, 9 May 2019, at 8–9, available at https://rm.coe.int/1680945a2d.

363 FRA, Forced return monitoring systems: 2019 update (2019), available at https://fra.europa.eu/en/publication/2019/forced-return-monitoring-systems-2019-update.

EU agencies are a well-known feature of EU composite administration, first developed in the field of governing the internal market. In migration policy, the involvement of agencies in 'mixed' or 'hybrid' procedures of decision-making is a more recent phenomenon. Since the establishment of Frontex in 2004 (renamed 'European Border and Coast Guard Agency' in 2016)[364], EASO in 2010[365] and eu-LISA (EU Agency for the Operational Management of Large-Scale IT Systems in the Area of Freedom, Security and Justice) in 2012,[366] agencies have played an increasing role in the implementation of EU migration policy.[367]

Due to the nature and structural features of EU agencies, this development poses a number of obstacles to the full respect for procedural safeguards, particularly concerning access to justice. Legal and political accountability for the decision taken is notoriously blurred, most notably by the structural entanglement of different actors.

The main task of Frontex is to support EU Member States in controlling the external borders of the Union and the Schengen area (see also Chapter 1). It does so by the deployment of European Border Guard Teams and the coordination of maritime operations or operations at external land borders. In 'joint operations' it coordinates the deployment of staff and equipment from one Member State in another EU Member State, or even in third countries. In such instances of operational cooperation between the agency and Member States, responsibility is often diffused – despite a moderately increased level of scrutiny since the 2018 renewal of Frontex's founding Regulation.[368] In recent years, evidence for the involvement of

---

364 See Regulation 2019/1896 on the European Border and Coast Guard (Frontex Regulation).

365 See Regulation 39/2010 establishing a European Asylum Support Office (EASO Regulation).

366 See Regulation 1726/2018 on the European Union Agency for the Operational Management of Large-Scale IT Systems in the Area of Freedom, Security and Justice (eu-LISA).

367 Tsourdi, 'Beyond the 'Migration Crisis': The Evolving Role of EU Agencies in the Administrative Governance of the Asylum and External Border Control Policies', in J. Pollak and P. Slominski (eds), *The Role of EU Agencies in the Eurozone and Migration Crisis* (2021) 175.

368 M. Gkliati and H. Rosenfeldt, *Accountability of the European Border and Coast Guard Agency: Recent Developments, Legal Standards and Existing Mechanisms* (2018), at 1, available at https://sas-space.sas.ac.uk/9187/.

Frontex officers in push-back operations, such as at the maritime Greek-Turkish border, has been abundant and sparked public criticism.[369]

EASO was originally more focused on gathering and sharing information among EU Member States – for example, on 'best practices in asylum matters' or on countries of origin of persons applying for international protection.[370] In recent years, it has considerably expanded its operational powers.[371] It has become more operationally involved in the asylum procedure (for which Member States remain primarily competent), as in the case of interviews conducted by deployed experts. This has nourished uncertainty as to the procedural rights available to migrants in such cases.[372]

In the case of eu-LISA, the agency allows for data exchange among EU Member States by providing the IT systems Eurodac (European Dactyloscopy – a fingerprint database for the identification of asylum seekers), SIS (Schengen Information System, containing certain information and alerts on persons, such as when a person's entry is to be refused) and VIS (Visa Information System, including information on applicants for visas to enter the Schengen area). Eu-LISA is also scheduled to set up a new large-scale IT system in 2022 for the automatic monitoring of the border crossing of third-country nationals, the Entry/Exit System (EES).[373] A variety of questions regarding such interoperable system remain unanswered –

369 See, e.g., European Parliament: LIBE Committee, Report on the fact-finding investigation on Frontex concerning alleged fundamental rights violations, Working Document, 14 July 2021, available at https://www.europarl.europa.eu/meetdocs/2014_2019/plmrep/COMMITTEES/LIBE/DV/2021/07-14/14072021FinalReportFSWG_EN.pdf; L. Karamanidou and B. Kasparek, *Fundamental Rights, Accountability and Transparency in European Governance of Migration: The Case of the European Border and Coast Guard Agency Frontex* (2020), at 55 et seq., available at https://respondmigration.com/wp-blog/fundamental-rights-accountability-transparency-european-governance-of-migration-the-case-european-border-coast-guard-agency-frontex.

370 See., e.g., Art. 3 and 4 EASO Regulation.

371 On EASO, see Nicolosi and Fernandez-Rojo, 'Out of Control? The Case of the European Asylum Support Office', in M. Scholten and A. Brenninkmeijer (eds), *Controlling EU Agencies: The Rule of Law in a Multi-jurisdictional Legal Order* (2020) 177.

372 Tsourdi, 'Bottom-up Salvation? From Practical Cooperation Towards Joint Implementation Through the European Asylum Support Office', 1 *European Papers* (2016) 997, at 1024, available at http://www.europeanpapers.eu/en/e-journal/bottom-up-salvation-from-practical-cooperation-towards-joint-implementation.

373 Based on Regulation 2017/2226 establishing an Entry/Exit System (EES).

for example, how to effectively ensure the right to access one's own data and have incorrect data rectified.[374]

Overall, the structure of such 'mixed administration' between agencies and Member State administrations, the entanglement of multiple actors in general, and the complex legal structure of the agencies lead to a lack of transparency and of information, making it difficult to determine who is actually responsible for potential rights violations.

To make matters worse, the conditions of admissibility for actions brought before the CJEU by individuals against measures taken by agencies are very restrictive (see Art. 263(4) TFEU). This is particularly true of the criteria for determining a reviewable act, the criteria for determining direct and individual concern caused by such acts, and the short time limit of two months for filing an action.[375]

3.2 *Legal evaluation*

3.2.1 General framework

In universal Human Rights law, procedural guarantees tend to be rather general and/or fragmentary compared to substantive rights. Procedural guarantees under customary international law form only a thin layer of International Migration Law. This relates to the prohibition of arbitrary detention, certain due process guarantees concerning the removal of migrants, and respect for human dignity in the enforcement of immigration control.[376] However, a growing awareness of the international community is reflected in the Global Compacts. The Global Compact for Migration restates that 'respect for the rule of law, due process and access to justice are fundamental to all aspects of migration governance' (GCM, para. 15) and establishes the non-binding objective to strengthen certainty and pre-

---

374 FRA, Fundamental Rights and the Interoperability of EU Information Systems: Borders and Security (2017), at 33 et seq.; R. Bossong, *Intelligente Grenzen und interoperable Datenbanken für die innere Sicherheit der EU: Umsetzungsrisiken und rechtsstaatliche Anforderungen* (2018), at 28 et seq., available at https://www.swp-berlin.org/fileadmin/contents/products/studien/2018S04_bsg.pdf.

375 M. Gkliati and H. Rosenfeldt, *Accountability of the European Border and Coast Guard Agency: Recent Developments, Legal Standards and Existing Mechanisms* (2018), at 10 et seq., available at https://sas-space.sas.ac.uk/9187/https://sas-space.sas.ac.uk/9187/.

376 V. Chetail, *International Migration Law* (2019), at 132 et seq.

dictability in migration procedures (GCM, para. 28). In the Global Compact on Refugees, States have acknowledged the importance of the rule of law in general (GCR, para. 9) as well as of procedural safeguards for identifying international protection grounds, particularly for those with specific needs (GCR, para. 59–61).

In universal Human Rights treaties, the ICCPR contains a general right to recognition as a person before the law (Art. 16 ICCPR) as well as a right to a fair trial and certain rights of the accused in criminal procedures (Art. 14 and 15 ICCPR). Stand-alone guarantees regarding administrative proceedings are not explicitly mentioned. In respect of migrants, the ICCPR stipulates a prohibition of arbitrary expulsions, but only of foreigners who are 'lawfully in the territory' of the State (Art. 13 ICCPR). In a similar vein, the 1951 Refugee Convention contains procedural safeguards against expulsions for refugees 'lawfully' in the territory of a Contracting State (Art. 32 Refugee Convention). A rare exception is the UN Convention on the Rights of the Child, which requires States to provide children with a comprehensive right to be heard in all judicial and administrative proceedings (Art. 12 CRC).

The ECHR contains a number of important provisions entailing procedural rights. However, most of them correlate with limitations *ratione materiae* or *ratione personae*. The right to a fair trial (Art. 6(1) ECHR), pursuant to its wording, only applies to 'civil rights and obligations' and to 'criminal charges', and thus not to immigration court proceedings per se. Art. 13 ECHR provides for the right to an effective remedy against any violation of Convention rights. Yet, because the right to an effective remedy is not an autonomous right but an auxiliary one, it can only be claimed in connection with a substantive right derived from the Convention. In addition, implied procedural guarantees that exceed the standard of Art. 13 ECHR can be derived from the prohibition of refoulement laid down in Art. 3 ECHR (see Chapter 1).

European Human Rights law provides for certain procedural guarantees that are applicable to migrants regardless of whether they are seeking international protection. Procedural safeguards relating to expulsion of aliens are provided by the 1984 Protocol No. 7 to the ECHR, ratified by all EU Member States except for Germany and the Netherlands. According to Art. 1(1) Protocol No. 7 ECHR, any 'alien lawfully resident' in a Convention State may only be expelled when such a decision was reached 'in accordance with law' and on the condition that she or he was allowed to submit reasons against the expulsion, have the case reviewed, and to be represented for these purposes.[377]

In light of the increasing importance of ensuring actual access to procedures with respect to the territorial admission in Europe, a procedural safeguard that has been under the spotlight in the past years is the 1963 Protocol No. 4 to the ECHR, ratified by all EU Member States except for Greece. Art. 4 of Protocol No. 4 ECHR simply states: 'Collective expulsion of aliens is prohibited.' As this provision outlaws any form of collective expulsion without the qualification of lawful residency, it applies to all persons irrespective of their immigration status. While the corresponding guarantee in unwritten universal Human Rights law is mostly regarded as a substantive right accorded to a group of persons, the case-law of the ECtHR has developed implied procedural guarantees protecting individual migrants, including but not limited to persons seeking international protection. Following the jurisprudence of the ECtHR, the provision requires a 'reasonable and objective examination of the particular case of each individual alien'.[378] Such a sufficiently individualized examination requires that each person 'has a genuine and effective possibility of submitting arguments against his or her expulsion' as well as an appropriate examination of those arguments by the state authorities involved.[379]

It is noteworthy that the ECtHR interprets the concept of expulsion not in a narrow but in a wider sense, encompassing different forms of removal, among other things in extraterritorial situations.[380] In its 2020 Grand Chamber judgment in the case *N.D. and N.T. v. Spain*, the ECtHR confirmed the view that the term 'expulsion' also covers non-admission of aliens at state borders,[381] notwithstanding its ultimate rejection of the application in the instant case on the basis of the applicants' own conduct

377 Exceptions are possible according to Art. 1(2) for reasons of public order or national security.

378 See, e.g., ECtHR, *Čonka v. Belgium*, Appl. no. 51564/99, Judgment of 5 February 2002, at para. 59.

379 ECtHR, *Khlaifia and others v. Italy*, Appl. no. 16483/12, Judgment of 1 September 2015, at para. 238 and 248.

380 ECtHR, *Hirsi Jamaa and others v. Italy*, Appl. no. 27765/09, Judgment of 23 February 2012; *N.D. and N.T. v. Spain*, Appl. no. 8675/15 and 8697/15, Grand Chamber Judgment of 13 February 2020, at para. 166 et seq.

381 ECtHR, *N.D. and N.T. v. Spain*, Appl. no. 8675/15 and 8697/15, Grand Chamber Judgment of 13 February 2020, at para. 173.

and conditional upon a supposedly present 'genuine and effective access to means of legal entry'.[382]

It follows that, according to the ECHR – and, hence, in European migration policy at large – any decision by public officials on the territorial admission of migrants must be sufficiently individualized in order to comply with the prohibition of collective expulsion.[383] In this sense, Art. 4 Protocol No. 4 ECHR constitutes a general due process clause in European migration law and, thus, a procedural corollary to the right to juridical personality in immigration proceedings.[384] The rights enumerated in Art. 1 Protocol No. 7 ECHR can serve as a point of reference for determining this minimum standard. This standard encompasses the rights to submit reasons against a decision adversely affecting the migrant, to have one's case reviewed, and to be represented for these purposes. Save for the carve-out in *N.D. and N.T. v. Spain*, the precise scope of which is still subject to debate, the requirement of lawful residence stipulated in Art. 1(1) Protocol No. 7 ECHR has become immaterial in order to avoid collective expulsions. In effect, the standards laid down in Protocol No. 7 constitute the procedural yardstick for all decisions granting or refusing lawful immigration status.[385]

The EU should not have any difficulties in meeting the minimum procedural guarantees derived from international Human Rights law. The relevant provisions are mirrored, specified, and, in many respects, extended by the fundamental rights laid down in the EU-CFR.

With regard to administrative procedures, Art. 41 EU-CFR sets a high standard by providing for a right to good administration,[386] comprising,

---

382 Ibid., at para. 201.

383 Leboeuf and Carlier, 'The Prohibition of Collective Expulsion as an Individualisation Requirement', in M. Moraru, G. Cornelisse and Ph. de Bruycker (eds), *Law and Judicial Dialogue on the Return of Irregular Migrants from the European Union* (2020) 455.

384 For a comparison with the American Convention on Human Rights, see Campbell-Duruflé, 'The Right to Juridical Personality of Arbitrarily Detained and Unidentified Migrants After the Case of the Guyaubin Massacre', *Revue Québécoise de droit international* (2013) 429, at 439.

385 Note that the ECHR may also apply to visa procedures, following the case-law of the former European Commission of Human Rights which ruled that a State may be held responsible under the ECHR for acts of visa officials in its embassy: EComHR, *X v. Germany*, Appl. no. 1611/62, Decision of 25 September 1965, Yearbook 8 (1965) 158, at 163.

386 It is not clear whether or not this right can also be considered as being part of the corpus of customary international law and/or a general principles of

among other things, the right to be heard and the obligation of the administration to give reasons for its decisions. Technically, Art. 41 EU-CFR is merely directed at EU institutions and bodies.[387] However, the CJEU has acknowledged that the right to good administration constitutes a general principle of EU law,[388] hence it applies also to Member State authorities when acting within the scope of EU law. This is particularly true for the right to be heard as part of the so-called 'rights of defence', which have been developed in the CJEU's case-law as cornerstones of any administrative proceedings governed by EU law.[389] While these rights have originally been recognized in proceedings that may lead to an administrative sanction, they have since been extended also to adverse decisions taken upon the initiative of the potential beneficiaries.[390]

As far as the right to an effective remedy is concerned, Art. 47 EU-CFR provides for a comprehensive guarantee that exceeds the standard established by Art. 13 ECHR in various respects. In particular, the effective remedy must be 'before a tribunal' (as compared to remedy 'before a national authority', which may be a quasi-judicial body), and any rights granted by EU law entail this protection (rather than the enumerated Convention rights, as provided by Art. 13 ECHR).[391]

Given that EU constitutional law generally provides for a higher level of protection in terms of procedural rights, both at the administrative and the judicial stages of immigration proceedings, one may even argue that there is no point in identifying the extent to which respect for these rights is required by Human Rights law. However, as our analysis of current trends

law within the meaning of Art. 38(1) of the ICJ Statute; see B. Fassbender, *Targeted Sanctions and Due Process: The Responsibility of the UN Security Council to Ensure That Fair and Clear Procedures are Made Available to Individuals and Entities Targeted With Sanctions Under Chapter VII of the UN Charter,* available at https://www.un.org/law/counsel/Fassbender_study.pdf. As far as the EU is concerned, however, the relevance of deciding this controversy is diminished by the applicability of Art. 41 EU-CFR.

387 CJEU, Cases C-141/12 and C-372/12, *YS* (EU:C:2014:2081), at para. 67.

388 CJEU, Case C-604/12, *H. N. v. Ireland* (EU:C:2014:302), at para. 49.

389 CJEU, Case C-166/13, *Mukarubega* (EU:C:2014:2336), at para. 45.

390 CJEU, Case C-277/11, *M.M.* (EU:C:2012:744), at para. 87; on the development of the case-law, see St. Bitter, *Die Sanktion im Recht der Europäischen Union* (2011), at 37–89.

391 For more recent case-law on the scope of Art. 47 EU-CFR, see CJEU, Case C-556/17, *Alekszij Torubarov v. Bevándorlási és Menekültügyi Hivatal* (EU:C:2019:626); Cases C-133/19, C-136/19 and C-137/19, *B. M. M.* (EU:C:2020:577).

and persistent patterns demonstrates, the EU and its Member States are not immune to the legacy of 'immigration exceptionalism'. Recalling that a basic layer of procedural guarantees owed to migrants is part of Human Rights law may be instrumental in overcoming this legacy, even in a polity that proudly claims to be 'a Union based in the rule of law'.

3.2.2 Specific issue: Application of procedural standards on visa decisions

On the basis of our construction of Art. 4 Protocol No. 4 ECHR as a general due process clause, it follows that all decisions of state officials on the territorial admission of non-resident foreigners, irrespective of their status or the nature of their claim, must be adequately individualized and respect certain procedural safeguards (see above, 3.2.1). Accordingly, the prohibition of collective expulsion would in principle also provide for procedural rights regarding visa decisions governed by EU law.

This conclusion may be challenged based on the ECtHR judgment in the *M.N. and others v. Belgium* case. According to the ECtHR, the Convention does not apply to visa applications filed at embassies and consulates abroad by persons seeking international protection. This follows from Art. 1 ECHR, which limits the applicability of the Convention to persons within the 'jurisdiction' of a Contracting Party. The Court holds that such jurisdiction, understood as territorial or extraterritorial effective authority or control, is not exercised by Convention States vis-à-vis foreign nationals who apply for a humanitarian visa at one of their diplomatic and consular missions.[392] While in the instant case the Court ruled out a potential violation of Art. 3 ECHR, the same rationale arguably applies to Art. 4 Protocol No. 4 ECHR.

However, we counter the presumed insignificance of Human-Rights-based procedural standards in the context of visa procedures by making two legal observations. First, the ECtHR's finding regarding the lack of jurisdiction in the *M.N.* case determines whether a Convention State (in this case, Belgium) has violated its treaty obligations under public international law. Given that the EU is not a party to this Convention anyway, this sheds no light on the issue as to whether the EU, and EU Member States when implementing EU law, meet the relevant obligation *in terms of substance*. We would like to recall here the argument developed in the introductory

392 ECtHR, *M.N. and others v. Belgium,* Appl. no. 3599/18, Grand Chamber Decision of 5 May 2020, at para. 112 et seq.

chapter that a strong assumption of homogeneity between the substance of Human Rights and the legal obligations under EU law applies, regardless of any international obligation on the part of the EU.

Second, the criteria for establishing the scope of application of EU fundamental rights and the jurisdiction under the ECHR are not identical. Accordingly, the ECtHR rationale regarding the construction of Art. 1 ECHR does not necessarily apply to the EU Charter of Fundamental Rights.[393] According to Art. 51(1) EU-CFR, Charter provisions are addressed to the EU and its Member States 'when they are implementing Union law'. According to our knowledge, neither territorial nor other forms of effective control has played a role in the relevant case-law of the CJEU. Rather, the jurisprudence of the CJEU is guided by the assumption that the scope of EU law (and hence, of the Charter) is determined by the scope of EU powers to the extent that the EU has actually exercised them. In other words, it is unthinkable that the EU has enacted any legislation the implementation of which is not limited by EU fundamental rights.

Accordingly, to the extent that the issuance or refusal of visas is covered by the EU Visa Regulation or any other piece of EU legislation, such action constitutes implementation of EU law in the sense of Art. 51(1) EU-CFR, irrespective of where the acting authority or the applicant sits.[394] In the case of such visa applications, the safeguards of Art. 4 Protocol No. 4 and Art. 1(1) Protocol No. 7 ECHR are thus not only mirrored but also extended and rendered applicable by the EU-CFR, in particular the right to good administration (Art. 41 EU-CFR), comprising the right to be heard and the obligation of the administration to give reasons for its decisions. Only in those instances where EU law, as it stands, does not provide for relevant legislation that triggers the application of EU fundamental rights, such as the issuance of 'humanitarian visas' pursuant to a contested ruling of the CJEU (see Chapter 1), does the rationale not apply.

For national visas (long-term visas), this means that decisions by Member States' consular or diplomatic missions constitute implementation of EU law if they are the pre-entry stage of a decision on granting a residence right defined by an EU instrument, such as decisions on a long-term

393 V. Moreno-Lax, *Accessing Asylum in Europe* (2017), at 292–294, with reference to pertinent CJEU case-law.

394 Moreno-Lax, 'Asylum Visas as an Obligation under EU Law: Case PPU C-638/16 X, X v État belge (Part II)', *EU Migration Law Blog* (2017), available at http://eumigrationlawblog.eu/asylum-visas-as-an-obligation-under-eu-law-case-ppu-c-63816-x-x-v-etat-belge-part-ii/.

visa for family reunification or a Blue Card. Consequently, in such cases the procedural guarantees following from the right to good administration must be respected. In some instances, certain aspect of this right are already specified in the relevant legal acts, e.g., in Art. 5(4) Family Reunification Directive.[395] National provisions limiting procedural rights in application procedures for long-term visas (such as Sec. 77(2) German Residence Act, mentioned above) are subject to the primacy of EU law and, hence, rendered inapplicable whenever the matter falls within the substantive scope of EU law.[396]

Short-term (Schengen) visas are comprehensively determined by EU law. In this regard, it is questionable whether the duty to give reasons is sufficiently reflected in Art. 32(2) Visa Code. This provision merely requires Member State officials to tick boxes on a list in a standard form. The same provision also renders it difficult to legally challenge refusals of Schengen visa without having a substantiated explanation for the refusal at hand. This puts into question the *effect utile* of the right to an effective remedy (Art. 47 EU-CFR). While this issue is not yet decided by the CJEU, there is ample case-law stressing the functional link between the duty to give reasons and the right to an effective remedy.[397] The CJEU already ruled that – contrary to the practice of some Member States – Art. 32(3) of the Visa Code, read in the light of Art. 47 EU-CFR, requires Member States to provide for an appeal procedure against decisions refusing visas, including a right to judicial review.[398]

395 R. Hofmann (ed.), *Ausländerrecht* (2nd ed. 2016), commentary on Sec. 77 AufenthG, at para. 3.

396 As to Sec. 77(2) German Residence Act (*Aufenthaltsgesetz*), an administrative circular acknowledges certain procedural rights in cases of family reunification (see Allgemeine Verwaltungsvorschrift zum Aufenthaltsgesetz vom 26. Oktober 2009, Sec. 77(2), available at http://www.verwaltungsvorschriften-im-internet.de/bsvwvbund_26102009_MI31284060.htm). However, this administrative circular has limited legal effect and refers only to German constitutional law (Art. 6 German Basic Law), not to EU law.

397 See, most notably, CJEU, Cases C-402/05 P and C-415/05 P, *Kadi I*, at para. 71–333; Cases C-584/10 P, C-593/10 P and C-595/10 P, *Kadi II*, at para. 97–137.

398 CJEU, Case C-403/16, *Soufiane El-Hassani* (EU:C:2017:960), at para. 42. Yet, many problems remain regarding the effectiveness of remedies against the refusal of Schengen visa, e.g. in cases of visa representation by another (Member) State, see CJEU, Case C-680/17, *Sumanan Vethanayagam, Sobitha Sumanan, Kamalaranee Vethanayagam* (EU:C:2019:627).

3.2.3 Specific issue: Decisions on territorial admission at land and sea borders

As far as push-back operations are concerned, they clearly violate the prohibition of collective expulsion (Art. 4 Protocol No. 4 ECHR, mirrored by Art. 19(1) EU-CFR), as entire groups of people are returned without adequate verification of the individual identities and circumstances of the group members. This follows from established case-law of the ECtHR on push-back operations on the high seas[399] and even inside the EU.[400] Push-backs often also constitute a breach of procedural guarantees implied in the principle of non-refoulement (Art. 3 ECHR, mirrored in this respect by Art. 19(2) EU-CFR) – as no individual assessment of the migrant's situation takes place regarding potential grounds for granting international protection – as well as a violation of Art. 13 ECHR (right to an effective remedy, mirrored by Art. 47 EU-CFR).[401]

As to the Spanish practices of 'hot returns' of migrants who crossed the fences separating the Spanish exclave of Melilla from Morocco, the ECtHR's Grand Chamber in 2020 revoked its 2017 Chamber decision in *N.D. and N.T. v. Spain*, finding no breach of the Convention in the particular cases.[402] The reasoning of the judgment is highly contextual, referring to the specific conduct of the applicants (storming the border fences together with a larger group of people) as well as supposedly available alternatives to access Spanish territory using legal pathways. In its ensuing case-law the ECtHR has clarified that being part of a group that has entered the territory without authorization does not, in itself, preclude the person from claiming a right not to be expelled collectively.[403] In any event, the aforementioned carve-out may only be considered regarding the application of Art. 4 Protocol No. 4 ECHR and not of Art. 3 ECHR. Whenever there is an arguable claim of refoulement risk, the procedural

---

399 ECtHR, *Hirsi Jamaa and others v. Italy*, Appl. no. 27765/09, Judgment of 23 February 2012.

400 ECtHR, *Sharifi and others v. Italy and Greece*, Appl. no. 16643/09, Judgment of 21 October 2014.

401 ECtHR, *Hirsi Jamaa and others v. Italy*, Appl. no. 27765/09, Judgment of 23 February 2012.

402 ECtHR, *N.D. and N.T. v. Spain*, Appl. no. 8675/15 and 8697/15, Grand Chamber Judgment of 13 February 2020.

403 ECtHR, *Shahzad v. Hungary*, Appl. no. 12625/17, Judgment of 8 July 2021, at para. 61.

dimension of Art. 3 ECHR always requires a thorough assessment of the individual circumstances (see Chapter 1).

However, it is not only the operational practice of push-backs that seems problematic; so too do the legal provisions in EU legislation regarding the treatment of migrants at the border requesting access to the territory. Most notably, Art. 14(3) of the Schengen Borders Code, while specifying that complaints against entry decisions shall *not* have a suspensive effect, does not set precise conditions for satisfying the guarantee of effective remedy. In particular, Art. 14(3) of the Schengen Borders Code does not specify that the possibility for remedies to not have suspensive effect only applies once it has been established that none of the grounds for international protection apply and the refusal does not violate relevant international law such as the Geneva Convention or the Convention on the Rights of the Child[404] (cf. Art. 4 Schengen Borders Code). At the same time, the right to an effective remedy as laid down in Art. 47 EU-CFR requires in such cases the possibility of obtaining a judicial order establishing suspensive effect of a remedy in an interim injunction before a court.

3.2.4 Specific issue: Scope of procedural safeguards in the Return Directive

The Return Directive provides for certain procedural safeguards that may be invoked in proceedings before national courts by those affected by return decisions (Art. 12–14 Return Directive). Among other things, a certain form is prescribed for such decisions; they must be issued in writing, give reasons, and provide information about legal remedies (Art. 12(1) Return Directive). However, the Return Directive does not contain an explicit right to be heard before a return decision is taken. Instead, the CJEU had to confirm that such a right to be heard 'is required even where the applicable legislation does not expressly provide for such a procedural requirement'.[405] This follows from the rights of the defence as a general principle of EU law.[406] The CJEU also made it clear that the right to be heard serves to enable the persons concerned to express their point of view on the legality of their stay and to provide information that might justify a return decision not being issued, particularly where such a decision may

404 Cf. CRC, *D.D. v. Spain*, Communication No. 4/2016, CRC/C/80/D/4/2016.

405 CJEU, Case C-166/13, *Mukarubega* (EU:C:2014:2336), at para. 49.

406 Ibid., at para. 45.

pose a threat to the rights of the person concerned enshrined in Art. 5 of the Return Directive (non-refoulement, best interests of the child, family life, and state of health).[407]

The current proposal for a recast Return Directive still does not contain any such (horizontal) provision on the right to be heard.[408] Although in the light of the CJEU case-law cited above the right to be heard must be respected under any circumstances, an explicit provision in the new Return Directive would significantly enhance legal clarity and access to legal safeguards.[409]

Instead, the Commission proposal for a recast Return Directive contains a considerable tightening of the provision on voluntary departure. The new Art. 9(4) would oblige Member States to automatically refrain from granting a voluntary period of departure, among other things, where there is a risk of absconding or a risk to public policy. This is contrary to the CJEU jurisprudence on the matter, which states that 'the right to be heard before the adoption of a return decision implies that the competent national authorities are under an obligation to enable the person concerned to express his point of view on the detailed arrangements for his return, such as the period allowed for departure and whether return is to be voluntary or coerced'.[410] Art. 9(4) of the proposed new Return Directive is, therefore, in breach of the right to be heard as guaranteed by EU constitutional law.[411]

Another procedural safeguard that plays a crucial role in the context of returns is the right to an effective remedy (Art. 13 ECHR, Art. 47 EU-CFR). Art. 13(1) of the Return Directive repeats this right 'to appeal against or seek review of decisions related to return … before a competent judicial or administrative authority or a competent body composed of members who are impartial and who enjoy safeguards of independence'. What seems to

---

407 CJEU, Case C-249/13, *Boudjlida* (EU:C:2014:2431), at para. 47–51. On the substantive implications of these references to Human Rights and EU fundamental rights, see below, Chapter 5.

408 European Commission, Proposal for a recast Return Directive, COM(2018) 634, 12 September 2018.

409 European Parliament Research Service, The proposed Return Directive (recast): Substitute Impact Assessment (2019), at 79 et seq., available at https://www.europarl.europa.eu/RegData/etudes/STUD/2019/631727/EPRS_STU(2019)631727_EN.pdf.

410 CJEU, Case C-249/13, *Boudjlida* (EU:C:2014:2431), at para. 51.

411 European Parliament Research Service, The proposed Return Directive (recast): Substitute Impact Assessment (2019), at 80.

be problematic about Art. 13 of the Return Directive, as it stands, is not only that it does not require judicial review (contrary to Art. 47 EU-CFR) but that it also lacks a provision guaranteeing automatic suspensive effect in the case of a potential violation of the principle of non-refoulement.

According to the case-law of the ECtHR on Art. 13 ECHR, effectiveness of the remedy requires that the person concerned should have access to a remedy with automatic suspensive effect when there are substantial grounds for fearing a real risk of treatment contrary to the right of life (Art. 2 ECHR) or the prohibition of torture (Art. 3 ECHR) in the case of a return.[412] In a similar vein, the CJEU decided that, despite the lack of an explicit provision in the Return Directive, the applicant for international protection must be guaranteed a remedy enabling automatic suspensory effect, based on the right to asylum (Art. 18 EU-CFR), the principle of non-refoulement (Art. 19(2) EU-CFR), and the right to an effective remedy (Art. 47 EU-CFR).[413]

The Commission's proposal for a new Return Directive clarifies in its Art. 16(1) that there is a right to 'judicial review' (as compared to administrative or other) to appeal return decisions. In Art. 16(3) and Art. 22(6), it would provide for an automatic suspensive effect of appeals in cases where there is a risk of breach of the principle of non-refoulement by the enforcement of return decisions. However, this shall not apply where 'no relevant new elements or findings have arisen or have been presented', as compared to the asylum procedure (Art. 16(3)(3) and Art. 22(6)(1) Proposal for a recast Return Directive). Depending on the interpretation in the Member States, this may lead to exclusion of the automatic suspension in cases where, for example, a serious health condition and absence of treatment in the country of origin was raised in the asylum procedure but was not sufficient to grant subsidiary protection.[414]

412 ECtHR, *De Souza Ribeiro v. France*, Appl. no. 22689/07, Judgment of 13 December 2012, at para. 82.

413 CJEU, Case C-181/16, *Gnandi* (EU:C:2018:465), at para. 52–56.

414 European Parliament Research Service, The proposed Return Directive (recast): Substitute Impact Assessment (2019), at 85, available at https://www.europarl.europa.eu/RegData/etudes/STUD/2019/631727/EPRS_STU(2019)631727_EN.pdf.

3.2.5 Specific issue: Monitoring of deportations by EU Member States

As to the execution of return decisions by actual deportations, Art. 8(4) of the Return Directive acknowledges that Member States may – as a last resort – use coercive measures to carry out the removal of a third-country national. However, such measures must be proportionate and shall be implemented in accordance with the fundamental rights of the person concerned. At the same time, Art. 8(6) Return Directive merely states that 'Member States shall provide for an effective forced-return monitoring system'. It does not prescribe in any detail what such a system should look like. It thus grants wide discretion to Member States.[415] However, the FRA considers a system 'effective' in the sense of Art. 8(6) Return Directive only when the monitoring entity is separate from the authority in charge of returns, which was not the case in all EU Member States in 2018 (see above, Trend 2).[416]

In line with general recommendations of the UN Human Rights Council,[417] all EU Member States should establish independent forced-return monitoring mechanisms with a wide scope of monitoring activities. The EU would have to provide a binding and detailed list of minimum requirements that such institutions must fulfill in order to be 'effective'.[418] However, the Art. 10(6) of the Commission's proposal for a recast Return Directive[419] does not suggest any amendment in this respect. Consequently, the determination of the shape and details of the monitoring systems will continue to be left to the discretion of the Member States.

3.2.6 Specific issue: Accountability of EU agencies

Procedural safeguards also come into play regarding the scrutiny of actions by EU agencies. Here, international Human Rights are particularly rele-

415 Cf. European Commission, Recommendation 2017/2338 establishing a common 'Return Handbook' to be used by Member States' competent authorities when carrying out return related tasks, at para. 42.

416 FRA, Forced Return Monitoring Systems: 2019 Update (2019).

417 UN Human Rights Council: Report of the Special Rapporteur on the human rights of migrants, A/HRC/38/41, 4 May 2018, at para. 78–79.

418 For a non-binding list, see European Commission, Recommendation 2017/2338 establishing a common 'Return Handbook', at para. 42–43.

419 European Commission, Proposal for a recast Return Directive, COM(2018) 634, 12 September 2018.

vant in their iterations as fundamental rights enshrined in the EU-CFR. As bodies of the EU, the provisions of the EU-CFR are directly applicable to all agencies (Art. 51(1) EU-CFR). Consequently, the right to good administration (Art. 41 EU-CFR) and to an effective remedy (Art. 47 EU-CFR) form the most important yardsticks for the evaluation of procedural guarantees in the context of possible rights violations by EU agencies toward migrants.

The shortcomings in the fulfillment of the requirements set up by Art. 41 and 47 EU-CFR can be illustrated by looking at the legal framework and practice of Frontex. Following amendments in the year 2011, the Frontex Regulation today contains a number of institutional and procedural safeguards for the protection of human and fundamental rights in the context of Frontex activities. A consultative forum on fundamental rights was established, comprising among others representatives of EASO, the FRA, and UNHCR (Art. 108 Frontex Regulation). Furthermore, the position of a fundamental rights officer, appointed by the management board (Art. 109 Frontex Regulation), was created. In 2016, following a 2013 own-initiative report of the European Ombudsman[420] supported by the European Parliament,[421] these instruments were supplemented by a complaints mechanism, providing the ability to file individual complaints against Frontex actions to the Frontex fundamental rights officer (Art. 111 Frontex Regulation).

Another possibility for addressing fundamental rights issues is to file a complaint to the European Ombudsman. The European Ombudsman examines complaints about maladministration by EU institutions and bodies, and can also conduct inquiries on her/his own initiative (Art. 228 TFEU, Art. 43 EU-CFR). The European Code of Good Administration,[422] drafted by the European Ombudsman and adopted in 2001 as a resolution by the European Parliament, serves as a specification of the right to good administration enshrined in Art. 41 EU-CFR, and thus as a basis for the work of the Ombudsman. However, the European Ombudsman

420 European Ombudsman, Decision closing own-initiative inquiry OI/5/2012/BEH-MHZ, 12 November 2013, available at https://www.ombudsman.europa.eu/en/decision/en/52477.

421 European Parliament, Resolution of 2 December 2015 on the Special Report of the European Ombudsman in own-initiative inquiry OI/5/2012/BEH-MHZ concerning Frontex, 2017/C 399/01, available at https://www.europarl.europa.eu/doceo/document/TA-8-2015-0422_EN.html.

422 European Ombudsman, The European Code of Good Administrative Behaviour (2015), available at https://www.ombudsman.europa.eu/de/publication/en/3510.

has no binding powers to compel compliance with her/his decisions. The Ombudsman has limited authority, reduced to offering recommendations, warnings, or advice to EU institutions and bodies. Correspondingly, the European Code of Good Administrative Behavior is not a legally binding instrument.[423] Furthermore, complainants must be either EU citizens or residents to have legal standing (Art. 43 EU-CFR). Thus, the administrative procedures installed by the Frontex Regulation and the complaints mechanism with the European Ombudsman can complement, but not replace, the possibility of judicial review as the core of the right to an effective remedy guaranteed by Art. 47 EU-CFR.[424]

The CJEU, according to Art. 263(1) TFEU, reviews the legality of acts adopted by bodies or agencies of the EU intended to produce legal effects vis-à-vis third parties. This review can also be initiated by a natural or legal person who is addressed by the act or to whom it is in other ways of direct and individual concern (Art. 263(4) TFEU). However, in the case of Frontex these requirements are nearly impossible to meet due to the structural features of Frontex operations. These are notoriously marked by an involvement of a plethora of multi-level authorities, often consisting of (local and deployed) officials from different (host and guest) Member States, Frontex staff, and actors from third countries (such as the Libyan coast guard). Given these complicated structures, it is legally and practically all but impossible for individuals to prove that the ultimate operational control in a particular situation rested with Frontex rather than with officials of third countries or of the host Member State, even though Frontex is widely regarded as playing a predominantly coordinating role. However, its acts are not final and supposedly do not have legal effects vis-à-vis individuals (see Chapter 1).[425]

A lack of information, on the side of the individual affected, about the details of Frontex operations often contributes to the difficulty of substan-

423 N. Vogiatzis, *The European Ombudsman and Good Administration in the European Union* (2018), at 33.

424 J. Rijpma, *The Proposal for a European Border and Coast Guard: Evolution or Revolution in External Border Management?* (2016), at 30, available at https://www.europarl.europa.eu/RegData/etudes/STUD/2016/556934/IPOL_STU(2016)556934_EN.pdf.

425 M. Fink, *Frontex and Human Rights: Responsibility in 'Multi-Actor Situations' Under the ECHR and EU Public Liability Law* (2018); R. Mungianu, *Frontex and Non-Refoulement: The International Responsibility of the EU* (2016); M. Lehnert, *Frontex und operative Maßnahmen an den europäischen Außengrenzen* (2014), at 337 et seq.

tiating her or his claim. While the principle of transparency and the rights of individuals to access documents of EU bodies (Art. 15 TFEU, Art. 42 EU-CFR), as concretized by secondary EU law,[426] also apply to Frontex (Art. 114(1) Frontex Regulation), and while persons without residence in the EU also have the right to address the agency and receive an answer (Art. 114(4) Frontex Regulation), there is no obligation of result and the content of the answer is left to the discretion of Frontex.[427]

Taken together, these circumstances render the guarantee of Art. 47 EU-CFR in the case of Frontex operations ineffective in practice, and leave individual migrants affected by these operations without proper access to justice, understood as the possibility of obtaining independent and binding judicial review.[428]

These problems could be mitigated by introducing an appeal procedure regarding the decisions of complaints against Frontex actions filed with the Frontex fundamental rights officer (Art. 111 Frontex Regulation). This remedy should provide for full judicial review of such cases by the CJEU. EU primary law already allows for this possibility, as acts setting up agencies of the Union may lay down specific conditions and arrangements concerning actions brought by natural or legal persons against acts of these agencies intended to produce legal effects in relation to them (Art. 263(5) TFEU). A good example of such a provision is Art. 94 of Regulation 1907/2006 (REACH Regulation),[429] which gives individuals the right to have decisions by the European Chemicals Agency reviewed by the CJEU.[430]

---

426 Regulation 1049/2001 regarding public access to European Parliament, Council and Commission documents.

427 M. Gkliati and H. Rosenfeldt, *Accountability of the European Border and Coast Guard Agency: Recent developments, legal standards and existing mechanisms* (2018), at 7, available at https://sas-space.sas.ac.uk/9187/. Furthermore, challenging such decisions before a court may come with a high financial risk for persons who claim their fundamental rights, as was shown by a 2019 judgment of the General Court: CJEU, Case T-31/18, *Izuzquiza* (EU:T:2019:815).

428 On the parallel issue of EU agencies' involvement in the administration of 'hot spots' at EU borders, see Ziebritzki, 'The Integrated EU Hotspot Administration and the Question of the EU's Liability', in M. Kotzur et al. (eds), *The External Dimension of EU Migration and Asylum Policies* (2020) 253.

429 Regulation 1907/2006 concerning the Registration, Evaluation, Authorisation and Restriction of Chemicals (REACH Regulation).

430 M. Gkliati and H. Rosenfeldt, *Accountability of the European Border and Coast Guard Agency: Recent developments, legal standards and existing mechanisms* (2018), at 5–6, available at https://sas-space.sas.ac.uk/9187/.

However, access to justice is also rendered difficult by the multiplicity and divergence of existing legal bases for the plethora of EU agencies. This plurality impedes transparency, accessibility, and predictability of procedural guarantees, not to mention requiring consistent interpretation of the relevant norms by the CJEU. In this respect, the far more numerous decentralized (or 'regulatory') agencies (like Frontex, EASO, or eu-LISA) must be distinguished from executive agencies, the latter being created by the European Commission for a fixed period. As to executive agencies, Regulation 58/2003[431] lays down common provisions on liability (Art. 21 Regulation 58/2003), the legality of acts (Art. 22 Regulation 58/2003), and access to documents and confidentiality (Art. 23 Regulation 58/2003). A similar horizontal regulation providing for common procedural guarantees for decentralized agencies could significantly increase the ability to hold EU agencies accountable and thus serve the *effet utile* of Art. 41 and 47 EU-CFR.

3.3 Recommendations

Recommendation 1: Provide comprehensive procedural safeguards for visa applications

Courts at all levels of European migration governance are called upon to safeguard the procedural rights of migrants in all immigration and asylum proceedings. Art. 41 EU-CFR sets high standards for safeguarding due process in EU migration law, which reflects and expands the Human Rights protected by Art. 4 of Protocol No. 4 and Art. 1 of Protocol No. 7 ECHR. According to Art. 41 EU-CFR and the corresponding guarantee recognized as a general principle of EU law, any processing of a visa application that is substantively governed by EU law must respect the right to be heard and the duty to submit reasons for a decision adversely affecting the applicant, and would have to provide for the possibility of review and representation before the competent authority.

As to EU legislation, the already existing sectoral provisions guaranteeing procedural rights in the case of refusal of a long-term visa should be supplemented by a horizontal provision applicable to all applications for

431 Regulation 58/2003 laying down the statute for executive agencies to be entrusted with certain tasks in the management of Community programmes.

granting a right to reside as far as the scope of EU law is affected, including applications for long-term (national) visas.

Recommendation 2: Clarify and strengthen procedural guarantees at the borders

Art. 14(3) of the Schengen Borders Code lacks legal clarity in respect of the guarantee of effective remedy. This provision should be reformulated accordingly. Due consideration is particularly to be given to the suspensive effect of legal remedies. In order to guarantee the Human Right to an individual assessment of one's case – including possible exceptional circumstances – it must always be possible to obtain a judicial order establishing suspensive effect of a remedy in an urgent preliminary ruling procedure.

Recommendation 3: Guarantee sufficient procedural rights when terminating residence

The revised Return Directive[432] should contain a clear and explicit reference to the right to be heard, especially as far as the rights enshrined in Art. 5 of the proposed new Directive ('Non-refoulement, best interests of the child, family life and state of health') are concerned, preferably in a horizontally applicable provision.[433] In a similar vein, Art. 9(4) of the Proposal should not be adopted, as a provision obliging Member States to automatically refrain from granting a voluntary period of departure (e.g., when there is a risk of absconding or to public policy) is in breach of the right to be heard according to the interpretation of the CJEU.

Moreover, the Return Directive should be amended so as to include ECtHR and CJEU case-law on the automatic suspensive effect of appeals against return decisions posing a real risk of a violation of the non-refoulement principle. The wording of the proposed amendments (Art. 16(3) and Art. 22(6) of the Commission proposal) may, however, render the changes ineffective. Most notably, the EU legislature must ensure that the require-

432 Cf. European Commission, Proposal for a recast Return Directive, COM(2018) 634, 12 September 2018.

433 European Parliament Research Service, The proposed Return Directive (recast) (2019), at 79, available at https://www.europarl.europa.eu/RegData/etudes/STUD/2019/631727/EPRS_STU(2019)631727_EN.pdf.

ment of 'new elements or findings' (cf. Art. 16(3)(3) and Art. 22(6)(1) Proposal for a recast Return Directive) will not lead to a very narrow interpretation by Member States of the scope of automatic suspensive effect.

Unlike the Return Directive as it stands (Art. 8(6)) or the Commission proposal for a recast Directive on the same matter (Art. 10(6)), the EU should provide a binding and detailed list of minimum requirements for forced-return monitoring mechanisms. In order to render this institution effective, its shape and independence should not be left to the discretion of the Member States.

Recommendation 4: Guarantee a right to an effective remedy against EU agencies

In face of the trend toward an agencification of EU migration policy, the EU must ensure that the relevant actors in the field remain accountable and their actions are legally reviewable. In order to achieve this aim, the EU should adopt a horizontal regulation for all EU agencies, including a general minimum standard for safeguarding procedural rights.

Such a horizontal provision is important to increase transparency as a precondition to effective and adequate access to justice. Such a horizontal regulation should be reinforced by procedural safeguards for the specific contexts of Frontex, EASO, and eu-LISA.

Chapter 4 – Preventing Discrimination

The inclusion of foreigners according to the principle of non-discrimination is a central goal of European integration. Ever since the Treaties of Rome were concluded in the 1950s, the European Communities have called upon the founding States to ensure equal treatment of migrants – be they migrant workers, entrepreneurs, service providers, or consumers. This principle of 'constitutional tolerance', as Joseph Weiler famously theorized it,[434] was later elevated to the status of a fundamental right (Art. 21(2) EU-CFR). However, the personal scope of this constitutional guarantee has always been limited to nationals of other Member States, even though this is not evident from the wording of the relevant Treaty provisions (cf. Art. 18 TFEU).[435] Hence, equality of status within the EU is a right of Union citizens, rather than a Human Right. Nonetheless, we argue in this chapter that equality of status, both of and among migrants, has a Human Rights dimension that is underexplored and widely underestimated as a source of legal obligations the EU is bound to respect when developing its migration policy.

Equality and non-discrimination of migrants is a complex issue that could be discussed at various levels of inquiry.[436] Everyday experiences of migrants are often characterized by discrimination, both in their interaction with members of the host societies and with public officials. Migrants are frequently labeled and treated as 'the Other', irrespective of their im migration status or nationality. In recent years, this shared experience

434 Weiler, 'In Defence of the Status Quo: Europe's Constitutional *Sonderweg*', in J.H.H. Weiler and M. Wind (eds), *European Constitutionalism Beyond the State* (2003) 7.

435 CJEU, Case C-122/96, *Saldanha and MTS* (EU:C:1997:458); Cases C-22/08 and C-23/08, *Vatsouras and Koupatantze* (EU:C:2009:344); on the genesis of the ambiguous wording, see S.A.W. Goedings, *Labor Migration in an Integrating Europe* (2005), at 309–343.

436 See, e.g., B. Fridriksdottir, *What Happened to Equality? The Construction of the Right to Equal Treatment of Third-Country Nationals in European Union Law on Labour Migration* (2017); MacCormack-George, 'Equal Treatment of Third-Country Nationals in the European Union: Why Not?', 21 *European Journal of Migration and Law (EJML)* (2019) 53.

of migrants is being voiced more loudly in public debate, catalyzed by incidents of racist police action against black citizens in the USA.

The claim of migrants not to be subject to racist and xenophobic discrimination has a strong legal basis in Human Rights law. However, the present chapter has a different focus – namely, discrimination embedded in the laws of migration governance. The EU's policy regarding discrimination based on 'racial or ethnic origin' is conceptually outside the field of migration law. Art. 19 TFEU and the relevant EU anti-discrimination legislation aim at providing protection that is not specific to migrants, whereas migration law proper is largely exempt from the scope of the EU's anti-discrimination policy.[437] The present chapter connects these separate fields and addresses non-equal treatment within the realm of immigration and asylum law. It discusses the issue of whether EU migration law is a cause of inequality in itself and, if so, what the Human Rights standards constraining EU policies are.

4.1 Structural challenges and current trends

Questioning inequality in migration law seems almost a contradiction in terms. The difference in treatment of citizens and non-citizens of a State – that is, 'discrimination' based on nationality – is at the very heart of migration law.[438] The relevant legal regimes emerged in the nineteenth century in the wake of the modern nation state, both in domestic law[439] and in international law.[440] Non-nationals are the subjects of a special set of rules that excludes them from hard-won citizens' rights and accords the former an inferior legal position in the host state. This largely holds true today, irrespective of the fact that the gradual expansion of the rule of law into the field of migration and the emergence of denizenship policies since the 1970s have reduced the degree of legal inequality between

437 Cf. Art. 3(2) of Directive 2000/43/EC implementing the principle of equal treatment between persons irrespective of racial or ethnic origin.

438 Thym, 'Ungleichheit als Markenzeichen des Migrationsrechts', 74 *Zeitschrift für öffentliches Recht (ZöR)* (2019) 905.

439 D. Gosewinkel, *Einbürgern und Ausschließen: Die Nationalisierung der Staatsangehörigkeit vom Deutschen Bund bis zur Bundesrepublik Deutschland* (2001).

440 R.B. Lillich, *The Human Rights of Aliens in Contemporary International Law* (1984).

citizens and non-citizens.[441] On that basis, a second layer of rules was gradually developed by state legislatures. Modern migration law provides for difference in treatment *among* non-citizens – that is, 'discrimination' based on immigration status. Depending on the respective purpose of admission, migration law coins various immigration statuses, with distinctive combinations of residence rights, access to employment, and access to the welfare system.[442] Historically, this new field of 'immigration law' (*Aufenthaltsrecht*, in German) emerged in the early twentieth century with the rise of the interventionist welfare state.[443] In essence, immigration law is about defining a plurality of immigration statuses, thus deliberately creating inequality among classes of migrants and causing a stratification of their rights.[444]

When the EU entered the stage in the theater of migration law, it almost naturally followed this line, adopting legislation that defines legal statuses of various classes of third-country nationals. Depending on the regulatory approach, the impact on the existing plurality of immigration statuses at the level of the Member States varies. On the one hand, a certain trend toward horizontal (transnational) convergence of immigration statuses is inherent in the Europeanization of migration policy. The emergence of the EU as a new actor in immigration law heralds a pan-European harmonizing effect. On the other hand, the activity of yet another legislature in the field adds to its complexity when newly created immigration statuses complement existing ones at the national level, rather than harmonizing or replacing them.[445] In this case, the EU actually contributes to new

441 Thym, 'Vom "Fremdenrecht" über die "Denizenship" zur "Bürgerschaft"', 57 *Der Staat* (2018) 77.

442 Bast, 'Zur Territorialität des Migrationsrechts', in F. von Harbou and J. Markow (eds), *Philosophie des Migrationsrechts* (2020) 17.

443 Lucassen, 'The Great War and the Origins of Migration Control in Western Europe and the United States', in A. Böcker et al. (eds), *Regulation of Migration* (1998) 45.

444 L. Morris, *Managing Migration: Civic Stratification and Migrants' Rights* (2002), at 19 et seq. and 103 et seq.

445 Examples include the denizen status under to Long-Term Residents Directive (Directive 2003/109/EC), which sits next to permanent residence statuses according to national law; subsidiary protection status according to Qualification Directive (Directive 2011/95/EU) sits next to complementary national protection statuses.

vertical (multi-level) divergence and, hence, increases inequality among migrants.[446]

Given these structural conditions, the impact of the EU legislature on the equality of migrant status is strongly policy-dependent. In this respect, we observe the following trends, which in sum reveal a growing number of status distinctions created by the EU.

Trend 1: Increasing sectoral divergence within the Europeanized fields of legal migration

There is a trend toward increasing sectoral divergence within the Europeanized fields of legal migration – that is, in immigration policy in the narrow sense as defined in Art. 79 TFEU. This is the result of the approach taken by the EU legislature to defining immigration statuses. The EU's approach features a number of aspects, the combined effect of which is the risk of maintaining, or actually creating, distinctions among classes of migrants that lack a reasonable foundation.

First, the EU has enacted incomplete or 'shallow' harmonization by, inter alia, inserting optional clauses, laying down discretionary requirements, or choosing an approach of partial non-regulation. The prime example of this approach is the Family Reunification Directive (Directive 2003/86/EC; see Chapter 5). This legislative approach is often a result of political disagreement within the Council, where Member States governments have pursued the goal of limiting the impact of particular legislative acts on existing domestic laws. This weakens the horizontal convergence or even contributes to new divergence. This, in turn, involves the risk of maintaining arbitrary distinctions among holders of residence permits whose immigration statuses are partly defined by EU law.

Second, the EU has followed a piecemeal approach to defining new immigration statuses based in EU law. This increases the risk of inconsistent outcomes of legislative processes that are insufficiently coordinated. This trend is even more marked since the Commission switched to a sectoral approach in the field of labor migration, after the political failure to garner sufficient support in the Council for a horizontal approach to European

446 Strumia, 'European Citizenship and EU Immigration', 22 *European Law Journal* (2016) 417, at 423–426.

labor migration policy.[447] The EU has failed to develop a meaningful body of law that lays down cross-sectoral standards and procedures applicable to all immigration statuses defined by EU law, or at least to broad classes thereof. The 'general body' (*Allgemeiner Teil*) of EU migration law is rather slim.[448]

Third, the EU's incremental legislative activity lacks a clear *Leitbild* – a model or overall concept – that could serve as a template for defining the immigration statuses of third-country nationals.[449] In the first period of legislation after the entry into force of the Amsterdam Treaty, the Tampere Program agreed by the European Council had raised expectations that the status of Union citizens would serve as such a *Leitbild* for the future statuses of third-country nationals. The ensuing negotiations led to the adoption of the Long-Term Residents Directive (Directive 2003/109/EC), which in turn served as a point of reference for other legislation (e.g., the Blue Card Directive 2009/50/EC). However, ten years later the Tampere *Leitbild* of near-equality between Union citizens and third-country nationals had all but disappeared, as many critically observed.[450] In the absence of such a model, the EU does not have a yardstick to distinguish unprincipled proliferation of statuses from sectoral differentiation that is reasonably related to the respective purposes of admission.

Because of this unprincipled approach, the EU's legislative activity in defining immigration statuses has maintained or created distinctions that seem to reflect little more than the ad hoc political compromises found in dealing with the latest dossier. This inconsistency causes a major challenge to EU migration policy. While a certain degree of inconsistent outcomes is inherent in any political decision-making that involves various actors and

447 B. Fridriksdottir, *What Happened to Equality?* (2017), chapter 3; von Harbou, 'Arbeits- und Ausbildungsmigration', in Wollenschläger (ed.) *Europäischer Freizügigkeitsraum: Unionsbürgerschaft und Migrationsrecht (EnzEuR vol. 10)* (2021) 621, at para. 97–98.

448 According to H. Tewocht, *Drittstaatsangehörige im europäischen Migrationsrecht* (2017), at 411–412 and 449, it consists of the Family Reunification Directive, the Long-Term Residents Directive, the Return Directive, and the Single Permit Directive. Only the latter provides rights that apply to a range of immigration statuses.

449 On the function of a *Leitbild* in immigration policy, see Gusy and Müller, 'Leitbilder im Migrationsrecht', *Zeitschrift für Ausländerrecht (ZAR)* (2013) 265.

450 Halleskov Storgaard, 'The Long-Term Residents Directive: A Fulfilment of The Tampere Objective of Near-Equality?', in E. Guild and P. Minderhoud (eds), *The First Decade of EU Migration and Asylum Law* (2011) 299; A. Wiesbrock, *Legal Migration to the European Union* (2010).

stretches over time, at some point the increasing sectoral divergence within the Europeanized fields of migration law encounters legal limits posed by Human Rights law.

Trend 2: Contradictory policy choices in respect of the asylum status in the EU

We observe a high degree of inconsistency in respect of the asylum status of persons enjoying international protection in the EU – that is, of refugees in the broad sense of the term. On the one hand, this is a particular case in point of the EU's unprincipled approach to defining immigration statuses, since to some extent it results from incomplete, incremental, and unguided decision-making. On the other hand, it is also – and perhaps primarily – a result of contradictory policy choices. This policy inconsistency unfolds on two levels: among the persons enjoying asylum in the EU, and between them and other migrants legally residing in the EU.

First, the EU legislature decided to create a uniform protection status called 'international protection (in the EU)', thereby fusing the protection of refugees as defined in the Geneva Refugee Convention with other Human Rights-based grounds of protection ('subsidiary protection').[451] The status of Convention refugees according to international law served as the template for the immigration status defined by EU law for all grounds of international protection. The choice in favor of equality of status includes the prospect of long-term residence according to the Long-Term Residents Directive. However, in certain instances the EU legislature deviates from that template and assigns an inferior status to people eligible for protection on subsidiary grounds. Such instances include the validity of the (renewable) residence permit and access to social assistance. The distinction between the two subgroups of migrants enjoying international protection is most pronounced in respect of the right to family reunification; persons enjoying subsidiary protection are excluded both from the privileged regime applicable to Convention refugees and from the standard regime applicable to migrants legally residing within the EU. The question thus arises as to whether this inequality of status is justified in light of Human Rights law (see below, section 4.2.4).

451 Bast, 'Vom subsidiären Schutz zum europäischen Flüchtlingsbegriff', *Zeitschrift für Ausländerrecht (ZAR)* (2018) 41.

Second, the EU legislature has elected to establish a privileged status for persons enjoying international protection in the EU. This is in line with the basic rationale of refugee law, which regards refugees as persons whose decision to migrate (or not to return) is non-voluntary and who thus cannot avail themselves of the citizens' rights in their home country. Accordingly, they deserve equal, or at least similar, treatment to the citizens of their host country as long as their need of protection persists. The EU (then still called the European Community) applied this rationale in 1958 when Regulation No. 3 on the coordination of social security systems granted refugees the same rights as nationals of the Member States. However, in certain respects the asylum status defined by EU law is less favorable than the immigration status of other, 'ordinary' migrants residing in the EU. This is particularly true in respect of mobility rights within the Union. Such rights are granted, albeit to a limited degree, to persons who are admitted as researchers, students, or highly qualified non-EU nationals. In contrast, such rights to relocate voluntarily are notably absent for refugees and other persons enjoying asylum in the EU. Their 'secondary movement' is even seen as a threat to the asylum system and is actively discouraged (on this issue, see Chapter 6). Here again, at some point the inequality of status created by the EU legislature may constitute a Human Rights violation.

4.2 Legal evaluation

4.2.1 General framework: Three objectionable grounds of distinction among migrants ('race', nationality, immigration status)

The section will develop the standards of determining which distinctions in immigration and asylum law constitute Human Rights violations. We have identified three grounds of distinction that are particularly relevant: distinctions that constitute direct or indirect discrimination on *racial grounds*, distinctions based on the *nationality* of the migrants concerned, and distinctions that relate to their *immigration status*. In the following, we shall set out the respective sources as well as the elements of the legal test for whether such distinctions constitute a discrimination prohibited by Human Rights law.

(1) First, Human Rights law prohibits any distinctions that amount to racial discrimination, including indirect discrimination on racial grounds. 'Race' – that is, any attribution of presumably unalterable characteristics

of human beings such as their skin color or ethnic origin – is a ground of distinction that Human Rights law most strongly condemns.[452] It is an 'objectionable' ground in the sense that such distinctions cannot be justified.[453]

Various sources of universal and regional Human Rights law unequivocally reject 'race' as a legitimate ground of distinctions. In EU law, the prohibition of racial discrimination is mirrored in Art. 21(1) EU-CFR and Art. 19 TFEU. The most general non-discrimination clause is Art. 2 UDHR, stating that everyone is entitled to all the rights and freedoms set forth in this Declaration, without distinction of any kind, such as, inter alia, 'race' or 'colour'. It is reproduced almost verbatim in Art. 2(1) ICCPR and Art. 14 ECHR. Various other Human Rights sources confirm and specify the right to non-discrimination on racial grounds within their respective scope of application (see, e.g., Art. 2(2) ICESCR and Art. 2(1) CRC). The right to non-discrimination on racial grounds is generally regarded as a norm of customary international law, even one of preemptory character (*ius cogens*).[454] This view is confirmed by numerous soft-law instruments, including the Global Compact for Migration (see, inter alia, Objectives 15 [para. 31] and 16 [para. 32]).

The most comprehensive prohibition of racial discrimination is laid down in the International Convention on the Elimination of All Forms of Racial Discrimination (ICERD). In this Convention, the term 'racial discrimination' means 'any distinction, exclusion, restriction or preference based on race, colour, descent, or national or ethnic origin which has the purpose or effect of nullifying or impairing the recognition, enjoyment or exercise, on an equal footing, of human rights and fundamental freedoms' in any field of public life (Art. 1(1) ICERD). The Convention lays down

452 On the historical context, see Van Boven, 'The Concept of Discrimination in the International Convention on the Elimination of all Forms of Racial Discrimination', in W. Kälin (ed.), *Das Verbot ethnisch-kultureller Diskriminierung: Verfassungs- und menschenrechtliche Aspekte* (1999) 9.

453 Cf. ECtHR, *Biao v. Denmark*, Appl. no. 38590/10, Grand Chamber Judgment of 25 March 2014, at para. 94.

454 ICJ, *Legal Consequences for States of the Continued Presence of South Africa in Namibia (South West Africa) Notwithstanding Security Council Resolution 276* (Advisory Opinion), General List No. 53 [1971], at para. 131; *Case Concerning the Barcelona Traction, Lights and Power Company Ltd. (Belgium v. Spain)* (Judgment), [1970] ICJ Reports 3 [32], at para. 33–34. For references to scholarly opinions, see V. Chetail, *International Migration Law* (2019), at 147, note 378.

various negative and positive obligations of States Parties to eliminate racial discrimination.

However, certain limitations as to the scope of ICERD apply. According to Art. 1(2) and (3) ICERD, this Convention does not apply to distinctions between citizens and non-citizens, and it does not affect provisions concerning nationality, citizenship, or naturalization, provided that such provisions do not discriminate against any particular nationality. It is noteworthy here that 'immigration law' is not excluded from the scope of ICERD. Moreover, the Committee on the Elimination of Racial Discrimination (CERD, the treaty body entrusted with the supervision of this Convention) has developed a consistent jurisprudence according to which non-equal treatment based on citizenship or immigration status may constitute racial discrimination.[455]

We recognize that this 'intersectional' approach of the CERD is not free from criticism, as evidenced by the judgment of the International Court of Justice in the case of *Qatar v. United Arab Emirates*.[456] However, it is generally acknowledged that Art. 1(1) ICERD prohibits not only direct discrimination but also measures that expose persons to indirect discrimination, as evidenced by the wording of the provision ('purpose *or* effect').[457] Developing the relevant legal test is not without its difficulties. The starting point of any indirect discrimination is a norm or practice characterized by distinctions based on apparently neutral criteria. The decisive factor is whether a specific group is particularly affected by the relevant measure, irrespective of the intention to expose it to discriminatory treatment.[458] CERD, in particular, is critical of the assumption that, when claiming

---

455 CERD, General Recommendation No. 30: Discrimination Against Non-Citizens, CERD/C/64/Misc.11/rev.3, at para. 4.

456 ICJ, *Application of the International Convention on the Elimination of All Forms of Racial Discrimination (Qatar v. United Arab Emirates)* (Provisional measures), Judgment of 4 February 2021, at para. 101. The ICJ held that the term 'national origin' in Art. 1(1) ICERD does not encompass current nationality, but it did not rule out that a measure targeting a particular group of non-citizens may constitute an 'indirect' racial discrimination; see ibid., at para. 112.

457 See CERD, General Recommendation No. 32: The meaning and scope of special measures in the International Convention on the Elimination of All Forms of Racial Discrimination, CERD/C/GC/32, at para. 7. In EU law, cf. Art. 2(1) and (2) of Directive 2000/43/EC implementing the principle of equal treatment between persons irrespective of racial or ethnic origin.

458 O. de Schutter, *International Human Rights Law* (3rd ed. 2019), at 722 et seq.; P. Thornberry, *The International Convention on the Elimination of All Forms of Racial Discrimination* (2016), at 114.

discriminatory treatment, it is necessary to demonstrate discriminatory intent.[459] The empirical examination of the prejudicial effects of such norms and practices is decisive in order to establish a discriminatory effect.[460] The proof of indirect discrimination can only ever be provided by considering the context and all relevant circumstances.[461]

Given the postcolonial conditions of global inequality, where 'race' and class are closely linked, it could be argued that many of the socio-economic selection criteria (such as income or skill requirements), frequently used in current immigration law in the Global North, are biased toward 'race' because they objectively affect the ethnic composition of the migrant population, to the disadvantage of certain groups defined by their 'race'. Such a line of reasoning would fundamentally challenge the mode of operation of immigration law, since States (and the EU) would have to demonstrate that their seemingly neutral socio-economic selection criteria do not entail discriminatory effects as defined in ICERD. While this line of reasoning seems perfectly logical according to established jurisprudence, we accept that it would amount to a 'progressive development' of the law, for which we do not find sufficient support in existing authorities.

(2) The second 'objectionable' ground in distinguishing among migrants relates to nationality. These distinctions are not prohibited per se, unless they constitute a hidden racial discrimination (see above). However, distinctions based on the nationality of a migrant must be justified by 'very weighty reasons', according to the case-law of the ECtHR.

'Nationality' is a technical term of international law that refers to a legal bond, established by national law, between a natural person and his or her State (or States, in the case of multiple nationalities). Note that none of the non-discrimination clauses referred to above explicitly lists nationality as a prohibited ground. Pursuant to the dominant understanding, the term 'national origin' mentioned in Art. 2 UDHR, Art. 2 ICCPR and Art. 2 CESCR pertains to particular groups within the citizenry of the relevant State, rather than foreign nationals.[462] In any event, nationality constitutes 'other

459 CERD, Concluding Observations on the fourth, fifth and sixth periodic reports of the USA, 8 May 2008, CERD/C/USA/CO/6, at para. 35.

460 O. de Schutter, *International Human Rights Law* (3rd ed. 2019), at 723. Cf. ECtHR, *Biao v. Denmark*, Appl. no. 38590/10, Grand Chamber Judgment of 25 March 2014, at para. 103.

461 CERD, *L. R. et al. v. Slovakia*, Communication No. 31/2003, CERD/C/66/D/31/2003, at para. 10.4.

462 V. Chetail, *International Migration Law* (2019), at 151.

status' according to the cited provisions (on this open-ended concept, see below).[463]

Seemingly an outlier in this regard is the EU Charter of Fundamental Rights. According to Art. 21(2) EU-CFR, any discrimination on grounds of nationality shall be prohibited within the scope of application of the EU Treaties. A historically informed construction of this provision (and of Art. 18(1) TFEU, its template) reveals that it merely establishes a prohibition of discrimination of nationals of other EU Member States, and not of third-country nationals. This traditional understanding has more recently been confirmed by the CJEU,[464] rejecting scholarly proposals to expand the meaning of the clause.[465] Distinctions based on the nationality of third-country nationals are therefore measured against the yardstick of Art. 21(1) EU-CFR, rather than Art. 21(2) EU-CFR. The wording of the former provision slightly differs from the cited non-discrimination clauses of Human Rights law, as it does not include a reference to 'other status'. However, while it lists additional grounds not mentioned in these sources, the omission of the phrase 'other status' was not meant to reduce the substantive scope of the guarantees or establish an exhaustive lists of discrimination grounds (see the wording 'such as' introducing the listed grounds).[466]

The most developed jurisprudence relating to discrimination based on nationality stems from the ECtHR's case-law on Art. 14 ECHR, which is the main source of inspiration for Art. 21(1) EU-CFR. The relevant line of reasoning was founded in 1996 with the judgment *Gaygusuz v. Austria*, when the Court for the first time held that excluding certain classes of migrants from a particular social welfare benefit constitutes discrimination based on nationality and therefore violates Art. 14 ECHR.[467]

---

463 HR Committee, *Ibrahima Gueye et al. v. France*, Communication No. 196/1985, CCPR/C/35/D/196/1985, at para. 9.4.

464 CJEU, Case C-291/09, *Francesco Guarnieri & Cie* (EU:C:2011:217); Case C-42/11, *Lopes de Silva* (EU:C:2012:517); Case C-45/12, *Hadj Hamed* (EU:C:2013:390).

465 See, e.g., Brouwer and De Vries, 'Third-country Nationals and Discrimination on the Ground of Nationality: Article 18 TFEU in the Context of Article 14 ECHR and EU Migration Law: Time for a New Approach', in M. van den Brink, S. Burri and J. Goldschmidt (eds), *Equality and Human Rights: Nothing but Trouble?* (2015) 123.

466 Opinion of AG Cruz Villalón, Cases C-443/14 and C-444/14, *Alo and Osso* (EU:C:2015:665), at para. 98.

467 ECtHR, *Gaygusuz v. Austria,* Appl. no. 17371/90, Judgment of 16 September 1996.

The legal test to determine a violation of Art. 14 ECHR consists of five elements.[468] First, the contested measure must affect the enjoyment of a right set forth in the ECHR or in one of its Protocols, and therefore falls within the ambit of the Convention. Second, the measure must be based on a discrimination ground covered by Art. 14 ECHR. Third, to establish prima facie discrimination against the person concerned, a relevant class of persons must be identified who are in analogous, or relevantly similar, situations but not adversely affected by the tested measure (comparability test). Fourth, the standard of review by the Court must be determined – that is, the extent to which States enjoy a margin of appreciation in making distinctions relating to the subject-matter concerned. Fifth, provided that comparable groups are treated differently according to the first three elements, the defending State must provide an objective and reasonable justification supporting the difference in treatment. That element essentially entails a proportionality test. A difference in treatment is discriminatory if it does not pursue a legitimate aim, or if there is no reasonable relationship of proportionality between the means employed and the aim sought to be realized. This proportionality test is to be conducted according to the standard of review determined in step four.[469]

In respect of legal distinctions made in migration law, it follows from the *Gaygusuz* judgment that 'nationality' is a discrimination ground covered by Art. 14 ECHR, although the Court never finally clarified why this is the case (it may fall under the rubric of 'national origin' or 'other status'). In any case, the applicable standard of review is high, since the Court requires the State to provide 'very weighty reasons' to justify distinctions based exclusively on the ground of nationality. The *Gaygusuz* case and the ensuing case-law also demonstrate that difference in treatment may be considered 'based exclusively' on nationality if a State discriminates against certain classes of non-nationals while other foreign nationals enjoy

468 See Arnardóttir, 'The Differences that Make a Difference: Recent Developments on the Discrimination Grounds and the Margin of Appreciation under Article 14 of the European Convention of Human Rights', 14 *Human Rights Law Review* (2014) 647; Gerards, 'The Discrimination Grounds of Article 14 of the European Convention on Human Rights', 13 *Human Rights Law Review* (2013) 99.

469 For a summary of the Court's approach to Art. 14 ECHR, see ECtHR, *Pajic v. Croatia*, Appl. no. 68453/13, Judgment of 23 February 2016, at para. 53–60.

equal treatment with the citizens of that State.[470] The comparability test conducted by the ECtHR usually enquires whether the claimant is in a like or analogous situation to a national of the responding State, irrespective of the treatment of other classes of migrants.[471] This doctrine is particularly noteworthy since immigration legislatures almost always distinguish between different classes of non-nationals, whereas rules and regulations that apply to all non-nationals without distinction are very rare.[472]

(3) A third layer of protection against discrimination in migration law relates to difference in treatment based on immigration status per se. As is the case with nationality, distinctions based on immigration status are unlawful unless the differentiation is duly justified, that is, supported by a legitimate aim and proportionate to achieve that aim. However, States usually enjoy a larger degree of discretion in making these types of distinctions.

Again, the most developed jurisprudence is provided by the ECtHR in its case-law on Art. 14 ECHR. This layer of protection against discrimination was added in several rulings of the ECtHR in 2011 and 2012.[473] The Court held that distinctions based on immigration status, either exclusively or in combination with the nationality of the person concerned, can amount to unlawful discrimination.

In *Ponomaryovi v. Bulgaria* (2011), the ECtHR held that the irregular immigration status of the claimant did not provide sufficient grounds to exclude him from access to a social benefit in the educational field. The case shows obvious similarities to the landmark *Plyler* case decided by the US Supreme Court.[474] In respect of the relevant discrimination ground, the ECtHR pragmatically acknowledged that in the instant case the exclusion of Mr. Ponomaryovi was based on a 'personal characteristic',

470 See, e.g., ECtHR, *Okpisz v. Germany*, Appl. no. 59140/00, Judgment of 25 October 2005; *Niedzwiecki v. Germany*, Appl. no. 58453/00, Judgment of 25 October 2005.

471 See, e.g., ECtHR, *Andrejeva v. Latvia*, Appl. no. 55707/00, Grand Chamber Judgment of 18 February 2009, at para. 87.

472 For a critical discussion on the actual impact of *Gaygusuz*, see Dembour, 'Gaygusuz Revisited: The Limits of the European Court of Human Rights' Equality Agenda', 12 *Human Rights Law Review* (2012) 689.

473 ECtHR, *Ponomaryovi v. Bulgaria*, Appl. no. 5335/05, Judgment of 21 June 2011; *Bah v. UK*, Appl. no. 56328/07, Judgment of 27 September 2011; *Hode and Abdi v. UK*, Appl. no. 22341/09, Judgment of 6 November 2012.

474 Cf. H. Motomura, *Immigration Outside the Law* (2014), at 105 et seq.

without making a clear distinction between 'nationality' and 'immigration status'.[475]

In *Bah v. UK* (2011), the Court confirmed its view that the legal position defined in immigration law constitutes a 'status' for the purposes of Art. 14 ECHR, irrespective of the fact it does not amount to an immutable or innate characteristic.[476] In the instant case, the difference in treatment was based purely on a distinction established in national immigration law (the irregular status of the applicant's son), which would have prevented Ms. Bah's family from having access to housing assistance even if she were a British national.

In *Hode and Abdi v. UK* (2012), the ECtHR reviewed a difference in treatment between different groups of refugees in respect of the right to family reunification. Again, the test conducted by the ECtHR enquired as to whether the State had provided objective and reasonable justification supporting the distinctions made in its asylum legislation, which resulted in non-equal treatment among different classes of non-nationals.

In *Bah v. UK*, however, the Court distinguished that type of case from the jurisprudence established in *Gaygusuz*. To justify a difference in treatment based on immigration status, the State need not necessarily provide 'very weighty reasons'. The Court explained that in order to determine the relevant standard of review, the 'nature of the status' is particularly relevant. Accordingly, in respect of immigration status the States enjoy a larger margin of appreciation; the Court will usually enquire only whether the difference is 'manifestly without reasonable foundation'.[477] As we will discuss in more detail below, this lower standard of review does not apply in all circumstances, particularly where migrants in vulnerable situations are concerned.

Having outlined the general jurisprudence on evaluating distinctions in immigration and asylum law in light of Human Rights, we shall proceed to apply this yardstick to the relevant trends and patterns of EU migration policy.

---

475 ECtHR, *Ponomaryovi v. Bulgaria*, Appl. no. 5335/05, Judgment of 21 June 2011, at para. 50 and 63.

476 ECtHR, *Bah v. UK*, Appl. no. 56328/07, Judgment of 27 September 2011, at para. 43–46.

477 Ibid., at para. 37.

4.2.2 Specific issue: Privileged and non-privileged nationalities in EU migration law

(1) According to our assessment, the existing immigration *acquis* of EU law does not make use of distinctions that amount to racial discrimination as defined in ICERD. As explained above, according to current jurisprudence the high-income requirements laid down, for example, in the Blue Card Directive 2009/50/EC in order to obtain the favorable status defined in this Directive do not amount to indirect discrimination on grounds of 'race', irrespective of the objectively biased effects that such criteria probably entail.

As a singular incident of what amounts to indirect racial discrimination, we identify the inclusion of Union citizens in the scope of Regulation 2019/816 to establish a centralized system for the exchange of criminal record information on convicted third-country nationals and stateless persons (ECRIS-TCN).[478] According to Art. 2 of this Regulation establishing a large-scale EU database, its provisions apply to citizens of the Union who also hold the nationality of a third country and who have been subject to convictions in the Member States, apart from minor exceptions. In effect, Union citizens with multiple nationalities are subject to a system that represents a typical instrument of 'aliens police' (*Fremdenpolizei*, in German) subordinating foreigners to a special layer of supervision.[479] While dual nationality is a seemingly neutral criterion in terms of 'race', in practice the majority of dual nationals are non-European migrants or their descendants and hence marked by their ethnic origin.[480] Commentators have convincingly argued that this difference in treatment between groups of Union citizens may constitute indirect racial discrimination.[481]

---

478 Regulation 2019/816 establishing a centralised system for the identification of Member States holding conviction information on third-country nationals and stateless persons (ECRIS-TCN).

479 On this older layer of immigration law, see J. Bast, *Aufenthaltsrecht und Migrationssteuerung* (2011), at 75–78.

480 See, e.g., CERD, *D.R. v. Australia*, Communication No. 42/2008, CERD/C/75/D/42/2008; Concluding observations on the eighteenth to twentieth periodic reports of Rwanda, 10 June 2016, CERD/C/RWA/CO/18–20.

481 Meijers Committee, *Policy Brief on 'Differential treatment of citizens with dual or multiple nationality and the prohibition of discrimination'* (CM 2016), 6 December 2020; Meijers Committee, *Creating second-class Union citizenship? Unequal treatment of Union citizens with dual nationality in ECRIS-TCN and the prohibition of discrimination* (CM 2104).

(2) The EU immigration *acquis* rarely uses 'nationality' as a factor in legal distinctions. The EU legislature follows the path of Member States with a developed system of immigration law in predominantly using *functional* criteria to define grounds of admission and the corresponding immigration statuses, regardless of the nationality of the persons concerned (see the introduction to this chapter). In some instances, however, the EU does draw distinctions between different nationalities in order to accord a privileged status exclusively to these nationals. This may raise issues of discrimination. We recall that 'very weighty reasons' must be provided to justify distinctions exclusively based on nationality.

The most fundamental distinction in EU law based on nationality is that between Union citizens and their family members, on the one hand, and third-country nationals, on the other hand.[482] Already in 1991 the ECtHR accepted the preferential treatment given to nationals of other Member States, on the ground that the Union (or, at the time, the European Communities) forms a 'special legal order'.[483] This rationale has been confirmed in more recent case-law.[484] However, it is important to note that the ECtHR does not understand the lawfulness of this distinction to be inherent in the concept of citizenship but, rather, requires reasonable grounds. In fact, in certain instances the ECtHR has found the drawing of a distinction between Union citizens and third-country nationals to be discriminatory for the purposes of Art. 14 ECHR.[485]

This rationale of a 'special legal order' is not readily applicable to the preferential treatment of nationals from particular third countries, which is granted in association agreements jointly concluded by the EU and its Members with those countries. While most external EU agreements do not include provisions that are immediately relevant for European immigration law, the EEA Agreement with Iceland, Lichtenstein, and Norway, and the bilateral agreements with Switzerland and with Turkey, do include far-reaching regulations concerning immigration law,[486] essentially grant-

482 On the conceptual basis, see Thym, 'The Evolution of Citizens' Rights in Light of the European Union's Constitutional Development', in D. Thym (ed.), *Questioning EU Citizenship* (2017) 111.

483 ECtHR, *Mustaquim v. Belgium*, Appl. no. 12313/86, at para. 49.

484 ECtHR, *Ponomaryovi v. Bulgaria*, Appl. no. 5335/05, Judgment of 21 June 2011, at para. 54.

485 See, e.g., ECtHR, *Dhahbi v. Italy*, Appl. no. 17120/09, Judgment of 8 September 2014, at para. 50 et seq.

486 Cf. D. Thym and M. Zoeteweij-Turhan (eds), *Rights of Third-Country Nationals under EU Association Agreements: Degrees of Free Movement and Citizenship* (2015).

ing the nationals of these association states free movement rights similar to those of EU citizens or, in the case of Turkish nationals residing in the EU, a denizen status that is even more favorable than the status defined in the Long-Term Residents Directive.[487] According to a traditional understanding, such distinctions are part of the unfettered discretion of States (and, by analogy, of the EU) to pursue their own migration policy. In light of modern Human Rights law, they constitute difference in treatment that requires justification. However, it is likely that the foreign policy considerations that sit at the heart of such external EU agreements would still satisfy the need to provide 'very weighty reasons'. The privileged status accorded to the nationals of the association states mirrors the privileged partnership between the respective subjects of international law and, hence, meets the requirement of objective and reasonable justification.

The critical case in respect of distinctions based exclusively on nationality is the Schengen visa regime laid down in the Visa List Regulation 2018/1806. Art. 3(1) in conjunction with Annex I to this Regulation establishes a list of States whose nationals must have a visa when crossing the external borders in order to stay in the Schengen area for up to 90 days, while nationals of States listed in Annex II are exempt from this requirement. Of course, one may take the view that the Schengen visa regime is beyond the scope of this study, since it concerns short-term travel rather than immigration. However, there are many legal and factual links between the two regimes that may bring about a situation whereby a short-term stay transforms into the first stage of an immigration process.[488]

The Visa List Regulation does not state the reasons for placing one particular State in Annex I (the 'black list'), and others in Annex II. Art. 1 of the Regulation refers to a 'case-by-case assessment of a variety of criteria relating, inter alia, to illegal immigration, public policy and security, economic benefit ... and the Union's external relations with the relevant third countries ...'. The actual composition of the lists seems to reflect a mixture of migration and foreign policy considerations.[489] In particular, the offer

487 Bast, 'European Community and Union, Association Agreements', in R. Wolfrum (ed.), *Max Planck Encyclopedia of Public International Law (MP-EPIL)*, online edition, last updated August 2010.

488 See, in the context of German immigration law, J. Bast, *Aufenthaltsrecht und Migrationssteuerung* (2011), at 233–234.

489 Martenczuk, 'Visa Policy and EU External Relations', in B. Martenczuk and S. van Thiel (eds), *Justice, Liberty, Security: New Challenges for EU External Relations* (2008) 21.

to conclude a bilateral Visa Facilitation Agreement has become a powerful tool in the EU's external relations.[490]

A scholarly debate on the legality of these distinctions based on the nationality of the traveler in light of non-discrimination law has begun only recently, drawing inspiration from the legal debate in the USA concerning selective travel bans against predominantly Muslim countries.[491] In respect of Art. 14 ECHR, one may doubt whether the matter falls within the ambit of the Convention. In instances of family-related travel, however, Art. 8 ECHR could serve as a connecting factor. Even in cases in which the more lenient standard of the general equality clause in Art. 20 EU-CFR applies, rather than Art. 21(1) EU-CFR mirroring Art. 14 ECHR, objective justification of the non-equal treatment is required under EU law. In any case, the lack of transparency regarding the 'case-by-case assessment' of the open-ended criteria laid down in the Regulation seem to originate from a tradition in which such decisions could still be taken without having due regard to the Human Rights of the persons concerned. A particular cause of concern is the fact that the placement of the large majority of countries on the 'black list' dates from the intergovernmental Schengen era and has never been properly justified.[492]

4.2.3 Specific issue: Differential treatment in respect of social assistance

It follows from the above legal analysis (section 4.2.1) that the EU must provide sufficient reasons to justify a difference in treatment between immigration statuses that are defined by EU law. This pertains, inter alia, to difference in treatment in respect of family reunification, social welfare, health care, access to the labor market, and mobility within the Union.[493]

The initial observation in this context is that it is very difficult to assess whether differences among the various categories of migrants established by the EU legislature are based on objective and reasonable justification,

490 N. Coleman, *European Readmission Policy* (2009), at 184–201.

491 Den Heijer, 'Visas and Non-discrimination', 20 *European Journal of Migration and Law (EJML)* (2018) 470, with references to earlier contributions.

492 Ibid., at 487.

493 For comparative analysis in the field of labor migration, see B. Fridriksdottir, *What Happened to Equality?* (2017). See also Farahat, 'Is There a Human Right to Equal Social Security?: EU Migration Law and the Requirements of Art 9 ICESCR', in M. Maes, M.-C. Foblets and Ph. de Bruycker (eds), *External Dimensions of European Migration Law and Policy* (2011) 529.

given that the recitals in the preamble to the Directives usually do not include any 'equality reasoning' explaining the legislative outcome in comparison to existing statuses. By way of example, we shall discuss in some detail the provisions related to social assistance. This is a crucial element of social welfare and is recognized in Art. 34(3) EU-CFR as a fundamental social right that the EU (and thus the Member States when they are implementing EU law) must respect.[494]

(1) First, we provide a brief outline of the relevant legislation, covering a selected number of immigration statuses.

A limited guarantee of access to social assistance is provided for in the Long-Term Residents Directive (Directive 2003/109/EC). According to point (d) of Art. 11(1), long-term residents shall enjoy equal treatment with nationals as regards, inter alia, social assistance. However, pursuant to Art. 11(4) of this Directive, Member States may limit the equal treatment to 'core benefits'.[495]

In contrast, in the Blue Card Directive (Directive 2009/50/EC) social assistance is not mentioned in the list of matters where EU Blue Card holders shall enjoy equal treatment with nationals of the Member State issuing the Blue Card (Art. 14 Blue Card Directive). When the EU Blue Card holder applies for social assistance, this may even be regarded as a ground for withdrawing or not renewing the Blue Card (Art. 9 Blue Card Directive). The latter clause is mitigated in the new Blue Card Directive 2021/1883, with effect from 19 November 2023.

A very similar approach is taken in the so-called REST Directive (Directive 2016/801/EU) regarding researchers and certain other third-country nationals whose stay is mainly related to educational purposes. Researchers are entitled to equal treatment with nationals of the Member State to the extent that this is provided for in another Directive, the Single Permit Directive 2011/98/EU. The equality of treatment of researchers is subject to certain further exceptions provided for in the REST Directive. Even more restrictions are permitted regarding trainees, volunteers, au pairs, and students.

---

494 CJEU, Case C-571/10, *Kamberaj* (EU:C:2012:233), at para. 80.

495 Recital 13 in the preamble to this Directive explains that this possibility of limiting the benefits is to be understood in the sense that this notion covers at least minimum income support, assistance in case of illness, pregnancy, parental assistance, and long-term care. On the construction of this derogation, see CJEU, Case C-571/10, *Kamberaj* (EU:C:2012:233), at para. 83 et seq.; Case C-94/20, *KV* (EU:C:2021:477), at para. 38–40.

The cited Single Permit Directive applies to 'third-country workers' as defined in this Directive, who are legally residing and are allowed to work in an EU Member State, including persons whose status is defined in national law. These workers enjoy a right to equal treatment in matters listed in Art. 12 of the Single Permit Directive (the clause referenced in the REST Directive). However, social assistance is not mentioned in this list. It does cover the branches of social security as defined in the relevant EU Regulations on the coordination of social security systems, but these branches usually do not include social assistance.

Yet another approach is taken by the EU legislature regarding refugees. According to Art. 29(1) of the Qualification Directive (Directive 2011/95/EU), Member States shall ensure that beneficiaries of international protection receive, in the Member State that has granted such protection, the 'necessary social assistance' as provided to nationals of that Member State. However, pursuant to Art. 29(2) of this Directive, Member States may limit social assistance granted to beneficiaries of subsidiary protection to 'core benefits'.

(2) The following legal evaluation is based on Art. 14 ECHR. Further applicable sources are Art. 2(2) ICESCR and Art. E of the revised European Social Charter. Note that in the Global Compact for Migration, States have also committed themselves 'to ensure that all migrants, regardless of their migration status, can exercise their human rights through safe access to basic services' (GCM, Objective 15, para. 31).

It is readily apparent that access to social assistance falls within the ambit of the ECHR, given that the ECtHR regards such benefits as a pecuniary right for the purposes of Art. 1 of Protocol No. 1 ECHR.[496] As discussed above, immigration status constitutes a personal characteristic within the meaning of Art. 14 ECHR. The relevant group of persons who are in a similar situation are other third-country nationals whose status is governed by EU law. Absent specific circumstances, the more lenient standard of review applies – that is, the difference in treatment must not be 'manifestly without reasonable foundation'.

The limited number of cases thus far decided by the ECtHR provides some guidance as to what arguments are sufficient to demonstrate a 'reasonable foundation'. The Court seems to accept that 'offering incentives

---

496 ECtHR, *Gaygusuz v. Austria*, Appl. no. 17371/90, Judgment of 16 September 1996, at para. 41.

to certain groups of immigrants' may provide such foundation.[497] More specifically, the need 'to stem or reverse the flow of illegal immigration' is explicitly recognized as a legitimate policy aim.[498] With respect to social benefits, the Court has pointed out that short-term and illegal immigrants do not contribute to the funding of public services.[499] The ECtHR acknowledges that the use of categorizations to distinguish between different groups in need is inherent in any welfare system, which may also justify distinctions between different categories of non-nationals.[500] On the other hand, the fact that the beneficial treatment of certain migrants fulfills the State's international obligations will not in itself justify the difference in treatment.[501] As to the proportionality of the differential treatment, the Court seems particularly concerned when migrants with a high level of de facto integration into the host society are excluded from certain benefits merely due to their status.[502]

To sum up the guidance from case-law, general considerations of migration policy ('offering incentives') may justify a difference in treatment with respect to the welfare system. In this context, States are entitled to use general categorizations. However, the difference in treatment must be reasonably related to the nature of the social benefit. Exclusions of migrants based on their temporary or irregular status serve a legitimate aim but may be disproportionate if they exclude migrants with strong ties to the host society.

(3) Applying these standards to the above examples from the EU immigration *acquis*, it seems reasonable to grant more favorable treatment in terms of social assistance to long-term residents and persons enjoying international protection in the EU. While the former are characterized by their strong social ties to and within the host societies, the latter are forced migrants who, by definition, cannot rely on social assistance in their

---

497 ECtHR, *Hode and Abdi v. UK*, Appl. no. 22341/09, Judgment of 6 November 2012, at para. 53.

498 ECtHR, *Ponomaryovi v. Bulgaria*, Appl. no. 5335/05, Judgment of 21 June 2011, at para. 60.

499 Ibid., at para. 54.

500 ECtHR, *Bah v. UK*, Appl. no. 56328/07, Judgment of 27 September 2011, at para. 49–50.

501 ECtHR, *Hode and Abdi v. UK*, Appl. no. 22341/09, Judgment of 6 November 2012, at para. 55.

502 See ECtHR, *Ponomaryovi v. Bulgaria*, Appl. no. 5335/05, Judgment of 21 June 2011, at para. 61; *Dhahbi v. Italy*, Appl. no. 17120/09, Judgment of 8 September 2014, at para. 52; see also ECtHR, *Biao v. Denmark*, Appl. no. 38590/10, Grand Chamber Judgment of 25 March 2014, at para. 118.

country of origin. Yet, the consistency of the detailed differences between the three groups concerned is less obvious. While the social assistance granted to long-term residents can be limited to 'core benefits', the same limitation does not apply to Convention refugees. However, in respect of the latter the social assistance from the host State must be 'necessary'. Both limitations to the right to equal treatment apply to persons with subsidiary protection status. In effect, it is difficult to see what these differences actually entail and what reasons potentially justify them. We will return to the issue of the difference in treatment between these two groups of internationally protected persons in the next section.

In respect of the other immigration statuses reported above, the striking feature is the lack of distinction made by the EU legislature in terms of social assistance. Highly qualified workers with a prospect of permanent stay and who are actively contributing to the funding of the social systems, such as EU Blue Card holders and researchers, are placed on equal footing with temporary visitors such as participants in training programs and pupil exchange schemes. Neither the validity of the residence permit, nor the actual duration of stay, nor the potential presence of social and family ties are taken into account. The same lack of regard to the actual situation of the migrants concerned pertains to third-country workers holding a 'single permit' under the Directive 2011/98/EU. This all the more surprising as the EU Charter recognizes that the right to social assistance is instrumental 'to ensure a decent existence for all those who lack sufficient resources' (Art. 34(3) EU-CFR), indicating that in various situations a Member State acts in violation of EU law (and corresponding Human Rights) when it refrains from granting the applicant the social assistance necessary to ensure a decent existence (see Chapter 6).

In sum, the scope of the right to equal treatment guaranteed in the Directives does not include all situations in which equal treatment in terms of social assistance would be required under Art. 14 ECHR. While such 'underinclusive legislation' may not per se violate EU law, since the Directives do not *oblige* the Member State to take decisions that would violate Art. 34(3) EU-CFR, such lack of consistency of EU legislation raises serious issues of compliance with the right to non-discrimination according to Art. 14 ECHR and Art. 21(1) EU-CFR.

4.2.4 Specific issue: Differential treatment among beneficiaries of international protection

A more detailed legal analysis is required in respect of the difference in treatment among beneficiaries of international protection as defined in the Qualification Directive 2011/95/EU, i.e., between Convention refugees and persons protected on subsidiary grounds. The leading authority is *Hode and Abdi v. UK*. At the time of writing, further potentially relevant cases are pending before the ECtHR.[503]

Two issues are of particular concern in light of Art. 14 ECHR. First, Member States may limit the social assistance to persons with subsidiary protection status to 'core benefits', whereas Convention refugees are entitled to equal treatment with nationals of the host State regarding 'necessary social assistance' (see above, 4.2.3). Second, in terms of the right to family reunification, Convention refugees benefit from a privileged regime laid down in the Family Reunification Directive 2003/86/EC (Art. 9–12), whereas EU law as it stands does not contain any regulations regarding family reunification of beneficiaries of subsidiary protection, since they are exempt from the scope of the Family Reunification Directive.[504] The background of this gap is that the first Qualification Directive 2004/83/EC was not yet adopted when the Family Reunification Directive was drafted.

Applying the settled doctrine regarding non-discrimination to these regulations, it is beyond dispute that they fall within the ambit of the ECHR[505] and that being entitled to subsidiary protection constitutes a 'status' for the purposes of Art. 14 ECHR. Obviously, there is a difference in the treatment of persons in comparable situations, namely other persons enjoying international protection in the EU (Convention refugees).

As to the standard of review, in view of the fact that the present case concerns a status defined in immigration law, States (and by analogy, the EU) would enjoy a wider margin of appreciation in assessing whether, and to what extent, differences in otherwise similar situations justify differen-

503 In ECtHR, *M.A. v. Denmark*, Appl. no. 6697/18, Grand Chamber Judgment of 9 July 2021, at para. 162, the Court did not rule on the issue of Art. 14 ECHR, after having concluded that stipulating a three-year waiting period for family reunifications requested by persons facing 'insurmountable obstacles to enjoying family life in the country of origin' breaches Art. 8 ECHR. The case *M.T. and others v. Sweden*, Appl. no. 22105/18, is still pending.

504 CJEU, Case C-380/17, *K. and B.* (EU:C:2018:877), at para. 33.

505 On family reunification, see ECtHR, *Abdulaziz, Cabales and Balkandali v. UK*, Appl. no. 9214/80, 9473/81 and 9474/81, Judgment of 28 May 1985.

tial treatment. However, we argue that very weighty reasons are required in cases involving persons in need of international protection since they are in a particularly vulnerable situation.[506] Among other things, the family life of these forced migrants cannot be maintained or established in the country of origin, nor can they rely on its systems of social welfare. In contrast, the 'element of choice' involved in obtaining an immigration status was a core argument put forward by the Court to determine that the justification required 'will not be as weighty as in the case of a distinction based, for example, on nationality'.[507] Such an 'element of choice' is notably absent where refugees or other forced migrants are concerned.[508]

Applying this standard of review, we now turn to the issue of whether the difference in treatment between the two classes of internationally protected persons has an objective and reasonable justification. The aims pursued by the EU legislature are somewhat difficult to identify, since the Qualification Directive reflects a compromise between contradictory policy approaches represented by different Member States in the Council. On the one hand, the EU legislature aimed at creating a uniform status for all beneficiaries of international protection and, therefore, chose to afford beneficiaries of subsidiary protection, as a general rule, the same rights and benefits enjoyed by beneficiaries of refugee status.[509] Accordingly, when implementing the Directive, a presumption of equality of status applies.[510] This conception constitutes a deliberate deviation from an or-

---

506 On this rationale for deriving a high standard of review, see ECtHR, *Alajos Kiss v. Hungary*, Appl. no. 38832/06, 20 May 2010, at para. 42: 'if a restriction on fundamental rights applies to a particularly vulnerable group in society, who have suffered considerable discrimination in the past, such as the mentally disabled, then the State's margin of appreciation is substantially narrower and it must have very weighty reasons for the restrictions in question.' Note that in *Hode and Abdi v. UK* (Appl. no. 22341/09, Judgment of 6 November 2012) the ECtHR did not elaborate on this point since the responding Government even failed to proof a 'reasonable foundation' (i.e., the more lenient standard) for the difference in treatment between groups of refugees (see at para. 52–54).

507 ECtHR, *Bah v. UK*, Appl. no. 56328/07, Judgment of 27 September 2011, at para. 47; the Court expressly noted that the applicant was not granted refugee status. See also ECtHR, *M.A. v. Denmark*, Appl. no. 6697/18, Grand Chamber Judgment of 9 July 2021, at para. 145.

508 This conclusion is supported by T. Gordzielik, *Sozialhilfe im Asylbereich: Zwischen Migrationskontrolle und menschenwürdiger Existenzsicherung* (2020), at 114–115.

509 CJEU, Cases C-443/14 and C-444/14, *Alo and Osso* (EU:C:2016:127), at para. 32; Case C-720/17, *Bilali* (EU:C:2019:448), at para. 55.

510 Cf. CJEU, Case C-662/17, *E.G. v. Slovenia* (EU:C:2018:847), at para. 42.

thodox approach to refugee protection, which tends to privilege refugees as defined in the Geneva Refugee Convention. This policy choice is even more marked since the reform of the Qualification Directive in 2011.[511] The central point of the new approach is that subsidiary protection is not characterized by a less urgent or otherwise reduced need for protection, which would potentially translate into an inferior asylum status.[512] Rather, subsidiary protection in the EU is based on other Human Rights-based grounds of protection and thus complements and adds to the protection of refugees enshrined in the Geneva Refugee Convention.[513] On the other hand, the traditional approach lingers on in certain provisions of the Qualification Directive and in the exemption from the scope of the Family Reunification Directive. According to this view, which is still prevalent within certain Member States, subsidiary protection is a secondary form of protection that goes beyond of what is required under international refugee law and is thus marked by a higher degree of discretion on the part of States and, consequently, by a less comprehensive set of rights for the beneficiaries. The regulations under review here, on family reunification and social assistance, are prime examples of the latter approach. The EU legislature has chosen to partially maintain this discretion, even at the cost of laying down contradictory policy choices.

However, in order for the resulting difference in treatment to be in line with Art. 14 ECHR (and Art. 21(1) EU-CFR), there must be a reasonable relationship of proportionality between the means employed and the aim sought to be realized. In other words, there must be objective reasons (in our view: very weighty reasons) demonstrating that the different status accorded to beneficiaries of subsidiary protection is reasonably related to the different grounds of protection that distinguish them from Convention refugees. We would like to recall that the different status under interna-

511 For a detailed analysis, see Bauloz and Ruiz, 'Refugee Status and Subsidiary Protection: Towards a Uniform Content of International Protection?', in V. Chetail, Ph. de Bruycker and F. Maiani (eds), *Reforming the Common European Asylum System: The New European Refugee Law* (2016) 240.

512 Hasel and Salomon, 'Differenzierungen zwischen Flüchtlingen und subsidiär Schutzberechtigen: Zu einem einheitlichen Schutzstatus', in St. Salomon (ed.), *Der Status im europäischen Asylrecht* (2020) 113, at 147–152, discussing the relevant arguments in legal scholarship.

513 Bast, 'Vom subsidiären Schutz zum europäischen Flüchtlingsbegriff', *Zeitschrift für Ausländerrecht (ZAR)* (2018) 41.

tional law as such does not suffice to justify the difference in treatment (see above, section 4.2.3).[514]

A single argument stands out as having the potential to demonstrate such reasonable relationship: the claim that subsidiary protection is of a more temporary nature than the protection of Convention refugees. Indeed, were subsidiary protection status conceived as a provisional status, as opposed to a more permanent refugee status, it would be plausible that Member States should have a higher degree of discretion to limit access to social assistance or postpone family reunification, although an individual assessment of the applicant's situation would be required anyway. This point has been made, inter alia, by the Austrian Constitutional Court in its evaluation of the relevant provisions of Austrian law in light of Art. 14 ECtHR.[515]

However, this argument was met with convincing critique.[516] First, the assumption that a change of circumstances in the country of origin is more likely in cases of the real risk of serious harm that led to the granting of subsidiary protection (such as civil war or systematic torture) in comparison with cases of a well-founded fear of persecution that led to recognition as a refugee, has until now not been sufficiently supported empirically.[517] Second, there is no compelling normative argument that subsidiary protection status, according to the conception of the EU legislature, is characterized by distinct temporality. Such construction of the Qualification Directive seems unduly influenced by national statuses of complementary protection, i.e., precisely the traditional approach not

---

514 See, again, ECtHR, *Hode and Abdi v. UK*, Appl. no. 22341/09, Judgment of 6 November 2012, at para. 55. The only difference that finds a strong explanation in international law is Art. 25 of the Qualification Directive on travel documents.

515 Verfassungsgerichtshof, E 3297/2016 (Erkenntnis of 28 June 2017, re minimum benefit system), at para. 21–22; VfGH, E 4248–4251/2017–20 (Erkenntnis of 10 October 2018, re family reunification), at para. 47.

516 Council of Europe: Commissioner for Human Rights, *Realising the right to family reunification of refugees in Europe* (2017), at 25–26 and 47; UNHCR, *Summary Conclusions on the Right to Family Life and Family Unity in the Context of Family Reunification of Refugees and Other Persons In Need Of International Protection* (2017), at 32; from legal scholarship, see, e.g., Immervoll and Frühwirth, 'Statusdifferenzierungen in der Familienzusammenführung', in St. Salomon (ed.), *Der Status im europäischen Asylrecht* (2020) 161, at 183.

517 See Hasel and Salomon, 'Differenzierungen zwischen Flüchtlingen und subsidiär Schutzberechtigen', in St. Salomon (ed.), *Der Status im europäischen Asylrecht* (2020) 113, at 153.

taken by the EU legislature. At first glance, the difference in respect of the validity of the first residence permit (three years for refugees, one year for beneficiaries of subsidiary protection, according to Art. 24 of the Qualification Directive) seems to provide evidence to the contrary. However, this argument apparently overlooks the fact that all persons enjoying international protection are entitled to have their residence permit renewed, as long as the need for protection persists. The relevant provisions on the cessation of the protection status are literally drafted in parallel (Art. 11 and 16 Qualification Directive). Moreover, both groups are entitled to the status of long-term residents according to exactly the same conditions (see Directive 2003/109/EC, as amended by Directive 2011/51/EU). Accordingly, the claim that the difference in treatment has a reasonable foundation in a more temporary nature of subsidiary protection must be rejected.

In sum, there is no objective justification for the difference in treatment between refugees and persons enjoying subsidiary protection, in respect of either social assistance or family reunification. Accordingly, these instances of non-equal treatment amount to a violation of Art. 14 ECHR.

The resultant legal question is: what level of European governance must provide for equal treatment – the EU legislature or the Member States? Usually, the answer to such a question is rather straightforward: the level of governance that has caused the Human Rights violation is responsible for remedying the situation. In the present instance, however, the responsibility is shared. The unlawful discrimination against persons enjoying subsidiary protection occurs in a situation of partial and underinclusive regulation by the EU legislature, on the one hand, and practices and regulations on the part of the Member States that are seemingly permitted (social assistance) or not covered (family reunification) by EU law, on the other hand. In other words, the problematic non-equal treatment is the result of the current distribution of legislative powers in the multi-level system of European migration governance.

This is a well-known problem of federal systems, which tend to produce, and constitutionally accept, non-equal treatment of comparable situations whenever the federal level has only partly exercised its shared legislative powers (or is not competent to legislate at all). In the context of EU law, this issue is familiar from internal market law that, at times, creates 'reverse discrimination' against national entities, which is not regarded as unlawful. Examples from the field of migration include family reunification where the sponsor is an EU national who has not exercised his or her freedom of movement.[518]

However, we argue that this doctrine of reverse discrimination does not apply to persons enjoying international protection in the EU. The crucial difference here is that both the EU and its Member States have legally committed themselves to observe the Human Rights standards defined by the ECHR. From the 'outside' perspective of the ECHR, the distribution of powers between the EU and its Members is not a valid argument to justify discrimination caused by disparate decisions between the two levels. Both are simultaneously obliged to provide for equal treatment of persons in analogous situations, each within their respective scope of powers. This view finds additional support in the ECtHR judgment in *Hode and Abdi v. UK*, where the Court explicitly rejected the argument that an international obligation to grant certain rights to one group of persons could justify denying these rights to another group.[519]

Applying this doctrine to the present case of persons enjoying international protection, we hold that the EU Member States are legally bound to immediately accord non-discriminatory treatment to persons protected on subsidiary grounds in respect of social assistance and family reunification, even if the EU legislature has so far failed to establish statutory obligations to this effect. This obligation follows from international law and, in the case of social assistance, from EU constitutional law.

In respect of the EU itself, it is more difficult to argue that a positive obligation to legislate to this effect exists, given that the EU is not a party to the ECHR and that the EU is constitutionally entitled to pursue an incremental approach to establishing the Common European Asylum System (Art. 78(1) TFEU).[520] For an interim period, this necessarily implies that certain elements of the system are only partly governed by EU law, including the asylum status (Art. 78(2)(a) and (b) TFEU). However, the EU legislature must refrain from adding to the disparities that already stem from the absence of full harmonization of national legislation, and work toward a comprehensive system.[521] Accordingly, we hold that it is unlawful, from a constitutional point of view, to maintain a situation of

---

518 See A. Walter, *Reverse Discrimination and Family Reunification* (2008).

519 ECtHR, *Hode and Abdi v. UK*, Appl. no. 22341/09, Judgment of 6 November 2012, at para. 55.

520 See, mutatis mutandis, CJEU, Case C-193/94, *Skanavi* (EU:C:1996:70), at para. 27; Case C-233/94, *Germany v. Parliament and Council* (EU:C:1997:231), at para. 43.

521 See, mutatis mutandis, CJEU, Case 41/84, *Pinna* (EU:C:1986:1), at para. 21.

underinclusive legislation in respect of the asylum status, a situation that in effect leads to a violation of the prohibition of discrimination based on immigration status.

4.3 Recommendations

Recommendation 1: Systematically ensure non-discrimination regarding social assistance

We recommend that the EU systematically review its asylum and immigration *acquis* to ensure that any distinctions between immigration statuses defined in EU law are based on objective and reasonable justification as required by Art. 14 ECHR, in order to ensure non-discrimination among these persons. The above legal analysis revealed that non-equal treatment in respect of social assistance is a critical case in point. For most categories of migrants, whose immigration status is (partly) defined by EU law, the EU legislature apparently permits Member States to deny access to social assistance entirely or to limit the assistance to 'core benefits'. The lack of guidance provided by this 'underinclusive legislation' invites the Member State to apply arbitrary distinctions and issue unlawful decisions in individual cases. We therefore recommend that the EU enact, as a minimum guarantee, a right to equal treatment in respect of social assistance necessary to ensure a decent existence for all migrants present in the Union for more than 90 days.

In order to prepare for comprehensive reform, the European Commission should conduct a systematic review of the asylum and immigration *acquis* to identify non-justified sectoral differentiation created by the EU legislature, including distinctions exclusively based on nationality. Any distinction that fails to meet the test enshrined in Art. 14 ECHR must be eliminated. This pertains, inter alia, to difference in treatment in respect of family reunification, social welfare, health care, access to the labor market, and mobility within the Union. Such review should result, where appropriate, in initiatives to revise existing legislation, including most notably the Qualification Directive (see Recommendation 2).

We further recommend that the Commission conduct a systematic review of Member States' laws and policies making use of optional clauses or derogations that allow for less favorable treatment of third-country nationals. The Commission should institute, where appropriate, infringement proceedings according to Art. 258 TFEU, and/or propose amendments to

EU legislation that currently provides for discretion on the part of the Member States, in all cases where the review reveals that such discretion leads in practice to violations of Human Rights law.

Recommendation 2: Eliminate any discrimination among persons granted international protection

We recommend that the EU exercise its legislative and supervisory powers to ensure that any discrimination among persons granted international protection in respect of their immigration status is eliminated, most notably regarding family reunification. Upholding the current situation of non-regulation of family reunification where the sponsor enjoys subsidiary protection status would violate Art. 21(1) EU-CFR.

As to the means of achieving that aim, the EU should accord a uniform asylum status defined in EU legislation. More specifically, all beneficiaries of international protection must be granted the same rights in respect of family reunification and access to social welfare, including social assistance. Such an approach would transpose existing legal obligations of Member States under Human Rights law onto parallel obligations under statutory EU law. Accordingly, we recommend deleting Art. 3(2)(c) and amending Art. 9 to 12 of the Family Reunification Directive, and deleting Art. 29(2) of the Qualification Directive, in order to establish a uniform asylum status for all persons enjoying international protection in the EU.

Pending such amendments, EU Member States are obliged, by virtue of Art. 14 ECHR, to apply the same legal regime in respect of the right to family reunification to refugees and persons eligible for subsidiary protection. In effect, Member States participating in the Area of Freedom, Security and Justice must grant the rights laid down in Chapter V of the Family Reunification Directive (Art. 9–12) to beneficiaries of subsidiary protection as defined in the Qualification Directive.

In respect of the right to social assistance, EU Member States are obliged, by virtue of Art. 14 ECHR and Art. 20(1) EU-CFR, to apply the same legal regime to Convention refugees and persons eligible for subsidiary protection. The possibility of limiting such assistance to core benefits pursuant to Art. 29(2) of the Qualification Directive is rendered inapplicable by EU fundamental rights. We recommend that the Commission conduct a systematic review of the relevant laws and policies of those Member States relying on Art. 29(2) of the Qualification Directive and, where appropriate, institute infringement proceedings according to Art. 258 TFEU.

Recommendation 3: Follow a legislative approach guided by the 'Leitbild' of status equality

As regards future legislation in migration law, we recommend that the EU follow a horizontal approach, in order to avoid creating new, potentially non-justified distinctions among immigration statuses. The EU should be guided by the *Leitbild* of status equality that serves as a template for the status of all third-country nationals residing in the EU.

Such an approach would not only foster consistency of legislative outcomes but also provide for conformity with the principle of non-discrimination. Defining such a *Leitbild* obviously involves political choices that are not determined by Human Rights law. The logical starting point for such determinations is the privileged status of migrants who are Union citizens. While Human Rights law does not necessarily require that the EU accord third-country nationals the same set of rights as Union citizens, the latter could nevertheless serve as a point of reference for the model immigration status of third-country nationals, in particular in respect of equal treatment in all fields governed by EU law and the freedom of movement within Union territory. Where legal and political discourse reveals that distinctions between EU citizens and non-citizens are supported by objective and reasonable justification, the status of a long-term resident as defined in the Long-Term Residents Directive could serve as secondary point of reference, providing the template for the 'general status' of third-country nationals residing in the EU.

Any deviation from this dual template should relate to the specific nature of the class of migrants at issue, in particular the purpose of admission to the EU, and to the specific right at hand. On a procedural level, the EU legislature should include explicit equality reasoning in the preamble to every new act, providing the reasons for which the immigration status of a particular class of migrants deviates from the templates.

Chapter 5 – Preserving Social and Family Ties

There is an obvious tension between, on the one hand, the interest of migrants to maintain and develop family and other social ties in the place of their residence and, on the other hand, the selective logic of States' migration governance. States may refuse to admit certain members of the migrant's family, thus hampering or rendering impossible a normal family life. States may also sever the family and other social ties developed in the host State by adopting measures to terminate a person's stay. The tensions are more pronounced the closer the ties, and the more vulnerable the migrants (e.g., children or refugees). The conflict seems almost irreconcilable when an irregular migrant claims a right to maintain their social ties in the host country, since this could only be achieved by way of regularizing his or her status.

The EU legislature has addressed these tensions in the two legislative projects that mark the very beginning of the EU's legislative activity in the field of immigration: Directive 2003/86/EC on the right to family reunification (the FR Directive) and Directive 2003/109/EC concerning the status of third-country nationals who are long-term residents (the LTR Directive). The 2003 Directives responded to the ECtHR's jurisprudence on Art. 8 ECHR, developed in the 1990s (see section 5.2.1, below), and the related political deliberations in the political bodies of the Council of Europe. These fora helped developing common ground for the 12 Member States originally participating in the EU's newly proclaimed Area of Freedom, Security and Justice.[522] Human Rights discourse in the Council of Europe thus formed the natural point of reference for the EU legislature.

In the FR Directive, the EU vested certain third-country nationals with an enforceable individual right to reunite in the host state with the members of their core family, subject to certain conditions that the sponsor and the family members must meet. In addition, refugee sponsors (in the narrow sense defined in the Geneva Refugee Convention) benefit from a privileged regime that waives some of these requirements. However, members of the wider family – such as the parents of adult sponsors, or

522 See Groenendijk, 'Long-term Immigrants and the Council of Europe', in E. Guild and P. Minderhoud (eds), *Security of Residence and Expulsion* (2001) 7.

siblings – are subject to discretionary decision-making by the Member States.

The LTR Directive also provides certain third-country nationals with an enforceable right to achieve an immigration status defined by the EU legislature. LTR status includes a wide range of rights, similar to those enjoyed by EU citizens. It can thus be classified as a denizenship – that is, a status that resembles the membership usually associated with the nationality of the host state.[523] In respect of security of residence, holders of LTR status benefit from reinforced protection against expulsion. This status element makes it less likely that the person will be subject to measures disrupting social ties developed in the host country, although the Directive falls short of laying down an absolute ban on expulsions.

Regarding irregular migrants, the EU legislature has thus far failed to recognize a legitimate interest in maintaining and developing such ties. On the contrary, not only are they excluded from the scope of the 2003 Directives, but irregular migrants are also subject to 'Directive 2008/115/EC on common standards and procedures for returning illegally staying third-country nationals' (the Return Directive). The Return Directive obliges Member States, as a rule, to conduct and expeditiously complete a procedure terminating the irregular residence of the migrant concerned.[524]

The political compromises laid down in the 2003 Directives still form the legal framework within which EU Member State practice unfolds. The only major development after that initial period was the decision, in 2011, to include all persons entitled to international protection into the scope of the LTR Directive.[525] In all other respects, the Commission made the choice *not* to propose a 'recast' of the FR Directive and the LTR Directive, despite ample indications that the discretion left to the Member States does give rise to Human Rights conflicts in light of Art. 8 ECHR. Moreover, to date the Commission has not returned to the earmarked legislative item to define a privileged regime for family reunification of persons enti-

523 Acosta Arcarazo, 'Civic Citizenship Reintroduced: The Long-Term Residence Directive as a Post-National Form of Membership', 21 *European Law Journal* (2015) 21; Bast, 'Denizenship als rechtliche Form der Inklusion in eine Einwanderungsgesellschaft', *Zeitschrift für Ausländerrecht (ZAR)* (2013) 353; for a narrower concept, see Thym, 'Vom "Fremdenrecht" über die "Denizenship" zur "Bürgerschaft"', 57 *Der Staat* (2018) 77.

524 CJEU, Case C-38/14, *Zaizoune* (EU:C:2015:260), at para. 31–32, 34.

525 Previously, only refugees as defined in the Geneva Refugee Convention but not persons entitled to subsidiary protection as defined in the Qualification Directive were eligible.

tled to subsidiary protection (see above, Chapter 4). The Commission does not intend to address Human Rights-based claims of irregular migrants, either, as evidenced by its 2018 proposal for a recast Return Directive.[526]

Despite this reluctance to complete and adapt the legislative framework protecting the family and social ties of migrants, the EU has occupied these subfields of migration policy to such an extent that it is henceforth accountable for any deviation from the relevant Human Rights standards. As we will demonstrate in the following sections, some of the gaps in the present framework can be closed by construing the relevant instrument in conformity with EU fundamental rights, which mirror Human Rights; others require further legislative activity by the EU.

5.1 Structural challenges and current trends

Trend 1: Requirements of socio-cultural integration are used to deny family reunification

We observe that several Member States have established, and are consistently applying, requirements of socio-cultural integration that are aimed at family members seeking to join the sponsor. Such requirements also take the form of pre-entry conditions – that is, legal requirements for admission that are examined before entering the country. The respective policies may have the effect that family reunification takes place only after a long waiting period, or is frustrated entirely.

Restrictive policies toward family migration are currently particularly salient with respect to reunification claims made by people seeking or enjoying international protection in the EU. We discuss these policies elsewhere in the study – in particular, from the angle of non-discrimination (see Chapter 4). However, there seems to be a consistent pattern of restrictive policies toward 'ordinary' migrants as well. Integration requirements play a vital role in this regard.[527]

---

526 European Commission, Proposal for a recast Return Directive, COM(2018) 634, 12 September 2018.

527 Goodman, 'Controlling Immigration Through Language and Country Knowledge Requirements', 34 *West European Politics* (2011) 235; see, e.g., K. de Vries, *Integration at the Border: The Dutch Act on Integration Abroad and International Immigration Law* (2013), chapter 2, on Dutch integration policy.

Within the framework of the FR Directive, imposing certain integration measures is explicitly permitted. Member States may adopt them pursuant to Art. 7(2) of the Directive.[528] They constitute optional requirements for exercising the right to family reunification, which complement the mandatory requirements of socio-economic integration laid down in other provisions in respect of the sponsor or the family member. Several Member States have used that discretion and require some kind of (pre- or post-departure) integration measures.[529] Language tests are a typical tool. Other measures include testing the migrant's knowledge about the State's legal and political system, or a pledge to respect the social habits of the host country as part of an 'integration contract' signed by the newly arriving migrant.[530]

Most of the requirements laid down in national law had not been in place when the FR Directive was adopted in 2003.[531] This reflects a general policy trend in EU Member States (and beyond) to defend established 'cultural compromises' of the host societies in view of increased ethnic and religious diversity.[532] The rise of socio-cultural integration requirements is seen as expressing legitimate expectations directed at migrants to adjust themselves to the dominant culture of the host society. In other words,

528 For an early account, see K. Groenendijk, R. Fernhout, D. van Dam, R. van Oers and T. Strik, *The Family Reunification Directive in the EU Member States: The First Year of Implementation* (2007) 27–28.

529 As of 2019: AT, BE, CZ, DE, EE, FR, LV, NL, SE, as well as DK and UK (which were by then already not bound by the Directive). See European Commission, Report on the implementation of Directive 2003/86/EC, COM(2019) 162, 29 March 2019, at 7–9. The Report was based on a study by the European Migration Network, see EMN, *Synthesis Report: Family Reunification of Third-Country Nationals in the EU plus Norway: National Practices* (2017), Migrapol EMN Doc 382.

530 For details, see S. Carrera, *In Search of the Perfect Citizen? The Intersection between Integration, Immigration and Nationality in the EU* (2009) 291–349; Groenendijk, 'Pre-departure Integration Strategies in the European Union: Integration or Immigration Policies?', 13 *European Journal of Migration and Law (EJML)* (2011) 1.

531 Strumia, 'European Citizenship and EU Immigration', 22 *European Law Journal* (2016) 417, at 431, providing references to France, Italy, Austria, Luxembourg, and the Netherlands.

532 On the role of 'cultural compromises' in immigration contexts, see Zolberg and Long, 'Why Islam Is Like Spanish: Cultural Incorporation in Europe and the United States', 27 *Politics & Society* (1999) 5; J. Bast, *Aufenthaltsrecht und Migrationssteuerung* (2011) 100–101.

they serve as a means of implementing assimilationist policies.[533]Though such policies are usually formulated in non-discriminatory terms, in practice they produce inequitable results due to the heterogeneity in the migrant population in terms of linguistic and cultural backgrounds.[534]Moreover, testing a defined level of 'knowledge' is inherently biased against migrants with limited access to education, particularly when the test must be performed before entering the country. Studies have shown that 'civic integration' testing has a chilling effect irrespective of the contents of the tests, which may conform with liberal or republican values.[535] In some cases, the very purpose of the measures is apparently to prevent 'unwanted' immigrants from entering the country in the first place. In fact, restrictionist measures taken by the Member States today are often legally shaped and politically justified in the language of 'integration'.[536] Arguably, this is also an indirect effect of the entry into force of the FR Directive, which narrows the scope for other, more overtly restrictionist policies in the field of family migration.

In sum, while the FR Directive aims to protect the family ties of migrants, its optional requirements for socio-cultural integration enable policies that effectively thwart family reunifications. Hence, the task of this chapter is to identify the Human Rights limits to such restrictionist policies.

Trend 2: Settled migrants are subject to security-driven policies of expulsions

In recent years there has been a new wave of expulsions specifically targeting elements of the migrant population perceived as an inherent threat to public security, mainly in the context of counter-terrorist measures or in response to public demands to be 'tough' on criminal foreigners.

533 On normative justifications of the 'culture defense' of collective/national identity, see L. Orgad, *The Cultural Defense of Nations: A Liberal Theory of Majority Rights* (2015).

534 E. Pochon-Berger and P. Lenz, *Language Requirements and Language Testing for Immigration and Integration Purposes: A Synthesis of Academic Literature* (2014) 20–21.

535 R. van Oers, *Deserving Citizenship: Citizenship Tests in Germany, the Netherlands and the United Kingdom* (2014) 275–277.

536 L. Block, *Policy Frames on Spousal Migration in Germany: Regulating Membership, Regulating the Family* (2016) 309–318.

Particularly alarming in this context is the fact that policies of expulsion are applied to settled migrants – that is, persons who immigrated long ago or were born in the country and may not even identify themselves as 'migrants'.[537]

And yet, as long as a settled migrant has not obtained the nationality of the host state, he or she is potentially subject to an order to leave the territory according to the traditional rules of Public International Law. Policing and, if necessary, expelling 'dangerous aliens' have always been features of States' policies toward migrants, even in periods in which they adopted fairly liberal admission policies.[538] From a long-term perspective, the combined effects of national constitutional law, Human Rights law, and EU legislation have substantially curtailed States' powers to expel unwanted foreigners, establishing both procedural and substantive limits to that power (on the procedural guarantees, see Chapter 3).[539]

More recently, however, the securitization of migration discourse[540] has triggered a backlash against a rights-based approach to expulsion, including in the Union. Expulsion has re-emerged as a policy tool in its own right, rather than being an instrument addressing the situation of individual migrants. The loss by members of targeted groups of a regular immigration status, and the ensuing enforcement of the duty to leave the country, are defined as policy goals in themselves.[541] Securitized policies of expulsion take different shapes and forms. As far as settled migrants are concerned, they mainly unfold on the level of the Member States and primarily affect, it appears, migrants who do not benefit from enhanced protection provided by EU law. Unfortunately, reliable data on actual expulsions by Member State authorities are difficult to obtain, particularly since a change in practice is not necessarily accompanied by a change in laws. Using case-law as evidence, there is a trend toward intensification of

537 Cf. the attribute 'post-migrant' used in academic literature; see Foroutan, 'Was will eine postmigrantische Gesellschaftsanalyse?', in N. Foroutan, J. Karakayali and R. Spielhaus (eds), *Postmigrantische Perspektiven* (2018) 269.

538 J. Bast, *Aufenthaltsrecht und Migrationssteuerung* (2011) 80.

539 D. Thym, *Migrationsverwaltungsrecht* (2010) 197–211.

540 J. Huysmans, *The Politics of Insecurity* (2006) 45–62; Karamanidou, 'The Securitisation of European Migration Policies: Perceptions of Threat and Management of Risk', in G. Lazaridis and K. Wadia (eds), *The Securitisation of Migration in the EU: Debates Since 9/11* (2015) 37.

541 Gibney, 'Asylum and the Expansion of Deportation in the United Kingdom', 43 *Government and Opposition* (2008) 146.

expulsions 'on the ground' that has not faced resistance from the courts.[542] Our impression is that the authorities have learned to speak the language of 'balancing', while the result is pre-determined by schemes that normalize expulsions. To this effect, States have established catalogs of serious offenses or other deviant behavior that entail, as a rule, an expulsion order being issued.[543]

Such security-driven policies target specific groups of the migrant population that have been identified in public discourse as inherently 'dangerous'. Two partly overlapping groups stand out in this regard.

First, expulsion policies in the Union specifically target members of Muslim communities. While these policies must be placed in the wider context of rising Islamophobia, they specifically emerged as part of the fight against militant jihadism, including in its most violent, terrorist forms.[544] However, the use of expulsion measures for the purposes of counter-terrorism fails to recognize the fact that such threats are, to a large extent, 'home-grown' – that is, the relevant processes of radicalization took place in the midst of our society. Such measures at times focus on prominent individuals susceptible of spreading jihadist ideologies ('hate preachers').[545] In other instances, migrants are labeled as 'dangerous persons' (*Gefährder*, in the language of German legal discourse) without compelling evidence of an actual threat to public security, connecting to lawful behavior such as worshiping in certain mosques or being member of a non-violent group of Islamists.[546] Note that expelling 'dangerous'

---

542 E.g., German courts have confirmed that expulsion may be ordered on general preventive grounds – that is, with a view to deterring other migrants – even under the new law introduced in 2016 that was meant to bring Germany in line with the ECtHR's jurisprudence. See K. Bode, *Das neue Ausweisungsrecht* (2020) 189 et seq.; J.-R. Albert, *Gefahrenprognose im Ausweisungsrecht nach strafrechtlicher Verurteilung* (2020).

543 On Spanish expulsion law and practice until recently, see the summary in CJEU, Case C-636/16, *López Pastuzano* (EU:C:2017:949), at para. 5–10 and 15; see also the extensive list of crimes which constitute, pursuant to Art. 54(1) of the German Residence Act, an 'especially serious public interest in expelling the foreigner', which weighs heavily in the balancing process. The list was last expanded in 2019.

544 Volpp, 'The Citizen and the Terrorist', in C. A. Choudhury and K. A. Beydoun (eds), *Islamophobia and the Law* (2020) 19.

545 A. Kießling, *Die Abwehr terroristischer und extremistischer Gefahren durch Ausweisung* (2012) 32–47.

546 E.g., according to Sec. 58a(1) German Residence Act, a 'deportation order' (*Abschiebungsanordnung*) that is immediately enforceable may be issued to avert 'a special threat to the security of the Federal Republic of Germany or a terrorist

persons is usually not ordered by a criminal court following a conviction (which would imply a higher standard of proof and enhanced procedural guarantees) but, rather, relies on information gathered by administrative authorities, including intelligence agencies.[547]

Second, policies of intensified and more systematic use of expulsion are directed at criminal offenders, in particular juveniles or young adults. Such policies must be situated against the background of the demographics of many immigration societies in Europe, which are marked by large segments who were born and have grown up in the host country but who remain non-citizens, not least due to restrictive citizenships laws. These settled migrants typically have developed strong connection to their country of residence. Much like their siblings with a 'native' passport, a few of these non-citizens fall foul of the law and end up being convicted by the criminal courts, some of them repeatedly. Here is where expulsion policies come into play. Criminal offenders who are non-nationals are not only subject to criminal sanction but also to the threat of being expelled following a conviction. From the perspective of a settled migrant, the latter may even be the more severe sanction.

While legal instruments to remove 'criminal aliens' are part of immigration law's DNA, the relevant legislative frameworks and administrative practices vary significantly over time and space. More restrictive expulsion policies toward migrant offenders emerge in waves, as evidenced by the clusters of cases that have reached the European Courts. Suffice it to mention the French Government targeting of juvenile offenders of Maghreb

---

threat'. The law merely requires the order to be 'based on the assessment of facts'. See Berlit, 'Umgang mit Gefährdern im Aufenthaltsrecht', *Zeitschrift für Ausländerrecht (ZAR)* (2018) 89.

547 The above policies are complemented by policies to deprive 'dangerous' citizens of their nationality. While in some Member States the deprivation of citizenship was on the rise for quite a while (see S. Mantu, *Contingent Citizenship: The Law and Practice of Citizenship Deprivation in International, European and National Perspectives* (2015) 173 et seq.), such measures have become more widespread after the fall of the Khalifate (the 'Islamic State') in Syria. Withdrawing the nationality of a person subjects him or her to expulsion measures or re-entry bans in the first place, measures which are not available vis-à-vis a country's own nationals. While policies of citizenship deprivation technically do not distinguish between migrants and non-migrants, they disproportionately concern naturalized citizens and persons holding more than one nationality, of whom many are actually (former) migrants; see Meijers Committee, *Policy Brief on 'Differential treatment of citizens with dual or multiple nationality and the prohibition of discrimination'* (CM2016), 6 December 2020, at 5–9.

origin in the late 1980s,[548] or the attempt of German *Länder* to get 'tough' on young Turkish migrants in the early 2000s that was eventually blocked by the CJEU.[549] Currently, Denmark seems to have taken the lead in more systematically resorting to such policies.[550] Overall, there are indications that a new wave of more restrictive policies is building across Europe. Policy-makers are more often, and more systematically, resorting to expulsion as a means to address criminal behavior, irrespective of its literally 'home-grown' nature.

As we discuss in more detail below, these patterns and trends in expulsion cause tensions with the ECtHR's jurisprudence, as the Strasbourg Court always requires that an individual decision be taken that balances all relevant factors, including the social ties developed in the country of residence. Hence, the re-emergence of a systematic policy of expelling settled migrants as a means to provide 'security' constitutes an important challenge to the EU's accountability for compliance with Human Rights in the field of migration.

Trend 3: Efforts to enforce irregular migrants' return disregard their social and family ties

Perhaps the most crucial challenge to Human Rights compliance in this field is migrants with an irregular immigration status ('illegally staying third-country nationals', in the language of the Return Directive). Both at the EU level and on the level of the Member States, we observe increased efforts to enforce the 'duty to leave' against irregular migrants, either by way of removing obstacles to deportation or by fostering voluntary returns. In this context, a persistent pattern of disregarding the social and family ties of irregular migrants seems to exist.

---

548 See the facts of the cases ECtHR, *Djeroud v. France*, Appl. no. 13446/87, Decision of 23 January 1991; *Beldjoudi v. France*, Appl. no. 12083/86, Judgment of 26 March 1992; *Nasri v. France*, Appl. no. 19465/92, Judgment of 13 July 1995; *Boughanemi v. France*, Appl. no. 22070/93, Judgment of 24 April 1996.

549 Case C-467/02, *Cetinkaya* (EU:C:2004:708); Case C-373/03, *Aydinli* (EU:C:2005:434); Case C-502/04, *Torun* (EU:C:2006:112).

550 See ECtHR, *Munir Johana v. Denmark*, Appl. no. 56803/18, and *Kahn v. Denmark*, Appl. no. 26957/19, Judgments of 12 January 2021. Both cases concerned the expulsion, following repeated convictions, of a person who had been living legally for decades in Denmark. The first applicant was born in 1994 in Denmark; the second applicant came to live there in 1990 at the age of four.

The reinforced return policies in the Union focus particularly on rejected asylum seekers, although the 'deportation turn' that has taken place in the early 2000s has a broader scope.[551] The toolbox of the EU's return policies comprises a wide range of measures, including readmission agreements with third countries that are conditioned by the EU's concessions in terms of aid and visa facilitation.[552] The alternative method of terminating illegal stay – namely, through regularization of the person concerned – is increasingly discouraged and, in any case, not systematically considered a policy option.[553]

Establishing the distinction between legal and illegal stay on state territory, between wanted and unwanted foreigners, is one of the fundamentals of immigration law.[554] Effectively enforcing this distinction is an entirely different matter. Although States are empowered to use force for that purpose – that is, to conduct deportations, or 'removals', as the EU prefers to call them – many obstacles can and do arise. The authorities may not be aware of the person being present in the first place. Even if he or she is under their effective control, or is actually willing to cooperate with the return procedure, international law requires a degree of cooperation on the part of the country of destination. If the latter questions the duty to admit the deportee – be it for undetermined nationality, lack of proper documentation, insufficient means of transportation, or any other reason – the deportation must be stalled, potentially even indefinitely.[555] This inter-state principle of non-intervention opens up a space for agency on the part of irregular migrants and their advocates, who may intentionally create obstacles to deportation – much to the annoyance of the authorities and politicians who have promised to be more effective on returns.

551 Gibney, 'Asylum and the Expansion of Deportation in the United Kingdom', 43 *Government and Opposition* (2008) 146.

552 Morticelli, 'The External Dimension and the Management of Irregular Migration in the EU', in M. Kotzur et al. (eds), *The External Dimension of EU Migration and Asylum Policies* (2020) 59; Carli, 'Readmission Agreements as Tools for Fighting Irregular Migration: An Appraisal Twenty Years on from the Tampere European Council', *Freedom, Security & Justice: European Legal Studies* no. 1 (2019) 11.

553 K. F. Hinterberger, *Regularisierungen irregulär aufhältiger Migrantinnen und Migranten* (2020), at 143–146.

554 Bast, 'Zur Territorialität des Migrationsrechts', in F. von Harbou and J. Markow (eds), *Philosophie des Migrationsrechts* (2020) 17, at 21–25.

555 Ellermann, 'The Limits of Unilateral Migration Control: Deportation and Interstate Co-operation', 43 *Government and Opposition* (2008) 168.

But such practical difficulties are not the whole of the matter. Not infrequently, migrants have been staying illegally with full knowledge of the authorities, who tolerated their presence either de facto or de jure. Moreover, there exists a considerable number of bona fide irregular migrants who are legally entitled not to be deported, as to do so would constitute a violation of Human Rights. The causes of rights-based obstacles to deportation are manifold. They relate, for example, to the serious illness of the person concerned. Other irregular migrants may have a strong claim not to be deported based in the principle of non-refoulement, yet fail to meet all requirements to achieve the status of international protection in the EU. The present chapter is specifically concerned with legal obstacles to deportation that follow from the fact that irregular migrants tend to develop social ties in the host country, including family ties, which may be as strong as those of regular migrants.[556] This is particularly true in respect of irregular migrants who have been staying for extended periods.

EU legislation only vaguely addresses claims of 'non-removables' to respect their social ties developed in the country of residence, and their interest in living together with family members. Pursuant to the general terms of Art. 5 of the Return Directive, Member States 'shall take due account of' the best interest of the child and of family life when implementing the Directive. Note that social ties other than family are not mentioned in this Article. The Return Directive merely permits States not to enforce a final return decision due to 'specific circumstances of the individual case' (Art. 9(2) Return Directive), without setting a maximum time for the deferral of enforcement ('for an appropriate period').[557] Moreover, the Return Directive recognizes Member States' discretion to grant a regular immigration status 'at any moment' of the return procedure (Art. 6(4) Return Directive).[558]

In summary, EU law as it stands does not require a return decision to be withdrawn, or not to be issued in the first place, on the grounds of social or family ties in the country of residence. The ensuing legal evaluation will discuss the extent to which the claims of irregular migrants not to be

---

556 Cf. Farcy, 'Unremovability under the Return Directive: An Empty Protection?', in M. Moraru, G. Cornelisse and Ph. de Bruycker (eds), *Law and Judicial Dialogue on the Return of Irregular Migrants from the European Union* (2020) 437, at 442.

557 Cf. CJEU, Case C-546/19, *BZ* (EU:C:2021:432), at para. 59.

558 Ibid., at para. 57.

deported, and consequently claims to have their presence regularized, are supported by Human Rights law.[559]

5.2 Legal evaluation

5.2.1 General framework: protection of migrants' family and social ties

The rights to marry and found a family and to conduct a family life free of arbitrary interference are firmly protected in Human Rights law (see, *inter alia*, Art. 12 and 16 UDHR, Art. 17 and 23 ICCPR, and, regarding discrimination against women, Art. 16(1) CEDAW). However, Human Rights catalogs are more reticent in recognizing and protecting the specific interests of migrant families – that is, families partly or entirely composed of foreign nationals. Such interests include the choice of the place where family life is conducted and not to being separated by measures terminating a residence. As regards the latter, Human Rights law provides for certain guarantees against arbitrary expulsion (see, inter alia, Art. 13 ICCPR, Art. 22 ICRMW, Art. 4 Protocol No. 4 ECHR and Art. 1 Protocol No. 7 ECHR). None of these, however, explicitly recognizes family unity as a protected interest.

The UN Convention on the Rights of the Child (CRC) and the UN Migrant Workers Convention (ICRMW) stand out in this regard. The CRC states that, in order to ensure that a child shall not be separated from his or her parents against their will, applications for family reunifications 'shall be dealt with by States Parties in a positive, humane and expeditious manner' (Art. 10(1) CRC). The ICRMW is even more explicit in requiring States to 'take appropriate measures to ensure the protection of the unity of the families of [regular] migrant workers' (Art. 44(1) ICRMW) and 'to facilitate the reunification of [such] migrant workers with their spouses ... as well as with their minor dependent unmarried children' (Art. 44(2) ICRMW). Moreover, the ICRMW calls on State Parties intending to expel a regular migrant that 'account should be taken of humanitarian considerations and of the length of time that the person concerned has already resided in the State of employment' (Art. 56(3) ICRMW). These carefully circumscribed provisions demonstrate that a self-standing Human Right to respect the family unity of migrants has not yet gained recognition

559 In Chapter 6 we will discuss the Human Rights requirements relating to the status of those 'non-removables' during their stay in the EU.

in universal Human Rights law, even leaving aside the ICRMW's low number of ratifications from the Global North.[560] An important step in this direction is the commitment by UN Member States in the Global Compact for Migration to devise pathways for regular migration 'in a manner that upholds the right to family life' (GCM, Objective 5, para. 21), and, more specifically, 'to facilitate access to procedures for family reunification for migrants at all skills levels through appropriate measures that promote the realization of the right to family life' (para. 21, point i).

The remainder of this section will be focused on Art. 8 ECHR and the relevant case-law of the ECtHR, since a right to respect for the unity of migrant families has clearly emerged in the regional context of Europe. This jurisprudence is immediately relevant for the construction of Art. 7 EU-CFR, which literally mirrors Art. 8 ECHR (cf. Art. 52(3) EU-CFR).

A right to family unity first gained recognition in expulsion cases, especially in cases affecting second-generation immigrants – that is, descendants of post-colonial or labor migrants who came to live in Northern or Western Europe between the post-War era and the mid-1970s. Building on earlier decisions of the EComHR[561] and a pioneer judgment in 1988,[562] the ECtHR held that such expulsions interfere with the right to family laid down in Art. 8(1) ECHR.[563] The right to stay implied in this provision is not unconditional, being subject to the limitations set out in Art. 8(2) ECHR. The ECtHR has assumed a broad understanding of the public interests listed therein, including general economic considerations and requirements of effective migration control.[564] At the same time, however,

---

560 On the positive obligations of States to facilitate family reunifications, see V. Chetail, *International Migration Law* (2019) 124–132, and D. C. Schmitt, *Familienzusammenführung und Rechtsschutz in Deutschland und den USA: Eine rechtsvergleichende Betrachtung unter Berücksichtigung des Völker- und Europarechts* (2020) 29–54, each with references to scholarly opinions and jurisprudence of the relevant treaty bodies.

561 See, e.g., EComHR, *Alan, Khan und Singh v. UK*, Appl. no. 2991/66 and 2992/66, Decision of 15 July 1967; *X v. UK*, Appl. no. 9088/80, Decision of 6 March 1982; for discussion, see M. Caroni, *Privat- und Familienleben zwischen Menschenrecht und Migration* (1999) 210 et seq.

562 ECtHR, *Berrehab v. the Netherlands*, Appl. no. 10730/84, Judgment of 21 June 1988.

563 ECtHR, *Mustaquim v. Belgium*, Appl. no. 12313/86, Judgment of 18 February 1991; *Beldjoudi v. France*, Appl. no. 12083/86, Judgment of 26 March 1992; *Nasri v. France*, Appl. no. 19465/92, Judgment of 13 July 1995.

564 See, e.g., ECtHR, *Berrehab v. the Netherlands*, Appl. no. 10730/84, Judgment of 21 June 1988, at para. 26; on more recent case-law, see *Osman v. Denmark*, Appl.

the ECtHR has insisted that any interference with the right to family life must be 'necessary in a democratic society', meaning that a 'fair balance' must be struck between the private and public interests involved. In the course of the 1990s, the ECtHR consolidated this jurisprudence, which has now matured into settled case-law.[565] The cornerstone of this doctrine is that expulsion of a family member is lawful only if due consideration was given to all relevant circumstances of the individual case. To this effect, the ECtHR has established a list of criteria States must take into account, the so-called *Boultif/Üner* criteria, which include, among other things, the strength of the social and family ties that would be severed were the person forced to leave the host country.[566] Accordingly, the proportionality test required by Art. 8 ECHR has both a procedural and a substantive dimension, in that the authorities must conduct a complete assessment of the case and the resulting decision must be 'fair' in the eyes of the ECtHR.[567]

The jurisprudence of the ECtHR is similar in respect of claims to family reunification – that is, when the family member refers to Art. 8 ECHR in order to be authorized to enter the country and join the sponsor (who may or may not be a migrant him/herself).[568] In this context, however, the ECtHR usually accepts a higher degree of discretion on the part of the States (a 'margin of appreciation'), placing particular emphasis on the territorial jurisdiction of States that implies, under general international

no. 38058/09, Judgment of 14 June 2011, at para. 58; *J.M. v. Sweden*, Appl. no. 47509/13, Decision of 8 April 2014, at para. 40.

565 For a summary, see P. Boeles et al., *Public Policy Restrictions in EU Free Movement and Migration Law: General Principles and Guidelines* (2021) 19–23.

566 ECtHR, *Boultif v. Switzerland*, Appl. no. 54273/00, Judgment of 2 August 2001, at para. 48; *Üner v. the Netherlands*, Appl. no. 46410/99, Grand Chamber Judgment of 18 October 2006, at para. 57–58; *Maslov v. Austria*, Appl. no. 1638/03, Grand Chamber Judgment of 23 June 2008, at para. 68.

567 Commentators have observed a recent trend in ECtHR case-law toward a more process-based review, which accepts a wider margin of appreciation of national courts in making the substantive assessment; see Feihle, 'Asylum and Immigration under the European Convention on Human Rights: An Exclusive Universality?', in H.P. Aust and E. Demir-Gürsel (eds), *The European Court of Human Rights: Current Challenges in Historical Perspective* (2021) 133, at 153–155.

568 Given the complexities of migration laws and migrant biographies, it may anyway be difficult in practice to make the distinction between termination of stay and non-admission, e.g., in cases regarding claims to readmission, renewal of residence permits, or reunification of 'tolerated' migrants.

law, the power to refuse the admission of 'aliens'.[569] Regardless of this, the ECtHR recognizes that Art. 8 ECHR also entails positive obligations that may give rise to a well-founded claim to family reunification – that is, a right to admission to preserve or establish a normal family life. The 'fair balance' test conducted by the Court is essentially the same as in expulsion cases. Such a claim was first deemed well-founded in the *Sen* case (2001), which concerned minors in complex transnational family relations.[570] Further successful petitions were decided in the following years,[571] although it should be noted that in a large number of cases the Court dismissed the claims and referred to the margin of appreciation accorded to the Convention States.[572] Nonetheless, in order to lawfully reject an application for family reunification, States are under the two-fold obligation to conduct an individual assessment and to arrive at a substantially 'fair' decision.

In summary, the ECtHR's jurisprudence on Art. 8 ECHR has established a Human Right to family unity, which means a right to maintain or establish the unity of a migrant family.[573] This right is not an unconditional one but, rather, is subject to limitations for reasons of public policy that States may pursue while observing the principle of proportionality.

A more complicated issue concerns the extent to which migrants' social ties other than those established in the context of family relations are protected in Human Rights law. Universal Human Rights treaties are basically silent on the topic, apart from the vague references to 'humanitarian considerations' and the duration of residence in Art. 56(3) ICRMW. In this regard, the ECtHR was even more a pioneer than in relation to migrant families. In its case-law on Art. 8 ECHR, the Court has developed a far-reaching scope of protection based on the right to respect for one's private life.

---

569 ECtHR, *Abdulaziz, Cabales und Balkandali v. UK*, Appl. no. 9214/80, 9473/81 and 9474/81, at para. 67; *Ahmut v. the Netherlands*, Appl. no. 21702/93, Judgment of 28 November 1996, at para. 63.

570 ECtHR, *Sen v. the Netherlands*, Appl. no. 31465/96, Judgment of 21 December 2001.

571 ECtHR, *Tuquabo-Tekle v. the Netherlands*, Appl. no. 60665/00, Judgment of 1 December 2005; *Nolan and K. v. Russia*, Appl. no. 2512/04, Judgment of 12 February 2009, at para. 83 et seq.; recently, in the context of international protection, see ECtHR, *M.A. v. Denmark*, Appl. no. 6697/18, Grand Chamber Judgment of 9 July 2021.

572 M.-B. Dembour, *When Humans Become Migrants* (2015), at 122.

573 Cf. M.A.K. Klaassen, *The Right to Family Unification: Between Migration Control and Human Rights* (2015), at 95–97 and 378, highlighting the inconsistencies of the case-law.

Again, this approach has first come to the fore in the context of expulsions. Young adults from the second generation of immigrants represent the critical case. The scope of protection derived from the notion of 'family life' was, at times, too narrow to cover this group of settled migrants: While the family ties connecting them to their parents had typically weakened, they were sometimes too young to have established their own family. Nevertheless, their interest in staying in the country in which they were born or had received their primary education did not appear less legitimate than that of other settled migrants. Hence, the Court recognized that this interest may be covered by the notion of 'private life' which, according to the Court, is a broad concept that encompasses the right to establish and develop relationships with other human beings, including relationships of a professional or business nature.[574] Accordingly, any expulsions interfering with a migrant's 'private life' must meet the *Boultif/Üner* criteria. In most cases concerning second generation immigrants, however, the Court continued to refer to their 'family life' – or, in generic terms, to 'private and family life' – to trigger Art. 8 ECHR.[575]

The conceptual breakthrough to an independent Human Rights guarantee was eventually brought about by the *Slivenko* case decided in 2003. The Court held that the applicants, a family of Russian origin living in the newly independent Latvian Republic, were removed from the country where they had developed 'the network of personal, social and economic relations that make up the private life of every human being'.[576] Henceforth, the Court would consider the totality of social ties an essential aspect of the 'private life' of a person within the meaning of Art. 8(1) ECHR.[577] Thus, the interest of any migrant in staying in the country where such ties exist is protected by Human Rights – subject, of course, to the limitations set out in Art. 8(2) ECHR.

574 ECtHR, *C. (Chorfi) v. Belgium*, Appl. no. 21794/93, Judgment of 7 August 1996, at para. 25; from the more recent case-law, see ECtHR, *Pajic v. Croatia*, Appl. no. 68453/13, Judgment of 23 February 2016, at para. 61.

575 See, e.g., ECtHR, *Mehemi v. France*, Appl. no. 25017/94, Judgment of 26 September 1997, at para. 27; *Jakupovic v. Austria*, Appl. no. 36757/97, Judgment of 6 February 2003, at para. 22.

576 ECtHR, *Slivenko v. Latvia*, Appl. no. 48321/99, Grand Chamber Judgment of 9 October 2003, at para. 96.

577 ECtHR, *Onur v. UK*, Appl. no. 27319/07, Judgment of 17 February 2009, at para. 46; *Levakovic v. Denmark*, Appl. no. 7841/14, Judgment of 23 October 2018, at para. 34.

The premises and implications of this doctrine are still subject to discussion in legal scholarship. Some have argued that the doctrine applies only to a narrow category of migrants, who are defined by being 'de facto citizens' (*faktische Inländer*, in German) or by their 'rootedness' (*Verwurzelung*, a term widely used by German courts) after an extensive period of lawful stay.[578] We consider this a misrepresentation of the ECtHR's case-law, which does not reserve the protection of one's private life to a privileged class of migrants, even if this may have originally motivated the jurisprudence. The ECtHR's conceptual point of departure is the question of whether a 'private life' (as defined by the Court) de facto exists, irrespective of the migration history, immigration status or duration of stay of the person concerned.[579] Whether the migrant's interest in maintaining his or her social ties actually prevails must be settled by balancing all relevant factors, rather than by determining that he or she belongs to a predefined category for which such balancing was reserved in the first place. Accordingly, given that virtually all migrants will, after a certain period of stay, develop some kind of social ties in the host country, the ECtHR has recognized a (conditional) right to abode in all but name.[580]

5.2.2 Specific issue: integration requirements restricting family reunifications

(1) The above analysis revealed that States must always provide justification if they interfere with the right to family unity. Such justification requires striking a 'fair balance' between the private and public interests involved.

Applying this standard to integration requirements, there is no doubt that the ECtHR accepts 'ensuring effective integration' as a policy goal that serves public interests recognized in Art. 8(2) ECHR. In this context,

578 Cf. D. Thym, *Migrationsverwaltungsrecht* (2010) 250–253 and 255; F. Fritzsch, *Der Schutz sozialer Bindungen von Ausländern* (2009) 148–189, arguing that lawful stay constitutes an inherent limitiation (*immanente Schranke*) of Art. 8 ECHR.

579 On the corresponding approach in respect of 'family life', see ECtHR, *Mengesha Kimfe v. Switzerland*, Appl. no. 24404/05, at para. 62, and *Agraw v. Switzerland*, Appl. no. 3295/06, at para. 45, Judgments of 29 July 2010.

580 On the parallel discussion of a right to abode in German constitutional law, see E. Weizsäcker, *Grundrechte und freiwillige Migration* (2007) 89–100; J. Bast, *Aufenthaltsrecht und Migrationssteuerung* (2011) 206–212.

the Court has specifically referred to 'preserving social cohesion' as a legitimate aim of migration policy.[581] The *Boultif/Üner* criteria and their application by the Strasbourg Court confirm this finding.[582] A lack of socio-cultural integration on the part of the migrant is regularly held against him or her when assessing whether a 'fair balance' has been struck. In some instances, the Court has even attributed excessive importance to such factors,[583] triggering criticism from commentators that it is employing an overly simplified, unidirectional model of migrants' integration.[584] In effect, restrictionist policies in the guise of 'integration measures' will only fail to satisfy the ECtHR if the relevant framework preempts the required balancing of interests or when the latter is systematically biased toward non-admission outcomes.

(2) This margin of appreciation granted by the Strasbourg Court in the context of family reunification is crucial to understanding the complex interplay between Human Rights and the FR Directive. From the outset, scholars have detected a tension between two competing paradigms of integration, both of which have found their way into the text of the Directive: a liberal approach according to which migrant integration is best fostered by granting a secure residence status ('integration qua rights'), and a restrictive approach according to which such a status should be reserved for migrants who prove their successful integration ('rights qua integration').[585] The optional 'integration requirements' pursuant to Art. 7(2) of the Directive reflect the latter approach.

The case-law of the CJEU has had to navigate this tension ever since the first case on the Directive was decided in 2006.[586] The EU Court held that the very point of the FR Directive is that it goes beyond the obligations under the ECHR, in that it lays down a clearly defined individual right to reunification with members of the sponsor's core family, without

581 ECtHR, *M.A. v. Denmark*, Appl. no. 6697/18, Grand Chamber Judgment of 9 July 2021, at para. 165.

582 Murphy, 'The Concept of Integration in the Jurisprudence of the European Court of Human Rights', 12 *European Journal of Migration and Law (EJML)* (2010) 23, at 27–28.

583 See, e.g., ECtHR, *Boughanemi v. France*, Appl. no. 27275/95, Judgment of 24 April 1996, at para. 44.

584 Farahat, 'The Exclusiveness of Inclusion: On the Boundaries of Human Rights in Protecting Transnational and Second-Generation Migrants', 11 *European Journal of Migration and Law (EJML)* (2009) 253.

585 Groenendijk, 'Legal Concepts of Integration in EU Migration Law', 6 *European Journal of Migration and Law (EJML)* (2004) 111.

586 CJEU, Case C-540/03, *Parliament v. Council* (EU:C:2006:429).

discretion on the part of the Member States.[587] Accordingly, the Directive represents a liberal political choice to promote family reunification.[588] To this end, the FR Directive preventively addresses potential Human Rights violations by defining a legal status vesting its holder with rights based in EU law that partly exceed what is necessary to comply with Human Rights obligations. The 'fair balance' between individual and public interests is struck in favor of the individual by virtue of a legislative framework set by the EU. In the context of the present study, we call such an approach 'overinclusive legislative balancing' that ensures outcomes that comply with Human Rights.

One cannot fail to observe, however, that in certain contexts the FR Directive does not counteract the danger of Human Rights violations in that it recognizes a margin for manoeuvre to reject applications for family reunification. The blunt discretion granted in Art. 7(2) is but one example of the Directive being 'underinclusive', as it apparently does not rule out unfairly weighing the interests involved. The CJEU has responded to this danger by establishing a general rule of interpretation, according to which all conditions, exclusions, and discretionary clauses of the FR Directive must be construed in the light of the fundamental rights and, more particularly, in light of the right to respect for family life enshrined in both the ECHR and the EU Charter.[589] This rule of interpretation may even force reconstruction of (thereby effectively overruling) the strict wording of certain provisions that seemingly exclude individual assessment of an application or that invite Member States to do so. According to the CJEU, EU legislation must never be construed in such a way as to fall short of the standards of Human Rights law.[590] In addition, the 'fair balance' test established by the ECtHR is mirrored in EU law's doctrines of proportionality and effectiveness. While in the latter line of reasoning the EU Court argues on the basis of legislative choices crystalized in the Directive's main objective to promote family reunification, in substance the statutory

587 Ibid., at para. 60.

588 CJEU, Case C-578/08, *Chakroun* (EU:C:2010:117), at para. 43.

589 CJEU, Case C-540/03, *Parliament v. Council* (EU:C:2006:429), at para. 58; Case C-578/08, *Chakroun* (EU:C:2010:117), at para. 44.

590 CJEU, Case C-540/03, *Parliament v. Council* (EU:C:2006:429), at para. 105–107; Case C-403/09 PPU, *Detiček* (EU:C:2009:810), at para. 34 and 54–55; Cases C-356/11 and C-357/11, *O., S. and L.* (EU:C:2012:776), at para. 76–78.

argument made by the CJEU converges with the constitutional argument based on fundamental rights.[591]

This general approach determined the path for the CJEU's leading case on integration requirements pursuant to Art. 7(2) FR Directive, decided in 2015.[592] The Court confirmed that a Member State – the Netherlands, in the instant case – may establish a requirement to pass a 'civic integration' examination prior to entry, which involves testing basic knowledge of the language and society of the host State.[593] However, the CJEU stressed that Art. 7(2) must be interpreted strictly and in line with the principle of proportionality.[594] The conditions of application of such a requirement must not make it impossible or excessively difficult to exercise the right to family reunification: that is to say, it must not form an insurmountable obstacle for the concrete person.[595] Accordingly, Member States' schemes must not automatically exclude persons who have demonstrated their willingness to pass the examination and have made every effort to achieve that objective.[596] An assessment on a case-by-case basis is required, taking into account individual circumstances, such as the age, illiteracy, level of education, economic situation or health of a sponsor's relevant family members.[597]

In view of the combined effects of the ECtHR's 'fair balance' jurisprudence and the EU legislature's approach of 'overinclusive legislative balancing', the present legal framework should do a good job in protecting migrants' right to family unity in the EU. However, 'integration measures' pursuant to Art. 7(2) FR Directive are a weak spot, as this provision enables Member State to pursue assimilationist and restrictionist policies that potentially violate Human Rights. The CJEU has mitigated this threat in stipulating that Member States must not automatically exclude persons who fail to meet formal integration tests. In practical terms, however,

591 This convergence, and the transformative potential of taking the Charter seriously, are underrated in Thym's reconstruction of the Court's case-law; see Thym, 'Between "Administrative Mindset" and "Constitutional Imagination": The Role of the Court of Justice in Immigration, Asylum and Border Control Policy', 44 *European Law Review (E.L.Rev.)* (2019) 139, at 145–148.

592 CJEU, Case C-153/14, *K. and A.* (EU:C:2015:453); for a similar ruling on language requirements in the context on the Association Agreement with Turkey, see Case C-138/13, *Dogan* (EU:C:2014:2066), at para. 38.

593 CJEU, Case C-153/14, *K. & A.* (EU:C:2015:453), at para. 53–54.

594 Ibid., at para. 50–51.

595 Ibid., at para. 59 and 71.

596 Ibid., at para. 56.

597 Ibid., at para. 58.

reinstating the 'fair balance' requirement on a case-by-case basis offers insufficient assurance that integration measures will not serve as an instrument of selective non-immigration policies.[598] The Court's approach fails to address the structural biases and hidden restrictionist agendas of integration narratives and practices. In this regard, the CJEU does not consider the competing concepts and goals of integration policies – sweepingly asserting that the stated aim of 'facilitating the establishment of connections in the host State' is genuine,[599] but not reviewing whether less burdensome alternatives would be available (such as language training after the arrival[600]). As a result, a narrative of legitimate national closure, and of discretionary inclusion, continues to prevail both at national and supranational levels.[601]

5.2.3 Specific issue: protection of settled migrants' right to abode

(1) Our analysis has detected a trend toward securitized policies of expulsion, including measures targeting settled migrants. Such measures interfere with the right to respect for private life as defined in the ECtHR jurisprudence. While the Strasbourg Court has always acknowledged that preventing crime and fighting terrorism are legitimate aims within the meaning of Art. 8(2) ECHR,[602] securitized policies of expulsion are likely to give rise to Human Rights violations, particularly when expulsion is

598 A requirement established by the CJEU; see ibid., at para. 57.

599 For a similar line of reasoning, see Case C-579/13, *P and S* (EU:C:2015:369), at para. 13. The CJEU also held that making an entitlement to housing assistance dependent on a language requirement does not amount to an indirect discrimination on grounds of ethnic origin pursuant to Art. 21 EU-CFR, provided that it applies without distinction to all third-country nationals; see CJEU, Case C-94/20, *KV* (EU:C:2021:477), at para. 56 and 63.

600 Moreover, integration measures may often be more effective in the host country; this was also observed by the European Commission: Communication on guidance for application of Directive 2003/86/EC, COM(2014) 210, 3 April 2014, at 16. On the practical difficulties of preparing for the tests abroad, see T. Strik et al., *The INTEC Project: Synthesis Report: Integration and Naturalisation Tests: The New Way to European Citizenship* (2010), at 33–36.

601 Strumia, 'European Citizenship and EU Immigration', 22 *European Law Journal* (2016) 417, at 434.

602 Suffice it to mention that 'the interest of public safety' and 'the prevention of disorder and crime' expressly feature in the list of Art. 8(2) ECHR.

ordered in a quasi-automatic manner or as a means of deterring other migrants.

(2) The EU legislature has thus far failed to adopt horizontal rules on expulsion. The LTR Directive is the main tool protecting settled migrants' right to abode. Like the FR Directive, the LTR Directive possesses a dual character: it results from an autonomous political choice by the EU legislature, while at the same time it mirrors and enhances Human Rights by means of EU law.[603] Embracing the first element, the CJEU has consistently held that the 'principal objective' of the LTR Directive is the integration of third-country nationals who are settled on a long-term basis in the Member States.[604] The CJEU stresses that, for that purpose, the EU legislature has established 'extensive rights attached to long-term resident status' with a view to bringing the rights of those nationals closer to those enjoyed by EU citizens.[605] The liberal choice to promote integration by creating a denizenship status consequently goes beyond what is required by Human Rights law.

However, the LTR Directive also serves the aim of protecting settled migrants' right to abode laid down in Art. 8 ECHR – in particular, by providing for reinforced protection against expulsion.[606] This is evidenced by the reference to the ECtHR's case-law in recital 16 of the LTR Directive. The criteria to be considered, pursuant to Art. 12(3) LTR Directive, before taking a decision to expel a long-term resident replicate the *Boultif/Üner* criteria. Here again, the EU legislature has chosen the approach of over-inclusive balancing. In excluding economic considerations from the equation (Art. 12(2)) and by requiring that the expellee poses 'an actual and

603 On such 'democratic iterations' of Human Rights, see S. Benhabib, *The Rights of Others: Aliens, Residents and Citizens* (2004) 176–181. It should be noted, however, that the EU legislature has established an independent set of eligibility criteria to claim LTR status. These criteria are only partly in consonance with the *Boultif/Üner* criteria; see Çali and Cunningham, 'The European Court of Human Rights and Removal of Long-term Migrants', in B. Çali, L. Bianku and I. Motoc (eds), *Migration and the Convention on Human Rights* (2021) 159, at 163–174, demonstrating the limited importance the ECtHR attaches to long-term stay as isolated factor.

604 CJEU, Case C-571/10, *Kamberaj* (EU:C:2012:233), at para. 86; Case C-508/10, *Commission v. Netherlands* (EU:C:2012:243), at para. 66; Case C-309/14, *CGIL and INCA* (EU:C:2015:523), at para. 21.

605 CJEU, Case C-557/17, *Y.Z., Z.Z. and Y.Y* (EU:C:2019:203), at para. 63–64.

606 The Human Rights dimension of the LTR Directive is only vaguely acknowledged by the CJEU; see Case C-636/16, *López Pastuzano* (EU:C:2017:949), at para. 24.

sufficiently serious threat' to public policy or public security (Art. 12(1)), the LTR Directive copied the special legal regime protecting Union citizens and certain Turkish nationals under the EEC-Turkey Association Agreement, and thus exceeds Human Rights standards. According to this special regime, expulsion cannot be ordered automatically on general preventive grounds following a criminal conviction or as a means of deterring other foreign nationals from committing offenses.[607] This jurisprudence now applies to the LTR Directive.[608] Hence, settled migrants who have achieved long-term resident status are firmly protected, by way of EU law, against quasi-automatic expulsion schemes and other trends of securitized expulsion.

On the downside, this 'safety net' is not available to those who have failed to apply for LTR status or do not meet all conditions established in the Directive. Indeed, only a limited number of settled migrants living in the EU have acquired LTR status. Statistical comparison between States bound by the Directive shows a highly uneven application of the LTR Directive.[609] In some Member States, such as Germany, the LTR Directive has had only limited impact since national law already provided for a similar status of permanent residence. Settled migrants have little incentive to apply for a change of status. In other Member States, administrative obstacles such as high administrative fees or restrictive interpretation of eligibility criteria seem to have discouraged eligible applicants.[610]

In other instances, the limited use of the LTR Directive may be due to the fact that the conditions laid down in the Directive are too demanding for a large number of persons who have developed strong social ties in the host country. Discretionary 'integration requirements' pursuant to Art. 5(2) of the LTR Directive again seem to play an important role here.[611]

---

607 CJEU, Case C-371/08, *Ziebell* (EU:C:2011:809), at para. 82–83.

608 CJEU, Case C-636/16, *López Pastuzano* (EU:C:2017:949), at para. 28; Case C-448/19, *W.T.* (EU:C:2020:467), at para. 25.

609 European Commission, Report on the implementation of Directive 2003/109/EC, COM(2019) 161, 29 March 2019, at 1. Four Member States (AT, CZ, EE, IT) account for 90 % of the LTR permits issued in 2017, with Italy alone having issued around 73 %.

610 See the first Report from the European Commission on the application of Directive 2003/109/EC, COM(2011) 585, 29 September 2011, at 5. Cf. also Case C-508/10, *Commission v. Netherlands* (EU:C:2012:243), on the Netherlands, and Case C-309/14, *CGIL and INCA* (EU:C:2015:523), on Italy; Cases C-503/19 and C-592/19, *UQ and SI* (EU:C:2020:629), on Spain.

611 See European Commission, (Second) Report on the implementation of Directive 2003/109/EC, COM(2019) 161, 29 March 2019, at 3. A majority of Member

The CJEU has yet to rule on this clause[612] but it is likely that the CJEU would employ its general approach to integration requirements mandated by the EU legislature. In its view, national immigration law may make the consolidation of the right to stay conditional upon the acquisition of knowledge of the language and society of the host State, subject to the principle of proportionality.[613] In the context of the LTR Directive, the additional requirements imposed by Member States must not jeopardize the effectiveness of the Directive – that is, compromise its principal objective of integration. Accordingly, requirements pursuant to Art. 5(2) LTR Directive must not make it impossible or excessively difficult to acquire LTR status, and States must consider the individual circumstances of the applicant. While such clarification by the CJEU could be helpful, it would presumably not suffice to counteract practices that prevent settled migrants from achieving secure status under the LTR Directive.[614]

5.2.4 Specific issue: obligations to regularize irregular migrants

(1) To what extent are the social ties, including family ties, of irregular migrants protected by Human Rights law? Part of the answer has already been discussed above: The ECtHR's case-law recognizes these private interests as falling within the scope of protection of the right to private and family life, irrespective of whether the migrants have a legal right to stay in the country in question (see section 5.2.1).[615]

States require applicants to comply with integration conditions (AT, BE, CY, EE, EL, FR, HR, IT, LT, LV, LU, MT, NL, PT, RO). In Germany, for example, level B1 of the Common European Framework of Reference for Languages is required – the same as for naturalization.

612 For an extensive legal discussion, see D. Acosta Arcarazo, *The Long-Term Residence Status as a Subsidiary Form of EU Citizenship* (2011) 203–223.

613 See CJEU, Case C-257/17, *C and A* (EU:C:2018:876), at para. 53 et seq., on Art. 15(1) and (4) of the FR Directive.

614 Cf. Böcker and Strik, 'Language and Knowledge Tests for Permanent Residence Rights: Help or Hindrance for Integration?', 13 *European Journal of Migration and Law (EJML)* (2011) 157, at 178.

615 On the procedural rights of irregular migrants in the context of expulsions and deportations, see the review of the relevant sources of Human Rights law in the Concurring Opinion of Judge Punto de Alberquerque, joined by Judge Vučinić, appended to ECtHR, *De Souza Ribeiro v. France*, Appl. no. 22689/07, Grand Chamber Judgment of 13 December 2012.

In effect, irregular migrants may have a well-founded claim to stay on the basis of Art. 8 ECHR, although this is less likely than in the case of settled migrants who are lawfully present. The leading authority is *Jeunesse v. the Netherlands*, decided by the Grand Chamber in October 2014,[616] which concerned a married couple living together with three children. The applicant, the only foreigner of the family, had been staying illegally in the Netherlands for more than 17 years, with the full knowledge of the authorities which never seriously tried to deport her. The Court found that the failure to issue a residence permit to regularize her stay amounted to a violation of Art. 8 ECHR, albeit the Court stressed the 'highly exceptional' circumstances of the case.[617] The judgment is in line with previous case-law on family reunification, in which the fact that the applicant was not lawfully resident in the responding State did not prevent the Court from determining that the State had failed to comply with its positive obligations under Art. 8 ECHR.[618]

This line of jurisprudence is complemented by another line that concerns claims to be regularized on the basis of strong social ties developed in the country of de facto residence. Such claims were first deemed well-founded in the context of former Soviet citizens of Russian origin who found themselves in a precarious legal situation in the newly independent Baltic republics. The Chamber decision in *Sisojeva v. Latvia* accepted the claim that the prolonged refusal of the Latvian authorities to grant the applicants the right to reside in Latvia on a permanent basis constituted an interference with the right to private life.[619] The Grand Chamber was more reserved, deferring to the national legal systems safeguarding Human Rights. It argued that Art. 8 ECHR cannot be construed as guaranteeing, as such, the right to a particular type of residence permit.[620] In principle, however, the Court has accepted that Art. 8 ECHR may entail a right to

---

616 ECtHR, *Jeunesse v. the Netherlands*, Appl. no. 12738/10, Grand Chamber Judgment of 3 October 2014.

617 Ibid., at para. 121–122; on the 'exceptional circumstances' test concerning irregular migrants, see *Butt v. Norway*, Appl. no. 47017/09, Judgment of 4 December 2012, at para. 78, with reference to previous case-law. In the latter case, the Court was satisfied that applicants' deportation from Norway would entail a violation of Art. 8 ECHR.

618 See, e.g., ECtHR, *Rodrigues da Silva and Hoogkamer v. the Netherlands*, Appl. no. 50435/99, Judgment of 31 January 2006.

619 ECtHR, *Sisojeva et al. v. Latvia*, Appl. no. 60654/00, Judgment of 16 June 2005, at para. 105.

620 ECtHR, *Sisojeva et al. v. Latvia*, Appl. no. 60654/00, Grand Chamber Judgment of 15 January 2007, at para. 90–91.

be regularized in order obtain a legal status that adequately reflects the personal, social, and economic relations of the person concerned within his or her de facto home country.[621]

This rationale was affirmed in 2012 by the Grand Chamber in the *Kurić* case, which dealt with the situation of former Yugoslav citizens in post-independence Slovenia ('the erased').[622] Despite the historical singularity of the instant case, the *Kurić* judgment is of general significance for irregular migrants.[623] The Court added another building block to its jurisprudence on Art. 8 ECHR: the doctrine that 'the positive obligations inherent in effective "respect" for private or family life or both, in particular in the case of long-term migrants' may lead to the conclusion that 'the regularisation of the residence status of [the applicants] was a necessary step which the State should have taken in order to ensure that [the adverse consequences of the applicable laws] would not disproportionately affect the Article 8 rights'.[624] Accordingly, Art. 8 ECHR is not only a potential source of a right not to be expelled or deported but also, in exceptional circumstances, of a right to be regularized.[625] The Court has thus opened a channel for Human-Rights-based 'immigration from within'.[626]

---

621 From the ensuing discussion, see Thym, 'Respect for Private and Family Life under Article 8 ECHR in Immigration Cases: A Human Right to Regularize Illegal Stay?', 57 *International and Comparative Law Quarterly (ICLQ)* (2008) 1; M.-B. Dembour, *When Humans Become Migrants: Study of the European Court of Human Rights with an Inter-American Counterpoint* (2015) 442–481; C. Costello, *The Human Rights of Migrants and Refugees in European Law* (2016) 79–83.

622 ECtHR, *Kurić et al. v. Slovenia*, Appl. no. 26828/06, Grand Chamber Judgment of 26 June 2012, at para. 356–359.

623 This has not yet been fully recognized in legal scholarship; see, e.g., Farcy, 'Unremovability under the Return Directive: An Empty Protection?', in M. Moraru, G. Cornelisse and Ph. de Bruycker (eds), *Law and Judicial Dialogue on the Return of Irregular Migrants from the European Union* (2020) 437, at 449; B. Menezes Queiroz, *Illegally Staying in the EU: An Analysis of Illegality in EU Migration Law* (2018) 109.

624 Ibid., at para. 358 and 359, respectively. Note that the quotes are not a mere *obiter dictum* but rather the decisive paragraphs of the GC judgment.

625 See, e.g., ECtHR, *Hoti v. Croatia*, Appl. no. 63311/14, Judgment of 26 April 2018, and *Sudita Keita v. Hungary*, Appl. no. 2321/15, Judgment of 12 August 2020, concerning stateless persons residing in Croatia and Hungary, respectively; in both cases the Court found a violation of Art. 8 ECHR due to a lack of effective and accessible procedures enabling further stay and status to be determined. See also ECtHR, *B.A.C. v. Greece*, Appl. no. 11981/15, Judgment of 13 October 2016: violation of the State's positive obligations under Art. 8 ECHR by not deciding the applicant's asylum request for more than twelve years.

(2) In the present legal framework at the EU level, irregular migrants do not benefit from either the FR Directive or the LTR Directive, since these require the lawful presence of the sponsor or the applicant respectively. Rare examples of the EU's legislative activity on matters of regularizations are the Directive on Victims of Trafficking (Directive 2004/81/EC)[627] and the Employers Sanctions Directive (Directive 2009/52/EC).[628] However, neither Art. 8 of the Directive on Victims of Trafficking nor Art. 6(5) and 13(4) of the Employers Sanctions Directive entail an enforceable right to be regularized.[629]

As explained above, the Return Directive is basically silent on the issue of a Human-Rights-based claim to regularization. It does, however, recognize that Member States may issue a residence permit at any stage of the return procedure – a decision seemingly left to the discretion of the Member States. The case-law of the CJEU on the fundamental rights of irregular migrants who are subject to return proceedings reiterates the wording of Art. 5 Return Directive, reminding Member States that, when they implement that Directive, they must 'take due account of' the best interests of the child, family life, and the state of health of the person concerned, without discussing what legal consequences such considerations might entail.[630] From the point of view of the CJEU, this provision is apparently mainly procedural in nature, in that it requires the Member States to hear the person concerned on that subject prior to the adoption

626 The term is borrowed from the French discussion in the 1960s on the widespread (and routinely legalized) practice of labor recruitment from the population of undocumented migrants (*l'immigration interne*). On the use of the concept in the present context, see Bast, 'Illegaler Aufenthalt und europarechtliche Gesetzgebung', *Zeitschrift für Ausländerrecht (ZAR)* (2012) 1, at 6.

627 Directive 2004/81/EC on the residence permit issued to third-country nationals who are victims of trafficking in human beings or who have been the subject of an action to facilitate illegal immigration, who cooperate with the competent authorities (Directive on Victims of Trafficking).

628 Directive 2009/52/EC providing for minimum standards on sanctions and measures against employers of illegally staying third-country nationals (Employers Sanctions Directive).

629 See Kau, 'Human Trafficking Directive 2004/81/EC', in K. Hailbronner and D. Thym (eds), *EU Immigration and Asylum Law: Commentary* (2nd ed. 2016), commentary on Art. 8, at para. 8; Schierle, 'Employers Sanctions Directive 2009/52/EC', ibid., commentary on Art. 14, at para. 12.

630 On the reluctance of the CJEU to engage with Human Rights jurisprudence in the context of the Return Directive, see T. Molnár, *The Interplay Between the EU's Return Acquis and International Law* (2021) 100–121.

of a return decision.[631] The scope of the right to be heard arguably extends, by analogy, to adverse consequences for the private life of the person concerned, which the EU legislature has failed to mention in Art. 5 of the Directive.

Regarding the consequences of compelling legal or practical obstacles to enforce a return decision, the Court has yet to clarify important aspects of the legal framework set out by the EU legislature. The Court has consistently held that Art. 6(1) Return Directive provides, principally, for an obligation on Member States to issue a return decision against any third-country national staying illegally on their territory.[632] Member States must not de facto tolerate the presence of irregular migrants, either by failing to issue a return decision in the first place[633] or by deliberately refraining from enforcing it in due time.[634] The idea of the Directive is precisely to avoid any 'gray area' between illegal and legal stay, between return and regularization.[635] Only on a temporary basis does the Return Directive, in Art. 9(2), provide for the possibility of postponing the removal of a third-country national, in which case a written confirmation of his or her situation must be provided.[636] The Court has yet to rule on the practice of certain Member States, notably Germany, of indefinitely iterating the postponement of deportations in view of persistent legal or factual obstacles (*Kettenduldung*). We concur with the legal scholarship that regards this practice as a violation of the Return Directive.[637] In particular, when persistent non-removability results from Human Rights – be it Art. 8 ECHR or, even more so, the principle of non-refoulement – the discretion under Art. 6(4) Return Directive is limited to only one possible lawful decision:

631 CJEU, Case C-249/13, *Boudjlida* (EU:C:2014:2431), at para. 48–49; Case C-82/16, *K.A. et al. (re family reunification in Belgium)* (EU:C:2018:308), at para. 102–103; see Ilareva, 'The Right to be Heard: The Underestimated Condition for Effective Returns and Human Rights Consideration', in M. Moraru, G. Cornelisse and Ph. de Bruycker (eds), *Law and Judicial Dialogue on the Return of Irregular Migrants from the European Union* (2020) 351. On the unwritten guarantee of the right to be heard in the context of the Return Directive, see above, Chapter 3 (section 3.2.4).

632 CJEU, Case C-61/11 PPU, *El Dridi* (EU:C:2011:268), at para. 35.

633 CJEU, Case C-38/14, *Zaizoune* (EU:C:2015:260), at para. 31–32.

634 CJEU, Case C-441/19, *TQ* (EU:C:2021:9), at para. 81.

635 CJEU, Case C-546/19, *BZ* (EU:C:2021:432), at para. 57.

636 CJEU, Case C-146/14 PPU, *Mahdi* (EU:C:2014:1320), at para. 88.

637 K. F. Hinterberger, *Regularisierungen irregulär aufhältiger Migrantinnen und Migranten* (2020) 161–163; Nachtigall, 'Die Ausdifferenzierung der Duldung', *Zeitschrift für Ausländerrecht (ZAR)* (2020) 271, at 276.

to regularize the status of the person concerned.[638] Given that the Member State act within a legal framework set by EU law and, hence, within the ambit of EU fundamental rights,[639] this right to be regularized is enforceable before national courts.

More recently, the CJEU has inched toward recognizing such a right in the context of unaccompanied minors. The Court held that a return decision against an unaccompanied minor must not be issued unless the authorities have verified that deportation can, in practice, be enforced. The alternative would be contrary to the requirement to protect the best interests of the child at all stages of the procedure, as laid down in Art. 5(a) of the Return Directive and Art. 24(2) of the Charter.[640] The essence of the Court's argument extends to the Human Rights of adult irregular migrants, as well: It would be unlawful to adopt or maintain a return decision which the State is satisfied cannot be enforced within a reasonable period of time.[641] The Court rightly observed: 'The [person] in question would … be placed in a situation of great uncertainty as to his or her legal status and his or her future, in particular as regards … the possibility of remaining in the Member State concerned.'[642] This reasoning echoes the ECtHR's finding of a 'legal vacuum' in which the applicants were trapped in the *Kurić* case.[643]

In view of the lack of clear guidance from EU law, the relevant policies are subject to a fragmented landscape of Member States' regulations and practices. A recent comparative study of Austrian, German, and Spanish law has demonstrated that regularization clauses are natural components

638 We concur with Acosta Acarazo, 'The Charter, Detention and Possible Regularization of Migrants in an Irregular Situation under the Returns Directive: *Mahdi*', 52 *Common Market Law Review (CMLRev.)* (2015) 1361, at 1375–1377; for a more cautious approach, see B. Menezes Queiroz, *Illegally Staying in the EU: An Analysis of Illegality in EU Migration Law* (2018) 107. Note that CJEU, Case C-562/13, *Abdida* (EU:C:2014:2453), at para. 54–55, did not rule on the consequences of a *permanent* obstacle to deportation arising from Art. 3 ECHR/Art. 19(2) EU-CFR.

639 See CJEU, Case C-441/19, *TQ* (EU:C:2021:9), at para. 45.

640 CJEU, Case C-441/19, *TQ* (EU:C:2021:9), at para. 52–54 and 80–82.

641 C. Hörich, *Abschiebungen nach europäischen Vorgaben* (2015) 92; K. F. Hinterberger, *Regularisierungen irregulär aufhältiger Migrantinnen und Migranten* (2020) 156–158.

642 CJEU, Case C-441/19, *TQ* (EU:C:2021:9), at para. 53.

643 ECtHR, *Kurić et al. v. Slovenia*, Appl. no. 26828/06, Grand Chamber Judgment of 26 June 2012, at para. 344 et passim.

of immigration law.[644] The clauses enabling individual regularizations cover a broad range of purposes, ranging from respecting the principle of non-refoulment, social ties, family unity, and particular vulnerability of migrants – all of which have some basis in international law or EU law – to reasons of public policy such as fostering employment, education, or criminal prosecution.[645] These authorizations are almost always subject to discretionary decision-making by immigration authorities.[646]

Given the prevailing focus on enforcing returns as the primary policy option in dealing with irregular migration, this situation is likely to lead to unlawful decisions that do not sufficiently consider the Human Rights of irregular migrants. The main issues of concern are the enforcement of return decisions regardless of social and family ties, and the indefinite suspension of return procedures, which keeps non-removable migrants in a legal limbo.

5.3 Recommendations

The above legal evaluations have reached the comforting conclusion that the EU does not establish mandatory policies that fall foul of its own obligation 'to respect' the private and family life of migrants. However, more efforts are required in response to Member State policies that potentially violate Human Rights. Our recommendations build on the EU's positive obligation 'to protect' these rights. EU legislation, as it currently stands, is not sufficiently specific or inclusive to counteract the trends observed in the first section of this chapter, notwithstanding the CJEU's doctrine of interpretation in conformity with fundamental rights.

As a general approach, we recommend that the EU refine its legislation to address typical situations in which violations of Art. 8 ECHR occur. The EU legislative bodies should follow the approach of 'overinclusive legislative balancing' by granting an individual right to family reunification and a right to a secure legal status, respectively, to *all* persons in critical situations. While there is no strict obligation under international law to adopt

644 K. F. Hinterberger, *Regularisierungen irregulär aufhältiger Migrantinnen und Migranten* (2020) chapter 5.

645 Ibid., at 125.

646 Lutz, 'Non-removable Returnees under Union Law: Status Quo and Possible Developments', 20 *European Journal of Migration and Law (EJML)* (2018) 50, at 46.

such an approach, the EU would more effectively prevent unlawful results in a field in which it is generally accountable due to earlier legislative activity occupying the fields of family reunification, long-term residence, and return policy.

Recommendation 1: Prohibit integration requirements that amount to violations of the right to family reunification

We recognize that discretionary requirements of socio-cultural integration laid down in the FR Directive must be construed in accordance with EU fundamental rights, which, in turn, mirror Human Rights. Pending a revision of this Directive, successful litigation strategies mobilizing national courts could further clarify the limits of using integration requirements as a means of restrictive immigration policies.

To address the issue more systematically, we recommend revising the FR Directive to circumscribe Member States' discretion through an enhanced agenda of 'overinclusive legislative balancing'. First, we recommend amending Art. 7(2) of the FR Directive with a view to abolishing policies of establishing pre-departure integration conditions. If this is not feasible politically, post-entry integration measures must be the only option whenever they would equally (or better) promote the integration of the family member. A maximum waiting period for the family members staying abroad should be established. Second, a horizontal clause should be included stipulating that integration measures or conditions established by Member States must not pursue the aim, nor have the practical effect, of preventing family reunification.

In terms of the personal scope of the FR Directive, beneficiaries of subsidiary protection need to be included, under the same conditions as Convention refugees. This systematic gap not only gives rise to violations of the right to non-discrimination pursuant to Art. 14 ECHR (see Chapter 4) but is also likely to produce substantive violations of Art. 8 ECHR.

Recommendation 2: Facilitate access to the status provided by the Long-term Residents Directive

In view of the security-driven policies of expulsions adopted by EU Member States, we recommend that the EU facilitate access to the status provided by the LTR Directive, to ensure that more settled migrants are effectively protected against expulsion.

In view of the uneven implementation of the Directive in the Union, the Commission should work with the Member States concerned and identify the grounds preventing eligible migrants from applying for, or being granted, long-term resident status. Hidden restrictive practices should be stopped and potential beneficiaries actively be encouraged. Such consistent policy would also serve as a safety net against policy changes in Member States that currently do not target settled migrants.

In addition, the requirements laid down in the Directive should be liberalized where they have the practical effect of preventing settled migrants from obtaining LTR status. We therefore recommend the following amendments. First, the EU legislature should clarify that integration conditions established by Member States in accordance with Art. 5(2) of the LTR Directive must be based on objective, non-discriminatory criteria and that the conditions of application of such criteria must not make it impossible or excessively difficult to achieve LTR status. To ensure that language requirements are proportionate in view of the purpose of facilitating the integration of long-term residents, the EU legislature should establish a maximum level according to the Common European Framework of Reference for Languages (CEFR); we suggest a level of A2. Second, in respect of the socio-economic requirements, the amended text of the Directive should explicitly state that the individual circumstances of each applicant must be considered. Third, the EU legislature should contemplate lowering the qualifying period from five years to three years, a proposal the Commission has already made relating to persons enjoying international protection in the EU.[647] In any case, for the purpose of calculating the period of legal and continuous residence, authorization to stay during the asylum procedure should be fully recognized.

Recommendation 3: Develop a comprehensive legislative framework on regularizations

Given the general trend in the Union toward policies that aim at more effective returns, it is very likely that actual Human Rights violation will occur whenever the relevant legislative framework does not provide for

647 European Commission, Proposal for a Regulation on Asylum and Migration Management, COM(2020) 610, 23 September 2020, Art. 71 and recital 39.

systematic assessment of these claims. It is imperative that the Return Directive explicitly stipulate that Member States shall 'respect' the rights to both private and family life of irregular migrants at all stages of the return procedure, rather than merely 'take due account of' the latter right. Art. 5 of the Return Directive should be amended accordingly.

Moreover, the Directive should recognize that EU law entails a right to regularization if a continuation of the return procedure would amount to a violation of Art. 7 EU-CFR/Art. 8 ECHR. To this end, the EU legislature should prohibit policies of unlimited postponement of deportations. We recommend amending the Return Directive to stipulate a strict maximum period for successive postponement of removal according to Art. 9(2) of the Return Directive; we suggest a maximum period of 18 months. This amendment would be based on Art. 79(2)(c) TFEU, which gives the EU the power to legislate on all matters related to illegal immigration and unauthorized residence. It would complement the regulation of socio-economic rights of irregular migrants, including but not limited to non-removable persons, to be defined in binding legal terms by the EU legislature (see Chapter 6).

Adopting a more comprehensive approach of replacing Member States' discretion by way of legislative balancing, the EU should work toward a legislative instrument that regulates claims to regularizations based on Art. 7 EU-CFR/Art. 8 ECHR. The Commission should draft a proposal for an EU Regularization Directive (a 'Directive of the European Parliament and the Council on common standards and procedures in Member States for regularizing illegally staying third-country nationals').[648] This new Directive should provide for minimum harmonization of the requirements for terminating the illegal stay of third-country nationals by way of regularization. The scope of the Directive should at a minimum include all persons who cannot be removed on Human Rights grounds, whether due to the situation in the country of origin (Art. 3 ECHR) or the host country (Art. 8 ECHR). This Directive would be based on Art. 79(2)(a) and (b) TFEU – that is, the comprehensive power of the EU to define the conditions of

---

648 We concur with a proposal made by K. F. Hinterberger, *Regularisierungen irregulär aufhältiger Migrantinnen und Migranten* (2020), chapter 6; Hinterberger, 'An EU Regularization Directive: An Effective Solution to the Enforcement Deficit in Returning Irregularly Staying Migrants', 26 *Maastricht Journal of European and Comparative Law (MJ)* (2019) 736; on the discussions of the topic at EU level, see Lutz, 'Non-removable Returnees under Union Law: Status Quo and Possible Developments', 20 *European Journal of Migration and Law (EJML)* (2018) 50, at 46–50.

entry and residence of third-country nationals (note that Art. 79(5) TFEU is not applicable since the beneficiaries are already present in the EU).

Chapter 6 – Guaranteeing Socio-Economic Rights

Not all migrants are in situations that render them particularly vulnerable. Many migrants, however, can face social and economic exclusion, compete in jobs in the low-skilled sector and have limited access to the host society's support systems. This puts them at a heightened risk of destitution and exploitation. This risk is partly caused by law, because it is conditioned by the migrants' legal status.[649]

Immigration statuses define the scope of migrants' rights, particularly in relation to the conditions of entry, residence and employment.[650] Immigration law classifies migrants into a stratified system, ranging from denizens to those with a much more precarious legal status.[651] These include asylum-seekers, non-removable returnees (such as those with toleration status in Germany or Austria, *Duldung*) as well as irregular migrants without documents (*sans papiers*).[652] We summarily refer to this marginal group as 'margizens'.[653]

Margizens are particularly vulnerable to violations of basic guarantees, in particular their socio-economic Human Rights. With a view to deterring

---

649 European Commission: Directorate-General for Employment, Social Affairs and Inclusion, *Study on Mobility, Migration and Destitution in the European Union: Final Report* (2014), chapter 5; Jesuit Refugee Service Europe, *Living in Limbo: Forced Migrant Destitution in Europe* (2010), at 139, available at https://jrseurope.org/wp-content/uploads/sites/19/2020/07/Living-in-Limbo.pdf.

650 J. Bast, *Aufenthaltsrecht und Migrationssteuerung* (2011), at 25–28.

651 On the concept of civic stratification, see Morris, 'Managing Contradiction: Civic Stratification and Migrants' Rights', 37(1) *The International Migration Review* (2003) 74, at 79 et seq.; L. Morris, *Managing Migration: Civic Stratification and Migrants' Rights* (2002), at 19 et seq. and 103 et seq.

652 S. Castles and A. Davidson, *Citizenship and Migration: Globalization and the Politics of Belonging* (2000), at 95–96; see also C. Janda, *Migranten im Sozialstaat* (2012), at 380; Mohr, 'Stratifizierte Rechte und soziale Exklusion von Migranten im Wohlfahrtsstaat', 34 *Zeitschrift für Soziologie* (2005) 383, at 388.

653 The term was coined by Marco Martiniello in *Leadership et pouvoir dans les communautés d'origine immigrée: l'exemple d'une communauté ethnique en Belgique* (1993), at 290–291; further developed in Martiniello, 'Citizenship of the European Union: A Critical View', in R. Bauböck (ed.), *From Aliens to Citizens: Redefining the Status of Immigrants in Europe* (1994) 29, at 42–44; in the context of current immigration law, see Nachtigall, 'Die Ausdifferenzierung der Duldung', *Zeitschrift für Ausländerrecht (ZAR)* (2020) 271, at 278.

present and future 'unwanted' migrants, States limit their freedom of movement, deny a right to family reunification, and restrict their access to the labor market and social benefits. This chapter focuses on the latter aspect.[654] Low levels of social support are used to deter potential candidates from entering, and to prompt (voluntary) returns.[655] We refer to situations where social and economic exclusion is used as a policy tool to control migration as 'planned destitution'.[656] These are contexts where EU and Member State migration policy choices lead to, build on, or condone destitution.

Planned destitution as a deterrent against (unwanted) migration, including forced migration,[657] generates acute tensions between migration policy and Human Rights protection.[658] The EU has only partly addressed these tensions in its legislation, with basic socio-economic rights of asylum seekers laid down in Directive 2013/33/EU (the Reception Conditions Directive). Regarding rejected asylum seekers or other migrants without a legal right to stay, the EU legislature has regulated around destitution and exploitation by focusing on preventing entry and increasing return rates. In view of the consistently low rates of actual returns, this policy approach is insufficient. Moreover, by definition this approach is not applicable to irregular migrants who are non-removable due to factors beyond their control. Provisions establishing minimum standards for the protection of individual rights of irregular migrants are largely absent at the EU level. Legal instruments whose regulatory scope touches on irregular migrants are Directive 2008/115/EC (the Return Directive), for those subject to a return decision, and Directive 2009/52/EC (the Employers Sanctions Directive) for clandestine or other migrants working irregularly.

---

654 On freedom of movement, see Chapter 2; on family reunification, see Chapter 5.

655 Da Lomba, 'Fundamental Social Rights for Irregular Migrants: The Right to Health Care in France and England', in B. Bogusz et al. (eds), *Irregular Migration and Human Rights: Theoretical, European and International Perspectives* (2004) 363, at 363.

656 Term coined by Eve Lester in *Making Migration Law* (2018), at 235. Catherine Woollard uses the term 'strategic destitution' in her 'Editorial: Strategic Destitution and the Politics of Migration', *ECRE Weekly Bulletin*, 8 March 2019, available at https://www.ecre.org/editorial-strategic-destitution-and-the-politics-of-migration/.

657 L. Slingenberg, *The Reception of Asylum Seekers under International Law: Between Sovereignty and Equality* (2014), at 2.

658 See also ECRE, *Withdrawal of Reception Conditions of Asylum Seekers: An Appropriate, Effective or Legal Sanction?*, July 2018, available at https://asylumineurope.org/wp-content/uploads/2020/11/aida_brief_withdrawalconditions.pdf.

Neither of these instruments comprehensively provide for socio-economic rights aimed at preventing destitution. However, as per Art. 2 TEU, the EU is committed to respect human dignity and Human Rights as foundational values of the Union. By virtue of Art. 78(2) TFEU for asylum, and Art. 79(2) TFEU for immigration policy, the EU has sufficient powers to address the legal position of margizens and protect the Human Rights of these migrants in most vulnerable situations. We argue that, as a necessary corollary of these tasks and powers, the EU is accountable for guaranteeing a minimum standard of socio-economic rights for all migrants in the EU, irrespective of their status, in order to live up to its constitutional commitments.

6.1 Structural challenges and current trends

In EU migration policy, three areas in particular give rise to concerns with regards to the protection of margizens' socio-economic rights. The first relates to policies sanctioning secondary movements of asylum-seekers. The second arises from policies that aim at incentivizing returns of non-removable migrants. The third relates to exploitation in labor relations involving clandestine or other irregular migrants.

Trend 1: Policies to prevent movements of asylum-seekers within the EU build on planned destitution

We observe that Member States resort to planned destitution to prevent so-called secondary movements of asylum seekers within the EU. The deprivation of socio-economic rights is explicitly used as a sanction for migrants who find themselves in a Member State different from the one in which they ought to be.

A core element of the Common European Asylum System is the allocation of responsibility for hearing claims of asylum seekers. The Dublin III Regulation (Regulation 604/2013) defines the Member State responsible according to a list of criteria in order to avoid asylum seekers applying for asylum in more than one Dublin State or choosing one according to their preferences ('asylum shopping'). Accordingly, asylum seekers do not enjoy freedom of movement in Europe but must remain in the State to which they have been allocated. Among the reasons given by policy-makers for largely disregarding asylum seekers' preferences is the assumption that higher standards of reception conditions or social security constitute 'pull factors' and, thus, would trigger onward movements – although the 'welfare-magnet' hypothesis is widely considered an overly simplistic explanation in migration research.[659]

If asylum seekers decide to move to countries within the EU other than the one responsible for their asylum request, such onward movement is referred to as 'secondary movement'. Preventing secondary movements has evolved into an (almost) generally agreed goal guiding the reform of the European asylum system. In its 2016 reform package, the Commission identified the tackling of secondary movements as a stand-alone policy priority to be pursued so as not to disrupt the 'first country of irregular entry' logic of the Dublin system and to prevent 'asylum shopping'.[660]

Against this backdrop, there is a trend among Member States to resort to cutting social benefits in order to sanction secondary movements of asylum seekers. This does not necessarily conform with the legal framework of EU law. The Reception Conditions Directive lays out material reception conditions in Art. 17–20 (just as Art. 13–16 of the previous Directive 2003/9/EC), including the circumstances under which these conditions may be cut. Sanctions for onward movement are not foreseen.

Regardless, some Member States have implemented legislation to that end. For example, France excluded allowances for asylum seekers in the Dublin procedure,[661] and Ireland limited access to the labor market, provided for in the Reception Conditions Directive, for those subject to a pending Dublin transfer.[662] While these policies have been found to be unlawful by the CJEU,[663] in 2019 Germany also introduced sanctions curtailing material reception conditions for asylum seekers subject to a Dublin transfer.[664] According to this legislation, protection-seeking migrants for whom it is been established that another Member State is responsible are

659 For a critical account of neo-classical assumptions about migration causation, see Massey et al., 'Theories of International Migration: A Review and Appraisal', 19(3) *Population and Development Review (PDR)* (1993) 431, at 432–454.

660 European Commission, Towards a Reform of the Common European Asylum System and Enhancing Legal Avenues to Europe, COM(2016) 197, 6 April 2016.

661 CJEU, Case C-179/11, *Cimade and GISTI* (EU:C:2012:594).

662 CJEU, Cases C-322/19 and C-385/19, *K.S.* (EU:C:2021:11).

663 CJEU, Case C-179/11, *Cimade and GISTI* (EU:C:2012:594); Cases C-322/19 and C-385/19, *K.S.* (EU:C:2021:11).

664 See Sec. 1a(7) of the Asylum Seekers Benefits Act (*Asylbewerberleistungsgesetz*), introduced by the Second Act on Better Enforcement of the Obligation to Leave the Country ('Orderly Return Act') which entered into force on 21 August 2019.

not entitled to regular benefits anymore. Until their departure or deportation, they are only granted benefits to cover their needs for food and accommodation, as well as physical and health care.[665]

In sum, while the Reception Conditions Directive aims to protect the basic socio-economic rights of asylum seekers, the conflicting policy aim of preventing secondary movements risks undercutting that protection.

Trend 2: Measures to enforce returns rely on creating 'hostile environments'

We also observe a pattern of policies using planned destitution as a means to enforce returns for a destination outside the EU. The trend is particularly marked vis-à-vis non-cooperative returnees.

The socio-economic rights of irregular migrants who cannot be returned and who continue to stay in the EU in a limbo situation remain largely outside the focus of policy debate (see also above, Chapter 5). Barriers to removal may be humanitarian, legal, or practical in nature, ranging from delays in obtaining the necessary papers from third countries to the non-refoulement principle and non-cooperation of individuals.[666]

In response, 'hostile environment' policies are mounting. Member States make access to basic needs conditional upon cooperation with return[667] and forcibly evict irregular migrants from makeshift homes.[668] The intention is to convince returnees that they will not be able to establish themselves within the EU. One key criterion used by Member States in this field relates to the existence of 'justified reasons for non-return' as opposed

665 For legal evaluation in light of EU law, see Hruschka, 'Die europäische Dimension von Leistungseinschränkungen im Sozialrecht für Asylsuchende', 34 *Zeitschrift für ausländisches und internationales Arbeits- und Sozialrecht* (2020) 113.

666 European Migration Network, *EMN Synthesis Report for the EMN Focussed Study 2016: The Return of Rejected Asylum Seekers: Challenges and Good Practices* (2016), Migrapol EMN Doc 000.

667 Rosenberger and Koppes, 'Claiming Control: Cooperation with Return as a Condition for Social Benefits in Austria and the Netherlands', 6 *Comparative Migration Studies* (2018) 1; Ataç, 'Deserving Shelter: Conditional Access to Accommodation for Rejected Asylum Seekers in Austria, the Netherlands, and Sweden', 17 *Journal of Immigrant & Refugee Studies* (2019) 44.

668 P. Mudu and S. Chattopadhyay (eds), *Migration, Squatting and Radical Autonomy* (2017); Slingenberg and Bonneau, '(In)formal Migrant Settlements and Right to Respect for a Home', 19 *European Journal of Migration and Law (EJML)* (2017) 335.

to 'non-justified reasons for non-return', with the latter encompassing all variations of non-cooperation, such as lack of cooperation in obtaining travel documents; lack of cooperation in disclosing one's identity; destroying documents; absconding; or otherwise hampering removal efforts.[669]

The term 'hostile environment' was coined in the United Kingdom, where the policies aimed explicitly at cutting undocumented migrants' access to any public services, including healthcare services. In addition, the British government pushed to make employment and rental accommodation impossible for migrants without adequate paperwork.[670] While the United Kingdom is no longer a Member State of the EU, similar policies have even longer traditions in Denmark and the Netherlands, for example. In Denmark, 'motivation enhancement measures' were introduced in 1997, intended to encourage asylum seekers and migrants to leave Denmark or cooperate in their own removal from the country.[671] In the Netherlands, the 1998 Linkage Act (*Koppelingswet*) coupled access to all public services with lawful migration status.[672] Non-removable migrants can only receive regular social benefits, such as social assistance and health insurance, if they obtain a residence permit based on a no-fault status (*buitenschuldvergunning*). This status provides access to social welfare but is granted on a remarkably limited scale.[673] Conditions for the no-fault status require the migrant to take concrete steps to arrange their own

669 Lutz, 'Non-removable Returnees under Union Law: Status Quo and Possible Developments', 20 *European Journal of Migration and Law (EJML)* (2018) 28, at 41.

670 See UK Immigration Act 2014 (c. 22), expanded by Immigration Act 2016 (c. 19). For an assessment of some of the measures, see Independent Chief Inspector of Borders and Immigration (D. Bolt), *An Inspection of the 'Hostile Environment' Measures Relating to Driving Licenses and Bank Accounts* (2016), available at https://www.gov.uk/government/publications/inspection-report-of-hostile-environment-measures-october-2016.

671 These measures are found in the Danish Aliens Act, among others in Sec. 34, 36, 40, 41, and 42a; J. Suarez-Krabbe, J. Arce and A. Lindberg, *Stop Killing Us Slowly: A Research Report on the Motivation Enhancement Measures and Criminalization of Rejected Asylum Seekers in Denmark* (2018), at 8 et seq., available at http://refugees.dk/media/1757/stop-killing-us_uk.pdf.

672 K. Zwaan et al., *Nederlands Migratierecht* (2018), at sec. 8.8.1. See the Dutch Aliens Circular (*Vreemdelingencirculaire*) 2000, at para. B8/4. As per Art. 10(1) Aliens Act (*Vreemdelingenwet*) 2000, social services are tied to regular migration status; the narrow exceptions are access to emergency medical care, children's education, and legal support, as per Art. 10(2) of the *Vreemdelingenwet*.

673 Cf. Ministry of Security and Justice, Parliamentary Questions 609 (2016), available at https://zoek.officielebekendmakingen.nl/ah-tk-20162017-609.

departure.[674] The goal of the Act is to ensure that undocumented migrants are discouraged from staying in the Netherlands.[675]

More recent changes to that effect occurred in Austria and in Germany. In Austria, the 2017 reform of the Aliens Act (*Fremdenrechtsgesetz*) laid down an obligation to cooperate in the return proceedings. Only if rejected asylum seekers are considered cooperative can they potentially receive a formal toleration status (*Duldungskarte*). In any case, reasons for postponement of deportation must not lie within the person's own responsibility.[676] In Germany, while non-cooperation with return does not prevent the issuance of toleration status (*Duldung*) entirely, legislative changes in 2019 have created the so-called *Duldung light* – a non-official term referring to the fact that the least favorable conditions are provided to this subgroup of documented irregular migrants – that is, those who are considered non-cooperative.[677] This is the case either if they make false statements regarding their identity or nationality, or if they fail to take reasonable steps to comply with the obligation to obtain a passport.[678] They are sanctioned with residence orders, a blanket ban on employment, and benefit cuts, to the extent that the latter only cover their needs for food and accommodation, including heating, as well as physical and health care.[679]

---

674 In addition, there are some shelters that are open for irregular migrants: *gezinslocaties* (for families with minor children), the VBL and the LVV. Currently, only the VBL is conditional upon cooperation in return procedures. The Dutch government recently announced, in accordance with the coalition agreement, to also make the LVV shelters conditional upon cooperation again. Both the VBL and the *gezinslocaties* have (quite) severe restrictions on freedom of movement and a daily reporting obligation. See https://www.rijksoverheid.nl/documenten/rapporten/2020/07/01/tk-bijlage-eindrapport-plan-en-procesevaluatie-lvv-regioplan.

675 Cf. Ombudsman Metropool Amsterdam, *Onzichtbaar: Onderzoek naar de leefwereld van ongedocumenteerden in Amsterdam en Nederland* (2021), available at https://www.ombudsmanmetropool.nl/uploaded_files/article/Rapport_Onzichtbaar.pdf.

676 As per Sec. 46a(1)(3) and 46a(3)(3) Aliens Police Act (*Fremdenpolizeigesetz*); see Rosenberger and Koppes, 'Claiming Control: Cooperation with Return as a Condition for Social Benefits in Austria and the Netherlands', 6 *Comparative Migration Studies* (2018) 1.

677 As per Sec 60b(5) Residence Act and Sec. 1a Asylum Seekers Benefits Act; see Nachtigall, 'Die Ausdifferenzierung der Duldung', *Zeitschrift für Ausländerrecht (ZAR)* (2020) 271, at 273 et seq.

678 As per Sec. 60b(2)(1) and 60b(3)(1) Residence Act.

679 As per Sec. 1a(1) Asylum Seekers Benefits Act.

As we shall develop below, the EU legislature has failed to enact legislation that successfully precludes such policies of planned destitution.

Trend 3: Persistent pattern of exploitation of irregular migrants in informal labor relations

Furthermore, we observe that European migration policy in general condones the exploitation of irregular migrants, especially clandestine migrants, in informal labor relations. They are subjected to severe exploitation and other kinds of abuse in firms, factories, and farms across the Union,[680] regularly facing underpayment or withholding of pay, unsafe working conditions and very long working hours, and substandard living conditions.[681]

Destitution resulting from the lack of a lawful residence status, of the right to work, and of access to any government support is a primary factor driving irregular migrants into exploitative work.[682] Be it intentional or otherwise, policies that increase destitution thereby secure an exploitable workforce that serves important labor market needs.[683] This 'adverse incor-

680 FRA, Protecting Migrant Workers from Exploitation in the EU: Workers' Perspectives (2019); see also the statement of the Global Migration Group, adopted on 30 September 2010, on the Human Rights of Migrants in an Irregular Situation, available at https://www.iom.int/news/statement-global-migration-group-human-rights-migrants-irregular-situation.

681 FRA, Protecting Migrant Workers from Exploitation in the EU: Workers' Perspectives (2019).

682 Anna Triandafyllidou and Laura Bartolini describe the connection between irregular migration and irregular work as a 'chicken and egg dilemma'; see Triandafyllidou and Bartolini, 'Irregular Migration and Irregular Work: A Chicken and Egg Dilemma', in S. Spencer and A. Triandafyllidou (eds), *Migrants with Irregular Status in Europe: Evolving Conceptual and Policy Challenges* (2020) 139.

683 Cheliotis, 'Punitive inclusion: The Political Economy of Irregular Migration in the Margins of Europe', 14 *European Journal of Criminology* (2017) 78.

poration'[684] into the labor market thus functions as a form of 'punitive inclusion'[685] in the EU migration management system.[686]

In addition to those margizens who are known to the authorities and subject to policies of planned destitution, undocumented migrants are particularly vulnerable to slavery-like work situations.[687] These *sans papiers* may have used the services of a facilitator (or 'human smuggler') to enter the Union territory and end up in bonded labor without ever having been registered with the authorities anywhere. Their immigration status – or, rather, the absence thereof – compounds situations of precarious employment and creates a situation of hyper-precarity.[688] Deportability creates exploitability. A set of generalized fears created by insecure status and non-existent rights to residence, welfare, and work can operate both directly – in the case of employers making threats to denounce workers to immigration authorities – but also indirectly to discipline workers by limiting their ability or willingness to exit or seek help.

At EU level, this issue is currently addressed in Directive 2009/52/EC (the Employers Sanctions Directive). However, as we shall discuss in more detail below (see section 6.2.5), the one-sided, repressive approach taken in this Act fails to effectively protect clandestine and other irregular migrants from labor exploitation.

---

684 Lewis and Waite, 'Asylum, Immigration Restrictions and Exploitation: Hyper-precarity as a Lens for Understanding and Tackling Forced Labour', 5 *Anti-Trafficking Review* (2015) 49, at 64; drawing on Phillips, 'Unfree Labour and Adverse Incorporation in the Global Economy: Comparative Perspectives on Brazil and India', 42 *Economy and Society* (2013) 171.

685 Cheliotis, 'Punitive Inclusion: The Political Economy of Irregular Migration in the Margins of Europe', 14 *European Journal of Criminology* (2017) 78.

686 Cf. Coddington, Conlon and Martin, 'Destitution Economies: Circuits of Value in Asylum, Refuge, and Migration Control', 110 *Annals of the Association of American Geographers* (2020) 1425; the authors argue that precisely the 'permanently temporary' status of irregular migrants is a useful part of capitalist 'destitution economies'; see also, in the US context, H. Motomura, *Immigration outside the Law* (2014), at 31–55.

687 FRA, Protecting Migrant Workers from Exploitation in the EU: Workers' Perspectives (2019); Amnesty International, *Exploited Labour: Migrant Workers in Italy's Agricultural Sector* (2012), available at https://www.amnesty.org/en/documents/EUR30/020/2012/en/.

688 Lewis and Waite, 'Asylum, Immigration Restrictions and Exploitation: Hyper-Precarity as a Lens for Understanding and Tackling Forced Labour', 5 *Anti-Trafficking Review* (2015) 49.

6.2 *Legal evaluation*

This section focuses on the Human Rights constraints on policies of planned destitution (trends 1 and 2) and the related positive obligation to address the situation of clandestine migrant workers (trend 3). We will then proceed to discuss whether the present EU legal framework sufficiently addresses these situations.

6.2.1 General legal framework regarding human dignity of margizens

At the universal level, the International Covenant on Economic, Social and Cultural Rights (ICESCR) protects the rights of 'everyone'. Thus, States are obliged to respect, protect, and fulfill the rights laid down in the Covenant of all individuals within their jurisdiction. The Committee on Economic, Social and Cultural Rights (CESCR), charged with overseeing the implementation of ICESCR, has clarified that the Covenant rights apply to everyone, including non-nationals, regardless of legal status and documentation.[689]

According to Art. 2 ICESCR, rights laid down in this Covenant are contingent upon availability of resources. In the situations analyzed here, however, States use arguments related to migration control, rather than a lack of resources, to justify restrictive measures. The relevant provision is Art. 4 ICESCR, which stipulates that States may subject the Covenant rights only to such limitations as are determined by law and only insofar as this may be compatible with the nature of these rights, and solely for the purpose of promoting the general welfare in a democratic society.[690] Differential treatment based on prohibited grounds will be viewed as discriminatory unless the justification for differentiation is reasonable and objective.[691] This includes an assessment as to whether the aim and effects of the measures or omissions are legitimate. The Limburg Principles on the Implementation of ICESCR, drafted by a group of experts in international law, suggest that 'promoting the general welfare' should be construed to mean 'furthering

689 CESCR, General Comment No. 20: Non-discrimination in economic, social and cultural rights, E/C.12/GC/20, at para. 13.

690 Müller, 'Limitations to and Derogations from Economic, Social and Cultural Rights', 9 *Human Rights Law Review* (2009) 557.

691 CESCR, General Comment No. 20: Non-discrimination in economic, social and cultural rights, E/C.12/GC/20, at para. 30.

the well-being of the people as a whole'.[692] Generally speaking, aims of migration policy such as preventing 'secondary movements' and fostering 'effective returns' might qualify for such justification.[693]

However, the measures or omissions must not entirely frustrate the rights granted in the Covenant – that is to say, there are minimum guarantees of socio-economic rights that must not fall prey to the goal of migration control.[694] On this point, the CESCR opined that 'a minimum core obligation to ensure the satisfaction of, at the very least, minimum essential levels of each of the rights is incumbent upon every State party. Thus, for example, a State party in which any significant number of individuals is deprived of essential foodstuffs, of essential primary health care, of basic shelter and housing, or of the most basic forms of education is, prima facie, failing to discharge its obligations under the Covenant.'[695] Even when resources are severely constrained, vulnerable members of society must be protected.[696] As regards asylum seekers and irregular migrants specifically, the CESCR found that States must refrain from 'denying or limiting equal access for all persons, including ... asylum seekers and illegal immigrants, to preventive, curative and palliative health services'.[697] Other treaty-monitoring bodies have also consistently described such migrants as a vulnerable group entitled to particular protection when States implement their treaty obligations.[698] The CESCR considers these core obligations as non-derogable and 'indivisibly linked' to the dignity of the human person. These obligations include access to basic shelter and minimum essential food for everyone, regardless of immigration status.[699]

692 The Limburg Principles on the Implementation of the International Covenant on Economic, Social and Cultural Rights, annexed to UN doc. E/CN.4/1987/17, 8 January 1987, at para. 52.

693 Although the limitation is to be construed narrowly, see Müller, 'Limitations to and Derogations from Economic, Social and Cultural Rights', 9 *Human Rights Law Review* (2009) 557, at 570–575.

694 Müller, 'Limitations to and Derogations from Economic, Social and Cultural Rights', 9 *Human Rights Law Review* (2009) 557, at 579–583.

695 CESCR, General Comment No. 3: The Nature of States Parties' Obligations, E/1991/23, at para. 10.

696 Ibid., at para. 12.

697 CESCR, General Comment No. 14: The right to the highest attainable standard of health (Art. 12), E/C.12/2000/4, at para. 34.

698 See, e.g., CMW, General Comment No. 1 on migrant domestic workers, CMW/C/GC/1, at para. 7 and 21.

699 CESCR, General Comment No. 12: The right to adequate food, E/C.12/1999/5, at para. 4 and 15; General Comment No. 4: The right to adequate housing,

Therefore, in order to preserve the human dignity of 'everyone', States must ensure a minimum core of the Covenant rights for irregular migrants who are actually present. For as long as a person falls within the jurisdiction of a State Party, this State must comply with its Human Rights obligations toward that individual, rather than referring the person to protection elsewhere.

At the regional level, Art. 3 ECHR provides for a source of minimum social guarantees. While the ECHR mainly sets forth civil and political rights, the ECtHR has recognized that many of them have implications of a social or economic nature.[700] Thus, although the ECHR does not explicitly lay down a right to human dignity, it is generally accepted that Art. 3 ECHR is derived from that principle. In its case-law, the Strasbourg Court has developed that a State's responsibility is engaged under Art. 3 ECHR when applicants who are wholly dependent on State support find themselves faced with official indifference in a situation of serious deprivation or want incompatible with human dignity.[701] In *M.S.S. v. Belgium and Greece*, the Court applied this principle to the situation of an asylum seeker from Afghanistan who had been transferred from Belgium to Greece, where he faced destitution without any support from Greece; the Court considered this to entail a violation of Art. 3 ECHR.[702] In its subsequent case-law relating to migrant destitution, the ECtHR has further clarified that violations of Art. 3 ECHR arise in situations where the persons concerned are highly vulnerable because of their dependency related to the inability to leave a difficult situation. Accordingly, the Court found no violation where the applicants were not found to be dependent on their relationship with the State – either because they did not have such a relationship in the first place,[703] or because they did not convince the

E/1992/23, at para. 6–7; General Comment No. 14: The right to the highest attainable standard of health (Art. 12); E/C.12/2000/4, at para. 43 and 47.

700 See ECtHR, *Airey v. Ireland*, Appl. no. 6289/73, Judgment of 9 October 1979, at para. 26.

701 ECtHR, *Budina v. Russia*, Appl. no. 45603/05, Admissibility Decision of 18 June 2009.

702 ECtHR, *M.S.S. v. Belgium and Greece*, Appl. no. 30696/09, Grand Chamber Judgment of 21 January 2011, at para. 252.

703 For example, because they did not formally apply for asylum, benefits or entry – see ECtHR, *Halimi v. Austria and Italy*, Appl. no. 53852/11, Admissibility Decision of 18 June 2013, at para. 70–72; *Miruts Hagos v. the Netherlands and Italy*, Appl. no. 9053/10, Admissibility Decision of 27 August 2013, at para. 38 and 44; *Ndikumana v. the Netherlands*, Appl. no. 4714/06, Admissibility Decision of 6 May 2014, at para. 45.

Court that the costs of leaving it were prohibitively high.[704] If the migrants in question can influence their destitute situation, such as by lodging an application for benefits or starting legal proceedings against a refusal – but also, for those subject to a return decision, by leaving the host country voluntarily or cooperating in a return procedure – there is no violation of Art. 3 ECHR.[705]

Beyond the ECHR, the European Social Charter of 1961 (ESC, extended by an Additional Protocol of 1988) and the Revised European Social Charter of 1996 which entered into force in 1999 (Revised ESC) contain comprehensive lists of social and economic rights. These rights are, as a rule, binding on the vast majority of European States. Yet, according to its Appendix, the Revised ESC in general exempts irregular migrants from the scope of its protection.[706] In its jurisprudence, however, the European Committee on Social Rights (ECSR) – the treaty body that monitors the implementation of the ESC and the Revised ESC and hears collective complaints in a quasi-judicial procedure since the 1995 Additional Protocol came into force in 1998 – has bridged this gap by setting out a minimum floor of social protection that should apply to all persons, including irregular migrants.[707] Relying on the preservation of human dignity as 'the fundamental value and indeed the core of positive European human rights

704 For example, because they left accommodation by choice – see ECtHR, *Abubeker v. Austria and Italy*, Appl. no. 73874/11, Admissibility Decision of 18 June 2013, at para. 61; *Hussein Diirshi and others v. the Netherlands and Italy*, Appl. no. 2314/10 et al., Admissibility Decision of 10 September 2013, at para. 140; or because they could leave for another country – see ECtHR, *A v. the Netherlands*, Appl. no. 60538/13, Admissibility Decision of 12 November 2013, at para. 50–53; *Hunde v. the Netherlands*, Appl. no. 17931/16, Admissibility Decision of 5 July 2016, at para. 53–59.

705 Slingenberg, 'The Right Not to be Dominated: The Case Law of the European Court of Human Rights on Migrants' Destitution', 19 *Human Rights Law Review* (2019) 291, at 312.

706 As laid down in the first paragraph of the Appendix, which is, according to Art. N of the Revised ESC, an integral part of this Charter.

707 ECSR, *International Federation of Human Rights Leagues (FIDH) v. France*, Complaint No. 14/2003, Decision of 8 September 2004 (on access to the health care system); *Defence for Children International (DCI) v. the Netherlands*, Complaint No. 47/2008, Decision of 20 October 2009 (on access to social housing); *DCI v. Belgium*, Complaint No. 69/2011, Decision of 23 November 2012 (on social assistance). See O'Cinnéide, 'Migrant Rights under the European Social Charter', in C. Costello and M. Freedland (eds), *Migrants at Work: Immigration and Vulnerability in Labour Law* (2014) 282, at 289–292.

law',[708] the ECSR has argued that the limited personal scope of the Revised ESC should not affect disadvantaged groups. In light of other international treaties ratified by all Parties, in particular the ECHR, the rights of the Revised ESC should be extended to non-nationals without distinction.[709] Therefore, it held, the denial of rights connected to life and dignity to foreign nationals within the territory of a State Party, 'even if they are there illegally', is contrary to the Revised Social Charter.[710] The Committee has since upheld and expanded this jurisprudence.[711] In subsequent reporting cycles, the ECSR has also begun to clarify the circumstances in which non-nationals, including those irregularly present on the territory of a Contracting State, are entitled to the protection of the Revised ESC.[712] As a result, the restriction on the scope of rights imposed by the Appendix does not apply when it comes to the enjoyment of the 'minimum core' of the rights set out in this Charter that are essential to maintain human dignity.[713] This minimum-floor logic converges with the obligation to meet 'minimum essential levels', as developed by the CESCR.

Although the ECSR makes reference to ECtHR jurisprudence, the Committee also explicitly observes that 'the scope of the Charter is broader [than that of the ECHR, as developed among others in *M.S.S. v. Belgium and Greece*] and requires that necessary emergency social assistance be granted also to those who do not, or no longer, fulfill the criteria of entitlement to assistance specified in the above instruments, that is, also to migrants staying in the territory of the States Parties in an irregular

---

708 ECSR, *FIDH v. France*, Complaint No. 14/2003, Decision of 8 September 2004, at para. 27–31.

709 ECSR, Conclusions XVII-1, Vol. 1 (2004), General Introduction, at para. 5.

710 ECSR, *FIDH v. France*, Complaint No. 14/2003, Decision of 8 September 2004, at para. 32.

711 ECSR, *DCI v. the Netherlands*, Complaint No. 47/2008, Decision of 20 October 2009, at para. 37; *Centre on Housing Rights and Evictions (COHRE) v. Italy*, Complaint No. 58/2009, Decision of 25 June 2010 at 33; *DCI v. Belgium*, Complaint No. 69/2011, Decision of 23 October 2012; *Conference of European Churches (CEC) v. the Netherlands*, Complaint No. 90/2013, Decision of 1 July 2014, at para. 144; *European Federation of National Organisations working with the Homeless (FEANTSA) v. the Netherlands*, Complaint No. 86/2012, Decision of 2 July 2014, at para. 58–61.

712 See also O'Cinnéide, 'Migrant Rights under the European Social Charter', in C. Costello and M. Freedland (eds), *Migrants at Work: Immigration and Vulnerability in Labour Law* (2014) 282, at 291.

713 ECSR, Conclusions XVII-1, Vol. 1 (2004), General Introduction, at para. 5.

manner, for instance pursuant to their expulsion.'[714] Specifically, the Committee held that emergency social assistance must be granted without any conditions and, in particular, cannot be made conditional upon the willingness of the persons concerned to cooperate in the organization of their own expulsion.[715]

(2) At EU level, both the ECHR and the Revised ESC are reflected in the EU-CFR. Art. 1 EU-CFR gives the right to human dignity a central place in the EU Charter. The prohibition of torture and inhuman or degrading treatment contained in Art. 3 ECHR is literally mirrored in Art. 4 EU-CFR. In addition, the EU Charter also transfers some provisions of the Revised ESC into the EU legal order, relating to labor, social security, social assistance, and healthcare; in some cases, the text is taken directly from the Revised ESC. Specifically, Art. 34 EU-CFR lays down the right to social security and social assistance and thus mirrors and specifies Art. 12 and 13 Revised ESC. Notably, pursuant to Art. 34(3) EU-CFR, the EU (and thus the Member States when they are implementing EU law) 'recognises and respects the right to social and housing assistance so as to ensure a decent existence for all those who lack sufficient resources'. The Explanations to the EU Charter note that Art. 34(3) EU-CFR inter alia draws on Art. 30 and 31 of the Revised Social Charter.[716] The CJEU has repeatedly referred to this social right to interpret the term 'core benefits' used in the Long-term Residents Directive (Directive 2003/109).[717]

This consonance speaks in favor of adopting the doctrines developed by the CESCR and the ECSR as part of the applicable EU law. However, their jurisprudence has a less certain legal status within EU law, as compared to the case-law of the ECtHR. While all EU Member States are Parties to the ICECSR and the ESC, five of them have signed but not yet ratified the Revised ESC.[718] The collective complaint procedure has been accepted

714 ECSR, *CEC v. the Netherlands*, Complaint No. 90/2013, Decision of 1 July 2014, at para. 117.

715 Ibid.

716 Explanations relating to the Charter of Fundamental Rights, 2007/C 303/02, on Art. 34 EU-CFR. The explanations only mention Art. 153 TFEU as a legal basis to implement this provision. This interpretation is too narrow; there is nothing in the text of Art. 34 EU-CFR that restricts its application to a particular legal basis.

717 CJEU, Case C-571/10, *Kamberaj* (EU:C:2012:233), at para. 80 and 92; Case C-94/20, *KV* (EU:C:2021:477), at para. 39 and 42.

718 Since Germany and Spain ratified the Revised ESC in 2021, Croatia, Czech Republic, Denmark, Luxembourg, and Poland are the remaining five EU Member States that have yet to ratify the Revised ESC (situation at 1 July 2021).

by 12 EU Member States,[719] while all EU Members are subject to the reporting system of the Social Charter. The EU Charter of Fundamental Rights does not establish an explicit link with the quasi-judicial practice of the CESCR or the ECSR (cf. Art. 52(3) EU-CFR). Moreover, the Revised ESC – like the ESC – has an 'à la carte' system, allowing acceding States, within certain limits, to choose which provisions they agree to be bound by – which leads to variable commitments across the States Parties.[720]

Against this backdrop, the CJEU unsurprisingly does not consider the ESC or the Revised ESC, in its entirety, as having 'de facto' binding force on the EU, unlike the ECHR – although the CJEU has repeatedly referred to the ESC and the Revised ESC in its case-law as a source of inspiration for interpreting EU law, including the Charter of Fundamental Rights.[721] The CJEU has also reminded the Member States that when they are implementing EU legislation – on family reunification, in the instant case – they must conform with their international obligations, including those derived from the ESC.[722] Consequently, where rights stipulated in the ESC or the Revised ESC have been incorporated into the EU Charter they shall be taken into account as a guide for the interpretation of the EU Charter. This naturally extends to the jurisprudence developed by the ECSR.[723] While there is no automatic relationship between these bodies of law, the presumption of substantive homogeneity between EU fundamental rights and Human Rights (see above, introduction to this volume) also applies in the realm of social and economic rights.

719 As of 1 July 2021, six EU Member States have signed but not yet ratified the relevant Additional Protocol of 1995 (CETS No. 158), see https://www.coe.int/en/web/conventions/full-list/-/conventions/treaty/158.

720 See Art. A Revised ESC and Art. 20 ESC.

721 See, e.g., CJEU, Cases C-119/19 P and C-126/19 P, *Commission and Council v. Carreras Sequeros et al.* (EU:C:2020:676), at para. 113–123; Case C-116/06, *Sari Kiiski*, (EU:C:2007:536), at para. 48–49; Case C-268/06, *Impact* (EU:C:2008:223), at para. 113–114.

722 CJEU, Case C-540/03, *Parliament v. Council* (EU:C:2006:429), at para. 107.

723 O. de Schutter, *The European Pillar of Social Rights and the Role of the European Social Charter in the EU Legal Order* (2017), at 47–48.

6.2.2 General legal framework regarding labor rights of irregular migrant workers

Human Rights law also protects the labor rights of irregular migrants.[724] At the universal level, Art. 7(a)(i) ICESCR protects the right of 'everyone' to just and favorable conditions of work without distinctions of any kind.[725] The CESCR specifically emphasizes that nationality and legal status should not bar access to the protection of rights under the ICESCR.[726] This has been reiterated in the CESCR's concluding observations on State Party reports.[727] In addition, Art. 5(e)(i) of the International Convention on the Elimination of All Forms of Racial Discrimination (ICERD) states that the protection of the right to work applies to all persons.[728] According to CERD, the relevant Committee, 'undocumented non-citizens' also fall within the scope of protection of ICERD.[729]

Building on these essentially uncontested general obligations, Part III of the UN Migrant Workers Convention (ICRMW) reiterates and specifies the Human Rights of all migrant workers and members of their families irrespective of their immigration status. The Committee on Migrant Workers (CMW) elaborates on the rights of migrant workers, particularly those in irregular migration situations, specifying that Art. 11 of this Convention requires States parties to take effective measures against all forms of forced or compulsory labor by migrant workers.[730]

---

724 See, e.g., E. Dewhurst, 'The Right of Irregular Immigrants to Back Pay: The Spectrum of Protection in International, Regional, and National Legal Systems', in C. Costello and M. Freedland (eds), *Migrants at Work: Immigration and Vulnerability in Labour Law* (2014) 216.

725 Art. 7(a)(i) ICESCR.

726 CESCR, General Comment No. 20: Non-discrimination in economic, social and cultural rights, E/C.12/GC/20, at para. 30; see also CERD, General Recommendation No. 30: Discrimination against non-citizens, CERD/C/64/Misc.11/rev.3.

727 See references in E. Dewhurst, 'The Right of Irregular Immigrants to Back Pay: The Spectrum of Protection in International, Regional, and National Legal Systems', in C. Costello and M. Freedland (eds), *Migrants at Work: Immigration and Vulnerability in Labour Law* (2014) 216, at 223, note 21.

728 Art. 5(e)(i) ICERD.

729 CERD, General Recommendation No. 30: Discrimination against non-citizens, CERD/C/64/Misc.11/rev.3, recital 3.

730 CMW, General Comment No. 2 on the rights of migrant workers in an irregular situation and members of their families, CMW/C/GC/2, at para. 60–61.

In addition, universal labor rights, as developed under the auspices of the International Labour Organization (ILO), also apply to irregular migrants. Indeed, the text of the ICRMW and the interpretations by the CMW derive the labor rights of irregular migrants from ILO standards, including Forced Labour Convention No. 29 (1930).[731] The ILO considers this Treaty one of the eight fundamental ILO Conventions that codify 'the fundamental principles and rights at work' – that is, the Human Rights core of international labor law, which all ILO Member States have committed to observe.[732] The Forced Labour Convention aims to suppress all forms of work or service that are exacted from a person under menace of a penalty and for which that person has not offered themselves voluntarily. More recently, the 2014 Protocol to ILO Convention No. 29 has further specified State obligations regarding the prevention of forced labor. It enshrines the general duty to 'prevent and eliminate' forced labor (Art. 1(1) Protocol of 2014), and the duty to create a national policy and plan of action to that end (Art. 1(2)). Specific efforts must be undertaken to ensure the coverage and enforcement of labor laws 'as appropriate' to 'all workers and all sectors of the economy' (Art. 2(c)(i)) and to strengthen labor inspection services (Art. 2(c)(ii)). Also required is specific protection, particularly for migrant workers, 'from possible abusive and fraudulent practices during the recruitment and placement process' (Art. 2(d)).

At the regional level, the two significant instruments that protect irregular migrants against exploitation are the ECHR and the Revised ESC. The Revised ESC provides an extensive list of labor rights in Art. 1–8; these are, however, subject to lawful residence status as per the Appendix. Regarding these Articles, the ESCR has not (yet) developed a minimum core exception for irregular migrants, although it could well be argued that the same reasoning applies to these rights. The remainder of this section therefore focuses on the ECHR.

While the ECHR does not generally protect labor rights due to its focus on civil and political rights, it does prohibit forced or compulsory labor (Art. 4 ECHR). The substance of this provision is part of EU law (see Art. 5(1) and (2) EU-CFR). Art. 4(1) ECHR requires that 'no one shall be

731 As well as ILO Convention No. 189 (2011) concerning Decent Work for Domestic Workers; and ILO Convention No. 111 (1958) concerning Discrimination (Employment and Occupation).

732 ILO Declaration on Fundamental Principles and Rights at Work (1998); see also ILO, *The Rules of the Game: An introduction to the standards-related work of the International Labour Organization* (4th ed. 2019), at 19.

held in slavery or servitude'. Note that, unlike most of the substantive clauses of the Convention, Art. 4(1) ECHR makes no provision for exceptions, and no derogation is permissible under Art. 15(2) ECHR even in the event of a public emergency threatening the life of the nation.[733] Given its absolute nature, this provision also extends to irregular migrants.[734] In view of Art. 52(3) EU-CFR, the same holds true in EU law; the general limitation clause of Art. 52(1) EU-CFR is not applicable.

By reference to international instruments specifically concerned with the issue, including the ILO Forced Labour Convention, the ECtHR has held that limiting compliance with Art. 4 ECHR only to direct action by State authorities would be inconsistent with these international instruments and would amount to rendering it ineffective.[735] It has, therefore, held that States have positive obligations under Art. 4 ECHR. The positive obligations are both substantive and procedural, including the obligation to investigate.[736]

In order to comply with their substantive obligations, Member States are required to put in place a legislative and administrative framework to prohibit and punish such acts.[737] Art. 4 ECHR may, in certain circumstances, also require a State to take operational measures to protect victims, or potential victims, of treatment in breach of that Article.[738] In order for a positive obligation to take operational measures to arise in a particular case, it must be demonstrated that the State authorities were aware, or ought to have been aware, of circumstances giving rise to a credible suspi-

733 ECtHR, *C.N. v. UK*, Appl. no. 4239/08, Grand Chamber Judgment of 13 November 2012, at para. 65; ECtHR, *Stummer v. Austria*, Appl. no. 37452/02, Grand Chamber Judgment of 7 July 2011, at para. 116.

734 Cf. also ECtHR, *Siliadin v. France*, Appl. no. 73316/01, Judgment of 26 July 2005; the applicant was unlawfully present in France. See for discussion Mantouvalou, 'Servitude and Forced Labour in the 21st Century: The Human Rights of Domestic Workers', 35 *Industrial Law Journal* (2006) 395. See also ECtHR, *Rantsev v. Cyprus and Russia*, Appl. no. 25965/04, Judgment of 7 January 2010.

735 ECtHR, *Siliadin v. France*, Appl. no. 73316/01, Judgment of 26 July 2005, at para. 89.

736 ECtHR, *S.M. v. Croatia*, Appl. no. 60561/14, Grand Chamber Judgment of 25 June 2020, at para. 306.

737 ECtHR, *C.N. v. UK*, Appl. no. 4239/08, Grand Chamber Judgment of 13 November 2012, at para. 66; *Siliadin v. France*, Appl. no. 73316/01, Judgment of 26 July 2005, at para. 112; *C.N. and V. v. France*, Appl. no. 67724/09, Judgment of 11 October 2012, at para. 105.

738 ECtHR, *Rantsev v. Cyprus and Russia*, Appl. no. 25965/04, Judgment of 7 January 2010, at para. 286; *C.N. v. UK*, Appl. no. 4239/08, Grand Chamber Judgment of 13 November 2012, at para. 67.

cion that an identified individual had been, or was, at real and immediate risk of being subjected to treatment in breach of Art. 4 ECHR. In the case of an answer in the affirmative, there will be a violation of that Article where the authorities fail to take appropriate measures within the scope of their powers to remove the individual from that situation or risk.[739] The preventive measures include measures to strengthen coordination at national level between the various anti-trafficking bodies and to discourage the demand for all forms of exploitation of persons. Protection measures include facilitating the identification of victims by qualified persons and assisting victims in their physical, psychological, and social recovery.[740]

The procedural requirements under Art. 4 ECHR are similar irrespective of whether the treatment has been inflicted through the involvement of State agents or private individuals. The requirement to investigate does not depend on a complaint from the victim or next-of-kin; rather, the authorities must act of their own motion once the matter has come to their attention.[741]

The Court has developed the positive obligations arising under Art. 4 ECHR mainly in its jurisprudence relating to human trafficking.[742] However, the ECtHR has specifically clarified that the notion of 'forced or compulsory labour' under Art. 4 ECHR aims to protect against instances of serious exploitation, irrespective of whether they are connected to a human trafficking context.[743] Thus, Art. 4 ECHR requires that member States penalize and prosecute effectively any act aimed at maintaining a person in a situation of slavery, servitude, or forced or compulsory labor.[744] In

739 ECtHR, *Rantsev v. Cyprus and Russia*, Appl. no. 25965/04, Judgment of 7 January 2010, at para. 286; *C.N. v. UK*, Appl. no. 4239/08, Grand Chamber Judgment of 13 November 2012, at para. 67; *V.C.L. and A.N. v. UK*, Appl. no. 77587/12 and 74603/12, Judgment of 16 February 2021, at para. 152.

740 ECtHR, *Chowdury and others v. Greece*, Appl. no. 21884/15, Judgment of 30 March 2017, at para. 110.

741 ECtHR, *S.M. v. Croatia*, Appl. no. 60561/14, Grand Chamber Judgment of 25 June 2020, at para. 312–320; *Rantsev v. Cyprus and Russia*, Appl. no. 25965/04, Judgment of 7 January 2010, at para. 288.

742 Cf. V. Stoyanova, *Human Trafficking and Slavery Reconsidered: Conceptual Limits and States' Positive Obligations in European Law* (2017).

743 ECtHR, *S.M. v. Croatia*, Appl. no. 60561/14, Grand Chamber Judgment of 25 June 2020, at para. 300 and 303.

744 ECtHR, *C.N. v. UK*, Appl. no. 4239/08, Grand Chamber Judgment of 13 November 2012, at para. 66; *Siliadin v. France*, Appl. no. 73316/01, Judgment of 26 July 2005, at para. 112; *C.N. and V. v. France*, Appl. no. 67724/09, Judgment of 11 October 2012, at para. 105.

Chowdury and others v. Greece the ECtHR held that, irrespective of the legal qualification of the circumstances as human trafficking or forced labor, the positive obligations generated by Art. 4 ECHR also apply to the severe exploitation of workers in employment relationships.[745] The Court found that the applicants' situation – irregular migrants working in difficult physical conditions and without wages, under the supervision of armed guards, in the strawberry-picking industry in a particular region of Greece – constituted human trafficking and forced labor.[746]

In sum, there is a comprehensive set of positive obligations imposed on both the EU and its Member States by virtue of Art. 4 ECHR/Art. 5 EU-CFR, to protect the rights of irregular migrant workers – in particular, from the risk of being subjected to severe exploitation. On a more fundamental level, this also raises the question of whether the positive obligations on States to avoid exposing individuals to forced labor encompass an obligation to rethink some features of how immigration is commonly regulated.[747]

6.2.3 Specific issue: Human Rights limits to sanctioning 'secondary movements'

It emerges from the above legal analysis that States must provide a socio-economic subsistence level to all migrants in order to safeguard their human dignity. This minimum core cannot be undercut by migration policy considerations. Measures sanctioning 'secondary movements' of asylum seekers within the Union by withdrawing material reception conditions regularly conflict with this obligation.

The relevant legislative instrument providing for the reception conditions of asylum seekers in the EU is the Reception Conditions Directive. Art. 17–19 of this Directive lay out the general rules and modalities for material reception conditions and health care. In addition, Art. 15 provides for the right to access employment. As per Art. 20, material reception conditions may be reduced or withdrawn in the event an applicant is

745 ECtHR, *Chowdury and others v. Greece,* Appl. no. 21884/15, Judgment of 30 March 2017.

746 Ibid., at para. 127.

747 See Costello, 'Migrants and Forced Labour: A Labour Law Response', in A. Bogg, C. Costello, A. Davies and J. Prassl (eds), *The Autonomy of Labour Law* (2014) 189.

considered to have abandoned the place of residence, not conformed with reporting duties, or lodged a subsequent application. Moreover, Member States may reduce reception conditions when an applicant has not lodged their application for international protection as soon as reasonably practicable, when an applicant has concealed financial resources, or when an applicant has seriously breached the rules of the accommodation center or demonstrated seriously violent behavior.

Legislation that reduces or withdraws reception conditions for other reasons than those foreseen in Art. 20 are contrary to the Directive. Specifically, sanctions for onward movement are not foreseen. This was confirmed in 2012 by the CJEU in its *Cimade and GISTI* judgment. The CJEU held that, under the current legislation, a Member State is obliged to provide material reception conditions even to an asylum seeker in respect of whom it decides to call upon another Member State to take charge of or take back that applicant under the Dublin Regulation. The obligation ceases only when the applicant is actually transferred.[748] Although access to the labor market is not, strictly speaking, a material reception condition, the CJEU later extended this reasoning to Art. 15 of the Reception Conditions Directive.[749] In both cases, the CJEU did not rely solely on the wording of the Directive but also buttressed its argument by reference to the preservation of human dignity.[750]

This reasoning links the construction of the Directive to Art. 1 EU-CFR, as well as to the broader legal discourse in Human Rights law discussed above. In its case-law on a dignified standard of living of asylum seekers, the CJEU initially turned to the ECHR and the case-law of the Strasbourg Court, transferring to Art. 4 EU-CFR the standard that the ECtHR first developed for Art. 3 ECHR *in M.S.S. v. Belgium and Greece*.[751] Yet, as discussed above, extreme material poverty in breach of Art. 3 ECHR is a narrower concept of human dignity than the one developed by the CESCR and the ECSR. This is beginning to be reflected in case-law, as the CJEU appears to be developing a notion of human dignity under Art. 1 EU-CFR that is more independent of the prohibition of torture and inhuman or de-

748 CJEU, Case C-179/11, *Cimade and GISTI* (EU:C:2012:594).

749 CJEU, Cases C-322/19 and C-385/19, *K.S.* (EU:C:2021:11), at para. 67–68.

750 CJEU, Case C-179/11, *Cimade and GISTI* (EU:C:2012:594), at para. 56; Cases C-322/19 and C-385/19, *K.S.* (EU:C:2021:11), at para. 69.

751 CJEU, Cases C-297/17, C-318/17, C-319/17 and C-438/17, *Ibrahim* (EU:C:2019:219), at para. 90 et seq.; Case C-163/17, *Jawo* (EU:C:2019:218), at para. 92 et seq.

grading treatment.[752] This would imply a higher standard of protection. In the case of *Haqbin*, interpreting the provision on reduction and withdrawal of reception conditions, the CJEU concluded, with reference to Art. 1 EU-CFR, that a sanction that consists in the full withdrawal of material reception conditions relating to housing, food, or clothing, even if only for a limited period of time, is irreconcilable with the requirement to ensure a dignified standard of living for the applicant.[753] Although the Court did not make explicit reference to the ECSR in that regard – which arguably reflects the uncertain legal status of the Revised ESC in EU law – it appears that the CJEU's notion of human dignity is closer to that developed by the ESCR. Hence, we argue that, in respect of a dignified standard of living, the CJEU has embraced the view that the relevant EU fundamental right in substance is consonant with the jurisprudence of the ECSR, rather than merely reflecting the Art. 3 case-law of the ECtHR.

Accordingly, EU law as it stands obliges Member States to provide for a socio-economic subsistence level that meets their obligations under international law. Policies to sanction secondary movements which resort to socio-economic deprivation are therefore unlawful if they fall below the core minimum as defined in international jurisprudence. According to our legal analysis, this is not only a matter of accurate interpretation of the Reception Conditions Directive but also enshrined in the EU Charter, read in light of the pertinent Human Rights law.

The reform proposal for a recast Reception Conditions Directive, tabled by the European Commission in 2016,[754] is, therefore, highly questionable. Rather than explicitly preventing such policies of planned destitution, the Commission proposed creating a legal basis for them. Unsurprisingly, in the ensuing political process the legislative bodies are struggling to develop a provision that both enables the possibility of withdrawing material reception conditions and, at the same time, is in line with the requirement for a socio-economic subsistence level to safeguard human dignity. According to a compromise text, prepared in 2018 by the Bulgarian Presidency of the EU Council that seems to reflect an agreement between the governments,[755] the general standard that Member States must provide for

752 CJEU, Case C-233/18, *Zubair Haqbin* (EU:C:2019:956), at para. 45–47.

753 Ibid., at para. 47.

754 Proposal for a recast Reception Conditions Directive, COM(2016) 465, 13 July 2016.

755 Council of the EU: Note from the Presidency to the Permanent Representatives Committee, Directive 2013/33/EU (recast): Conditional confirmation of the final compromise text with a view to agreement, 10009/18 ADD 1, 18 June

asylum seekers under Art. 17–19 of the Directive is formulated as follows: 'an *adequate* standard of living for applicants, which guarantees their subsistence, protects their physical and mental health and respects their rights under the Charter of Fundamental Rights of the European Union' (emphasis added). In addition to the existing reasons for reductions and withdrawals, as currently laid down in Art. 20 (which, in an amended form, corresponds to Art. 19 of the compromise text), the Presidency suggested a new provision according to which material reception conditions will be withdrawn from the moment an applicant has been notified of a transfer decision under the Dublin Regulation (Art. 17a of the compromise text).

Assuming that this text will eventually be signed into law, the ambiguous wording leaves considerable leeway for conflicting interpretations. Unlike the current Directive, the draft avoids the term 'dignified standard' as a limit on reductions and withdrawals.[756] When called upon to interpret the 'dignified standard of living' as laid down in Art. 20(5) of the Reception Conditions Directive, the Court has held that the most basic needs cover, inter alia, food, personal hygiene and a place to live.[757] In contrast, for sanctions for non-cooperation within the Dublin State (as per Art. 19 in the compromise text), as well as for sanctions for unauthorized secondary movements (as per its Art. 17a), the new reduced fallback standard in the proposal is 'a standard of living in accordance with Union law, including the Charter of Fundamental Rights of the European Union, and international obligations'. This wording would certainly still be open to a construction that ensures the socio-economic subsistence level as it emerges from both ICESCR and Revised ESC. However, in light of the political context, we have serious concerns that the 'core minimum' would be undercut, especially because the distinction between the normal standard ('adequate') and the reduced standard (only 'standard') invites Member States to test the bottom line – and frequently cross it in practice.

Taken together, by introducing the legal possibility of sanctioning secondary movements with the withdrawal of material reception conditions,

---

2018; leaked document available at https://www.statewatch.org/media/1429/eu-council-reception-conditions-conditional-confirmation-text-10009-18-add1.pdf. For discussion, see S. Carrera et al., *When Mobility is not a Choice: Problematising Asylum Seekers' Secondary Movements and Their Criminalisation in the EU* (2019), at 8–11, available at https://www.ceps.eu/wp-content/uploads/2019/12/LSE2019-11-RESOMA-Policing-secondary-movements-in-the-EU.pdf.

756 See recital 25 and Art. 20(5) Reception Conditions Directive.

757 CJEU, Case C-163/17, *Jawo* (EU:C:2019:218), at para. 92.

the current reform proposals risk creating a new category of asylum seekers vulnerable to destitution.

6.2.4 Specific issue: Human Rights limits to sanctioning non-cooperation in return proceedings

Our analysis revealed a trend toward the use of policies of socio-economic deprivation in order to incentivize returns of (non-cooperative) non-removable returnees. Such policies risk interfering with the right to a minimum socio-economic subsistence level as developed above.

Art. 9 of the Return Directive (Directive 2008/115/EC) acknowledges that the actual deportation of a person to whom a return decision has been addressed and has become final may nevertheless be postponed. This raises the question of the status of those persons whose stay is technically 'illegal' and at the same time 'tolerated' – in particular, in terms of their social and economic rights.

The Return Directive falls short of comprehensively regulating this status. Art. 14(1) merely establishes a list of 'principles' that 'are taken into account as far as possible' pending return:

> *Member States shall, with the exception of the situation covered in Articles 16 and 17 [i.e., in situations of detention], ensure that the following principles are taken into account as far as possible in relation to third-country nationals during the period for voluntary departure granted in accordance with Article 7 and during periods for which removal has been postponed in accordance with Article 9:*
> *(a) family unity with family members present in their territory is maintained;*
> *(b) emergency health care and essential treatment of illness are provided;*
> *(c) minors are granted access to the basic education system subject to the length of their stay;*
> *(d) special needs of vulnerable persons are taken into account.*

The protective scope of this provision is limited in both its personal and material dimension, as well as in terms of the nature of the obligations it creates.

Unlike the initial proposal from the Commission,[758] the Return Directive does not cross-reference the corresponding rights of asylum seekers laid down in the Reception Conditions Directive.[759] Member State governments had expressed concerns during the negotiations that references to the Reception Conditions Directive might be perceived as 'upgrading' the situation of irregular migrants and thus 'send a wrong message'.[760] In terms of substance, the list of safeguards is less comprehensive than the rights provided for asylum seekers. As far as social and economic rights are concerned, it merely mentions emergency healthcare (point b) and basic education for minors (point c). The most notable omission relates to access to employment and material reception conditions, which were not even included in the Commission proposal. The provision does not foresee the coverage of basic needs, such as food or housing.

The status and the rights of unremovable migrants should be primarily defined at national level, as the preamble suggests: Recital 12 specifically stipulates that the situation of people 'who are staying illegally but who cannot yet be removed should be addressed', and that their basic conditions of subsistence should be defined according to national legislation. As a result, EU law possibly creates a legal vacuum that needs to be filled by domestic law. This is flanked by non-binding recommendations from the Commission. In its 2014 Communication, the Commission stressed that 'protracted situations' should be avoided and non-deportable people

---

758 European Commission, Proposal for a Directive on common standards and procedures in Member States for returning illegally staying third-country nationals, COM(2005) 391, 1 September 2005. This proposal was accompanied by an Impact Assessment (SEC(2005) 1057) and a Commission Staff Working Document (SEC(2005) 1175), containing detailed comments.

759 Commission Proposal COM(2005) 391, Art. 13: 'Member States shall ensure that the conditions of stay of third-country nationals for whom the enforcement of a return decision has been postponed or who cannot be removed for the reasons referred to in Article 8 of this Directive are not less favourable than those set out in Articles 7 to 10, Article 15 and Articles 17 to 20 of Directive 2003/9/EC.' The referenced Articles essentially cover family unity, health care, schooling and education for minors as well as respect for special needs of vulnerable persons.

760 Lutz, 'Return Directive 2008/115/EC', in K. Hailbronner and D. Thym (eds), *EU Immigration and Asylum Law: Commentary* (2nd ed. 2016), commentary on Art. 14, at para. 2; F. Lutz, *The Negotiations on the Return Directive* (2010), at 64; see also Majcher and Strik, 'Legislating without Evidence: The Recast of the EU Return Directive', 23 *European Journal of Migration and Law (EJML)* (2021) 103, at 123.

should not be left indefinitely without basic rights.[761] The Commission's Return Handbook, which is equally non-binding, states that 'there is no general legal obligation under Union law to make provision for the basic needs of *all* third country nationals pending return', but notes that 'the Commission encourages Member States to do so under national law, in order to assure humane and dignified conditions of life for returnees'.[762]

Moreover, the fact that the safeguards are framed as 'principles' that are to be 'taken into account as far as possible', raises further questions as to the legal nature of the obligations they contain, if any. In *Abdida* the Court partly mitigated this gap by relying on the effectiveness principle to argue that emergency healthcare also includes the provision for the basic needs of the person concerned.[763] Referring to Art. 14(1)(b) Return Directive, the Court ruled that Member States have an additional obligation to provide for the basic needs of a third-country national suffering from a serious illness where such a person lacks the means to make such provision for themselves.[764]

Based on this reasoning by the CJEU, the obligation to cater for the basic needs of non-removable migrants could be derived from their effective enjoyment of the other rights enumerated in Art. 14(1) Return Directive.[765] Whereas a lower Belgian Court applied this principle with regard to family life,[766] the Netherlands' highest administrative court, the *Raad van State*, ruled that the *Abdida* rationale was not applicable to the situation of a third-country national who could not be returned to

---

761 European Commission, Communication on EU Return Policy, COM(2014) 199, 28 March 2014.

762 European Commission, Recommendation 2017/2338 establishing a common 'Return Handbook' to be used by Member States' competent authorities when carrying out return-related tasks, at para. 64 (emphasis in original).

763 CJEU, Case C-562/13, *Abdida* (EU:C:2014:2453), at para. 58–60; confirmed in Case C-402/19, *LM* (EU:C:2020:759), at para. 52–53. Note that in *Mahdi*, a detention case, the Court did not deal with Art. 14 Return Directive: CJEU, Case C-146/14 PPU, *Mahdi* (EU:C:2014:1320).

764 CJEU, Case C-562/13, *Abdida* (EU:C:2014:2453), at para. 60.

765 Opinion of Advocate General Bot in Case C-562/13, *Abdida* (EU:C:2014:2167), at para. 149; Lutz, 'Non-removable Returnees under Union Law: Status Quo and Possible Developments', 20 *European Journal of Migration and Law (EJML)* (2018) 28, at 36.

766 Tribunal du travail de Bruxelles, R.G.15/1/C, Judgment of 23 January 2015, cited in M. Moraru and G. Renaudiere, *European Synthesis Report on the Judicial Implementation of Chapter III of the Return Directive Procedural Safeguards* (2016), REDIAL Research Report 2016/03, at 38.

Côte d'Ivoire because his request for a laissez-passer was rejected by the embassy.[767]

While the expansive reading of Art. 14 Return Directive by the CJEU adds to the safeguards following from this provision, the nature of the obligation remains less clear. The Court's reasoning seems to imply that the 'principles' laid down therein give rise to binding obligations under EU law, since it held that Member States 'are required to provide' the safeguards of Art. 14.[768] On the other hand, this requirement is limited to 'in so far as possible',[769] and Member States 'determine the form' that such provision of basic needs takes.[770] As a result, the Court only partly addresses the legal and material situation of irregularly staying migrants whose removal is postponed.[771] In addition, the safeguards laid down in Art. 14 Return Directive only apply for the period granted for voluntary departure and cases where removal is temporarily postponed in accordance with Art. 9.

Still, provided that Art. 14 Return Directive is applicable, there is nothing in the wording of this Directive, nor in the reasoning of the CJEU, that authorizes sanctions for non-cooperation with return. On the contrary, the reference to technical reasons due to lack of identification in Art. 9(2)(b) appears to extend to situations where the returnee is unwilling to cooperate with his or her own deportation.[772]

In sum, the Return Directive creates a particularly vulnerable category of migrants – non-returnable people – who cannot be removed (yet) but

---

767 Raad van State, Uitspraak 201502872/1/V1 (NL:RVS:2015:4001), Judgment of 15 December 2015.

768 CJEU, Case C-562/13, *Abdida* (EU:C:2014:2453), at para. 58.

769 Ibid., at para. 59.

770 Ibid., at para. 61.

771 Farcy, 'Unremovability under the Return Directive: An Empty Protection?', in M. Moraru, G. Cornelisse and Ph. de Bruycker (eds), *Law and Judicial Dialogue on the Return of Irregular Migrants from the European Union* (2020) 437, at 446.

772 While the distinction is not explicitly foreseen in the Return Directive, the Commission's 'Return Handbook' uses this distinction in the chapter on criminal sanctions: Recommendation 2017/2338, at para. 19. The 2013 'Ramboll study' on the implementation of the Return Directive suggested including the distinction between cooperating and non-cooperating returnees generally in legislation: M. Heegaard Bausager, J. Köpfli Møller and S. Ardittis, *Situation of Third-country Nationals Pending Postponed Return/Removal in the EU Member States and the Schengen Associated Countries* (2013), HOME/2010/RFXX/PR/1001, at 93 et seq.

who are not granted a comprehensive status under EU law.[773] EU legislation currently does not prevent – in any case, not with the necessary clarity – their minimum core of socio-economic rights required by Human Rights law being denied.

6.2.5 Specific issue: Human Rights obligations to combat exploitation of irregular migrants

As developed above, Member States have positive obligations to combat the exploitation of persons with irregular immigration status, including non-documented migrants. These obligations involve, inter alia, putting in place a legislative framework for prevention (see section 6.2.2).

In the context of the Union, the responsibility for meeting this obligation to legislate is shared between the EU and its Member States. The respective powers to combat social exclusion in the field of migration are categorized, in Art. 4(2) points (a), (b) and (j) TFEU, as shared competence between the Union and the Member States. According to the principle of subsidiarity, the Union shall act in such areas if the objectives of the proposed action cannot be sufficiently achieved by the Member States, but can rather be better achieved at Union level (Art. 5(3) TEU). Accordingly, in order to meet its constitutional obligations under Art. 5 EU-CFR (which mirrors the international obligation of Member States under Art. 4 ECHR), the EU is requested to use its legislative powers whenever the objective of preventing exploitation of irregular migrants cannot be sufficiently achieved by Member State action alone.

The EU legislature has addressed the issue of clandestine and other irregular migrant workers via the Employers Sanctions Directive (Directive 2009/52/EC). Pursuant to Art. 1, the Directive is designed as a measure to combat illegal immigration by setting Union-wide minimum standards for imposing sanctions against employers of third-country nationals who are staying irregularly. The Employers Sanctions Directive obliges EU Member States to prohibit the 'employment of illegally staying third-country nationals' and to criminalize certain forms of employment – for example,

773 B. Menezes Queiroz, *Illegally Staying in the EU: An Analysis of Illegality in EU Migration Law* (2018), at 84–85; Majcher and Strik, 'Legislating without Evidence: The Recast of the EU Return Directive', 23 *European Journal of Migration and Law (EJML)* (2021) 103, at 125.

when employers subject workers to particularly exploitative working conditions, as set out in Art. 9(1)(c).

This repressive approach is complemented by very limited protection of the labor rights of the irregular migrant workers concerned. The provisions laid down in the Directive primarily address the employers. The Preamble does refer to fundamental rights – but the considerations are concerned with the rights of the employers rather than those of the affected migrants.[774] The protective elements that are laid down in the Directive mainly emerge indirectly from the duties of the employers or Member States. For example, in accordance with Art. 6(1) Employers Sanctions Directive, employers are liable to make back-payments.

This reflects a lack of political interest in protection of Human Rights of irregular migrants. The legislative process of the Directive is illustrative of this finding. Member States opposed provisions on strict monitoring of employers, while the more rights-based approach of the European Parliament, supported by trade unions, has left only a light footprint in the final version of the Directive.[775] Further evidence is provided by the lack of or late implementation and de facto non-application of this Directive, and in particular its protective elements.[776] Especially as regards the core of the protective measures designed to redress injustices suffered by irregular migrants, and to access to justice and facilitate complaints (Art. 6(2) to (5) and Art. 13 Employers Sanctions Directive), Member States have implemented weak (if any) mechanisms to promote enforcement.[777]

The existence of an effective complaints mechanism, which enables exploited workers to access justice and receive compensation, is the cornerstone of protecting migrant workers from exploitation and abuse. Art. 14 of the Directive requires Member States to 'ensure that effective and adequate inspections are carried out' to control the employment of migrants of irregular status. However, there is a lack of safeguards to ensure that this data is not used for immigration enforcement. In 20 out of 25 Member States bound by the Employers Sanctions Directive, labor inspectorates report irregular migrants identified during inspections to the immigration law enforcement authorities. This discourages victims from reporting abus-

774 Employers Sanctions Directive, recital 37.

775 Schierle, 'Employers Sanctions Directive 2009/52/EC', in K. Hailbronner and D. Thym (eds), *EU Immigration and Asylum Law: Commentary* (2nd ed. 2016), commentary on Art. 1, at para. 17–18; on Art. 13, at para. 2–6.

776 European Commission, Communication the application of Directive 2009/52/EC, COM(2014) 286, 22 May 2014, at 7–8.

777 Ibid.

es and violations of labor law.[778] Similarly, when labor inspectorates conduct inspections jointly with the police or immigration law enforcement authorities, this may discourage exploited workers from reporting their experiences; it may also cause them to hide to avoid apprehension and removal.[779] The issue also has been raised by the HR Committee, which called upon Belgium to ensure protection for the right to an effective remedy for irregular immigrants, which is 'jeopardised by the fact that police officers are obliged to report their presence' at court.[780] Absent such safeguards, migrants facing exploitation in their work place will not call labor inspectors.

In its repressive approach, the Employers Sanctions Directive contrasts with early (albeit abortive) legislative initiatives from the 1970s on the basis of Art. 100 EEC Treaty. This provision empowered the European Community to legislate with a view to the establishment or functioning of the Common Market, including on matters relating to the rights and interests of employed persons. Essentially the same power is today laid down in Art. 115 TFEU (cf. Art. 114(2) TFEU). On that legal basis, the European Commission proposed a 'Council directive on the harmonization of laws in the Member States to combat illegal migration and illegal employment'[781] in November 1976. As the Commission noted then, clandestine migrants facing the constant threat of discovery and deportation are particularly vulnerable to exploitation and intimidation.[782] The proposal contained strong references to Human Rights and justified the need to harmonize Member States' laws in terms of combating abusive

778 FRA, Protecting Migrants in an Irregular Situation from Labour Exploitation: Role of the Employers Sanctions Directive (2021), at 7 and in particular Annex II, Table A5. See also PICUM, *A Worker is a Worker: How to Ensure that Undocumented Migrant Workers Can Access Justice* (2020), available at https://picum.org/wp-content/uploads/2020/03/A-Worker-is-a-Worker-full-doc.pdf.

779 FRA, Protecting Migrants in an Irregular Situation from Labour Exploitation (2021), at 7.

780 HR Committee, Concluding observations on State reports: Belgium, A/59/40 vol. I (2004), at 72, para. 11; see also CESCR, Consideration of reports submitted by States parties: Russian Federation, E/2004/22 (2003), at para. 487–490.

781 Commission of the European Communities, Proposal for a Council Directive on the Harmonisation of Laws in the Member States to Combat Illegal Employment, COM(76) 331, 3 November 1976.

782 Commission of the European Communities, Action Programme in Favour of Migrant Workers and Their Families, COM(74) 2250, 18 December 1974, at 21; Proposal for a Council Directive on the Harmonisation of Laws in the Member States to Combat Illegal Employment, COM(76) 331, 3 November 1976, at 1 (Explanatory Memorandum).

employment relationships, protecting the rights of workers, and moving forward the general social aims of the then European Community.[783] The rationale for this approach was to deter the employment of irregular migrants by ensuring that, as a consequence of the fulfillment of employer obligations and safeguarding the rights of migrant workers, the cost of irregular labor would equate with or even exceed that of the lawful labor force.[784] The proposal was amended in April 1978[785] in response to criticism by the European Parliament and the Economic and Social Committee that it failed to devote sufficient attention to the protection of irregular migrants.[786] The proposal also foresaw the implementation of 'adequate control, especially of employers and persons and undertakings supplying manpower to third parties'.[787] However, the Commission's efforts were not pursued in the Council due to a lack of political consensus among the Member States.[788] When the file was reopened more than 30 years later with the Employers Sanctions Directive, it not only moved from internal market policy to the field of immigration policy, based on Art. 79(2)(c) TFEU, but also lost much of its protective rationale.

This could be remedied in reform efforts by picking up the rights-based approach of the Commission and Parliament from the 1970s. In order to meet its obligations to combat exploitation of migrants in particularly vulnerable situations, the EU should not only consider offering entitlements to regularization to victims of exploitation (see Chapter 5) but also use the

783 Kraler, 'Fixing, Adjusting, Regulating, Protecting Human Rights: The Shifting Uses of Regularisations in the European Union', 13 *European Journal of Migration and Law (EJML)* (2011) 297, at 303.

784 Commission of the European Communities, Amended Proposal for a Council Directive concerning the Approximation of the Legislation of the Member States, in order to Combat Illegal Migration and Illegal Employment, COM(78) 86, 3 April 1978, at para. 12 (Explanatory Memorandum).

785 Ibid., at para. 1 (Explanatory Memorandum).

786 Cholewinski, 'European Union Policy on Irregular Migration: Human Rights Lost?', in B. Bogusz, R. Cholewinski and A. Cygan (eds), *Irregular Migration and Human Rights: Theoretical, European and International Perspectives* (2004) 159, at 165.

787 Commission of the European Communities, Amended Proposal for a Council Directive concerning the Approximation of the Legislation of the Member States, in order to Combat Illegal Migration and Illegal Employment, COM(78) 86, 3 April 1978, Art. 3.

788 Cholewinski, 'European Union Policy on Irregular Migration: Human Rights Lost?', in B. Bogusz, R. Cholewinski and A. Cygan (eds), *Irregular Migration and Human Rights: Theoretical, European and International Perspectives* (2004) 159, at 166.

broad range of its powers to strengthen the rights of irregular migrants. To this effect, the EU could combine the legal bases to regulate the rights and interests of employed persons with a view to ensuring fair competition in the internal market (Art. 115 TFEU), to provide minimum harmonization in the field of social policy (Art. 153 TFEU), and to legislate in the area of illegal immigration and unauthorized residence (Art. 79(2)(c) TFEU). One important element to render the policy effective is the establishment of non-reporting obligations for the labor inspectors (so-called 'firewalls' between labor law and immigration law).[789]

6.3 Recommendations

The above legal evaluations revealed that enhanced efforts are required in response to Member States policies that potentially violate the Human Rights of margizens. Our recommendations build on the EU's positive obligation 'to protect' the relevant socio-economic rights. As a general approach, we recommend that the EU embrace the standards developed by the European Committee of Social Rights, irrespective of the disputed status of its jurisprudence in EU law. The EU legislative bodies should require States to ensure a decent existence for all migrants actually present, regardless of their legal status. Moreover, we recommend that the EU legislature adopt a level of protection that builds a safety margin against the absolute minimum, in order to avoid implementation deficits that violate Human Rights.

While there is no strict obligation under international law to choose such an approach, the EU would more effectively use its powers to prevent unlawful results in a field in which the EU is generally accountable, delivering on its commitment to human dignity as one of its foundational values.

789 Crépeau and Hastie, 'The Case for "Firewall" Protections for Irregular Migrants', 17 *European Journal of Migration and Law (EJML)* (2015) 157; see also Costello, 'Migrants and Forced Labour: A Labour Law Response', in A. Bogg et al. (eds), *The Autonomy of Labour Law* (2014) 189.

Recommendation 1: Stop using restrictions to socio-economic rights to sanction 'secondary movements' of asylum seekers

We urge the EU to prevent Member States from using restrictions to socio-economic rights as a means to disincentivize 'secondary movements' of asylum seekers. Counterfactual assumptions that the person ought not be present according to the terms of asylum laws cannot justify a real risk of violating the Human Rights of persons who do not respond to the incentive to leave.

Specifically, we recommend that the rights stipulated in the Reception Conditions Directive be available to all asylum seekers irrespective of the place of asylum jurisdiction according to the Dublin III Regulation or any follow-up Regulation. The text of the Directive should explicitly rule out any reduction or withdrawal of benefits as a tool to promote compliance with the Dublin rules. The Commission should amend its proposal for a recast Reception Conditions Directive accordingly, in particular in withdrawing the proposed Art. 17a.

Note that this approach does not amount to recognizing a general right to freedom of movement within the EU, as the States reserve their powers to perform Dublin transfers in accordance with EU law. Whenever they actually fail to enforce the obligation to leave, however, they must provide access to basic socio-economic rights without any discrimination based on (irregular) immigration status.

Recommendation 2: Provide equal treatment between asylum seekers and irregular migrants in respect of socio-economic rights

We recommend that the EU extend the rights and benefits granted to asylum seekers under the Reception Conditions Directive to all irregular migrants who are subject to the Return Directive, regardless of whether they are considered to cooperate in the return procedure. Art. 14 of this Directive should be amended accordingly.

Building on that minimum guarantee accorded to all irregular migrants, the EU should consider according more favorable treatment to irregular migrants whose removal has been postponed due to Human Rights concerns, including the principle of non-refoulement, or other legal or practical obstacles to removal likely to be persistent. The status of these 'non-removables' should be comprehensively regulated by EU law, next to stipulating a maximum period of successively postponing removals (see

Chapter 5). The status of being 'tolerated' in the EU should include, among others things, immediate access to the labor market of the respective Member State.

The power necessary to adopt these legislative acts follows from Art. 79(2)(c) TFEU, which enables to EU to comprehensively regulate the status of persons who are subject to return proceedings.

Recommendation 3: Adopt a rights-based approach toward undocumented irregular migrants to better protect them from exploitation and forced labor

We recommend that the EU move beyond a sanctions approach vis-à-vis employers in addressing labor relations involving irregular migrants. The EU should adopt an approach empowering irregular migrants to more effectively protect them from exploitation and forced labor. The Employers Sanctions Directive should be revised in the light of the positive obligations arising from Art. 5 EU-CFR/Art. 4 ECHR. In that regard, we recommend revisiting the proposals from the Commission in the 1970s.

In contrast to the revision of the Return Directive – recommended above, which addresses well-documented irregular migrants – the revision of the Employers Sanctions Directive should specifically target the situation of the most precarious (that is, undocumented or clandestine) irregular migrants. Next to legislating on their labor-related rights, the EU should foster their non-discriminatory access to other socio-economic rights, in particular health services and primary education provided according to national law. These regulations should also establish non-reporting obligations for the relevant authorities ('firewalls'). We consider the relevant powers of the EU to follow from Art. 79(1)(c), Art. 115 and Art. 153 AEUV.

Chapter 7 – Fostering Human Rights Infrastructure

Human Rights protection does not exist in a vacuum. The substantive and procedural guarantees of Human Rights law depend on infrastructure to render them effective. Such structures and procedures exist on a political and administrative level, a judicial level, and a civil-societal level. In line with the UN Declaration on Human Rights Defenders,[790] we consider a range of supervisory bodies, the judiciary, and civil society actors – each contributing by different means to the effective protection of migrants' individual rights – to form the vital Human Rights infrastructure in the field of European migration policy.

International and national supervisory bodies such as UNHCR, UN Special Rapporteurs, the Council of Europe's Commissioner for Human Rights, National Human Rights Institutions (NHRI), ombudspersons (including the European Ombudsman), and the EU Agency for Fundamental Rights (FRA) play particularly important roles in protecting migrants' Human Rights. Regarding the judiciary, independent, effective, and respected judges and courts form the heart of any Human Rights infrastructure. In the case of the EU this is true both at the Union and the Member State level. The ECtHR plays a pivotal role in the interpretation of international law, alongside the 'quasi-judicial' UN treaty bodies (the Human Rights Committee or the Committee Against Torture, among others). But apart from any public institutions, the implementation and protection of Human Rights depends on civil society actors, be they individuals or associations, most notably lawyers, journalists, NGOs, and volunteers.[791] These may be involved in various ways in protecting the interests of migrants – for example, by engaging in actual rescue operations at sea, in providing social assistance and legal advice to migrants, or in reporting on the Human Rights situation in countries of origin or transit, and in drawing public attention to instances of Human Rights violations.

790 UN General Assembly, Declaration on the Right and Responsibility of Individuals, Groups and Organs of Society to Promote and Protect Universally Recognized Human Rights and Fundamental Freedoms, Resolution adopted on 9 December 1998, A/RES/53/144, available at https://undocs.org/A/RES/53/144.

791 On the important role of NGOs as 'entities acting in the collective interest of European civil society', see P. Staszczyk, *A Legal Analysis of NGOs and European Civil Society* (2019).

While these structures and activities evolved, for the most part, independently from the EU, the EU has committed itself to preserving and fostering them. This follows from Art. 2 TEU as well as from the EU-CFR, which reaffirms in its preamble that the EU is based on the 'indivisible, universal values of human dignity, freedom, equality and solidarity'. Furthermore, with the creation of the FRA the EU has established an institution for, among other things, the implementation of 'activities in the field of promotion of fundamental rights and capacity building'.[792]

7.1 Structural challenges and current trends

The legitimacy of the historically grown, multi-layered infrastructure of Human Rights protection in Europe has long been widely accepted, and was by some even considered as self-evident. Recent years, however, have seen a number of developments that cast doubt on this general acceptance. Various political actors, including governments, have made attempts to limit, or even abolish, essential elements of this Human Rights infrastructure. In our view, three developments stand out: the criminalization of civil society actors supporting migrants (trend 1), the growing populist pressure on judges protecting the rights of migrants (trend 2), and challenges to the role of the ECHR as guardian of migrants' Human Rights (trend 3).

Trend 1: Criminalization of civil society actors supporting migrants

We observe a trend in several EU Member States toward restricting the activities of civil society actors promoting and striving for the protection

792 FRA Strategy 2018–2022, at 4; see Art. 2 Regulation 168/2007 establishing a EU Agency for Fundamental Rights (FRA Regulation): 'The objective of the Agency shall be to provide the relevant institutions, bodies, offices and agencies of the Community and its Member States when implementing Community law with assistance and expertise relating to fundamental rights in order to support them when they take measures or formulate courses of action within their respective spheres of competence to fully respect fundamental rights.' Notably, in the years 2018–2022, such FRA activities are supposed to focus among other things on 'migration, borders, asylum and integration of refugees and migrants'. Cf. Art. 2(e) of the Council Decision 2017/2269 establishing a Multiannual Framework for the European Union Agency for Fundamental Rights for 2018–2022.

and realization of Human Rights, including the rights of migrants. These Human Rights defenders – as individuals or organizations – have increasingly come under pressure from state authorities in many respects, including restricted access to public funding (and, in some instances, also to private funding), administrative and judicial harassment, abusive inspections (sometimes referred to as 'discriminatory legalism'[793]), and missing protection against hate speech by other private actors.[794]

This development has been accurately labeled by numerous observers and institutions such as the European Parliament, FRA or the Council of Europe's Commissioner for Human Rights as a 'shrinking space for civil society'[795] or 'shrinking space for human rights organisations'.[796] The restrictions affect civil society actors in general and those supporting migrants in particular.[797] For example, attempts to intimidate humanitarian actors in this area aim to restrict the access of asylum seekers to protection or to facilitate the return of irregular migrants. These attempts take different forms and are not confined to Member States marked by semi-authoritarian tendencies.[798]

An outstanding example is the criminalization of activities by humanitarian actors to rescue migrants in distress at sea by Member State authori-

793 J.W. Müller, *What Is Populism?* (2016), at 28.

794 See St. Kleemann, *Human Rights Defenders under Pressure: 'Shrinking Space' in Civil Society* (2020), at 55–83.

795 European Parliament, Shrinking space for civil society: the EU response, Study (2017), available at http://www.europarl.europa.eu/RegData/etudes/STUD/2017/578039/EXPO_STU(2017)578039_EN.pdf; FRA, Challenges Facing Civil Society Organisations Working on Human Rights in the EU (2017), at 18.

796 Council of Europe: Commissioner for Human Rights, The Shrinking Space for Human Rights Organisations, Statement (2017), available at https://www.coe.int/mk/web/commissioner/-/the-shrinking-space-for-human-rights-organisations.

797 For an overview: S. Carrera et al., *Policing Humanitarianism: EU Policies against Human Smuggling and Their Impact on Civil Society* (2019); Amnesty International, *Europe: Punishing Compassion: Solidarity on Trial in Fortress Europe,* 3 March 2020, available at https://www.amnesty.org/en/wp-content/uploads/2021/05/EUR0118282020ENGLISH.pdf.

798 For example, in spring 2019, the German Ministry of Interior proposed in its first draft of a new legislation (*Geordnete-Rückkehr-Gesetz*) to introduce a provision that would have allowed punishing those who publish or disseminate deportation dates with up to three years imprisonment. Similarly, humanitarian organizations would have been criminalized if they informed irregular migrants about identification measures. The project was only dropped following massive protest from civil society and the Council of Europe's Commissioner for Human Rights. See https://rm.coe.int/letter-to-andrealindholz-%20%20chairwoman-of-the-committee-on-internal-affa/168094799d.

ties. Private rescue operations became a form of 'transnational maritime civil disobedience'.[799] While this is not an entirely new phenomenon,[800] since the end of 2016, Italy, Greece, and Malta have increased their efforts to de-legitimize and criminalize Search and Rescue (SAR) operations in the Mediterranean Sea conducted by NGOs, including through the seizure of rescue ships,[801] the imposition of a binding 'code of conduct' for SAR NGOs in August 2017 by the Italian government,[802] and the actual criminal prosecution of humanitarian actors for their rescue activities.[803] By 2019, most of the SAR vessels operated by NGOs or private actors had been either seized or had ceased activity due to political pressure and legal prosecution of their crews.[804] What is more, since 2020 the COVID-19 pandemic has been used as a pretext for closing ports to NGO rescue vessels[805] or for putting further constraints on the crew members of the few remaining private SAR vessels. Italian health authorities, for example, required crew to undergo a two-week quarantine on board after the disembarkation of rescued migrants.[806]

Other instances of the criminalization of migrants' Human Rights defenders can be observed in semi-authoritarian EU Member States like Hungary. Severe restrictions were imposed on Hungarian civil society

799 Mann, 'The Right to Perform Rescue at Sea: Jurisprudence and Drowning', 21 *German Law Journal* (2020) 598, at 616.

800 For an early example, see the 2004 *Cap Anamur* boat incident: Cuttitta, 'Repoliticization Through Search and Rescue? Humanitarian NGOs and Migration Management in the Central Mediterranean', 23 *Geopolitics* (2018) 632.

801 For further references, see S. Carrera et al., *Fit for purpose? The Facilitation Directive and the Criminalisation of Humanitarian Assistance to Irregular Migrants: 2018 Update* (2018), at 69 et seq. and 107, available at https://www.europarl.europa.eu/RegData/etudes/STUD/2018/608838/IPOL_STU(2018)608838_EN.pdf.

802 Ibid., at 68.

803 Ibid., at 69 et seq. and 107; see also: Global Legal Action Network, 'Case filed against Greece in Strasbourg Court over Crackdown on Humanitarian Organisations', Press statement, 18 April 2019, available at https://www.glanlaw.org/single-post/2019/04/18/Case-filed-against-Greece-in-Strasbourg-Court-over-Crackdown-on-Humanitarian-Organisations.

804 For an overview, see FRA, Fundamental Rights Considerations: NGO Ships Involved in Search and Rescue in the Mediterranean and Criminal Investigations (2018); FRA, 2019 Update: NGO Ships Involved in Search and Rescue in the Mediterranean and Criminal Investigations (2019).

805 Deutsche Welle, 'Coronavirus crisis hampering Mediterranean migrant rescues', 17 April 2020, available at https://www.dw.com/en/coronavirus-crisis-hampering-mediterranean-migrant-rescues/a-53168399.

806 FRA, June 2021 Update: Search and Rescue (SAR) Operations in the Mediterranean and Fundamental Rights (2021).

organizations in 2017 with the so-called 'Stop Soros' legislation – which, among other things, requires every NGO in Hungary to register as an 'organisation receiving foreign funds' once a certain threshold of donations is reached.[807] This was found to be in breach of EU law by the CJEU in 2020.[808] Specifically directed against migrants' Human Rights defenders, a 2018 modification of the Hungarian Criminal Code ensures that criminal sanctions can be imposed on NGOs and individuals providing legal or other types of aid to migrants arriving at Hungarian borders; a new provision of the Hungarian Criminal Code was introduced that criminalizes 'facilitating illegal immigration' by extending already existing prohibitions to a wide range of organizational activities related to migration.[809] According to an official press statement issued by the Hungarian government, this was to be regarded as a 'strong action' directed 'against the organisers of migration'.[810] While a complaint against the new law was rejected by the Hungarian Constitutional Court in 2019,[811] the European Commission instituted an infringement proceeding and in late 2019 decided to refer Hungary to the CJEU concerning this legislation.[812]

807 An unofficial English translation of the 'Act LXXVI of 2017 on the Transparency of Organisations Receiving Foreign Funds' by the Hungarian Helsinki Committee is available at https://www.helsinki.hu/wp-content/uploads/LexNGO-adopted-text-unofficial-ENG-14June2017.pdf.

808 CJEU, Case C-78/18, *Commission v. Hungary* (transparency of associations) (EU:C:2020:476).

809 Alongside the new Art. 353/A of Act C of 2012 of the Hungarian Criminal Code, a subheading 'Facilitating illegal immigration' was introduced.

810 Hungarian Government, 'Strong Action is Required Against the Organisers of Migration', 24 May 2018 (the document has been removed from the official website).

811 Hungarian Constitutional Court, Decision 3/2019 on the Support of Illegal Immigration, 28 February 2019, available at https://hunconcourt.hu/uploads/sites/3/2019/05/3_2019_en_final.pdf. Cf. also Kazai, 'Stop Soros Law Left on the Books: The Return of the "Red Tail"?', *Verfassungsblog* (2019), available at https://verfassungsblog.de/stop-soros-law-left-on-the-books-the-return-of-the-red-tail/

812 Case C-821/19, *Commission v. Hungary (Criminalisation of assistance for asylum seekers)*, application submitted on 8 November 2019. See also the Opinion of Advocate General Rantos in this Case, delivered on 25 February 2021 (EU:C:2021:143).

Trend 2: Populist pressure on judges protecting the rights of migrants

We also observe a trend in several Member States of growing public pressure on judges in charge of asylum and other migration law cases to take a restrictive approach and to deny applicants an adequate level of Human Rights protection. This development may be observed particularly in Member States marked by strong populist movements – either governing the Member State or as an influential faction of the opposition.

Populist pressure on the independence of the judiciary extends across a continuum and takes various forms, reaching from rather diffuse exertion of political influence, to the defamation of critical judges through 'smear campaigns', the selective and arbitrary application of legal provisions, to actual institutional reforms. Some Member States have also formally limited judicial independence. Enhanced political control – for example, by tightened disciplinary regimes for judges – undermine the guarantee of impartial and effective adjudication and protection of rights, including the effective implementation of EU law, thus threatening the stability of existing Human Rights and rule of law infrastructures.

In recent years, systemic and repeated assaults on the independence of the judiciary in general, and among the branches in charge of asylum and migration cases in particular, have become a prominent issue in a number of EU Member States, in particular Bulgaria, Hungary, Poland, and Romania. These assaults are identified as an essential ingredient of what is referred to as the 'rule of law crisis' in the EU.[813]

Examples of this trend are numerous. For instance, since December 2015 Poland has passed a number of legislative acts on judicial reform, leading the Commission, as early as in January 2016, to activate the so-called rule of law framework in the context of Art. 7 TEU for the very first time.[814] According to the Commission, the Polish reforms pose 'systemic threats' to the rule of law.[815] One example of the problematic legislative

---

813 For an overview, see C. Closa and D. Kochenov (eds), *Reinforcing Rule of Law Oversight in the European Union* (2016).

814 European Commission, 'Rule of law in Poland: Commission starts dialogue', Press release, 13 January 2016, available at https://ec.europa.eu/commission/presscorner/detail/en/WM_16_2030.

815 European Commission, 'Rule of Law: European Commission refers Poland to the European Court of Justice to protect the independence of the Polish Supreme Court', Press release, 24 September 2018, available at http://europa.eu/rapid/press-release_IP-18-5830_en.pdf.

acts on the matter[816] is Poland's 2018 Law on the Supreme Court,[817] lowering the retirement age and applying it to current Supreme Court judges, thus terminating the mandate of more than a third of serving judges, as well as establishing a new disciplinary regime for Supreme Court judges, among other things. The law was partly reversed in 2018 following interim relief by the CJEU.[818] In 2021 the ECtHR ruled that the appointment of three judges to the Polish Constitutional Tribunal in 2015 was unlawful – with the consequence that the current composition of the Polish Constitutional Tribunal violated the right to a 'tribunal established by law', as the right to a fair trial enshrined in Art. 6(1) ECHR requires.[819]

Similar developments concern the independence of the judiciary and the rights of judges in Hungary. In 2011, a controversial law lowered the retirement age of Hungarian judges and other legal professionals, removing judges, prosecutors, and notaries from office. This law was later determined to be unlawful by the CJEU for infringing the Equal

816 Other examples include:
the 2017 Law on the National School of Judiciary, allowing among other things assistant judges – without being subject to Constitutional guarantees protecting judicial independence – to act as single judges in district courts (Law amending the law on the National School of Judiciary and Public Prosecution, the law on Ordinary Courts Organization and certain other laws, published in Polish Official Journal on 13 June 2017, in force since 20 June 2017);
the 2017 Law on Ordinary Courts Organization, reducing the retirement age of ordinary judges while giving the Minister of Justice the power to decide on the prolongation of judicial mandates, among other things (Law amending the law on the Ordinary Courts Organization, published in the Polish Official Journal on 28 July 2017, in force since 12 August 2017);
the 2018 Law on the National Council on the Judiciary, providing for the premature termination of the mandate of all judges-members of that Polish institution and, by establishing a new regime for the appointment of its judges-members, guaranteeing strong political influence (Law amending the law on the National Council for the Judiciary and certain other laws of 8 December 2017, published in the Polish Official Journal 2018, item 3, entry into force in March 2018);
the 2018 Supreme Court Act, constituting the basis for the jurisdiction of a Disciplinary Chamber of the Supreme Court (Law of 8 December 2017, Official Journal 2018, item 5), found unlawful in CJEU, Case C-791/19, *Commission v. Poland* (EU:C:2021:596).

817 Law on the Supreme Court (*Ustawa o Sądzie Najwyższym*) of 8 December 2017, Polish Official Journal 2018, item 5, which entered into force on 3 April 2018.

818 CJEU, Case C-619/18, *Commission v. Poland* (EU:2018:852), in French.

819 ECtHR, *Xero Flor v. Poland*, Appl. no. 4907/18, Judgment of 7 May 2021.

Treatment Directive.[820] Further concerns over violations of the rule of law led the European Parliament in September 2018 to activate a breach of value procedure under Art. 7 TEU against Hungary (see section 7.2.4 for details).[821] The Hungarian government argued that this step was an act of 'revenge' by 'pro-immigration politicians' reacting to Hungary's stance on migration.[822] Additionally, two laws[823] passed in December 2018 were intended to create a separate administrative court system in Hungary as of 1 January 2020, in charge of asylum cases but also of cases concerning elections or freedom of assembly. These courts would be placed under the supervision of the Minister of Justice. However, following heavy criticism, in mid-2019 the reform was suspended.[824] At about the same time, the initiation of disciplinary proceedings in 2019 against a Hungarian judge for referring questions to the CJEU, supposed to have a 'chilling effect' on other judges in terms of discouraging them from fully applying EU and

---

820 CJEU, Case C-286/12, *Commission v. Hungary* (EU:C:2012:687).

821 European Parliament, Resolution of 12 September 2018 on a proposal calling on the Council to determine, pursuant to Art. 7(1) of the Treaty on European Union, the existence of a clear risk of a serious breach by Hungary of the values on which the Union is founded, available at https://www.europarl.europa.eu/doceo/document/TA-8-2018-0340_EN.html?redirect. In 2020, the European Parliament complained that the rule of law situation in Hungary (as well as in Poland) had deteriorated since the triggering of the procedure and that the Council had failed to make effective use of it, cf. European Parliament, Resolution of 16 January 2020 on ongoing hearings under Article 7(1) of the TEU regarding Poland and Hungary, available at https://www.europarl.europa.eu/doceo/document/TA-9-2020-0014_EN.pdf.

822 R. Staudenmaier, 'EU Parliament votes to trigger Art. 7 sanctions procedure against Hungary', Deutsche Welle, broadcasted on 12 September 2018, available at https://p.dw.com/p/34k9I.

823 Act on Public Administration Courts and Act on the Coming into Force of the Act on Public Administration Courts and Certain Transitional Regulations, both adopted by the National Assembly on 12 December 2018.

824 Hungarian Government: Ministry of Justice, 'Government to postpone the coming into force of the Act on Public Administration Courts', Press release, 30 May 2019 (the document has been removed from the official website). For an example of the criticism, see the report of the Venice Commission from 19 March 2019 on the legislative acts (Opinion no. 943/2018), available at https://www.venice.coe.int/webforms/documents/default.aspx?pdffile=CDL-AD(2019)004-e.

Human Rights law,[825] furnishes yet another example of the many faces of the rule of law crisis.

Despite the trend just described, we also notice that a considerable number of judges in the countries most affected by populist assaults on the independence of the judiciary resist the pressure. One means by which they draw attention to these developments, and seek to restore the rule of law in their countries, is referring questions to the CJEU, indicated for example by the multitude of preliminary references to the CJEU by Polish and Hungarian courts.[826]

Cases of assaults on judicial independence and the rule of law are not limited to one particular group of EU Member States. For example, in a case widely discussed by the German public in 2018, a Tunisian national living in Germany for more than a decade and suspected of posing a threat to public security was deported to Tunisia despite a pending injunction procedure and concerns of the first instance court that the deportee could face torture in his home country. The Higher Administrative Court of North Rhine-Westphalia later ruled that the deportation was 'evidently unlawful' and that the behavior of the ministry of the State involved in the case – namely, the admittedly deliberate concealment of the deportation date despite request from the court of first instance – was 'incompatible with the rule of law and the separation of powers'.[827]

Trend 3: Challenges to the ECtHR as a guardian of migrants' Human Rights

We furthermore observe a tendency in Europe to challenge the relevance and legitimacy of the ECHR as interpreted by the ECtHR. This trend also comes in a variety of forms.

First, the development concerns the domestic implementation of ECtHR judgments in Member States. There appears to be a growing reluctance in recent years to fully implement ECtHR decisions, leading inter alia to a high number of 'repetitive cases' hindering the effective work

825 Hungarian Helsinki Committee, Disciplinary Action Threatens Judge for Turning to EU Court of Justice, Statement, 7 November 2019, available at https://www.helsinki.hu/en/disciplinary-action-threatens-judge-for-turning-to-cjeu/.

826 See Bárd, 'Luxemburg as the Last Resort', *Verfassungsblog* (2019), available at https://verfassungsblog.de/luxemburg-as-the-last-resort/.

827 Higher Administrative Court of North Rhine-Westphalia (*Oberverwaltungsgericht Nordrhein-Westfalen*), Decision of 15 August 2018 (17 B 1029/18).

of the Court.[828] In a similar vein, efforts were made to limit the ambit of ECtHR decisions by stressing the particular context of the Court's decisions.[829] These developments concern not only specific Member States but have been described as a wider European trend of 'principled resistance' to the ECHR and the full implementation of ECtHR judgments.[830]

At the same time, the overloading and resulting backlog of cases waiting to be heard by the ECtHR, and the length of proceedings, further weakens the impact of the Court. Justice delivered too late often does not have substantial impact on domestic discourse, and governments may even reckon with the considerable delay of remedies when resorting to practices of questionable conformity with Convention rights, knowing that the measures may already be completed by the time the ECtHR renders a decision.

Beyond these questions of implementation of ECtHR decisions, there have also been Member State initiatives, particularly in the context of the so-called Interlaken reform process (2010–2019), to change the architecture and legal basis of the ECHR and ECtHR itself – in particular, by strengthening the principle of subsidiarity and, by implication, lowering the standard of scrutiny applied by the Court.[831] Most notably, in 2018 Denmark spearheaded an initiative intending to massively limit the competence of the ECtHR in asylum and immigration cases to 'the most exceptional circumstances'.[832] Arguably, the message sent by this initiative has had a

828 On this problem, see Council of Europe: Committee of Ministers, Supervision of the execution of judgments and decisions of the European Court of Human Rights 2018: 12th Annual Report, April 2019, at 13, available at https://rm.coe.int/annual-report-2018/168093f3da. Repetitive cases – those cases 'relating to a structural and/or general problem already raised before the Committee in the context of one or several leading cases' (at 91) – account for the vast majority of new cases coming to the Court – in 2018, 88 % of the 1272 new cases were classified as repetitive cases (at 52). Several EU Member States (Bulgaria, Greece, Hungary, Italy and Romania) are among the main states with cases under 'enhanced supervision' (at 71).

829 Cf. Federal Constitutional Court of Germany (*Bundesverfassungsgericht*), Judgment of 12 June 2018 (2 BvR 1738/12).

830 M. Breuer (ed.), *Principled Resistance to ECtHR Judgments: A New Paradigm?* (2019).

831 Cf. Spano, 'The Future of the European Court of Human Rights. Subsidiarity, Process-Based Review and the Rule of Law', 18 *Human Rights Law Review* (2018) 473.

832 See, e.g., the draft Copenhagen Declaration, 5 February 2018, at para. 26, available at https://menneskeret.dk/sites/menneskeret.dk/files/media/dokumenter/nyheder/draft_copenhagen_declaration_05.02.18.pdf. On the wider

lasting impact on the ECtHR judges, even if it was defused in the final version of the Copenhagen Declaration.[833]

7.2 *Legal evaluation*

7.2.1 General legal framework regarding Human Rights infrastructure

Duties to provide for functioning and effective institutions and mechanisms to protect Human Rights already follow as an annex or logical implication from all substantive guarantees of Human Rights in international law. As normative principles always depend on certain structures and institutions to take effect, these principles presuppose a legal and political endorsement of Human Rights infrastructures. For example, due respect of the Human Right to non-refoulement requires a functioning administration to assess claims of protection as well as a judiciary ready to examine and correct possible breaches of this right by state officials.

In light of this inference, it comes as no surprise that explicit provisions specifically referring to institutional aspects of the protection of Human Rights are rather sparse in international law. The concrete shaping of these institutions is often regarded as a prerogative of States, so long as the substantive Human Rights guarantees are (somehow) implemented. However, some abstract (re-)statements of the obligations of States to render Human Rights effective, as well as a few more specific provisions, can be found in international law and in EU law, including provisions of soft law.

The preamble of the UDHR recalls the pledge of States to the 'promotion' of the observance of Human Rights under the UN Charter, as does the preamble to the ICCPR. States Parties to the ICCPR are also required to 'give effect' to the rights under the Covenant by domestic legislation or other measures. More specifically, they must provide for effective remedies before 'competent authorities', having the power to enforce such remedies when granted (Art. 2 ICCPR). UN Human Rights treaties also stipulate procedures before treaty bodies (such as the Human Rights Committee

---

historical context, see Feihle 'Asylum and Immigration under the European Convention on Human Rights: An Exclusive Universality?', in H.P. Aust and E. Demir-Gürsel (eds), *The European Court of Human Rights: Current Challenges in Historical Perspective* (2021) 133, at 150.

833 Council of Europe: High Level Conference of the States Parties, Copenhagen Declaration, 12–13 April 2018, available at https://www.echr.coe.int/Documents/Copenhagen_Declaration_ENG.pdf.

or the Committee against Torture) to monitor the observance of Human Rights by States Parties. Importantly, the treaties oblige States Parties to submit periodic reports on the implementation of their treaty obligations (see, e.g., Art. 40 ICCPR, Art. 16 ICESCR, Art. 19 CAT, Art. 44 CRC). Some treaties also provide for individual complaints procedures (e.g., First Optional Protocol to the ICCPR, Art. 22 CAT, Optional Protocol to CRC on a communications procedure).

In a similar vein, Art. 1 ECHR obliges the Contracting Parties to 'secure' the substantive rights enshrined in this Convention. Effective remedies for violations of Convention rights have to be provided before national authorities (Art. 13 ECHR), and, of course, the ECtHR in Strasbourg is vested with the power to receive individual complaints from victims of Human Rights violations (Art. 34 ECHR). Other Human Rights treaties in the framework of the Council of Europe – such as the European Convention for the Prevention of Torture, which provides the legal basis for the work of the Committee for the Prevention of Torture (CPT) – are also essential parts of the Human Rights infrastructure in Europe.

At the universal level, the UN Member States committed to implement the Global Compact for Migration promise to 'ensure' the 'effective respect for and protection and fulfilment of the human rights of all migrants' (GCM, para. 15, point f), while the Global Compact on Refugees urges States to do likewise (GCR, para. 9). A more specific catalog of the rights of civil society agents in defense of Human Rights was provided by the UN General Assembly in the 1998 Declaration on Human Rights Defenders.

The interconnectedness of the Human Rights regime and the respect for the rule of law has already been discussed in Chapter 3. Respect for the rule of law and for judicial independence is a prerequisite for Human Rights protections to become alive and effective. As early as 1948, the preamble of the UDHR stated that it was 'essential' for Human Rights to be 'protected by the rule of law'. More recently, the GCM and GCR have reaffirmed the importance of the rule of law, the former by stating that it is 'fundamental to all aspects of migration governance' (cf. GCM, para. 15, point d; GCR, para. 9). Particular significance has always been attributed to the rule of law in the Council of Europe. Its importance was acknowledged by references in the preambles to the 1949 Statute of the Council of Europe[834] and to the ECHR. Furthermore, the Statute of the 1990 Euro-

834 Art. 3 of the Statute makes respect for the principle of the Rule of Law even a precondition for accession of new Member States to the Organisation.

pean Commission for Democracy through Law ('Venice Commission') – an advisory body of the Council of Europe, which provides politically important (though not legally binding) opinions on constitutional law – refers to the rule of law as a priority objective.[835]

The commitment to both effective Human Rights protection and the rule of law is mirrored in the EU Treaties. Human Rights and the rule of law are not only referred to in the preamble to the TEU but characterized as foundational values of the Union and its Member States in Art. 2 TEU. The preamble of the EU-CFR repeats that the Union is 'based' on the rule of law and not only affirms the ECHR but even explicitly embraces the case-law of the ECtHR. The Charter furthermore gives specific meaning to the rule of law in providing for the rights to good administration (Art. 41 EU-CFR) and to an effective judicial remedy (Art. 47 EU-CFR). The latter also follows from the TEU, which obliges Member States to ensure effective legal protection through sufficient remedies in the fields governed by EU law (Art. 19(1) TEU). According to the CJEU, this implies a comprehensive duty of all Member States to respect the independence of the national judiciary.[836]

7.2.2 Specific issue: Criminalization of private actors involved in SAR activities and other migrants' Human Rights defenders in civil society

Providing search and rescue (SAR) – that is, assistance to people in distress at sea – is a duty of all States and shipmasters under international law. This duty to SAR follows from a number of provisions of international law, most notably the 1974 International Convention for the Safety of Life at Sea (SOLAS), the 1979 International Convention on Maritime Search and Rescue (SAR Convention), and the 1982 UN Convention on the Law of the Sea (UNCLOS). Shipmasters both of private and governmental vessels are obliged to assist those in distress at sea, irrespective of their nationality, status, or the circumstances in which they were found (Art. 98(1) UNCLOS; Annex 2.1.10 to the SAR Convention).

---

835 Art. 1 Revised Statute of the European Commission for Democracy through Law, Resolution (2002)3, 21 February 2002, available at https://www.venice.coe.int/WebForms/pages/?p=01_01_Statute.

836 CJEU, Case C-64/16, *ASJP (Trade Union of Portuguese Judges)* (EU:C:2018:117); Case C-619/18, *Commission v. Poland* (EU:C:2019:531).

The criminalization of NGOs and other private actors conducting SAR operations, including the seizure of SAR vessels, thus constitutes a violation of international law as it prohibits the fulfillment of the duties mentioned above. There is, arguably, even a positive obligation of EU Member States bordering the Mediterranean Sea to actively conduct SAR in order to assist people in distress at sea.[837] Following this assumption, the failure to do so would constitute a first rights violation (by omission) while the hindrance of private SAR activity would constitute a second violation. UNHCR,[838] the European Parliament,[839] and the FRA[840] have come to similar conclusions, asking EU Member States to prevent humanitarian assistance in SAR from being criminalized.

The criminalization of Human Rights defenders from civil society assisting migrants in distress at sea, as well as, more generally, those assisting migrants who try to enter EU territory irregularly, is also at odds with the UN Protocol against the Smuggling of Migrants by Land, Sea and Air, supplementing the 2000 Palermo Convention against Transnational Organised Crime. The Protocol defines 'smuggling of migrants' as 'procurement, in order to obtain, directly or indirectly, a financial or other material benefit, of the illegal entry of a person into a State Party of which the person is not a national or a permanent resident'.[841] As an *argumentum a contrario*, one may infer that support of irregular migration in the case of an altruistic motivation does not amount to 'smuggling' and, thus, is to be exempted from criminalization.

837 This may follow from Art. 98(2) UNCLOS; see A. Farahat and N. Markard, *Places of Safety in the Mediterranean: The EU's Policy of Outsourcing Responsibility*, February 2020, at 37 et seq., available at https://eu.boell.org/en/2020/02/18/places-safety-mediterranean-eus-policy-outsourcing-responsibility. On disembarkation, see also Chapter 1 of this volume.

838 UNHCR, General legal considerations: Search-and-rescue operations involving refugees and migrants at sea (2017), available at https://www.refworld.org/docid/5a2e9efd4.html.

839 European Parliament, Guidelines for Member States to prevent humanitarian assistance from being criminalized, Resolution of 5 July 2018, P8_TA(2018)0314, available at https://www.europarl.europa.eu/doceo/document/TA-8-2018-0314_EN.pdf?redirect.

840 FRA, Fundamental Rights Considerations: NGO Ships Involved in Search and Rescue in the Mediterranean and Criminal Investigations (2018); FRA, 2019 Update: NGO Ships Involved in Search and Rescue in the Mediterranean and Criminal Investigations (2019).

841 Art. 3 UN Protocol against the Smuggling of Migrants; see also the enumeration of certain criminal acts enabling the smuggling of migrants in Art. 6 UN Protocol against the Smuggling of Migrants.

Furthermore, the criminalization of SAR activities and other forms of altruistic assistance for irregular migration is contrary to the UN Declaration on Human Rights Defenders. According to this Declaration, '[e]veryone has the right, individually and in association with others, to promote and to strive for the protection and realization of human rights and fundamental freedoms at the national and international levels' (Art. 1 Declaration on Human Rights Defenders). The Declaration also protects the right of individuals and associations of individuals to 'participate in peaceful activities against violations of human rights and fundamental freedoms' (Art. 12(1) of the Declaration). In this regard, 'everyone is entitled, individually and in association with others, to be protected effectively under national law in reacting against or opposing, through peaceful means, activities and acts, including those by omission, attributable to States that result in violations of human rights' (Art. 12(3) of the Declaration).

Despite these provisions, EU law not only fails to outlaw criminalization of humanitarian actors but even buttresses such measures, most notably by way of the Facilitation Directive (Directive 2002/90/EC).[842] This Directive, as it stands, asks Member States to sanction 'any person who intentionally assists a person who is not a national of a Member State to enter, or transit across, the territory of a Member State in breach of the laws of the State concerned on the entry or transit of aliens' (Art. 1(1)(a) Facilitation Directive), while leaving it up to the Member States' discretion to refrain from such sanction 'where the aim of the behaviour is to provide humanitarian assistance to the person concerned' (Art. 1(2) Facilitation Directive).

The EU's definition of facilitation of entry and transit in the Directive thus suffers from two main deficiencies: It does not insist on any requirement of 'financial or other material benefit' nor does it oblige Member States to exempt 'humanitarian assistance' from the definition. On the contrary, it rather leaves discretion to Member States to decide whether they want to criminalize humanitarian actors.[843] The Facilitation Directive

842 Directive 2002/90/EC defining the facilitation of unauthorised entry, transit and residence (Facilitation Directive). On this matter, see also Ghezelbash, Moreno-Lax, Klein and Opeskin, 'Securitization of Search and Rescue at Sea: The Response to Boat Migration in the Mediterranean and Offshore Australia', 67(2) *International and Comparative Law Quarterly* (2018) 315, at 347 et seq.

843 S. Carrera et al., *Fit for purpose? The Facilitation Directive and the Criminalisation of Humanitarian Assistance to Irregular Migrants* (2016), available at https://www.europarl.europa.eu/RegData/etudes/STUD/2016/536490/IPOL_STU(2016)536490_EN.pdf; S. Carrera et al., *Fit for purpose? The Facilitation Directive and the Criminalisation of Humanitarian Assistance to Irregular Migrants: 2018 Update*

thus falls foul of the UN Smuggling Protocol which it intends to implement. This is partly recognized in a 'Guidance' on the implementation of the Facilitation Directive issued by the European Commission in 2020.[844] However, this is an insufficient remedy to the flaws of the Facilitation Directive, as the 'Guidance' only calls on States to not criminalize humanitarian assistance that is 'mandated by law', in particular SAR operations at sea, and, crucially, is not legally binding.

In the absence of a reform of the Facilitation Directive to introduce an explicit exemption for humanitarian assistance, Member States, when making use of their discretionary power, are required to interpret the law as it stands in conformity with Human Rights law, and thus must not criminalize anybody for rescuing persons in distress or for supporting immigration in other ways driven by an altruistic motivation. However, in view of Member State practice to the contrary, these obligations derived from international law does not obliterate the EU's accountability for reiterating and specifying them in EU law (see above, introductory chapter).

7.2.3 Specific issue: Requirements to strengthen migrants' Human Rights defenders

The positive obligation on the part of the EU to foster Human Rights by supporting civil society actors in Member States defending the rights of migrants is of a very general nature. Nevertheless, the EU is accountable for such support within the scope of its powers. The EU's general commitment to Human Rights implies obligations to support such measures as are necessary to render Human Rights effective (see section 7.2.1 above).

These obligations have been specified in a number of documents. Notably, the 1998 UN Declaration on Human Rights Defenders states the duty of States to effectively guarantee the rights of civil society engaged in the defense of Human Rights through, inter alia, appropriate legislative and administrative acts (Art. 2(1) of the Declaration) in general and, for example, by promoting and facilitating the teaching of Human Rights at

(2018), at 106, available at https://www.europarl.europa.eu/RegData/etudes/STUD/2018/608838/IPOL_STU(2018)608838_EN.pdf.

844 European Commission, Commission Guidance on the implementation of EU rules on definition and prevention of the facilitation of unauthorised entry, transit and residence, 23 September 2020, C(2020) 6470, available at https://ec.europa.eu/info/sites/info/files/commission-guidance-implementation-facilitation-unauthorised-entry_en.pdf.

all levels of education, such as the training of lawyers, law enforcement officers and public officials (Art. 15 of the Declaration). A UN Special Rapporteur on the situation of Human Rights defenders monitors the implementation of the Declaration.[845] A 2008 Declaration by the Committee of Ministers of the Council of Europe reaffirms the importance of the 1998 UN Declaration and, among other things, calls upon Council of Europe Member States to 'take effective measures to prevent attacks on or harassment of human rights defenders', to 'take effective measures to protect, promote and respect Human Rights defenders and ensure respect for their activities' and to provide for a legal basis to enable individual or associated Human Rights defenders 'to freely carry out activities'.[846]

These requirements are mirrored and further specified in EU law. While the general obligation to protect and promote Human Rights is stated in Art. 2 TEU, numerous provisions, institutions and programs establish, or require, specific measures. Interestingly, the 2004 EU Guidelines on Human Rights Defenders[847] endorse the UN Declaration on Human Rights Defenders – but focus on the support for Human Rights defenders *outside* the EU as, at the time, this was regarded as an issue of external relations. In contrast, the mandate of the FRA, according to its founding Regulation, requires the Agency to 'closely cooperate with non-governmental organisations and with institutions of civil society, active in the field of fundamen-

845 The mandate was established in 2000 by the UN Commission on Human Rights Resolution 2000/61 and renewed by the UN Human Rights Council Decision 43/115 in 2020.

846 Council of Europe: Committee of Ministers, Declaration on Council of Europe action to improve the protection of human rights defenders and promote their activities, adopted on 6 February 2008, available at https://search.coe.int/cm/Pages/result_details.aspx?ObjectID=09000016805d3e52. In a similar vein, the 2014 OSCE Guidelines on the Protection of Human Rights Defenders identify the right to defend human rights as a 'universally recognized right', requiring states not only to refrain from acts that violate the rights of human rights defenders because of their work and to protect human rights defenders from abuses by third parties but also to take 'proactive steps' to promote the full realization of the rights of human rights defenders, available at https://www.osce.org/odihr/guidelines-on-the-protection-of-human-rights-defenders.

847 Council of the EU, Ensuring Protection: European Union Guidelines on Human Rights Defenders, 10056/1/04, 14 June 2004, available at https://www.refworld.org/docid/4705f6762.html. On the lack of implementation of the guidelines: European Parliament, Resolution of 17 June 2010 on EU policies in favour of human rights defenders, 2009/2199(INI), available at https://www.europarl.europa.eu/sides/getDoc.do?type=TA&language=EN&reference=P7-TA-2010-0226.

tal rights' within the framework of the Fundamental Rights Platform as a cooperation network (Art. 10(1) FRA Regulation).

7.2.4 Specific Issue: Obligations and options to ensure the independence of judges deciding on migration law cases

As to the populist pressure on judges protecting the rights of migrants and the more general rule of law crisis in a number of EU Member States identified in the first section of this chapter, legal questions arise both in respect of identifying the legal obligations and in relation to the EU's options for responding to such rule of law deficits.

Legal definitions of the exact meaning of the rule of law are rare, and it remains notoriously contested as a concept, with the rule of law, *Rechtsstaat* or *État de droit* understood differently in each EU Member State due to different constitutional traditions. However, a comprehensive definition is not needed for the present purposes (the assessment of Member State challenges to an independent judiciary). It suffices to state here that, among other important elements such as the principle of legality, there is a solid consensus that access to justice provided by impartial and independent courts is an indispensable requirement of the rule of law.[848]

While the importance of the rule of law is reaffirmed in numerous documents of international law (see section 7.2.1), it is frequently referred to in preambles in a rather general way, so that its legal status often remains questionable. Specific and legally binding obligations concerning the rule of law are rather scarce in international law. The rights to a fair trial and to a fair procedure, enshrined in Art. 6 and 13 ECHR, are important exceptions in this respect and protect essential parts of the rule of law (for details on these provisions, see Chapter 3).

As to dealing with the rule of law crisis in a number of EU Member States in the past years, rule of law guarantees in EU constitutional law have proven to be of paramount importance, especially the recognition of the rule of law as a foundational value (Art. 2 TEU) and the substantive

848 See, e.g., the definitions by the European Commission and the Venice Commission: European Commission, Further strengthening the Rule of Law within the Union: State of play and possible next steps, COM(2019) 163, 3 April 2019, at 1; Venice Commission, Report on the rule of law, CDL-AD(2011)003rev, 25–26 March 2011, at 10, available at https://www.venice.coe.int/webforms/documents/?pdf=CDL-AD(2011)003rev-e.

provisions in Art. 41 and 47 EU-CFR and Art. 19(1) TFEU. For example, regarding Poland's 2018 Law on the Supreme Court, mentioned in section 7.2.1 above,[849] the CJEU has confirmed that the lowering of the retirement age for Polish Supreme Court judges undermines, where serving judges are affected, the principle of irremovability of judges and judicial independence and, thus, infringes EU law.[850] Irrespective of the wording of Art. 19(1) TEU, which limits its scope of application to 'the fields covered by Union law', the value of the rule of law has gained great importance for the protection of judicial independence in the Member States: As the CJEU has established, Art. 19(1) TEU guarantees judicial independence of every Member State court that *could* apply EU law – even if it does not actually apply it in the specific case at hand.[851] Further significance could be attributed to other values proclaimed in Art. 2 TEU. The actual status of the foundational values enshrined in this provision – among them, democracy and Human Rights – needs further elaboration. This, however, is beyond the focus of this study.[852]

When it comes to the rule of law, procedural aspects may be as important as substantive guarantees. There is already a wide array of procedures at EU level to protect the rule of law in its Member States.[853] Most important among these are infringement proceedings (Art. 258 TFEU), preliminary references from national courts (Art. 267 TFEU), and breach of value procedures (Art. 7(1) and (2) TEU procedures), possibly leading to the suspension of certain (e.g., voting) rights of the Member State concerned. These are supplemented by the EU Justice Scoreboard monitoring

---

849 Law on the Supreme Court (*Ustawa o Sądzie Najwyższym*) of 8 December 2017, Polish Official Journal 2018, item 5, which entered into force on 3 April 2018.

850 CJEU, C-619/18, *Commission v. Poland* (EU:C:2019:531).

851 Ibid.; CJEU, C-64/16, *ASJP (Trade Union of Portuguese Judges)* (EU:C:2018:117).

852 On their applicability and primacy, see von Bogdandy and Spieker, 'Countering the Judicial Silencing of Critics: Art. 2 TEU Values, Reverse Solange, and the Responsibilities of National Judges', 15 *European Constitutional Law Review (EuConst)* (2019) 391; for a short version, see von Bogdandy and Spieker, 'Countering the Judicial Silencing of Critics: Novel Ways to Enforce European Values', *Verfassungsblog* (2019), available at https://verfassungsblog.de/countering-the-judicial-silencing-of-critics-novel-ways-to-enforce-european-values/.

853 For an overview, see European Parliament, Protecting the rule of law in the EU: Existing mechanisms and possible improvements, Briefing (2019), available at https://www.europarl.europa.eu/RegData/etudes/BRIE/2019/642280/EPRS_BRI(2019)642280_EN.pdf.

instrument,[854] the Cooperation and Verification Mechanism (CVM) for Bulgaria and Romania,[855] and the 2014 European Commission Framework for addressing systemic threats to the rule of law in any of the Member States, allowing for a staged dialogue with the States affected. Since 2021, breaches of the rule of law in a Member State can also have budgetary consequences, such as the suspension of EU payments, provided that the specific violation of the rule of law risks affecting financial interest of the Union in a 'sufficiently direct' way.[856]

Despite this arsenal of different instruments, their application by the EU in response to the rule of law crisis has been described as 'too late, too long, too mild'.[857] Some have criticized the idea of a staged dialogue as part of the pre-Art. 7 TEU procedure as ineffective, particularly in comparison with infringement proceedings and preliminary references. However, the Art. 7 TEU procedure may be the most appropriate legal instrument to respond to a 'systemic deficiency',[858] while infringement proceedings and preliminary references may be very helpful as auxiliary thereto, as well as in dealing with more specific cases.

In a political context, however, further consequences with a focus on the anti-immigration policies of Member States, often underlying assaults on the rule of law, should be considered. Thus far, the European Commission has been rather reluctant to address violations of the rule of law as targeted attacks on the asylum and immigration *acquis*.[859] Without prejudice to whether this blind spot is to be attributed to deficient analysis or – to a

854 European Commission, EU Justice Scoreboard, available at https://ec.europa.eu/info/policies/justice-and-fundamental-rights/effective-justice/eu-justice-scoreboard_en.

855 European Commission, Cooperation and Verification Mechanism for Bulgaria and Romania, available at https://ec.europa.eu/info/policies/justice-and-fundamental-rights/effective-justice/rule-law/assistance-bulgaria-and-romania-under-cvm/cooperation-and-verification-mechanism-bulgaria-and-romania_en.

856 Art. 4(1) Regulation 2092/2020; see Łacny, 'The Rule of Law Conditionality Under Regulation No 2092/2020: Is it all About the Money?', 13 *Hague Journal on the Rule of Law* (2021) 79.

857 Kustra-Rogatka, 'The Rule of Law Crisis as the Watershed Moment for the European Constitutionalism', *Verfassungsblog* (2019), available at https://verfassungsblog.de/the-rule-of-law-crisis-as-the-watershed-moment-for-the-european-constitutionalism/.

858 Cf. von Bogdandy, 'Principles of a Systemic Deficiencies Doctrine: How to Protect Checks and Balances in the Member States', 57 *Common Market Law Review (CMLRev.)* (2020) 705.

859 For example, migration and asylum issues are hardly treated at all in the Commission's 2020 Rule of Law Report, COM(2020) 580, 30 September 2020.

certain extent – to tacit toleration, disclosing and discussing the political objectives of the breaches may help to more effectively protect both the institutions and persons affected as well as the authority of the EU's provisions and values called into question by such policies.

7.3 Recommendations

Recommendation 1: Strengthen migrants' Human Rights defenders by amending the Facilitation Directive and adopting consistent EU supporting policies

The criminalization of civil society SAR activities is contrary to the international law of the sea and to the UN Declaration on Human Rights Defenders which specifies positive obligations derived from Human Rights law. It is also incompatible with the Union's commitment to protect Human Rights. We therefore recommend the EU to develop consistent support policies for NGOs and other civil society actors engaged in defending migrants' Human Rights. These measures should encompass both protection from and support against attacks from Member State governments as well as active assistance, such as funding, training, and fostering information exchange.

As a first and necessary step, the EU should decriminalize rescue operations of civil society actors and amend the Facilitation Directive 2002/90 accordingly. Art. 1(1)(a) and Art. 1(2) of this Directive currently do not insist on a requirement of 'financial or other material benefit' in defining the facilitation of entry or transit, and do not oblige Member States to exempt 'humanitarian assistance'. The exemption of humanitarian actors should be obligatory: it must not be an option seemingly offered by EU law to criminalize humanitarian assistance.

On a more operational level, the European Commission should also take a much clearer stance on the criminalization of activities of humanitarian actors by Member States. While the FRA has – albeit cautiously – addressed this issue in the past, the Commission has remained largely silent on the question in the context of, for example, the imposition of sanctions against the crews of NGO SAR vessels. This contradicts not only the general EU commitment to the protection of Human Rights as enshrined in Art. 2 TEU but also specific promises made by the Commission in 2013 in the aftermath of the Lampedusa tragedy: '*Shipmasters and merchant vessels* should be reassured once and for all that helping migrants in distress will not lead to sanctions of any kind and that fast and safe disembarkation points will be available. It has to be clear that, provided they are acting in good faith, *they would not face any negative legal consequences for providing such assistance*.'[860] This declaration stands in sharp contrast with the subsequent silence and inactivity of the Commission regarding the persecution by Member States of humanitarian actors rescuing migrants in distress at sea.

As to positive measures, the FRA's Fundamental Rights Platform (FRP) already provides for a forum and network for cooperation with civil society organizations from across the EU.[861] As the FRA mandate encompasses capacity-building for civil society organizations, it should increase its efforts in those Member States in which humanitarian actors have come under the most severe political and legal pressure in recent years. A positive example of such support is the 2019 training of NGO lawyers in Hungary and from neighboring EU Member States with an external EU border, conducted by the FRA in cooperation with UNHCR.[862]

Recommendation 2: Take a firm stance on violations of EU migration law

We recommend the EU take a firm stance on, and adopt a systematic approach to, violations of the EU asylum and immigration *acquis* in Member States. The EU should not tolerate political pressure on migration law judges in Member States.

On a more general level, a clear stance should be taken by the EU on any developments in Member States undermining Human Rights infrastructures and the rule of law. The European Commission should, therefore, thoroughly pursue ongoing infringement and Art. 7 TEU procedures regarding judicial reforms in Member States. The independence of the judiciary in Member States is indispensable to guarantee the effective

860 European Commission, 'Lampedusa follow up: Concrete actions to prevent loss of life in the Mediterranean and better address migratory and asylum flows', Press release, 4 December 2013, available at http://europa.eu/rapid/press-release_IP-13-1199_en.htm (emphasis added).

861 Art. 10 FRA Regulation; for further information on the Fundamental Rights Platform, see https://fra.europa.eu/en/cooperation/civil-society.

862 FRA, 'Training NGO lawyers on the Schengen Borders Code and fundamental rights', Press release, 26 April 2019, available at https://fra.europa.eu/en/news/2019/training-ngo-lawyers-schengen-borders-code-and-fundamental-rights.

application of EU law in general, and the asylum and immigration *acquis* in particular.

However, before any measure that could be interpreted as 'punitive' is taken, all possible effects and alternatives should be carefully examined and weighed. Infringement and Art. 7 TEU procedures can only have short- and medium-term effect in preventing the actual dismantling of democratic institutions in a Member State and as a normative assertion of the validity and effectiveness of the fundamental values of the EU. In the long term, respect for Human Rights and the rule of law in Member States cannot be based on the motivation of avoiding sanctions, but must instead be grounded in an actual commitment to shared values.

Finally, any such measures must also respect the principles of coherence and equality before the law. For example, the EU should systematically examine the possibility of taking legal actions and, ultimately, launching Art. 7 TEU procedures against Greece, Italy, and Malta regarding the policies of criminalizing humanitarian actors.

Recommendation 3: Strengthen the role of the ECtHR as a 'migrants court' by acceding to the ECHR

We call upon the EU to adopt a clear political stance on any Member State attempt to challenge the legitimacy and relevance of the ECHR and the ECtHR. There should be no doubt that full respect for the ECHR and the decisions of the ECtHR are an integral aspect of membership in the EU and feature among its core commitments.

Furthermore, we recommend the EU actively strengthen respect for the ECHR and the decisions of the ECtHR by prioritizing the resumed accession process of the EU to the ECHR as foreseen in Art. 6(2) TEU, despite the negative Opinion issued by the CJEU in 2014.[863] This would credibly underline the EU's commitment to the Convention and, at the same time, would send an important message to the Member States.

A duty of the EU to accede to the ECHR does not follow from international law but it is a legal obligation under Art. 6(2) TEU. However, the accession process has stagnated since the CJEU's Opinion. Despite some rather vague public statements in favor of completing the accession process and the formal resumption of negotiations with the Council of Europe in

863 CJEU (Full Court), Opinion 2/13, *ECHR II* (EU:C:2014:2454).

September 2020,[864] the Commission does not seem eager to do so quickly. This does not come as a surprise, considering that accession to the ECHR would also limit the Commission's discretion by submitting the EU legislature to the judicial review of the ECtHR regarding its compliance with Human Rights.

Legal scholarship has convincingly demonstrated that it is possible to reconcile the autonomy of EU law (the CJEU's core concern) with membership in the pan-European Human Rights protection system.[865] The reluctance on the part of the EU institutions to explore these possibilities is all the more worrying as the EU is apparently determined to shield the gaps in its own system of fundamental rights protection, including Human Rights violations in the context of the Dublin system, against 'outside' interference. If the EU, at long last, were to accede to the ECHR, this would also reinforce the ECtHR's role as a crucial component of the Human Rights infrastructure defending the rights of migrants.

---

864 European Commission, 'The EU's accession to the European Convention on Human Rights: Joint statement on behalf of the Council of Europe and the European Commission', Press statement, 29 September 2020, available at https://ec.europa.eu/commission/presscorner/detail/es/statement_20_1748. On further meetings and the status of the accession process, see European Parliament, Completion of EU accession to the ECHR: Area of Justice and Fundamental Rights, Legislative Train Schedule 06.2021 (2021).

865 Halberstam, '"It's the Autonomy, Stupid!" A Modest Defense of Opinion 2/13 on EU Accession to the ECHR, and the Way Forward', 16 *German Law Journal (GLJ)* (2015) 105.

Summary

The REMAP study rests on the observation of two long-term processes: increasingly dense obligations under Human Rights law that are recognized as relevant to migration, and the emergence of the EU as a powerful player in migration policy. Their encounter has resulted in a growing number of instances in which European migration policies conflict with Human Rights. The REMAP study identifies these instances, outlines the applicable legal standards, and provides recommendations to ease the tension. It is based on an understanding of Human Rights as legal norms of international law that are rich in content but that must be construed by means of interpretation that are methodologically sound – a 'positivist Human Rights maximalism', as it were.

The study looks into acts or omissions that actually violate Human Rights and their corresponding provisions of EU fundamental rights, or instances in which current policies and practices run the risk of doing so. In our view, the EU is primarily accountable for European migration policy being in conformity with Human Rights. Accordingly, the legal analysis encompasses EU Member States acting in situations principally covered by EU legislation. The EU is also required to answer for its failure to enact a comprehensive legal framework that is sufficiently specific or broad to address cases in which Human Rights violations by Member States frequently occur (we call such situations 'underinclusive legislation').

The REMAP study is organized according to the interests of migrants protected by Human Rights guarantees. Each chapter identifies the main challenges to these protected interests: major trends in European migration policy that pose increasing and/or structural conflicts with Human Rights. These trends and patterns are analyzed as to their conformity with relevant provisions of Human Rights law. Based on the ensuing findings, we offer specific recommendations to stop ongoing Human Rights violations and prevent them from occurring. We also make suggestions where our findings indicate that legislative action on the part of the EU is required, naturally involving a higher degree of political discretion. This is in line with our understanding of Human Rights both as 'guardrails', setting strict and justiciable limits to policy choices, and 'directive principles' that legally guide policy-making. Calling for the EU legislature to act may sound politically naïve, given that the current political climate tends to lower Human Rights standards for migrants. And yet, we imagine ourselves being the trusted legal advisors of a 'bona fide' policy-maker who would like to know what a European migration policy based on Human Rights must and should entail.

1. *Ensuring Access to Asylum*

Chapter 1 addresses access to asylum, arguably the most pressing challenge to European migration policy. The EU and its Member States have developed a range of policies that prevent potential asylum seekers from gaining access to status determination procedures and, hence, from seeking and enjoying asylum in the EU as promised in Art. 18 EU-CFR. The EU not only fails to effectively offer legal and safe passages to asylum but has also actively implemented policies that aim at circumventing international obligations toward refugees by way of non-exercise of asylum jurisdiction. According to our analysis, these policies take three forms: tacitly avoiding, normatively contesting, and transferring jurisdiction.

First, we observe increased efforts among the EU and its Member States to avoid asylum jurisdiction through the externalization of mobility control – that is, via cooperation with third countries. Policies of cooperative externalization aim at preventing migrants from leaving their country of origin or a transit country in the first place ('non-departure policies'). The EU–Turkey Statement of 2016 serves as a model for this approach. In addition, the EU and its Member States implement 'non-arrival policies' aiming at 'pulling back' migrants before arrival on EU territory. The latter approach is exemplified by the ongoing cooperation of Italy and Malta with the so-called Libyan Coast Guard. The EU is actively involved in this particular cooperation by providing technical and financial assistance and conducting aerial surveillance coordinated by Frontex. Moreover, Frontex has concluded a growing number of status agreements and working arrangements with third countries on matters of border control, contributing to the EU's non-departure as well as non-arrival policies.

Second, policies of contesting asylum jurisdiction strategically challenge, and possibly reverse, the scope of Human Rights protection through calculated acts of non-compliance with legal obligations. We observe a growing trend among EU Member States of disregarding their Human Rights obligations (and corresponding obligations under EU law) to migrants who demand access to asylum. Such practices include push-back measures at or near the external border ('hot returns') and the closure of ports to the disembarkation of migrants rescued at sea. We read this trend as an expression of principled resistance; that is, as a political attempt at reversing Human Rights jurisprudence post-*Hirsi*, rather than singular infringements of rights.

Finally, the Common European Asylum System provides for, and embraces, policies of transferring asylum jurisdiction by referring migrants to other States. Such measures delegating international responsibilities are mandated both within the Union (in the context of the Dublin system) and beyond, to non-European countries through the use of the 'safe third country' concept. We observe increased efforts to implement such schemes that refer migrants to presumed protection in countries other than their actual residence, even when effective 'protection elsewhere' is based on counterfactual assumptions. Recent legislative initiatives at EU level even aim at lowering the standards for a third country to be considered 'safe'.

Regarding the standards used to legally evaluate these trends, a Human Right to asylum has yet to emerge as an undisputed part of international law. The most important rule of international law that, to some extent, ensures access to asylum is the principle of non-refoulement. It prohibits States from expelling or returning anyone to a place where his or her fundamental Human Rights are threatened. The prohibition of refoulement amounts to an unconditional right to be admitted and protected whenever the possible alternative to provisionally granting access to the territory would entail the risk of Human Rights violations. The principle is enshrined in various sources of international law, including the prohibition of torture and inhuman or degrading treatment as laid down in Art. 3 ECHR. In its case-law on this Article, the European Court of Human Rights (ECtHR) has consistently held that 'push-backs' are illegal, both at the land borders and on the High Seas. Note that this jurisprudence was not reversed in the controversial Grand Chamber judgment *N.D. and N.T. v. Spain*, which invented a limited exception to the prohibition of collective expulsion enshrined in Art. 4 Protocol No. 4 ECHR.

When the EU or Member States cooperate with third countries, they often do not exercise direct and exclusive control over the migrants concerned but, rather, facilitate the commission of Human Rights violations by others. We find that this does not necessarily absolve them from being responsible according to the rules of international law. Art. 16 of the relevant Articles on State Responsibility (ASR) establishes international responsibility through complicity – that is, by 'aiding or assisting' internationally wrongful acts commissioned by others. Insofar as Art. 16 ASR requires 'knowledge' of the circumstances of the violation on the part of the complicit State, we argue that a due diligence standard must be applied. Applying this standard of 'reasonably foreseeable threats', it would be hard to deny the fulfillment of the knowledge criterion in the context of lasting cooperation with third countries, such as Libya, that have a well-documented record of Human Rights violations. Moreover, we argue that the jurisdiction clause of Art. 1 ECHR has to be read in light of Art. 16 ASR, with the result that effective control may extend to cases of complicity.

Regarding rescue at sea and disembarkation, an additional layer of protection is achieved through the International Law of the Sea. The duty to render assistance to persons in distress at sea, expressed in various provisions of the Law of the Sea, requires that rescued persons be delivered to a 'place of safety'. This obligation must be construed in light of Human Rights law. Disembarkation policies must therefore respect the principle of non-refoulement and any positive obligations arising from other Human Rights. These may well leave the requested coastal state with no other option but to allow for disembarkation on its own soil.

In a similar manner, shifting responsibility through transferring jurisdiction must respect Human Rights. While international refugee law, as it stands, does not categorically rule out schemes based on the concept of 'protection elsewhere', they must be implemented in compliance with Human Rights obligations. These include not only the non-refoulement principle but also other guarantees such as Art. 8 ECHR or the Convention on the Rights of the Child (CRC). Accordingly, any 'safe third country' policies must ensure the safety of the person based on a good faith empirical assessment, in which the burden of proof lies with the country where asylum application was filed. Human Rights (and the corresponding EU fundamental rights) also demand transfers under the Dublin system to guarantee access to a fair asylum procedure. Finally, we argue that Human Rights entail a broadly framed, but nonetheless existing, positive obligation to facilitate legal pathways of accessing the asylum system (that is, to provide for 'genuine and effective access to means of legal entry', in the language of the ECtHR).

Building on this legal evaluation, we recommend that the EU and its Member States strictly condition any cooperation with third countries in the area of migration management on Human Rights compliance. Accordingly, cooperation with States known for systematic violations of Human Rights must be suspended. Any 'migration partnership' should be established or maintained only if the third country is able and willing to effectively protect Human Rights and is sufficiently stable at the time of concluding the agreement. To guarantee a certain level of protection over time, Human Rights compliance in third countries should be objectively and independently evaluated through a monitoring mechanism. We recommend that such a mechanism consist of a politically responsible management body as well as an independent body for risk assessment of Human Rights violations, composed of experts from the EU Fundamental Rights Agency (FRA), UNHCR and NGOs.

Furthermore, we recommend that the Human Rights obligations at external borders as well as at EU ports be spelled out and detailed in EU legislation in order to foster compliance by Member State authorities. The legislative agenda includes, inter alia, the Schengen Borders Code that should specify the conditions that apply to any border control measures carried out by Member States.

As regards 'safe third country' policies and transfers within the Dublin system, any reform must respect Human Rights obligations, including the right to access a functioning asylum procedure and reception system, and respect for the applicant's family and social ties. Specifically, the notion of partial territorial protection should not allow for qualification as a 'safe third country'. A new Dublin Regulation must not reverse the achievements in terms of Human Rights and EU fundamental rights brought about through case-law, most notably the protection against transfers to Member States where there is a threat of Human Rights violations, and the guarantee of effective legal remedies. In order to ensure sufficient flexibility of Member States to comply with Human Rights obligations, the system must continue to provide for an open-ended discretionary clause allowing Member States to assume responsibility for a particular asylum claim.

Finally, in order to comply with its positive obligations to protect and promote Human Rights, the EU must become proactive in providing safe and legal pathways to refuge within the EU. While there are a number of different avenues to reach this goal, we are of the view that the most accessible, fair, and reliable mechanism would be the creation of a European Humanitarian Visa. We recommend that the EU follow the 2018 initiative report by the European Parliament to adopt a Regulation to this effect.

2. *Ensuring Liberty and Freedom of Movement*

Chapter 2 focuses on immigration detention and other restrictions on the freedom of movement. Detention is understood as 'deprivation of liberty or confinement to a particular place' and can take place in a variety of locations such as specialized administrative facilities, prisons, or transit zones at the external borders. The EU has developed a broad regulatory framework on this type of administrative detention (as opposed to detention in the context of criminal proceedings), spanning the Reception Conditions Directive, the Dublin Regulation, and the Return Directive. Although these regulations are rather fragmentary, particularly in terms of detention conditions, together they cover all relevant situations of detaining migrants who are present on Union territory. The EU has therefore assumed for itself primary responsibility for Human Rights compliance in this field of European migration policy.

However, we observe an overall trend toward a tightening of the regime, moving toward a more restrictive and repressive approach – at the level of Member State practice as well as in legislative initiatives at EU level. First, we note an increased use of immigration detention for a wider range of reasons. This is particularly acute in the context of so-called border procedures, where some Member States systematically resort to detaining asylum seekers. This trend is, secondly, accompanied by a proliferation of other measures limiting migrants' freedom of movement that technically do not amount to detention (such as house arrest with reporting obligations or the restriction of movement to a small island). These less severe restrictions are sometimes misleadingly referred to as 'alternatives to detention' (ATD, which can be implemented when there is otherwise a ground for detention). Both in fact and in law, area-based restrictions are an independent policy tool that is available in addition to detention, widening the net of restrictive measures against migrants. They may also function as a pathway to detention, in cases where the failure of a migrant to respect the restriction provides a legal ground for detention. And, finally, we observe a persistent pattern of problematic conditions in detention facilities. Member States frequently disregard the fact that migrants are detained merely for administrative purposes rather than because they committed a crime.

Four interrelated layers of legal standards are particularly relevant to ensuring liberty and freedom of movement. The first layer of universal and regional Human Rights protects against arbitrary detention per se. Substantively speaking, the most comprehensive standard of protection is provided for in the International Covenant on Civil and Political Rights (ICCPR) and the jurisprudence of the relevant quasi-judicial body, the Human Rights Committee. According to this jurisprudence, detention is unlawful unless there are circumstances specific to the individual – such as a risk of absconding or a risk of acts against national security – that make it necessary and proportionate to resort to this ultimate measure. Restrictions of liberty that are based on abstractly formulated criteria, establishing irrebuttable presumptions to the detriment of migrants, are considered arbitrary. The UN standard supersedes the level of protection provided for in Art. 5(1)(f) ECHR according to the contested *Saadi* case-law of the ECtHR, which fails to require a full proportionality test in cases of immigration detention. Considering that Art. 52(3) EU-CFR recognizes that EU law may provide more extensive protection than the ECHR, the higher standard developed at universal level is applicable in the EU.

A second layer of Human Rights law protects against other forms of arbitrary limitation of movement. This is laid down in both Art. 12(1) ICCPR and Art. 2 of Protocol No. 4 ECHR. In line with these provisions, third-country nationals have a conditional right to freedom of movement within each EU Member State. The EU must also respect these guarantees when exercising its legislative powers to provide for the freedom of movement of third-country nationals within Union territory. In both instruments, however, the right to intra-territorial mobility is limited to persons staying 'lawfully'. According to our legal evaluation, this includes registered asylum seekers, documented migrants who are qualified as non-deportable (such as persons with toleration status in Germany), and those with a pending request to have their immigration status regularized. Restrictions on movement of other irregular migrants must be tested against Art. 8 ECHR, which equally requires a proportionality assessment. This layer of protection tends to be overlooked, as it is not explicitly mirrored in one of the provisions of the EU-CFR. Applying the presumption of substantive homogeneity between EU fundamental rights and Human Rights, these sources nonetheless are incorporated into EU law as general principles in the sense of Art. 6(3) TEU.

The third layer of Human Rights protection pertains to detention conditions. Art. 3 ECHR constitutes an absolute guarantee of detention conditions that preserve the detainee's human dignity. In addition, the ECtHR has frequently found immigration detention to be in violation of Art. 5(1)(f) ECHR due to the concrete detention conditions, notably when more vulnerable migrants such as minors were involved. The right to respect for family and private life enshrined in Art. 8 ECHR provides a fourth layer of protection, relating also to area-based restrictions of any kind. Since personal liberty is an indispensable condition for the development of the person – that is, his or her private life – any infringement of this right must be duly justified in accordance with the principle of proportionality. Given that these standards to measure the conditions of detention or other forms of liberty-restricting measures are developed by judicial and quasi-judicial bodies based on broadly framed provisions in international treaties, more detailed international soft law is of key importance to specifying the contents of Human Rights. Here, the existing rules adopted in the UN and the Council of Europe for the management of prison facilities and the treatment of prisoners are a relevant source of inspiration, although one must acknowledge that the criminal detention standards are neither directly applicable to, nor necessarily adequate for, immigration detainees.

Using the above Human Rights yardstick to evaluate European migration policy, we identify several shortcomings. On a positive note, any immigration detention governed by EU law can only be imposed by Member State authorities when the decision meets the principle of proportionality. According to the EU Court of Justice (CJEU), this is a constitutional requirement even in the absence of a statutory provision to this effect. This doctrine is in line with the UN standard and partly compensates for the insufficient protection under Art. 5(1)(f) ECHR. However, our detailed analysis of the relevant provisions in EU legislation reveals that the EU has defined the possible grounds for immigration detention too broadly, and in overly ambiguous terms, for it to be consonant with Human Rights. A consistent interpretation would render several clauses inapplicable or substantially limit the remaining scope of application. For pre-removal detention, the Return Directive provides for two broadly framed grounds for detention; arguably the list is not even exhaustive. Recent reform proposals intend to add new grounds and make the list explicitly non-exhaustive. For asylum seekers, the Reception Conditions Directive lays down a list of grounds for detention which exceeds the permissible grounds pursuant to Human Rights law. The Directive also contains a cross-reference to the Dublin Regulation that is entirely self-referential, adding to the indetermination of the current regime.

As regards area-based restrictions, Art. 7 of the Reception Conditions Directive authorizes Member States to impose restrictions on the movement of asylum seekers 'for reasons of public interest', a broad notion which would encompass measures taken for mere bureaucratic convenience. This is not in conformity with Human Rights law, which permits such limitations only for reasons of the narrower notions of 'public order' (*ordre public*) and 'national security' (see Art. 12(3) ICCPR and Art. 2(3) Protocol No. 4 ECHR). This layer of protection has further gained in significance since the European Commission proposed, in its legislative package of 2020, to expand the use of area-based restrictions in the context of border procedures. The new Asylum Procedures Regulation would make imposing such restrictions mandatory for certain types of asylum claims, without an assessment on a case-by-case basis. We consider quasi-automatic imposition of mobility restrictions on asylum seekers, based on statutory assumptions set by the EU, to be manifestly unlawful in light of Human Rights and EU fundamental rights, regardless of whether such measures would amount to de facto or de jure detention.

In order to counteract the expansive use of immigration detention and to prevent actual violations of Human Rights, we recommend that the EU enact a horizontal provision on detention grounds across all relevant legal instruments, which exhaustively defines and carefully circumscribes the permissible grounds for detention. We suggest that detention should be allowed only when strictly necessary in order to prevent 'absconding' or 'acts against national security'. We also recommend that the EU abstain from enacting or encouraging legal presumptions regarding grounds for detention, such as those for asylum seekers who are subject to border procedures. Specifically, we recommend deleting Art. 8(3) Reception Conditions Directive, which presumably provides a general legal basis for detention during border procedures. The same approach should guide the reform of Art. 7 Reception Conditions Directive regarding area-based restrictions. For reasons explained above, the EU must refrain from requiring Member States to impose area-based restrictions on migrants based on abstractly defined criteria.

With a view to detention conditions, we find that legislation at EU level is underinclusive with regard to existing standards in Human Rights law to prevent inhuman or degrading treatment in detention. EU law as it stands hardly provides for any specific regulation in respect of conditions of immigration detention, e.g., on how a detention center is to be designed and what facilities it must provide. The EU therefore fails to live up to its primary responsibility for Human Rights compliance in this field. In the absence of such comprehensive legislation, we recommend that the EU expand the provisions on reception conditions of asylum seekers to provisionally serve as a general standard for all persons in immigration detention and reception centers. An independent monitoring mechanism in these places should be established, including inspections without notice. With regard to further developing international soft law on detention conditions, we recommend that the EU take an active role within the Council of Europe to implement a Human Rights-based approach to defining the adequate conditions for administrative detention.

Finally, although there is no undisputed prohibition in Human Rights law of detaining children and other persons in situations of particular vulnerability, the requirements of necessity and proportionality will almost always render their administrative detention unlawful. We therefore recommend that the EU legislature, by way of legislative balancing, explicitly prohibit immigration detention of these groups of people.

3. Guaranteeing Procedural Standards

Chapter 3 focusses on the procedural rights of migrants. Procedural guarantees complement the substantive rights discussed in other chapters, recognizing migrants' agency as legal subjects in immigration or asylum proceedings, and thus their human dignity. In a community based on Human Rights, individuals must be heard before adverse decisions are taken, public authorities must give reasons for such decisions, and effective legal remedies must be at hand to challenge them.

In the EU, these standards are in principle accepted to be inherent in the rule of law, one of the foundational values stipulated in Art. 2 TEU, and considered to constitute general principles of the Union's law. The Charter of Fundamental Rights has given them the status of procedural fundamental rights, enshrined in the right to good administration (Art. 41 EU-CFR) and the right to an effective remedy and a fair trial (Art. 47 EU-CFR). The EU has, therefore, assumed legal responsibility, and is politically accountable, for ensuring that these standards are observed in all administrative and judicial proceedings that fall within the substantive scope of EU migration law.

However, the EU and its Member States are not immune to the legacy of 'immigration exceptionalism' – that is, the notion that non-citizens are subject to the discretionary power of state authorities, justifying a diminished set of procedural rights in comparison to citizens. This mindset is particularly marked in the admission of migrants (decisions on visa applications and admission at the borders) and regarding the termination of residence (decisions taken in the context of return procedures).

Concerning the first type of decisions, we observe a persistent pattern of denying procedural guarantees in such proceedings. Notoriously little attention is given to standards in visa application procedures conducted at Member States' consular or diplomatic missions. The relevant EU legislation is shallow and fragmentary, particularly in respect of so-called national visas for long-term stays (although the ground of admission may be governed by EU law). The trend of avoiding asylum jurisdiction, described in Chapter 1, frequently amounts to decisions of collective non-admission at the land or sea borders. The fact that such decisions do not necessarily qualify as 'decisions' according to the terms of procedural codes is precisely the point of concern.

We also observe, secondly, a persistent pattern of disregarding procedural standards in deportation procedures (or 'removals', as the EU calls them). The Return Directive fails to comprehensively regulate sufficient procedural guarantees, including the right to be heard and independent forced-return monitoring. Provisions that do exist are repeatedly ignored by Member State authorities, which leads to unlawful deportations.

Moreover, migrants' enjoyment of procedural rights has become even more difficult as the EU agencies Frontex, EASO and eu-LISA gain in importance in European migration policy. Increasing causes of concern are (1) the diffusion of responsibility in mixed administrative proceedings and joint operations that involve both EU agencies and Member State authorities, (2) the agencies' complex and opaque structures, and (3) the limited possibilities to challenge acts of EU agencies directly. Hence, the trend toward 'agencification' of European migration policy tends to blur accountability and menace the effective protection of procedural rights.

The relevant constitutional guarantees of EU law build on and enhance procedural guarantees derived from international law, involving a higher level of protection in the EU. Still, we argue that recalling the fact that a basic layer of procedural guarantees owed to migrants is part of Human Rights law may be instrumental in overcoming the legacy of 'immigration exceptionalism'. The ECHR contains a number of important provisions in this context, including the right to a fair trial (Art. 6(1) ECHR) and to an effective remedy (Art. 13 ECHR) as well as even stronger procedural guarantees derived from the principle of non-refoulement (Art. 3 ECHR). In our legal evaluation, we pay particular attention to the prohibition of collective expulsion of aliens laid down in Art. 4 of Protocol No. 4 to the ECHR, which – unlike Art. 1(1) Protocol No. 7 ECHR – does not require the migrant to be 'lawfully resident' in a Convention State. According to the ECtHR's case-law, Art. 4 Protocol No. 4 ECHR requires a reasonable and objective examination of the particular case of each individual who is subject to a non-admission or removal procedure. In this sense, the prohibition of collective expulsion constitutes a general due process clause in European migration law. The rights enumerated in Art. 1(1) Protocol No. 7 ECHR can serve as a point of reference for determining the minimum standard for all migrants seeking admission, notwithstanding the carve-out established in 2020 in the case *N.D. and N.T. v. Spain*. As far as visa decisions are concerned, we argue that the EU, and EU Member

States when implementing EU law, must meet the standards defined in the ECHR in terms of substance, regardless of whether the applicant is 'within their jurisdiction' as defined in Art. 1 ECHR. Decisions taken by Member States' missions abroad are acts 'implementing Union law' for the purposes of Art. 51(1) EU-CFR if they are the pre-entry stage of granting a residence right defined in an EU instrument.

Against this background, EU migration law falls short of what is required by Human Rights in several instances. In our view, it does not suffice that the gaps concerning procedural rights in the relevant pieces of legislation could be closed, on a case-by-case basis, by way of judicial construction relying on fundamental rights or unwritten general principles of EU law.

First, we recommend that the EU legislature provide for comprehensive procedural safeguards for visa applications according to the standards of Art. 41 and 47 EU-CFR. Any processing of applications that are substantively governed by EU law must respect the right to be heard and the duty to submit reasons for a decision adversely affecting the applicant, and would have to provide for the possibility of review and representation before the competent judicial authority. The existing sectoral provisions should be supplemented by a horizontal regulation applicable to all applications for granting a right to reside that falls within the scope of EU law, irrespective of where the acting authority or the applicant are located.

Second, the Schengen Borders Code should be amended in order to provide for automatic suspensive effect of legal remedies whenever there is an arguable claim of the risk of refoulement, and for a right to seek an interim injunction before a court in all other cases.

Third, we recommend amending the Return Directive to explicitly provide for a right to be heard before a return decision is taken. Moreover, the Directive should provide for a clearly drafted provision on automatic suspensive effect of appeals against decisions related to return in the case of a potential violation of the principle of non-refoulement.

Fourth, the EU should set up a binding and detailed list of minimum requirements that a forced-return monitoring mechanism must fulfill in order to be effective, including its institutional separation from the authority in charge of returns.

Finally, in view of the trend toward agencification of EU migration policy, we call for the mechanisms ensuring accountability and legal responsibility of the agencies to be strengthened. The EU should adopt a horizontal regulation pertaining to all EU agencies, providing for a general minimum standard for safeguarding procedural rights. Such horizontal regulation would increase transparency as a precondition to effective and adequate access to justice. This regulation should be complemented by reinforced procedural safeguards in the specific context of each agency, providing, inter alia, for an appeals procedure in the case of complaints filed with the Frontex fundamental rights officer in order to render its decisions reviewable by the CJEU.

4. Preventing Discrimination

The next chapter addresses the challenge to prevent discrimination in EU migration policy. Establishing differences in treatment between citizens and non-citizens, and among groups of non-citizens, is at the very heart of modern migration law. Nevertheless, Human Rights law poses limits to inequality of status in the realm of migration. Distinctions in immigration and asylum law that lack an objective and reasonable justification amount to discrimination and, therefore, constitute a violation of Human Rights.

The activity of the EU legislature has contributed to a plurality of immigration statuses and the ensuing stratification of migrants' rights. While a certain trend toward a pan-European harmonization of statuses is inherent in the Europeanization of migration policy, the dominant trend is one of increasing sectoral divergence within the Europeanized fields of migration. This results from incomplete harmonization, incremental decision-making, and the absence of a clear *Leitbild* (a model or overall concept) on the part of the EU legislature. All too often, the EU's unprincipled approach has produced inconsistencies and contradictory policy choices with questionable legal justification. We demonstrate this finding using the example of the right to equal treatment, or the lack thereof, in respect of social assistance enshrined in the various EU Directives. Another, partly overlapping case in point is the difference in treatment among beneficiaries of international protection as defined in the Qualification Directive – that is, legal distinctions between Convention refugees and persons protected on subsidiary grounds.

In determining which distinctions embedded in the laws of migration governance amount to unlawful discrimination, three objectionable grounds of distinction stand out: 'race', nationality, and immigration status.

The most important Human Rights instrument that stipulates a comprehensive prohibition of racial discrimination is the International Convention on the Elimination of All Forms of Racial Discrimination (ICERD).

ICERD does apply in the field of immigration law, and it also protects against indirect forms of racial discrimination, although the details of the related jurisprudence developed by the relevant Committee, the CERD, are subject to debate. Adopting a cautious reading of Human Rights law as it stands, we consider the bulk of EU migration law to be in line with ICERD. However, a centralized system for the exchange of criminal record information, the so-called ECRIS-TCN established by Regulation 2019/816, entails indirect racial discrimination as it in effect distinguishes between groups of migrants according to their ethnic origin.

The main source preventing discrimination on grounds of nationality is Art. 14 ECHR. According to the case-law of the ECtHR, distinctions based exclusively on the nationality of a migrant must be justified by 'very weighty reasons' – provided that the matter substantively falls within the ambit of the ECHR, e.g., in cases relating to family migration or social benefits. The Court has long held that distinctions between Union citizens and third-country nationals are in principle justified due to the special (read: federal) nature of EU law. Arguably, the privileged treatment of certain third-country nationalities resulting from EU association agreements is also supported by sufficiently weighty reasons, since these privileged immigration statuses mirror the privileged partnership between the respective subjects of international law. A critical case in point is the visa regime under the EU Visa List Regulation, which imposes a visa requirement based exclusively on the nationality of the travelers (and hence, of the potential migrants). A particular cause of concern here is the fact that placement of a large majority of countries on the visa 'black list' has never been properly justified on a case-by-case basis.

Yet, the main focus of Chapter 4 is the quest for objective and reasonable justification for any difference in treatment based on immigration status per se. Again, the most developed jurisprudence is provided in the case-law on Art. 14 ECHR, in particular since a series of ECtHR judgments in 2011 and 2012, the impact of which has yet to be digested in scholarship. This jurisprudence, analyzed here in some detail, has established that the legal position defined in immigration law constitutes a 'status' for the purposes of Art. 14 ECHR. However, the ECtHR held that the required justification supporting distinctions among groups of migrants need not involve 'very weighty reasons'. Rather, the Court will usually enquire only whether the difference in treatment is 'manifestly without reasonable justification'.

Regarding the inconsistent EU legislation in respect of social assistance, we doubt that the relevant Directives address all situations in which equal treatment would be required under Art. 14 ECHR. We suggest that the EU legislature remedy the situation by enacting, as a minimum guarantee, a right to equal treatment in respect of social assistance for all migrants present in the Union for more than 90 days. Regarding the difference in treatment between Convention refugees and persons protected on subsidiary grounds, most strikingly in respect of the right to family reunification, we conclude that these distinctions plainly lack a reasonable justification (let alone being supported by very weighty reasons – that is, the standard of review that we consider applicable in cases involving persons in need of international protection). Accordingly, we hold that EU Member States are legally bound to immediately accord non-discriminatory treatment to persons protected on subsidiary grounds in respect of social assistance and family reunification. In terms of EU legislation, these obligations should be explicitly stated in the Qualification Directive and the Family Reunification Directive respectively. We hold that it would be unlawful to maintain a situation of incomplete ('underinclusive') legislation in respect of the asylum status that invites the Member States to apply arbitrary distinctions based on immigration status.

Next to amending the specific pieces of legislation referred to above, we recommend that the EU systematically review its asylum and immigration *acquis* to ensure that any distinctions between immigration statuses defined in EU law are based on objective and reasonable justification. This pertains, inter alia, to difference in treatment in respect of family reunification, social welfare, health care, access to the labor market, and mobility within the Union. Moreover, the Commission should conduct a systematic review of Member States' laws and policies that use optional clauses or derogations provided for in the relevant legal instruments that seemingly allow for less favorable treatment of third-country nationals. The Commission should institute, where appropriate, infringement proceedings and/or propose amendments to EU legislation.

Future EU legislation in migration law should be guided by a *Leitbild* of status equality that serves as a template for the status of all third-country nationals residing in the EU. Union citizenship and the status defined in the Long-Term Residents Directive could serve as a dual point of reference for such a 'general status'. Any deviation from that template should relate to the specific nature of the class of migrants concerned and the specific right at hand. On a procedural level, the EU legislature should include explicit 'equality reasoning' in the preamble to every new act.

5. Preserving Social and Family Ties

Chapter 5 discusses the Human Rights of migrants and their family members to preserve their social ties, established among themselves and in relation to the host society. These rights often involve claims to a continued stay in, or being admitted to, the country of their choice and, hence, tend to conflict with the selective logic of immigration law. The EU legislature has convincingly addressed certain aspects of the conflict, in particular in two Directives adopted in 2003, the Family Reunification Directive (FR Directive) and the Long-Term Residence Directive (LTR Directive). In other respects, however, the EU has failed to sufficiently counteract problematic trends and persistent patterns on the part of its Member States that entail Human Rights violations.

First, restrictive policies in the area of family reunification are oftentimes legally shaped and politically justified in the language of socio-cultural 'integration'. Establishing integration requirements, including predeparture language tests, is basically permitted according to the FR Directive. The CJEU's approach to limit this discretion left to Member States via a proportionality assessment is not sufficient to counter covert non-admission policies. Second, we observe a new wave of security-driven policies of expulsions against 'dangerous' migrants in many Member States, which also concerns settled migrants. Such policies tend to specifically target members of Muslim communities labeled as potential 'terrorists', and criminal offenders, often of a young age. Notwithstanding their strong social ties within the country of residence (which frequently is their native country, too), many of the settled migrants addressed by such policies do not benefit from the secure immigration status provided by the LTR Directive. Third, neither of the two Directives applies to irregular migrants. The relevant Return Directive only vaguely mentions Human Rights of persons who are subject to a return procedure. It therefore fails to protect the social and family ties de facto developed in the host country by irregular migrants, even in cases in which the legal or practical obstacles to removal are likely to be persistent.

Universal Human Rights law has yet to develop a meaningful jurisprudence that specifically protects the unity of migrant families and recognizes a right to abode in the country of residence. The ECtHR's case-law on Art. 8 ECHR is pioneering in this regard. According to its jurisprudence, the entirety of social ties developed in the host country constitutes a protected interest for the purposes of Art. 8 ECHR, including, but not limited to, the ties developed among family members. The ensuing protection is not unconditional in nature: the Court recognizes goals of migration policies, such as 'ensuring effective integration' or sanctioning criminal offenses, as legitimate public interests that may justify an interference with this right. However, when exercising their discretion under Art. 8 ECHR, States are under the two-fold obligation to assess each individual case and arrive at a substantially 'fair' (balanced) decision that gives sufficient weight to the private interests of the migrants. These obligations equally apply in expulsion and family reunification cases.

While the essentials of this case-law, developed and consolidated during the 1990s, are well-established legal knowledge, legal doctrine and practice tend to overlook that the obligation to respect the social and family ties of migrants may also amount to a well-founded claim to achieve a lawful and secure immigration status. An important authority is the Grand Chamber judgment in the *Kurić* case of 2012. The ECtHR held that the positive obligation inherent in effective 'respect' for private or family life, or both, may lead to the conclusion that 'the regularization of the residence status of [the applicants] was a necessary step which the State should have taken to ensure that [the adverse consequences of the applicable laws] would not disproportionately affect the Article 8 rights'. Accordingly, the protection provided by Art. 8 ECHR is not limited to a pre-defined category of lawfully staying migrants but may amount, in exceptional circumstances, to a right of irregular migrants to have their status regularized.

In light of that jurisprudence, current EU legislation is not sufficiently specific and inclusive to prevent Human Rights violations from occurring in individual cases, even though Member States would be obliged, as a matter of EU constitutional law, to implement the relevant Directives in conformity with their international obligations. We therefore recommend that the EU consistently follow an approach of 'overinclusive legislative balancing' to meet its own positive obligations to protect the rights derived from Art. 8 ECHR. The EU legislature should address the typical situations in which Human Rights violations may occur, and grant enforceable individual rights to family reunification and to a secure legal status respectively to all persons in these situations. Such legislation would prevent the Member States from exercising their discretion under Art. 8 ECHR with potentially unlawful results.

To this effect, the EU legislature should amend the provisions in the FR Directive relating to 'integration measures'. In its present form, the legal framework fails to address the structural biases and hidden restrictionist agendas of integration narratives and practices. We recommend, inter alia, that the EU prohibit pre-departure integration requirements or, at the least, define a maximum waiting period for the family members staying abroad.

The LTR Directive seems to provide a well-functioning safety net against securitized policies of expulsion. In practice, however, few people that are clustered in a limited number of Member States have actually acquired the status under the LTR Directive. We recommend that the EU facilitate access to that status. Hidden restrictive practices should be remedied and potential beneficiaries actively be encouraged. In addition, the legal requirements laid down in the Directive should be liberalized. Among other things, a maximum level of language skills which States may require should be stipulated, and the qualifying period be lowered from five years to three.

In its present form, the Return Directive seemingly leaves to the discretion of Member States whether, and under what conditions, they regularize the status of a migrant who is subject to a return procedure. In light of Human Rights, however, we argue that in certain instances regularization is the only option to lawfully exercise that discretion. In order to prevent Human Rights violations, the Directive should explicitly stipulate that claims based on the private or family life of the migrants concerned shall be heard at all stages of the return procedure. Moreover, we recommend amending the Return Directive to establish a strict maximum period for repeatedly postponing removals. In the medium-term, the EU should work toward a comprehensive legislative framework on regularizations. The Commission should propose an EU Regularization Directive providing for minimum harmonization of the standards and procedures in Member States for regularizing illegally staying third-country nationals. This Directive should address the situation of all irregular migrants who cannot be removed on Human Rights grounds, whether due to the situation in the country of origin (Art. 3 ECHR) or the host country (Art. 8 ECHR).

6. *Guaranteeing Socio-Economic Rights*

Chapter 6 discusses the risks of destitution and exploitation and maps the ensuing challenges to guaranteeing socio-economic rights of migrants. Those risks are particularly acute for migrants with a precarious immigration status, notably asylum seekers and irregular migrants (be they documented or undocumented). We summarily refer to these migrants as 'margizens'.

The EU legislature has insufficiently regulated the socio-economic rights of margizens, and thus fails to prevent policies of planned destitution and practices of labor exploitation. Member States implement policies of planned destitution to combat 'secondary movements' of asylum seekers within the Dublin area. Similar policies are meant to deter irregular entry and enforce the obligation to leave the country and are directed in particular against 'non-cooperative' irregular migrants ('hostile environment' policies). These policies involve cutting or denying access to basic services as a sanction against unwanted migrant behavior. The resulting destitution is an additional factor driving irregular migrants into exploitative work. There is a persistent pattern of exploiting marginalized migrants in informal labor relations, notably regarding undocumented migrants – which EU migration policy fails to fight effectively, or even condones.

Human Rights provide for the protection of essential social and economic rights of all migrants irrespective of their status under immigration law. At the universal level, socio-economic rights are laid down in the International Covenant on Economic, Social and Cultural Rights (ICESCR). The Committee on Economic, Social and Cultural Rights (CESCR) has developed a doctrine of 'minimum core obligations', according to which everyone is entitled to essential socio-economic rights that must not fall prey to goals of migration control. At the regional European level, the ECtHR has found that States' responsibility is engaged under Art. 3 ECHR when applicants who are wholly dependent on State support are faced with official indifference leading to destitution. An even wider scope of protection is afforded pursuant to the revised European Social Charter. According to the jurisprudence of the relevant Committee, the ECSR, the provision of a 'minimum core' of the rights set out in the revised European Social Charter that are essential to maintain human dignity cannot be made conditional upon the legal status of the persons concerned, nor upon their cooperation in the organization of their own expulsion. Recognizing the uncertain legal force of that jurisprudence in the EU legal order, we still argue that it informs the notion of human dignity pursuant to Art. 1 EU-CFR as well as the fundamental right to social and housing assistance laid down in Art. 34 EU-CFR. Accordingly, the presumption of substantive homogeneity between EU fundamental rights and Human Rights extends to the jurisprudence developed by the CESCR and the ECSR.

Regarding the positive obligations of States to address the exploitation of marginalized migrants, the Human Rights core of international labor law regarding the prevention of forced labor, and Art. 4 ECHR prohibiting slavery and servitude, are the most relevant sources. The ECtHR's case-law on Art. 4 ECHR relating to human trafficking and forced labor has specified the relevant substantive and procedural obligations. These not only entail operational measures to protect victims of treatment in breach of Art. 4 ECHR, including the obligation to investigate *proprio motu*, but also the duty to establish a legislative framework to systematically fight such practices.

The present EU legislation fails to meet the above obligations to effectively ensure equal access to basic services and to fight exploitation of margizens. Current legislative trends at EU level even tend to weaken the level of protection in this regard. Concerning asylum seekers subject to a Dublin transfer, the existing legal framework would actually not allow for the withdrawal of material reception conditions as a sanction against unwanted 'secondary movements'. However, pending proposals for reform are problematic to the extent that they attempt to find vague formulations for a reduced 'standard of living' – which invites Member States to test the bottom line and frequently cross it in practice. In the context of enforcing returns via a 'hostile environment', the Return Directive merely lists vaguely framed 'principles' that Member States should take into account in the treatment of persons subject to a return procedure. Such fragmentary legislation falls short of implementing the 'minimum core' of socio-economic rights, let alone defining a comprehensive status of the persons concerned. The principal legal instrument relating to exploitation, the Employers Sanctions Directive, is also insufficient to provide protection for migrants who are in an irregular employment situation. The Directive adopts a punitive approach toward employers rather than a rights-based approach toward migrants. The protection it provides is undercut by the lack of 'firewalls' separating labor law from immigration law, disincentivizing irregular migrants from making complaints.

Accordingly, we recommend that the EU embrace the standards of socio-economic protection developed by the CESCR and the ECSR. The level of protection defined by the EU legislature should establish a safety margin against the absolute minimum, in order to avoid implementation deficits that violate Human Rights. In addition, the Reception Conditions Directive should explicitly rule out any reduction or withdrawal of benefits as a tool to promote compliance with the Dublin rules. Regarding irregular migrants, we recommend that the EU extend the rights and benefits granted to asylum seekers under the Reception Conditions Directive to all migrants who are subject to the Return Directive. Building on that minimum guarantee accorded to all irregular migrants, the EU should consider according more favorable treatment to documented irregular migrants whose removal has been postponed due to Human Rights concerns or other obstacles to removal likely to be persistent. Such comprehensive regulation of the status of 'non-removable' migrants would be complementary to the EU Regularization Directive recommended in Chapter 5.

Regarding labor relations involving irregular migrants, the revision of the Employers Sanctions Directive should specifically address the situation of the most precarious (that is, undocumented or clandestine) irregular migrants. Such regulations could draw inspiration from earlier proposals from the Commission in the 1970s, fostering non-discriminatory access to labor-related and other socio-economic rights, and should establish non-reporting obligations for the relevant authorities ('firewalls').

7. Fostering Human Rights Infrastructure

The last chapter addresses the actors and arrangements that are vital prerequisites for the legal guarantees, discussed in the other chapters, to be effective. We call such structures and procedures the 'Human Rights infrastructure'. We consider a plethora of supervisory bodies, judicial institutions, and civil society actors – each contributing by different means to the effective protection of migrants' rights – to form the Human Rights infrastructure in the field of European migration policy.

In the EU, the Human Rights infrastructure has increasingly come under pressure over the last years. Three developments stand out in this regard. First, we observe a trend in several Member States to criminalize civil society actors supporting migrants. These measures must be seen in the context of a 'shrinking space for civil society' – that is, a general trend toward restricting the activities of civil society actors, be they individuals or associations, in promoting and striving for the protection of Human Rights. Examples of pressure exerted on Human Rights defenders include the amendments to the Hungarian Criminal Code in 2018, penalizing a wide range of activities related to the support of migrants, as well as the comprehensive de-legitimization of Search and Rescue (SAR) operations conducted by NGOs in the Mediterranean Sea. Striking examples of the latter are the seizure of vessels and criminal charges brought against crew members in Italy under the Salvini government. Since 2020, the COVID-19 pandemic has been used as a pretext for closing ports and putting further constraints on the few remaining private SAR vessels.

Second, we also observe a trend in several Member States of growing public pressure on judges protecting the rights of migrants. Populist pressure on the independence of the judiciary – a cornerstone of the Human Rights infrastructure – takes various forms, reaching from rather diffuse exertion of political influence to the defamation of judges through smear campaigns and the formal limitation of judicial autonomy by way of institutional reform. In the last of these, the pressure on judges in charge of migration cases to take a more restrictive approach is intrinsically linked to the assaults on the independence of the judiciary as a whole – that is, the 'rule of law crisis' in parts of the EU. It is all the more remarkable that a considerable number of judges in countries most affected by assaults on their independence nevertheless resist the pressure, by, for example, making preliminary references to the CJEU.

Third, we observe a growing tendency in Europe to question the legitimacy of the ECtHR and its role as a guardian of migrants' Human Rights. Politically motivated challenges to the Strasbourg court are manifold. There appears to be an increased reluctance to fully implement ECtHR decisions, leading, inter alia, to repetitive cases and governments reckoning with the delay of remedies when resorting to questionable practices. The wider trend of 'principled resistance' to ECtHR judgments has also found expression in initiatives to change the architecture of the entire system, in particular by lowering the standard of scrutiny applied by the Court. In the draft Copenhagen Declaration of 2018, tabled by the Danish government, this goal was explicitly linked to the role of the ECtHR in asylum and immigration cases.

The duty to provide for functioning institutions to protect Human Rights is implied in the substantive guarantees of Human Rights treaties, entailing positive obligations of States to maintain and foster an adequate Human Rights infrastructure. These obligations are confirmed and specified in various sources of international soft law, such as the Global Compact for Migration which expresses the commitment of UN Member States to 'ensure' the 'effective respect for and protection and fulfilment of the human rights of all migrants' (GCM, para. 15). In terms of civil society actors and their essential role in effectively protecting Human Rights, a comprehensive set of rights was provided by the UN General Assembly in the 1998 Declaration on Human Rights Defenders. According to this declaration, '[e]veryone has the right, individually and in association with others, to promote and to strive for the protection and realization of human rights and fundamental freedoms at the national and international levels' (Art. 1 of the Declaration). These rights are complemented by various measures that States are expected to take in order to strengthen the work of Human Rights defenders.

In light of these obligations, the aforementioned trends are highly problematic. Criminalizing SAR activities and other forms of altruistic assistance for irregular migrants is contrary to the UN Declaration on Human Rights Defenders, in addition to violating various provisions of the Law of the Sea regarding the duty of shipmasters (and States) to provide assistance to persons in distress at sea. Since Human Rights defenders are acting for altruistic reasons, their criminalization is also at odds with the 2000 UN Protocol against the Smuggling of Migrants, which penalizes 'smuggling of migrants' only if the illegal entry of a person was procured in order to obtain a 'material benefit'. Against this backdrop, the relevant EU legislation (the so-called Facilitation Directive) falls foul of the UN Smuggling Protocol which it intends to implement. The Directive seemingly leaves discretion to EU Member States to decide whether they want to criminalize humanitarian actors. We therefore recommend that the Facilitation Directive be amended to make the exemption of altruistic assistance mandatory under EU law.

As regards the threat to judicial independence in various Member States, it is the rule of law and thus a foundational value of the Union that is at stake. While systemic deficiencies, particularly in Poland, have been addressed more boldly in recent years by the Commission and the Court of Justice, this is less evident with regard to the anti-immigration policies often underlying assaults on the rule of law. The Commission has been rather reluctant to address attacks on the EU's asylum and immigration *acquis*. We recommend that the EU take a firm stance on violations of the EU asylum and immigration law in any Member State, and that it not tolerate political pressure on migration law judges. Next to thoroughly pursuing infringement proceedings and Art. 7 TEU procedures regarding judicial reform, the Commission should examine the possibility of taking legal action against policies of criminalizing humanitarian actors.

Finally, we recommend that the EU adopt a clear political stance on any attempts to challenge the legitimacy and relevance of the ECtHR. Respect for the ECHR and the decisions of the ECtHR are integral aspects of EU membership. The EU should also complete its own accession to the ECHR as foreseen in Art. 6(2) TEU. This would send an important message to the Member States and reinforce the ECtHR's role as a crucial component of the Human Rights infrastructure defending the rights of migrants.

Annex: Panel of Experts

Individual Experts

Dr. Alberto Achermann, LL.M. (EUI), University of Bern, Associate Professor of Migration Law, and Vice President of the Swiss National Commission for the Prevention of Torture (NCPT)

Dr. Adam Bodnar, LL.M. (CEU), (former) Polish Commissioner for Human Rights, Warsaw

Dr. Cathryn Costello, Hertie School Berlin, Professor of Fundamental Rights and Co-Director of the Centre for Fundamental Rights

Dr. Marie-Bénédicte Dembour, DPhil (Oxford), Ghent University, Human Rights Centre, Professor of Law and Anthropology

Dr. Anuscheh Farahat, LL.M. (Berkeley), Friedrich-Alexander-University Erlangen-Nuremberg, Professor of Public Law, Migration Law and Human Rights Law

Dr. Kees Groenendijk, Radboud University Nijmegen, Emeritus Professor of Sociology and Migration Law

Dr. Matthias Lehnert, Attorney-at-Law, Berlin (panel member until June 2019)

Dr. Nora Markard, MA (King's College), University of Münster, Professor of International Public Law and International Human Rights

Dr. Violeta Moreno-Lax, MA (College of Europe), Queen Mary University of London, Professor of Law

Dr. Marei Pelzer, Fulda University of Applied Sciences, Professor of Law of Social Work and Social Services

Dr. Lieneke Slingenberg, Vrije Universiteit Amsterdam, Professor of Migrants and the Rule of Law

Expert Institutions

German Institute for Human Rights (Deutsches Institut für Menschenrechte, DIMR), Berlin

European Center for Constitutional and Human Rights (ECCHR), Berlin